SUSTAINABILITY LAW IN MINING AND ENERGY

ELGAR ENERGY LAW AND PRACTICE

The Elgar Energy Law and Practice series is a library of works by leading practitioners and scholars covering key areas in the field of Energy Law. Each title is analytical in approach, highlighting and unpicking the legal issues that are most critical and relevant to practice. Designed to be detailed, focused reference works, the books in this series aim to offer an authoritative statement on the law and practice in key topics within the field.

For a full list of Edward Elgar published titles, including the titles in this series, visit our website at www.e-elgar.com.

SUSTAINABILITY LAW IN MINING AND ENERGY

A Guide to the Sustainability Requirements

JOHN A.P. CHANDLER

Professor of Law and Co-Director, Centre for Mining, Energy and Natural Resources Law, University of Western Australia

ELGAR ENERGY LAW AND PRACTICE

EE Edward Elgar PUBLISHING

Cheltenham, UK · Northampton, MA, USA

Published by

Edward Elgar Publishing Limited
The Lypiatts
15 Lansdown Road
Cheltenham
Glos GL50 2JA
UK

Edward Elgar Publishing, Inc.
William Pratt House
9 Dewey Court
Northampton
Massachusetts 01060
USA

Authorised representative in the EU for GPSR queries only: Easy Access System Europe – Mustamäe tee 50, 10621 Tallinn, Estonia, gpsr.requests@easproject.com

A catalogue record for this book is available from the British Library

Library of Congress Control Number: 2025940922

This book is available electronically in the **Elgar**online
Law subject collection
https://doi.org/10.4337/9781035341320

MIX
Paper | Supporting responsible forestry
FSC® C013604

ISBN 978 1 0353 4131 3 (cased)
ISBN 978 1 0353 4132 0 (eBook)
ISBN 978 1 0353 7288 1 (ePub)

Printed and bound by CPI Group (UK) Ltd, Croydon, CR0 4YY

This book is in memory of Barbara Elizabeth Chandler, 1952–2023

CONTENTS

Extended contents viii
Preface and acknowledgements xiii
Abbreviations and definitions xv
Table of cases xix
Table of legislation xxi

1 Sustainability law in mining and energy: an introduction 1

2 Sustainability organisations 28

3 Governance and sustainability 53

4 Sustainable Development Goals 87

5 Intergenerational and intragenerational equity and mining and energy 107

6 Environmental approvals in mining and energy 120

7 Project development approvals and sustainability standards 153

8 Examples of company sustainability reporting 172

9 Regulation of company sustainability reporting 203

10 The future of sustainability law in mining and energy 230

Index 240

EXTENDED CONTENTS

Preface and acknowledgements xiii
Abbreviations and definitions xv
Table of cases xix
Table of legislation xxi

1 Sustainability law in mining and energy: an introduction
AIM OF THE BOOK 1.01
THE APPROACH OF THIS BOOK TO SUSTAINABILITY 1.08
The importance of ecological systems and biodiversity 1.11
Social and economic pillars 1.13
OTHER THEMES OR ELEMENTS OF SUSTAINABILITY 1.14
Profitability 1.14
The modern emphasis on combining development and environmental protection 1.18
Equity 1.20
A suggestion for elements of environmental sustainability 1.22
FOCUSING ON MINERALS AND ENERGY AND RELATED POLICY AND REGULATION 1.24
Minerals and energy as natural resources 1.24
Phases of a mining or fossil fuel energy project 1.29
Differences with renewable energy projects 1.32
The meaning of principles and rules 1.33
A SNAPSHOT OF THE MINERALS AND ENERGY SECTOR 1.35
Minerals 1.35
Energy from fossil fuels and nuclear 1.37
Renewable energy 1.40
COMPANY REPORTING OBLIGATIONS: ESG AND OTHER APPROACHES 1.43
Compulsory reporting of climate change and sustainability risks is increasing 1.43
Other sources of rules and guidance 1.48
AGENDA AND CHAPTER OVERVIEW 1.52
REIMAGINING SUSTAINABILITY IN MINING AND ENERGY 1.55

2 Sustainability organisations
INTRODUCTION 2.01
THE UNITED NATIONS 2.02
Conferences 2.02
UN Department of Economic and Social Affairs and Sustainable Development Solutions Network 2.04
The United Nations and human rights 2.05
United Nations Environment Programme 2.06
United Nations Development Programme 2.07
United Nations Educational, Scientific and Cultural Organization 2.08
OECD and World Bank 2.09
INTERGOVERNMENTAL BODIES 2.11
MINING AND ENERGY REGULATORS AND POLICY-SETTING 2.14
INDUSTRY BODIES IN MINING 2.19
INDUSTRY BODIES IN PETROLEUM AND ENERGY 2.21

REPORTING AND THE ESG LANDSCAPE 2.24
- Overview 2.24
- Global Reporting Initiative 2.26
- Task Force on Climate-related Financial Disclosures 2.28
- International Financial Reporting Standards 2.29
- US GAAP and national accounting standards 2.30
- Natural capital accounting 2.32
- Sustainable finance 2.34
- Rating and ranking 2.35

CORPORATE REGULATORS 2.36

SECURITIES EXCHANGES 2.37

CONCLUSIONS: GUIDANCE AND KEY PRINCIPLES 2.40
- Checklist 2.43

3 Governance and sustainability

INTRODUCTION 3.01
- *Cadbury Report*: example of general governance principles – corporations 3.06
- Corporate sustainability governance 3.08
- Examples of general governance principles – government 3.12
- The WFGW – the Welsh example of sustainability governance 3.18
- The UN and sustainability governance 3.24

THE IMPORTANCE OF CULTURE AND REGULATION 3.26
- Government policy on mining and energy operations 3.28
- The focus of regulation where the state owns the resources 3.35
- Public policy sustainability objectives and increased reporting requirements 3.39
- Governance of renewable energy 3.40

COMPANY LAW 3.42
- Outline 3.42
- Duties to act within powers, in good faith, and in the interests of the corporation 3.44
- Duty of care 3.46
- Duty to report on financial and non-financial matters 3.50

SECURITIES EXCHANGES AND MARKET REGULATION 3.51

ACCOUNTING STANDARDS AND IFRS S1 SUSTAINABILITY FINANCIAL DISCLOSURE 3.57
- Introduction 3.57
- IFRS S1 and sustainability financial disclosure 3.59

CONCLUSIONS, GUIDANCE, AND KEY PRINCIPLES 3.62

4 Sustainable Development Goals

INTRODUCTION 4.01

THE EARLY HISTORY AND SUSTAINABLE DEVELOPMENT 4.02
- Early history and the UN 4.02
- The flexible nature of sustainable development 4.06
- The Sustainable Development Goals (SDGs) 4.10

REPORTING ON THE SDGS – THE UN 4.12
- The UN 4.12
- UN high-level political forums and VNRs 4.18

COUNTRY EXAMPLES 4.19
- Canada 4.19
- Philippines 4.22

CORPORATE SDG REPORTING 4.25
- Overview of mining 4.25
- Mining companies 4.29
- Overview of oil and gas 4.33
- Oil and gas companies 4.35
- Renewable energy companies 4.37

CONCLUSIONS, GUIDANCE, AND KEY PRINCIPLES 4.38

5 Intergenerational and intragenerational equity and mining and energy
INTRODUCTION 5.01
Equity 5.03
CONCEPTUAL AND LEGAL DIFFICULTIES IN INTERGENERATIONAL EQUITY 5.06
Defining needs 5.06
Valuation and apportionment 5.07
CONCEPTUAL AND LEGAL DIFFICULTIES IN INTRAGENERATIONAL EQUITY 5.08
Distributional equity and energy justice 5.08
Analysis of costs and benefits 5.10
ACHIEVING THE FAIR DISTRIBUTION OF COSTS AND BENEFITS 5.13
Making fair decisions 5.13
The growing importance of soft law 5.14
CREEPING INTERGENERATIONALISATION AND ENERGY JUSTICE IN INTERNATIONAL AND DOMESTIC LAWS 5.16
Lack of treaties requiring intergenerational equity 5.16
The International Court of Justice 5.18
CONCLUSIONS, GUIDANCE, AND KEY PRINCIPLES 5.24

6 Environmental approvals in mining and energy
INTRODUCTION 6.01
REVIEW OF PROJECTS LIKELY TO HAVE A SIGNIFICANT ENVIRONMENTAL IMPACT 6.03
Two streams of environmental approvals 6.03
Federal approval in the USA for major federal actions significantly affecting the quality of the human environment 6.04
Federal review in Canada of designated projects 6.05
Review at the Saskatchewan province level of developments 6.08
Federal review in Australia of significant impacts on matters of national environmental significance 6.10
Review at the Western Australian state level of proposals likely to have a significant effect on the environment 6.14
Other offences 6.15
Environmental impact assessment, the public interest, and sustainability 6.16
MINING ENVIRONMENTAL APPROVALS 6.21
Introductory comments about Nevada, Saskatchewan, and Western Australia 6.21
Nevada mining 6.24
Saskatchewan mining 6.30
Western Australia mining 6.36
OIL AND GAS ENVIRONMENTAL APPROVALS 6.40
Introductory comments 6.40
Nevada oil and gas 6.42
Saskatchewan oil and gas 6.45
Western Australia oil and gas 6.50
RENEWABLE ENERGY ENVIRONMENTAL APPROVALS 6.54
Introductory comments 6.54
Renewable energy in Nevada 6.56
Renewable energy in Saskatchewan 6.59
Renewable energy in Western Australia 6.61
CONCLUSIONS, GUIDANCE, AND KEY PRINCIPLES 6.64

7 Project development approvals and sustainability standards
INTRODUCTION 7.01
What are development approvals? 7.01
Questions on development 7.02
BACKGROUND TO APPROVALS FOR DEVELOPMENT 7.04

MINING DEVELOPMENT APPROVALS 7.09
Mining in Nevada 7.09
Saskatchewan mining 7.12
Western Australia mining 7.16
OIL AND GAS DEVELOPMENT APPROVALS 7.18
Introduction 7.18
Nevada oil and gas 7.19
Saskatchewan oil and gas 7.22
Western Australia oil and gas 7.24
RENEWABLE ENERGY DEVELOPMENT APPROVALS 7.30
Introduction 7.30
Renewable energy in Nevada 7.31
Renewable energy in Saskatchewan 7.32
Renewable energy in Western Australia 7.33
DEVELOPMENT FINANCE 7.35
CONCLUSIONS, GUIDANCE, AND KEY PRINCIPLES 7.37

8 Examples of company sustainability reporting
INTRODUCTION 8.01
The nine companies 8.01
Reporting required by law 8.03
Process and guidance for reporting 8.04
Common features of the reports examined 8.07
THE MINING COMPANIES 8.12
Introduction 8.12
Barrick 8.13
Cameco 8.17
MinRes 8.20
THE OIL AND GAS COMPANIES 8.23
Introduction 8.23
TotalEnergies 8.24
Conoco 8.31
Cenovus 8.35
THE RENEWABLE ENERGY COMPANIES 8.39
Introduction 8.39
Iberdrola 8.40
Vestas 8.46
CSI 8.48
FLEXIBLE OPTIONS AND BEST PRACTICE 8.53
Flexible options 8.53
Guidance on best practice 8.54
CONCLUSIONS, GUIDANCE, AND KEY PRINCIPLES 8.56

9 Regulation of company sustainability reporting
INTRODUCTION 9.01
Regulation of disclosure 9.01
Australia, USA, Canada, and the European Union examined 9.02
AUSTRALIA 9.04
IFRS and Australia's new climate disclosure rules 9.04
The Australian climate-related disclosure legislation 9.05
Amendments to Australian companies legislation 9.06
Other reporting obligations of directors 9.10
The structure of AASB S2 9.11
Main requirements of AASB S2 9.12
The focus of IFRS S2 and AASB S2 9.13

	USA	9.18
	The SEC	9.18
	The SEC's new climate disclosure rules	9.19
	CANADA AND SASKATCHEWAN	9.27
	Canadian Securities Administrators	9.27
	Canadian federal regulation	9.28
	The Canadian Finance Taxonomy and Sustainability Standards	9.29
	Saskatchewan	9.31
	THE EUROPEAN UNION AND THE CSRD	9.32
	CSRD	9.32
	ESRS	9.35
	Reporting areas under ESRS for disclosure	9.36
	Disclosure and the double materiality test	9.37
	CSDDD	9.47
	CONCLUSIONS, GUIDANCE, AND KEY PRINCIPLES	9.48
10	The future of sustainability law in mining and energy	
	INTRODUCTION: THE CURRENT APPROACH	10.01
	The five themes	10.01
	Theme 1: Mining and energy regulators do not test sustainability as such	10.02
	Theme 2: Mining and energy regulators test environmental and safety matters	10.06
	Theme 3: Compulsory disclosure of sustainability is increasing	10.09
	Theme 4: Material on reporting and good practice is increasing	10.10
	Theme 5: Companies are producing sustainability reports	10.12
	REDUCING THE DISCLOSURE AND REPORTING REGIMES	10.13
	Multiplicity of regimes	10.13
	Reduction and simplification	10.16
	Meeting the energy transition	10.17
	REIMAGINING SUSTAINABILITY LAW IN MINING AND ENERGY	10.18
	Mining and energy regulators are increasing their focus on sustainability	10.18
	Other forces for change	10.19
	A rationale for sustainability law	10.23
Index		240

PREFACE AND ACKNOWLEDGEMENTS

This book is intended as a guide to the growing body of sustainability law in mining and energy for those trying to make sense of an increasingly complex picture as the world struggles with the energy transition and climate change. It covers basic concepts for students and those unfamiliar with the area, but also more advanced ideas for company directors, government officials, and company executives relating to mining and energy environmental and development rules, governance, company law, reporting, and disclosure.

ACKNOWLEDGEMENTS

The underlying philosophy behind this book is that there is a moral duty to try to leave the world in a better condition than we found it – that is the core of intergenerational equity. It is of course extremely difficult to implement that because of the numerous challenges faced by many people and a lack of political will and leadership. So I want to reflect briefly on the human qualities which are an essential underpinning of sustainability, and where we can all make a difference from day to day. These were qualities of my late wife Barbara, to whom this book is dedicated. First, we need to understand the challenges that others face. Women in particular still face many difficulties, especially in some parts of the world. Barbara graduated in law from the University of Western Australia in 1974, when women represented less than 10% of the law students. She had to overcome long-standing traditions to become the inaugural female partner in a leading commercial law firm and a Commissioner of some of Western Australia's leading institutions. It goes without saying that she was a great lawyer, but completely without ego. But, next, she modelled qualities which helped others overcome the challenges they faced: integrity, courage, compassion, sharing and enjoying life's simple pleasures, treating everyone with respect, and wishing the best for them. Throughout her life Barbara always trod lightly, and that is a key to sustainability.

There are many people I would like to thank for their help with this book: Richard Bartlett, John Paterson, Barbara Gordon, Sharon Mascher, Brian

Sullivan, Ruth Shean, Jim Butler, Jacqui Lane, Mike Scott, Tanya Perry, Erika Techera, Damien Cronin, Bodhi Hardinge, Susie Corlett, Lyndie Bayne, and Jess Dyer. I would like to thank Barbara's son James, my children and grandchildren and Tanya McDowell for their love and support. You all make such a difference to this writer.

SOURCES

This book has relied, where possible, on primary sources from government, legislatures, and companies. But it has also referred to secondary material such as commentary and scholarly works. The footnotes give references. Unless the context requires otherwise, to the best of my knowledge the law proferred in this book as current is up to date as at 2nd February 2025.

Interviews were conducted with industry personnel on the basis that they could be published without attribution. In the footnotes they have been cited only by reference to the date of the interview.

John A.P. Chandler
Law School, University of Western Australia
john.chandler@uwa.edu.au

ABBREVIATIONS AND DEFINITIONS

AEP	Australian Energy Producers
AOPGGSA	*Offshore Petroleum and Greenhouse Gas Storage Act 2006* (Cth)
APSLA or PSLA	*Petroleum (Submerged Lands) Act 1967* (Cth)
ASIC	Australian Securities and Investment Commission
ASN	Australian Strategy for Nature 2019–2030 (Commonwealth of Australia, 2019)
ASX	Australian Securities Exchange Ltd
BCM of gas	Billion cubic metres of gas
BLM	Bureau of Land Management (USA)
BMRR	Bureau of Mining Regulation and Reclamation (Nevada)
BOE	Barrels of Oil Equivalent
Brundtland Report	World Commission on Environment and Development, *Our Common Future* (Oxford University Press, 1987)
CASK	*The Business Corporations Act 2021* (S)
CAUK	*Companies Act 2006* (UK)
CAWA	*Corporations Act 2001* (Cth)
CSG	Coal Seam Gas
CSN	Nevada Revised Statutes Chapter 78 Private Companies
DCF	Discounted Cash Flow
DECC	Department of Energy and Climate Change (UK)
DEFRA	Department for Environment, Food and Rural Affairs (UK)
DMIRSWA	Department of Energy, Mines, Industry Regulation and Safety (Western Australia)
EIA	Environmental Impact Assessment
E&P	Exploration and Production

EP	Environment Plan (NOPSEMA)
EPAUSA	Environmental Protection Agency (USA)
EPAWA	Environment Protection Authority (Western Australia)
EPBCA	*Environmental Protection and Biodiversity Conservation Act 1999* (Cth)
ESG	Environmental, Social and Governance
Euro	Euro (EU)
EU	European Union
FCA	Financial Conduct Authority (UK)
FDP	Field Development Plan
G250	250 largest global companies
GAAP	Generally Accepted Accounting Principles
GBP	Pound sterling (UK)
GDP	Gross Domestic Product
GRI	Global Reporting Initiative
GSE	Government Sponsored Enterprises
GST	Goods and Services Tax
GTL	Gas-to-liquids
GWh	Gigawatt hours
ICMM	International Council of Minerals and Mines
IEA	International Energy Agency
IFC	International Finance Corporation
IFC Sustainability Practices	Focus 15 Sustainability Committees, Structures and Practices
IFRS	International Financial Reporting Standards
IGF	International Forum on Mining, Minerals, Metals and Sustainable Development
IMF	International Monetary Fund
Infrastructure	Generally used to mean the mining processing plant, wells, pipelines, railways, platforms, treatment and storage facilities, worker accommodation, generators, electricity networks and other infrastructure and facilities required for production and storage of minerals and energy; excluding ships and similar facilities
IOC	International Oil Company

IOGP	International Association of Oil and Gas Producers
Ipieca	International Petroleum Industry Environmental Conservation Association
Ipieca Reporting Guidance	Ipieca/API/IOGP Sustainability reporting guidance for the oil and gas industry (4th ed.)
IRENA	International Renewable Energy Agency
ISO	International Organization for Standardization
JV	Joint Venture
KPI	Key Performance Indicator
LNG	Liquefied Natural Gas
LPG	Liquefied Petroleum Gas
MBEIS	Ministry for Business, Energy and Industrial Strategy (UK)
MMbbl	One million barrels
NEA	Norwegian Environment Agency
NGL	Natural Gas Liquids
NMPE	Norwegian Ministry of Petroleum and Energy
NOC	National Oil Company
NOK	Norwegian Krone
NOPSEMA	National Offshore Petroleum Safety and Environmental Management Authority (Cth)
NOPTA	National Offshore Petroleum Titles Administrator (Cth)
NPA	*Petroleum Act 1996* (Norway)
NPCR	*Pollution Control Regulations* (Norway)
NPD	Norwegian Petroleum Directorate
NPDO	Plan for Development and Operation (Norway)
NPSA	Norwegian Petroleum Safety Authority
NSTA	North Sea Transition Authority, formerly the OGA
NYSE	New York Stock Exchange
OECD	Organisation for Economic Co-operation and Development
OGA	Oil and Gas Authority (UK)

OPEC	Organization of Petroleum Exporting Countries
OPGGSA	*Offshore Petroleum and Greenhouse Gas Storage Act 2006* (Cth)
OPP	Offshore Project Proposal (NOPSEMA)
PGERA	*Petroleum and Geothermal Energy Resources Act 1967* (WA)
PRT	Petroleum Revenue Tax
PSC	Production Sharing Contract
SASB	Sustainability Accounting Standards Board
SDG	Sustainable Development Goal (UN)
SEAUSA	*Securities Exchange Act 1934* (USA)
SEC	Securities and Exchange Commission (USA)
SEC CDRs	SEC Climate Disclosure Rules (2024)
SIA	Strategic Impact Assessment
TCFD	Task Force on Climate-related Financial Disclosures
TSX	Toronto Stock Exchange
UKCA	*Competition Act 1998* (UK)
UKCS	United Kingdom Continental Shelf
UKIA	*Infrastructure Act 2015* (UK)
UKPA	*Petroleum Act 1998* (UK)
UN	United Nations
UNCED	United Nations Conference on Environment and Development (Rio de Janeiro, 1992)
UNDP	United Nations Development Program
UNEP	United Nations Environment Program
UNCLOS	*United Nations Convention on the Law of the Sea 1982*
USD or US$	United States dollars
Weiss IFFG	Elizabeth Brown Weiss, *In Fairness to Future Generations: International Law, Common Patrimony and Intergenerational Equity* (United Nations University Tokyo and Transnational Publishers New York, 1988)
WFGW	*Well-being of Future Generations (Wales) Act* 2015

TABLE OF CASES

INTERNATIONAL

International Court of Justice

Case Concerning Pulp Mills on the River Uruguay (Argentina v Uruguay) [2010] ICJ Rep 14 — 5.18

Case Concerning the Gabcikovo-Nagymaros Dam (Hungary/Slovakia) [1997] ICJ Rep 7 — 5.18

Legality of the Threat or Use of Nuclear Weapons, Advisory Opinion [1996] ICJ Rep 226 — 5.18

Oposa v Factoran (1994) 33 ILM 173 — 5.20

Whaling in the Antarctic (Australia v Japan: New Zealand Intervening) [2014] ICJ Rep 262 — 5.18

NATIONAL

Australia

Church of Scientology v Woodward [1982] HCA 78, (1982) 154 CLR 25 — 3.17

Gloucester Resources Limited v Minister for Planning [2019] NSWLEC 7 — 3.34, 5.11, 5.12, 5.13, 6.16

Minister for Resources: ex parte Cazaly Iron Pty Ltd., Re (2007) 37 WAR 403 — 3.36

The Commonwealth of Australia v The State of Western Australia (1999) 196 CLR 392 — 3.36

Walker v Minister for Planning [2007] NSWLEC 741 — 6.11

Minister for Planning v Walker [2008] NSWCA 224 — 6.11

Waratah Coal Pty Ltd v Youth Verdict Ltd & Ors (No 6) [2022] QLC 21 — 5.21, 6.16

Canada

Borys v Canadian Pacific Railway Co [1953] D.L.R. 65 — 6.22

Labrador Inuit Association v Newfoundland (Minister of Environment and Labour), 1997 CanLII 14612 (NL CA) — 6.16

Reference re Impact Assessment Act [2023] SCC 23 — 6.05

Netherlands

State of the Netherlands v Urgenda [2019] ECLI:NL:GHDHA:2018:2591 (Supreme Court of the Netherlands) 5.21

Vereniging Milieudefensie and Others v Royal Dutch Shell PLC [2021] ECLI:NL: RBDHA:2021:5339 5.21

Norway

Foreningen Greenpeace Norden and others v The Government of Norway, case number 16-1666741TVI-OTIR/06 (Norwegian Supreme Court) 5.21

United Kingdom

R (application of Finch on behalf of the Weald Action Group) v Surrey County Council and Others [2024] UKSC 20 5.21, 6.16

United States of America

Basic Inc. v Levinson 488 US 224, 231, 232, and 240 (1988) 9.23

Illinois Central Railroad Company v Illinois, 146 U.S. 387 (1892) 3.38

Gould v Greylock Reservation Commission, 350 Mass. 410, 215 N.E. 2d 144 (1966) 3.38

Riggs v Palmer 115 N.Y. 506 (1889) 1.33

TABLE OF LEGISLATION

EU LEGISLATION

Commission Delegated Regulation (EU) 2023/2772 of 31 July 2023, supplementing Directive 2013/34/EU of the European Parliament and of the Council as regards sustainability reporting standards 9.35

Corporate Sustainability Reporting (CSRD), EU Directive 2022/2464 1.43, 2.25, 8.07, 8.26, 9.32, 9.35, 9.46, 9.48, 10.09, 10.14, 10.19, 10.20

Directive on Corporate Sustainability Due Diligence (CSDDD) EU Directive 2024/1760 8.26, 9.32, 9.47, 10.16

  Art 2 9.47

EU Taxonomy for Sustainable Activities (EU Taxonomy), Regulation 2020/852/EU 8.26, 9.32, 9.35, 10.16, 10.20

European Financial Reporting Advisory Group (EFRAG) 1.45, 9.35, 10.16, 10.23

European Financial Reporting Advisory Group Standards (ESRS) 9.35–39, 10.23

Sustainable Finance Disclosure Regulation (SFDR) Regulation 2019/2088 9.32, 9.35

Non-Financial Reporting Directive (NFRD) Directive 2014/95/EU 9.32, 9.33

INTERNATIONAL TREATIES AND CONVENTIONS

Convention on Biological Diversity, 1993 1.54

International Convention for the Regulation of Whaling 161 UNTS 75 (1946) 3.03, 5.17, 5.19

  Art III 3.01

Nuclear Test Ban Treaty, 1963 1.54

Paris Agreement to the United Nations Framework Convention on Climate Change, 12 December 2015, T.I.A.S. No. 16-1104 1.54, 2.02, 2.04

  Arts 2, 3 2.02

UN Framework Convention on Climate Change, 1992 1.54, 2.02

United Nations Convention on the Law of the Sea (UNCLOS), 1994 1.54

United Nations Universal Declaration of Human Rights, A/RES/217(III) (December 10, 1948) 1.54, 2.05

INTERNATIONAL SOFT LAW INSTRUMENTS

Convention on Long-range Transboundary Air Pollution (1979) 5.19

Equator Principles 2.34, 7.36

Global Reporting Initiative Guidelines 1.44, 2.25, 2.26–27, 8.05, 8.21, 8.40, 8.53, 9.35, 10.09, 10.10, 10.13, 10.14, 10.16

Intergovernmental Panel on Climate Change (IPCC), 1998 1.54

International Financial Reporting Standards (IFRS) 1.43, 1.45, 2.29, 9.04, 10.09, 10.10. 10.13, 10.14, 10.16

  IFRS S1 1.43, 1.45, 2.29, 3.07, 3.57–61, 9.04, 9.11, 9.29, 10.09, 10.20

  IFRS2 1.43, 1.45, 2.29, 3.07, 9.04, 9.11, 9.13–17, 9.24, 9.26, 9.29, 9.48, 9.49, 9.50, 10.49

  IFRS Sustainability Disclosure Standards 3.58

Report of the United Nations Conference on Environment and Development (12 August 1992) UN Doc A/CONF.151/6/Rev1 (Rio Declaration on Environment and Development) 4.04, 4.05, 5.17
Report of the United Nations Conference on the Human Environment (1972) UN Doc A/CONF.48/14 1.18, 1.54, 4.02
Task Force on Climate-related Financial Disclosures 1.43, 2.24, 2.28, 2.29, 3.07, 8.05, 8.16, 8.21, 8.40, 8.47, 9.02, 9.23, 9.28, 9.35, 9.48, 9.51, 10.09, 10.16
Final Report Recommendations of the Task Force for Climate Related Financial Disclosure, June 2017 (TFCD Final Report) 2.28, 8.05, 9.02, 9.49, 10.16
United Nations Charter 3.03
United Nations General Assembly Resolution, Permanent Sovereignty over Natural Resources, GA Res 1803 (XVII), UN Doc A/RES/1803(XVII) (14 December 1962) 4.04
United Nations General Assembly Resolution, Declaration on the Establishment of a New International Economic Order, GA Res 3201 (S-VI), UN Doc A/RES/3201(S-VI) (1 May 1974) 4.04
United Nations Framework Convention on Climate Change (1992) 5.19
United Nations General Assembly Resolution, Charter of Economic Rights and Duties of States, GA Res 3281 (XXIX) (12 December 1974) 4.04
United Nations General Assembly Resolution, Declaration on the Right to Development, GA Res 41/128, UN Doc A/RES/41/128 (4 December 1986) 4.04
United Nations Guiding Principles 2.05
United Nations Global Compact 2000, Global Compact Strategy 2021–2023 2.05
United Nations, Plan of Implementation of the World Summit on Sustainable Development (4 September 2002) UN Doc A/CONF.199/20 3.24
UN Resolution A/RES/44/228 (22 December 1989) 4.04
UN Resolution A/RES/70/1 'Transforming Our World: The 2030 Agenda for Sustainable Development' (25 September 2015) 1.10, 1.13, 1.52, 2.01, 2.04, 2.07, 2.10, 2.40, 4.04, 4.10–19, 4.38, 5.02, 5.14, 5.15, 5.22, 5.24, 8.07
World Commission on Environment and Development (WCED), Our Common Future (Brundtland Report) 1.08, 1.13, 1.19, 1.54, 3.20, 4.03, 4.06, 4.07, 4.08, 5.03, 5.04, 5.05, 5.23, 10.23
  Ch 2 4.06, 5.03
  Ch 12 1.22
World Commission on Environment and Development, Report of the World Commission on Environment and Development, UN Doc A/42/427 (4 August 1987) 1.08
World Conservation Strategy 1980 (WSC) 4.02

NATIONAL

Australia

Clean Energy Regulator Act 2011 2.18
Climate Change Act 2022 3.13
Corporations Act 2001 (CAWA) 1.48, 2.36, 3.43, 3.47, 9.05, 9.06, 9.07
  ss 3–5 2.36
  s 9 9.07
  s 180 3.43, 3.47
  s 181 3.43
  s 182 3.43
  s 183 3.43
  s 184 3.43
  s 285 9.07
  s 286A 9.07
  s 292A 9.07, 9.08
  s 296A 9.06, 9.07
  s 296D 9.09
  s 297 3.50
  s 298 1.48, 3.43, 3.50, 9.10

s 301A 9.07
s 307A 9.07
ss 793, 1101 3.54
Environmental Protection and Biodiversity Conservation Act 1999 (EPBCA) 6.10, 6.11, 6.13, 6.15, 6.18, 6.19, 6.36, 10.18
s 3 6.11, 6.36
s 18 6.10
s 133 6.13
Modern Slavery Act 2018 2.05
National Greenhouse and Energy Reporting Act 2007 (NGERA) 9.08
s 13 9.08
Native Title Act 1993 6.22
Offshore Electricity Infrastructure Act 2021 3.41
Offshore Petroleum and Greenhouse Gas Storage Act 2006 6.50, 7.24
Public Governance, Performance and Accountability Act 2013 3.13
Public Service Act 1999 3.13
Renewable Energy (Electricity) Act 2000 2.18
Renewable Energy (Electricity) (Large-scale Generation Shortfall Charge) Act 2000 2.18
Treasury Laws Amendment (Financial Market Infrastructure and Other Measures) Act 2024 (CRF, 9.51) 9.05, 9.06, 9.48, 9.49, 9.50, 9.51, 10.09
Sch 4 9.05

Soft Law

Australian Accounting Standards Board (AASB) 2.31, 8.21
AASB S1 General Requirements for Disclosure of Sustainability-related Financial Information (AASB S1) 9.04, 9.05, 9.17
AASB S2 Climate-related Disclosures (AASB S2) 9.04, 9.11, 9.17

New South Wales

Environmental Planning and Assessment Act 1979 5.12
s 451 5.12

Victoria

Mining Act 1852 3.29
Petroleum Act 1958 7.08
ss 34, 47 7.08

Western Australia

Corporations (Commonwealth Powers) Act 2001 3.42
Environmental Protection Act 1986 (WAenvpAct1986) 6.14, 6.15, 6.36, 6.37, 6.38, 6.63, 7.16, 7.34
s 3 6.15, 10.18
s 4 6.36
ss 38 6.14, 6.37
s 40 6.14
ss 44, 45 6.14
s 49 6.15
Environmental Protection Regulations 1987 (WAenvpRegs) 6.37
Land Administration Act 1967 6.61
Mining Act 1904 7.07
Mining Act 1972 (MAWA) 6.36, 6.37, 6.38, 7.16, 7.17
s 6 6.36
s 8 6.36, 7.16
s 27 6.36
s 66 6.36, 7.16
s 74 6.38, 7.16
s 85 6.36
Mining Act 1978 3.36
Petroleum Act 1936 7.07
s 9 7.07
Petroleum and Geothermal Energy and Resources Act 1967 (PGERA) 6.50, 6.52, 6.53, 7.04, 7.24
s 9 7.04
Petroleum and Geothermal Energy Resources (Environment) Regulations 2012 (PGERAER) 6.51, 6.52, 7.24, 7.25, 7.26
Reg 3 6.52
Reg 7 6.51, 7.24
Reg 11 6.52
Reg 14 6.51

Petroleum and Geothermal Energy Resources (Management of Safety) Regulations 2010 (PGERASR) 6.50, 7.24
Petroleum and Geothermal Energy Resources (Resource Management and Administration) Regulations 2014 (PGERRMA) 6.50, 6.53, 7.24, 7.26, 7.27, 7.28
Reg 47 7.27
Sch 3 7.28
Petroleum Submerged Lands Act 1982 6.50, 7.24

Canada

Canada Business Corporations Act (CBCA) 2024 9.28
Environmental Assessment Act 2012 6.05
Environmental Enforcement Act 6.15
Environmental Protection Act 1999 6.15
Gold Fields Act of British Columbia 1859 7.05
Impact Assessment Act 2019 (CIAA) 6.05, 6.06, 6.07, 6.08, 6.18, 6.19, 6.30, 6.32, 6.47, 6.64, 10.18
s 6 6.05
s 9 6.05, 6.47
s 7 6.06
s 21 6.06
s 31 6.07
s 63 6.07
s 65 6.06
s 99 6.06
s 102 6.07
Saskatchewan Natural Resources Act 1930 6.22, 7.12
s 1 7.12
Saskatchewan Oil and Gas Conservation Act 1952 7.08

Saskatchewan

Business Corporations Act 2021 (CASK) 2.36, 3.42, 3.48
9-21–9-23 3.43
9-23 3.45, 3.48
Crown Minerals Act (CMASAS) 6.33, 6.45, 7.13, 7.22
s 4 7.13
Energy and Mines Act 6.33
Environmental Assessment Act 1980 (EAASAS) 6.08, 6.09, 6.17, 6.30, 6.32, 6.48, 6.49, 6.60, 7.15, 7.23
s 2 6.08, 6.32
s 8 6.08, 6.30, 7.15, 7.23
ss 21, 22 6.08
s 25 6.09
Environmental Management and Protection Act 2010 6.06, 6.08, 6.15, 6.31
s 8 6.15
Financial and Consumer Affairs Authority of Saskatchewan Act 9.31
s 3 9.31
Mineral Disposition Regulations 1986 6.33
Mineral Exploration Incentive Regulations 6.33
Mineral Exploration Tax Credit Regulations 6.33
Mineral Industry Environmental Protection Regulations 1996 6.31, 7.15
Reg 2 7.13
Regs 23, 24 6.31, 7.15
Mineral Tenure Registry Regulations 2012 (MTRAC) 6.33, 7.13, 7.14
Regs 32, 35, 38, 41 6.33
Reg 48 7.13
Regs 51, 52 6.33
Regs 60, 62 7.14
Mineral Resources Act 1985 (S) 6.33
Mineral Taxation Act 1983 (S) 6.33
Oil and Gas Conservation Act 1978 (OGCASAS) 6.46, 6.49, 7.23
ss 3, 8 6.46, 7.23
Oil and Gas Conservation Regulations 2012 (OGRS) 6.46, 6.49
Regs 51, 70 6.46
Oil and Gas Tenure Registry Regulations (OGTRR) 6.45, 6.46, 7.22
Regs 6-6, 9-4 7.22
Planning and Development Act 2007 7.32
Securities Act 1988 (SAS1988) 9.31
Subsurface Mineral Tenure Regulations 2015 7.13
Reg 30 7.13

Norway

Constitution 5.21
Petroleum Act 1996 3.37

Philippines

Constitution 1987 5.20

United Kingdom

Canada Act 1982 6.22
Sch B 6.22
Climate Change Act 2008 3.13
Companies Act 2006 2.36, 2.42, 3.42, 3.45–46, 3.47, 3.48, 3.49, 3.50, 8.03, 9.01
s 171 3.42, 3.44
s 172 3.43, 3.45, 3.49
s 173 3.43
s 174 3.43, 3.46
s 171–177 3.42
s 182 3.43
s 414A 1.48, 3.43, 3.50, 3.59, 8.03, 9.01
s 414C 1.48, 3.50
Constitution Act 1867 6.22
s 109 6.22
Constitution Act 1982 6.22
ss 50, 51, 92 6.22
Energy Act 2016 3.37
Joint Stock Companies Act 1844 3.04
Modern Slavery Act 2015 2.05
Saskatchewan Act 1905 6.22, 7.12
s 21 6.22

Wales

Well-being of Future Generations (Wales) Act 2015 3.13, 3.18–23, 3.27, 3.62, 5.23
s 1 3.18
s 2 3.19
s 3 5.23
s 4 3.21
s 5 1.19, 3.20, 3.22, 5.23
ss 36, 39 3.19
Sch 2 3.19

United States of America

17 Code of Federal Regulations (CFR) 230.105 9.23
43 CFR 3100 6.42, 7.19
43 CFR 3101 7.19
43 CFR 3160 6.42, 7.19
43 CFR 3162 7.10, 7.19
43 CFR 3715 7.11
43 CFR 3802 7.11
43 CFR 3809 7.11
43 CFR 3833 7.09
Administrative Procedure Act 3.17
Clean Air Act 42 U.S.C. §7401 et seq. (1970) 6.28
Clean Water Act 33 U.S.C. §§ 131 6.15, 6.28
Constitution of the United States of America (ratified 1798) 3.14
Foreign Corrupt Practices Act 2.05
Inflation Reduction Act 2022 2.17
Mineral Leasing Act 1920 31 USC 181 6.42, 7.04, 7.18
Mining Law 1872 30 USC §29 1.53, 3.29, 6.23, 6.24, 7.04, 7.09
National Environmental Policy Act 1969 42 U.S.C. §4321 et seq. (1969) (NEPA) 6.04, 6.40
ss 101, 102, 106 6.04
Safe Drinking Water Act 6.28
Sarbanes-Oxley Act 2002 2.39
Securities Act 1933 2.39, 3.51, 9.18
Securities and Exchange Act 1934 2.39, 3.51, 9.18

Soft Law

Securities and Exchange Commission Rules 1.47, 1.54, 2.39, 3.51, 9.03, 9.18–26, 9.49, 9.50, 10.16
Climate Disclosure Rules (SECCCDIS2024) 1.47, 1.54, 9.03, 9.18, 9.19

Delaware

General Corporation Law, Chapter 1 of Title 8 of the Delaware Code 2.36

Nevada

Nevada Administrative Code 522 on Oil and Gas 6.64, 7.20, 7.21
Nevada Administrative Code 704.8831 to 704.8899 6.57
Nevada Revised Statutes – Chapter 78 Private Corporations (CSN) 3.42, 3.48, 3.49
78.138 3.43, 3.48
78.140 3.43
Nevada Revised Statutes, Chapter 86 Limited Liability Companies 2.36
Nevada Revised Statute 278 7.32
Nevada Revised Statutes Chapters 703 and 704 6.56, 7.31
Nevada Statutes Chapter 522 on Oil and Gas 6.44, 7.20

1

SUSTAINABILITY LAW IN MINING AND ENERGY: AN INTRODUCTION

AIM OF THE BOOK 1.01
THE APPROACH OF THIS BOOK TO SUSTAINABILITY 1.08
The importance of ecological systems and biodiversity 1.11
Social and economic pillars 1.13
OTHER THEMES OR ELEMENTS OF SUSTAINABILITY 1.14
Profitability 1.14
The modern emphasis on combining development and environmental protection 1.18
Equity 1.20
A suggestion for elements of environmental sustainability 1.22
FOCUSING ON MINERALS AND ENERGY AND RELATED POLICY AND REGULATION 1.24
Minerals and energy as natural resources 1.24
Phases of a mining or fossil fuel energy project 1.29
Differences with renewable energy projects 1.32
The meaning of principles and rules 1.33
A SNAPSHOT OF THE MINERALS AND ENERGY SECTOR 1.35
Minerals 1.35
Energy from fossil fuels and nuclear 1.37
Renewable energy 1.40
COMPANY REPORTING OBLIGATIONS: ESG AND OTHER APPROACHES 1.43
Compulsory reporting of climate change and sustainability risks is increasing 1.43
Other sources of rules and guidance 1.48
AGENDA AND CHAPTER OVERVIEW 1.52
REIMAGINING SUSTAINABILITY IN MINING AND ENERGY 1.55

AIM OF THE BOOK

The aim of this book is to explain and analyse the application of sustainability principles and rules in mining and energy and to provide a guide for those trying to understand them. Because of the energy transition revolution,[1] mining and energy companies are facing a tidal wave of increased disclosure and reporting requirements mainly focused on climate change risks, as well as changes to the more traditional forms of regulation. The picture is becoming increasingly complex, which is why a stocktaking and guide are timely. The early chapters will review some of the underpinnings of sustainability such as the rise of concern about the environment, the Sustainable Development 1.01

1 Industry interview, January 2025, describing the energy transition as a revolution, not an evolution.

Goals, and intergenerational equity. These form the base for other ideas that will be discussed, such as the trend over the last 50 years for regulators of minerals and fossil fuels to increase their scrutiny of environmental protection and health and safety. These are essential elements of sustainability and provide examples of sustainability principles and rules. But they have not generally been recognised as forming a discrete area of 'sustainability law' and regulators have been slow to use the term 'sustainability'. The reason for the book is that minerals and energy are both vital to the global economy. Without them, society could not function. This book explores sustainability principles and rules and their impact on mineral and energy production, including renewable energy. Are they just regulatory red tape, or do they have the potential to improve the availability and quality of minerals and energy? What would be required for them to realise that potential? This chapter sets the scene for the examination of issues like that by briefly introducing the reader to the history, the concepts, and the nature of the industry. The Agenda and Chapter Overview section at 1.52 contains the plan for a closer examination of important areas.

1.02 Dealing first with the importance of energy, modern lifestyles are increasingly dependent on electricity. Demand for electricity is going to grow as the world population increases and nations become wealthier. As a result, their desire for things like electric cars, data storage, artifical intelligence, and air conditioning will also increase.[2] Electricity has been generated to a great extent from the fossil fuels of coal, oil, and gas, which produce greenhouse gases. Those gases contribute to adverse changes in the climate, and many countries have moved to reduce emissions, that is, to decarbonise their economies. That shift has, in turn, led to a once-in-a-generation increase in the use of renewable energy sources such as solar and wind, which reduces emissions.[3] It has also required adjustments to the way in which energy is regulated, supplied, and used. A simple example is that electric cars need to have their batteries charged, leading to a growth in public charging stations. Electricity networks have also had to be expanded to deal with supply from renewable energy

2 *BP's Energy Outlook 2023 Edition* (BP 2023 Outlook) predicts that demand for electricity globally will increase by 75% in the period to 2050. See https://www.bp.com/content/dam/bp/business-sites/en/global/corporate/pdfs/energy-economics/energy-outlook/bp-energy-outlook-2023.pdf, 62. See also, International Energy Agency, *World Energy Outlook 2023* (IEA 2023 Outlook) https://www.iea.org/reports/world-energy-outlook-2023, 277; and the more detailed explanation in Chapter 6 of the IEA report.

3 Other options to generate energy include nuclear energy, hydroelectricity, and geothermal. See Table 6.7 at page 293 in the IEA 2023 Outlook (n 2). Nuclear contributes 10% of world electricity generation and hydropower contributes more than 10% (ibid, 281 and 294).

projects and increased and fluctuating supply and demand. Additionally, products like hydrogen, and its derivatives such as ammonia, are being examined not only for their potential as a green energy source but also as a medium to transport energy from countries like Australia and Chile with significant renewable power sources in sun and wind to countries like Germany, where they are less available.

Dealing next with mining, the world continues to have a significant appetite for minerals. The growth in renewable energy, artificial intelligence, and computing has meant an increased demand for the minerals required, such as lithium, copper, nickel, and rare earths, which in turn has caused enormous growth in the exploration and production of those minerals. At the same time, expanding economies like that of China continue to require huge quantities of more traditional minerals like iron ore and bauxite. 1.03

The mining and petroleum industries are having to respond to demands, not only that they take steps to reduce their emissions, but that their activities are conducted in a sustainable manner more broadly. The requirement to act sustainably goes further than achieving net zero emissions.[4] The next section will suggest what that means in definitional terms and how 'sustainability' will be used in this book. What we can say here is that the list of items that could fall under the umbrella of sustainability goes well beyond emissions and environmental damage to include things that can affect the operations of companies, and which are often dealt with in their ESG (environmental, social, and governance) reports. Examples include modern slavery and anti-corruption rules. In essence, sustainability requirements affect the way in which minerals and energy are produced, the extent of production, and the quality and characteristics of the product. They also have the potential to affect their availability by restricting opportunities to those companies with a good record. They also tend to make them more expensive to produce, which will cause problems for the sustainable producers until such time as a green premium is recognised and accepted by purchasers of minerals and energy. 1.04

The rules governing sustainability are becoming more stringent, and they are increasing in volume and complexity. This book aims to explain the critical ideas that underpin the governance of sustainability and extract key principles to help the reader solve sustainability problems in mining and energy. It provides a resource for those trying to develop or maintain mineral and energy 1.05

4 'Net zero' refers to achieving an overall balance between emissions produced and emissions removed from the atmosphere.

production and those trying to develop policy and regulations in relation to them.

1.06 The difficulty of their task is enhanced by a number of factors. They can be put into the following loose groups. The first is terminology and lack of balanced debate. There is disagreement as to the meaning and impacts of the terms used, including the term 'sustainability'. Different interest groups hold strong views on matters like the further development or use of fossil fuels. The debate is often highly charged and not balanced. Companies and governments falsely state that their products or services are sustainable, so-called 'greenwashing'. Next is politics and economics. On the one hand, governments are keen to reduce emissions, but on the other, they want to maintain growth and ensure that their populations have access to the economic benefits they currently enjoy. When you add in the huge cost of substituting renewable energy for energy from fossil fuels, you have a recipe for governments to continually revise down their decarbonisation and sustainability targets. Governments and interest groups often shy away from sensible discussion of these matters. Third and lastly is industry culture. In the mining jurisdictions like the USA, Australia, and Canada, there are very strong industry lobby groups who unsurprisingly want to continue to generate profits for their shareholders and therefore oppose changes which will impact their ability to do that. There are several good reasons why they take that position. The first, explored in Chapter 3, is the duty of company directors to act in the best interests of their shareholders rather than society. The second, explored in Chapters 6 and 7, is the historical approach of the industry to 'free mining' – basically that a miner or energy producer had the right to go onto land and explore and produce minerals with limited government interference. That culture persists. However, that is not the entire picture, as many companies are now embracing decarbonisation and sustainability, as other chapters will explore. Yet they too face economic challenges and there are examples of companies pulling back from decarbonisation objectives because of their impact on profits.

1.07 The world is in a period of mineral and energy transition in which the rules are changing, but there is considerable uncertainty. The move away from fossil fuels is taking time. Renewable energy sources like wind and solar are variable and intermittent if, for example, the wind does not blow or the sun is not shining. That means that fuels like gas can play an important role in bridging gaps in electricity generation. It is a simple but not well-understood point that electricity networks can only function with a constant and adequate supply of power, which wind and solar cannot provide without support. Energy networks need to be in balance so that supply and demand match each other. That means being able to deal with shortfalls in supply if, say, solar is not producing because it is nighttime or there is a spike in demand, for example, if very hot weather increases the use of air conditioning. If a part of a network falls out of balance, then the nature of electricity means that that part will shut down, and that can have a knock-on effect causing a total blackout in a region. In simple terms, the engineering works a bit like a circuit breaker or series of circuit breakers in a person's home. So, fossil fuels can still be an important part of the fuel mix for energy supply until there is an improved technological solution, such as more or improved batteries. But also, fossil fuels continue to have their essential uses, such as the production of medicines, fertilisers, and building materials. The ongoing production and use of fossil fuels to meet these needs add to the difficulty of plotting a decarbonisation pathway and, importantly, being able to justify it.

THE APPROACH OF THIS BOOK TO SUSTAINABILITY

It is notable that many organisations do not define sustainability. That is also **1.08**
the case with some of the accounting and other standards.[5] Some treat sustainability as having the same meaning as sustainable development. Those that define it often focus on the ecological and intergenerational aspects, sometimes using the well-known quote from the report of the World Commission on Environment and Development (WCED), *Our Common Future* (Brundtland Report), of the meaning of sustainable development:[6] 'development that meets the needs of the present without compromising the ability of future generations to meet their own needs'.[7] There are numerous examples of definitions, many of which note the economic and social pillars of sustainability.[8]

---

5 A matter explored in Chapters 3 and 10

6 The Brundtland Report is the report of the World Commission on Environment and Development, *Our Common Future* (Oxford University Press, 1987); see also World Commission on Environment and Development, *Report of the World Commission on Environment and Development*, UN Doc A/42/427 (4 August 1987) annex (Brundtland Report)

7 Brundtland Report Chapter 2: Towards Sustainable Development, para 1.

8 The Charter of the UCLA Sustainability Committee defines sustainability as: 'the integration of environmental health, social equity and economic vitality in order to create thriving, healthy, diverse and resilient communities for this generation and generations to come. The practice of sustainability recognizes how these issues are interconnected and requires a systems approach and an acknowledgement of complexity.' UCLA Sustainability Charter https://www.sustain.ucla.edu/wp-content/uploads/UCLA-Sustainability-Charter.pdf. See also: The property of being environmentally sustainable; the degree to which a process or enterprise is able to be maintained or continued while avoiding the long-term depletion of natural resources. https://www.oed.com/dictionary/sustainability_n.

1.09 The approach of this book to the meaning of sustainability in mining and energy is based on the older dictionary definitions – that something is capable of enduring for the long term[9] – or more recently, the quality of being sustainable 'at a certain rate or level'.[10] The proposed definition of sustainability is:

> Sustainability for a mining or energy project means that it will operate effectively for its intended life, cover its costs in that period, including environmental and social costs, comply with applicable laws and policies and continually improve its performance, the total quality of life and the ecological processes affected by it.

Factors that affect the performance of companies and the availability of minerals and energy for future generations need to be borne in mind – notably the extent and complexity of applicable laws. Performance is also brought out in the definition of sustainability used by Focus 15 Sustainability Committees: Structures and Practices (IFC Sustainability Practices), published by the International Finance Corporation (IFC) arm of the World Bank Group: 'the environmental and social factors that have an impact on the long-term performance of companies'.[11] Impact, whether financial or non-financial, is a very common theme in the disclosure and reporting regimes for companies reviewed in Chapter 9. Impact can be positive as well as negative. The rationale for the importance of sustainability in the view of the IFC lies not just in the compliance aspects but in its importance for long-term successful operational performance.[12] That distinction is important because many of the laws are directed at compliance requirements – for example, reporting on environmental performance, climate change, and modern slavery, and complying with the applicable regulations. Those compliance requirements have the potential to limit long-term supplies of minerals and energy. Performance involves broader questions about planning the future of the company and the profitable continuance and improvement of its operations. Not only are these more fundamental, but they are intrinsically more difficult.

1.10 Two themes support a wider view of sustainability going beyond the environment. The first is the focus on sustainable development flowing from the UN's Sustainable Development Goals. Sustainable development is regarded as

9 The Australian Concise Oxford Dictionary, Definition 1 of 'sustain', which is 'support, bear the weight of, especially for a long period' (Oxford University Press Australia, 3rd ed, 1967).

10 Oxford Dictionaries, Definition 2a of 'sustainability' https://www.oed.com/dictionary/sustainability_n.

11 IFC Sustainability Practices 2, quoting from IFC Toolkit for Disclosure and Transparency, 2018, 5. It goes on to say that 'the economic contribution (effect) of the company, and how the broader economy affects it and its customer base, surrounding communities, and other stakeholders, are implied in the performance dimension'.

12 IFC Sustainability Practices 4.

having three pillars: environmental, social, and economic. Companies report on all three areas. The second theme is the idea of a social licence to operate. Increasingly, companies are having to justify their existence by showing that they deal positively not just with their shareholders, but with people and societies affected by their operations. Even companies producing renewable energy, who at first glance would appear to be well positioned to benefit from sustainability, can have issues with their supply chains and modern slavery if their solar equipment is produced by underpaid workers in poor conditions.

The importance of ecological systems and biodiversity

A starting point in understanding sustainability is that it is inextricably linked to nature. As a report for the United States Environmental Protection Agency put it in 2011: **1.11**

> Sustainability is based on a simple and long-recognized factual premise: Everything that humans require for their survival and well-being depends, directly or indirectly, on the natural environment.[13] The environment provides the air we breathe, the water we drink, and the food we eat. It defines in fundamental ways the communities in which we live and is the source for renewable and non- renewable resources on which civilization depends. Our health and well-being, our economy, and our security all require a high-quality environment.[14]

At the same time, the definition used by the committee writing the report, which was taken from United States Executive Order 13514, indicated that the purpose of sustainability is to allow a productive relationship with nature which fulfils the social, economic, and other requirements of present and future generations.[15]

In activities that society has engaged in for thousands of years, such as agriculture, forestry, and water management, there are many examples of sustainable practices.[16] An example is that in many countries the management of forests **1.12**

---

13 G. P. Marsh, *Man and Nature; or, Physical Geography as Modified by Human Action* (Belknap Press of Harvard University Press, 1964).

14 National Academy of Sciences, *Sustainability and the U.S. EPA* (National Academy Press, 2011), 1.

15 Sustainability: 'to create and maintain conditions, under which humans and nature can exist in productive harmony, that permit fulfilling the social, economic, and other requirements of present and future generations' (NEPA [1969], EO 13514 [2009], 2).

16 Many were reviewed by the then Vice President of the International Court of Justice, Judge Christopher G. Weeremantry, in his separate minority opinion in the 1997 *Case Concerning the Gabcikovo-Nagymaros Project* (*Hungary v* Slovakia), where he unsuccessfully sought to apply customary law to sustainable development, saying that 'the principle of sustainable development is thus a part of modern international law by reason not only of its inescapable logical necessity, but also by reason of its wide and general acceptance by

for the long term has historically been given a high priority, with detailed regulations that have evolved over centuries.[17] But as the world has become more industrialised and urbanised, the fundamental connection between human society and the natural environment has weakened. That has made maintaining the quality of the environment much more difficult.

Social and economic pillars

1.13 The linkage to social and economic objectives is encapsulated in the term 'sustainable development', which is discussed in a sub-section below. The UN's Sustainable Development Goals (SDGs) are listed in Chapter 4. A UN website puts the linkage like this:

> For sustainable development to be achieved, it is crucial to harmonize three core elements: economic growth, social inclusion and environmental protection. These elements are interconnected and all are crucial for the well-being of individuals and societies.[18]

Slightly different forms of words are used to describe the three pillars, depending on the source. Sometimes the social pillar is described as 'social development' and the economic pillar as 'economic development'. The underpinning for the linkage is clear from the Brundtland Report discussed below, in that development is necessary to improve the position of poor nations but must also benefit society, or, as the UN website just mentioned puts it, result in 'social inclusion'. Sometimes the word 'equity' is used instead of social development. However, it is also important to ensure that decision-makers, in making 'social and economic development decisions do not disregard environmental considerations and not undertake environmental protection without taking into account relevant economic and social considerations'.[19] It is also important to recognise that the three elements are not always in balance or to be given equal weight in every situation. What can be said here is that the importance of the point that human survival depends on the natural environment cannot be overstated. The danger of having three pillars of sustainable development is that incompetent or self-interested decision-makers are not able to fairly balance them in a way in which the environment is sufficiently preserved.

---

the global community'. *Gabcikovo-Nagymaros Project (Hungary/Slovakia)* I.C.J. Reports (Judgment of 25 September 1997), 95 https://www.icj-cij.org/en/case/92/judgments.

17 See, for example, Klaus Bosselmann, *The Principle of Sustainability – Transforming Law and Governance* (Ashgate, 2008) (Bosselmann Sustainability).

18 UN, *The Sustainable Development Agenda*, 'What is sustainable development', https://www.un.org/sustainabledevelopment/development-agenda-retired/#:~:text=Sustainable%20development%20has%20been%20defined,to%20meet%20their%20own%20needs.

19 Cordonier Segger and Khalifan, *Sustainable Development Law* (OUP 2004), 104.

OTHER THEMES OR ELEMENTS OF SUSTAINABILITY

Profitability

Profitability is vital for the sustainability of a mining or energy operation in private ownership. For that to endure or be maintained at a certain level, production is profitable, otherwise the business will fail. An important step in achieving profitability is to ensure that operations cover the direct costs of production, such as the cost of extraction, the cost of treatment, the cost of energy, the cost of labour, the cost of ancillary services, and government royalties and taxes. The other important element here is the price that can be obtained for the mineral, which is often variable. Minerals and fossil fuels are notorious for booms followed by busts – companies rush in to produce minerals like lithium, nickel, and copper when the price is high, only to find that the resulting increased production or less robust demand causes an oversupply and falling prices, followed by mine closures.[20] Another element can be that companies with higher environmental and sustainability standards have higher production costs, so they can be undercut by companies with lower standards.[21] There is another layer of costs – indirect costs – which need to be taken into account. Indirect costs include damage to the environment and rehabilitation costs. In recent times, damage to the environment has started to include the greenhouse gas emissions from the activity. **1.14**

While climate change is seen by many as the most important crisis faced by humanity currently, it is suggested that it is only one, albeit very important, aspect of damage to the environment. Loss of biodiversity and the scenic value of landscapes are two others. Social costs of mining and energy activity are also relevant. These can include injuries to the workforce, but also the negative impacts of poor working conditions on a community; examples are the harm to health caused by coal and asbestos dust. These are all costs which can be taken into account if the true cost of a sustainable mining operation is to be evaluated. **1.15**

In the past, mining and energy companies and governments were not accustomed to taking the holistic approach that assessing sustainability in such a **1.16**

20 For example, in January 2024, Australia's ABC reported that the price of lithium had fallen by more than 80% in the last 12 months and that of nickel by more than 40%, causing several mines to close down. Darya Zadvirna, 'What's behind the drastic downturn in nickel and lithium prices and what does it mean?' (ABC News, updated 31 January 2024) https://www.abc.net.au/news/2024-01-26/examining-the-drastic-downturn-in-nickel-and-lithium-prices/103388902.

21 Ibid.

complete sense requires. A contributing factor is that sustainability has developed gradually as environmental science has developed and as governments have progressively tightened up controls over pollution and rehabilitation and security for the cost. Governments have often done this because ultimately it is the government that commonly has to deal with the domestic consequences of pollution. Rehabilitation obligations are much more rigorous now than they were one hundred years ago. Nevertheless, there have been many occasions, and there will continue to be many occasions, when the full cost of a mining or energy operation only becomes known after the company has ceased operations. Then equity considerations come into play, and these are discussed below.

1.17 As will be discussed in Chapter 6, the regulators have processes to manage the risk of what can be described as the escape of costs. Environmental impact assessment is one of those. It is aimed at examining and mitigating the environmental risks associated with a project before it commences, rather than dealing with them when the project is in operation and change is more difficult. But examples of a full cost–benefit analysis of a project at the outset are rare.

The modern emphasis on combining development and environmental protection

1.18 In modern times, there has been an increased emphasis on environmental protection. The increasing attention on the environment can be traced back to the United Nations (UN) conferences on general environmental issues, the first of which was the 1972 Stockholm Conference on the Human Environment.[22] The UN conferences were prompted by the growing crisis in the environment brought about by human activity, which has contributed to pollution, land degradation, loss of biodiversity, and climate change. Principle 1 of the Stockholm Declaration's 26 Principles expressed a general obligation to protect the environment for both present and future generations.[23] From about this time, many countries enacted environmental protection legislation and ratified international conventions protecting threatened species, habitat, and heritage.

1.19 In this period, it became increasingly clear that the interrelated issues of widespread poverty and growing environmental degradation around the world were

22 UN Doc A/CONF.48/14 (1972).

23 Ibid.

not being effectively addressed, and that the development model needed to be modified to combine conservation and development in a way that benefited present and future generations. That occurred as a result of the Brundtland Report. The Brundtland Report set out to encourage development to improve the position of poor nations in a way that did not further damage the environment. It developed the concept of sustainable development as: 'development that meets the needs of the present without compromising the ability of future generations to meet their own needs'.[24] This definition can be found in numerous statutes.[25] As already mentioned, sustainable development is viewed as having three elements or pillars: environment, society, and economy. The economic pillar supports a substantial purpose of sustainable development, which is the economic development of poor nations to relieve poverty. But at the same time without that pillar, there is little incentive for change.

Equity

Equity can refer to equity between generations and within a generation. It can also be used as part of, or instead of, the second, 'social', pillar of sustainable development. Intra-generational equity has mainly concerned access to energy and the price of access. It requires that part of the population is not disadvantaged in its ability to get energy or to get it at prices comparable with the rest of the population. That has led to the development of the study of energy justice discussed in Chapter 4. **1.20**

Intergenerational equity is mainly about timing and the matching of benefits and burdens. In relation to timing, during the development and production phases, the generations alive at that time can enjoy the benefits of employment, dividends paid to shareholders in the mining or energy company, and revenue to local businesses and different levels of government through royalties, rates, and taxes. When production ceases, the burden of tax refunds to the mining and energy company and rehabilitation costs will fall on the generation alive at that time. So, there will commonly be a problem in matching benefits and burdens. One way to deal with that is to set aside a portion of current profits into a future fund, which will only be available to meet the needs of future generations. **1.21**

---

24 Brundtland Report Chapter 2: Towards Sustainable Development, para 1.

25 For example, section 5(2)(1) of the *Well-being of Future Generations (Wales) Act 2015* says that 'a public body must act in a manner which seeks to ensure that the needs of the present are met without compromising the ability of future generations to meet their own needs'.

A suggestion for elements of environmental sustainability

1.22 Another way to look at sustainability is to break it down into component elements. That is not generally done in the literature, but it is possible to extract component elements from commentary and the statutes.[26] They cover the following environmental matters:

- Ecosystems necessary for human life: Physical quality of life for humans is conserved;
- Biodiversity: Diversity of nature is conserved;[27]
- Culture and aesthetic value of nature: Amenity is maintained;[28]
- Restoration: Ecosystems improve.

1.23 If an organisation or company is examining or challenging its approach to sustainability or particular sustainability policies, it can frame questions based on these elements:

- How does this policy protect or improve the ability of the planet to support human life?
- How does this policy protect or improve the ability of the planet to support ecosystems and biodiversity?
- How does this policy protect or improve cultural, heritage, and similar values?
- How does this policy restore damaged ecosystems?

FOCUSING ON MINERALS AND ENERGY AND RELATED POLICY AND REGULATION

Minerals and energy as natural resources

1.24 The focus of this book is minerals and energy. The purpose of this section is to explain how they fit within the broader concept of natural resources. The Organisation for Economic Co-operation and Development (OECD)

---

26 For more on this, see John A. P. Chandler, 'Improving outcomes for future generations in petroleum licensing regimes – an assessment of the United Kingdom's regime: Part 1 – the assessment methodology' (2021) 39(3) *Journal of Energy & Natural Resources Law*, 271.

27 For the first two, see, for example, paragraph 83 of Chapter 12 of the Brundtland Report.

28 See, for example, Edith Brown Weiss, *In Fairness to Future Generations: International Law, Common Patrimony and Intergenerational Equity* (United Nations University Tokyo and Transnational Publishers New York, 1988), 38. See also Edith Brown Weiss, 'Implementing Intergenerational Equity' in Malgosia Fitzmaurice, David M. Ong, and Panos Merkouris (eds), *Research Handbook on International Environmental Law* (Edward Elgar, 2010), 102.

definition of natural resources is: 'natural assets (raw materials) occurring in nature that can be used for economic production or consumption'.[29]

The OECD then subdivides them into four categories: mineral and energy resources, soil resources, water resources, and biological resources.[30] Minerals and energy are the resources that will be focused on in this book. It is outside its scope to consider the specialised solutions and regulations applicable to soil resources, water resources, and biological resources. For example, forests are a timber resource that fits within the descriptor of biological resources.[31] What minerals, energy, and forests have in common is the production of the resource leading to its sale or consumption. 1.25

A critical difference is that forests, like agricultural crops, require cultivation and are renewable in the sense that once a crop has been harvested, a further crop can be grown on the same ground. But minerals and energy are not renewable and have finite limits. What also follows is that change to the environment is an inevitable result of mining, and also of non-renewable energy production. An obvious starting point is that the minerals or fossil fuel will be extracted. In the case of many minerals, that will leave a significant open cut or underground mine, which often will be too large to fill in and restore at the conclusion so that the surface of the land is identical to how it was before operations commenced. There are also differences in terminology and approach. Getting minerals and energy into production requires significant risk and also capital: first, it is necessary to explore and find a commercial deposit; then it has to be evaluated and production planned. The expression 'development' is used in the mining and energy context to describe the process of getting a mine or petroleum well into production with the creation of the infrastructure and facilities required. 1.26

Development can be defined more broadly as 'the modification of the biosphere and the application of human, financial, living and non-living resources 1.27

29 Organisation for Economic Co-operation and Development (OECD), *Glossary of Statistical Terms*, 'Glossary of Environment Statistics, Studies in Methods', Series F, No. 67 (United Nations, New York, 1997) https://www.oecd.org/content/dam/oecd/en/publications/reports/2008/09/oecd-glossary-of-statistical-terms_g1gh9ad7/9789264055087-en.pdf.

30 It gives as context: 'The naturally occurring assets that provide use benefits through the provision of raw materials and energy used in economic activity (or that may provide such benefits one day) and that are subject primarily to quantitative depletion through human use. They are subdivided into four categories: mineral and energy resources, soil resources, water resources and biological resources', ibid.

31 OECD definition of biological resources, Glossary of Statistical Terms https://www.oecd-ilibrary.org/oecd-glossary-of-statistical-terms_5kzfczx4w8t.pdf?itemId=%2Fcontent%2Fpublication%2F9789264055087-en&mimeType=pdf.

to satisfy human needs and improve the quality of life'.[32] This definition brings out the modification of the biosphere, which has reached a critical stage in recent times because of climate change, rising temperatures, and loss of biodiversity, to name some of the environmental problems caused by humans. The weakness of approaches like that of the OECD (see 1.24) is that a focus on production and consumption does not deal with the negative effects of those things or with things like climate and air temperature that are essential to the quality of human life, but are not easily viewed as producible or consumable.[33] Hence, there has been an increasing emphasis on accounting for nature which is explained in Chapter 2.

1.28 This book does not consider the implications of the use of the product when produced. So, it does not deal with the environmental and other consequences of the use of the product – for example, if hydrocarbons are turned into plastics. It also does not consider the implications of the creation of the facilities required for exploration, development, and production – for example, the greenhouse gas emissions produced in the manufacture of solar panels or wind turbines.

Phases of a mining or fossil fuel energy project

1.29 Large mining and energy projects will usually require numerous environmental approvals, which track the phases of the project. A mining or fossil fuel energy project usually comprises the following phases: exploration, appraisal, development, production, and decommissioning/rehabilitation. In the exploration phase, the explorer is searching for an economically viable resource – that is, one where the resource can be extracted and sold profitably. Appraisal requires a more detailed evaluation of the resource and how it will be developed – this can involve feasibility studies of increasing rigour and detail. Development involves the design, construction, and commissioning of the facilities, plant, and machinery necessary for production. For a mine, that will require the design and construction of conveyors, crushers, loaders, treatment plants, energy supply, and accommodation and facilities for workers. The extraction of the ore will require mining plant and equipment. For an onshore oil and gas project, the focus will be on the wells and pipelines required to

32 International Union for Conservation of Nature and Natural Resources, *World Conservation Strategy: Living Resource Conservation for Sustainable Development* (World Conservation Strategy), section 1, paragraph 3, United Nations Environment Programme and World Wildlife Fund, Gland, Switzerland, 1980.

33 The OECD's approach can be explained on the basis that the purpose of the glossary is to inform the SEEA (System of Environmental-Economic Accounting) https://seea.un.org.

extract the resource before it is treated. In both cases, the product will have to be transported to customers, whether by truck, rail, pipeline, or ship.

In mining and fossil fuel energy, there will also usually be parallel procedures to check that operations will be safe for employees and others involved. The body responsible for environmental and safety approvals varies between countries. In some cases, it is the mining or petroleum regulator, often a department set up for that purpose. In other cases, particularly safety, there is a dedicated and separate safety regulator. So, there are a number of separate streams of regulation. Mining laws developed earlier than those regulating petroleum because petroleum only started being produced in commercial quantities at the end of the 19th century. Environmental legislation developed in the middle of the 20th century and occupational health and safety legislation around the same time. **1.30**

The discussion of state and corporate governance and environmental and development approvals in Chapters 6 and 7 will use examples focusing particularly on the United States of America (USA), Canada, and Australia. All three are leading mining and energy economies and have well-developed mining and energy regulatory systems which are public and in the English language. All of them have a federal structure, which means that there are two levels of government, federal and state/provincial, with an interest in the regulation of mining and energy matters. Federal governments tend to be focused on matters of national interest, which should mean that day-to-day regulation is mainly conducted at the state level. However, there are exceptions, for example, where the federal government has significant public lands, as in Nevada, or has exclusive jurisdiction, such as in some offshore areas. The states that will be used in the examples are Nevada,[34] Saskatchewan, and Western Australia. A snapshot of the mineral and energy sector globally is given in a later section of this chapter. **1.31**

Differences with renewable energy projects

Renewable energy projects are different for several reasons. First, there is no need for wells, except water wells if water is essential, for example, in the **1.32**

34 According to the US Government Mineral Review 2022, Nevada ranked second among the states in the USA by the size of its mineral production https://apps.usgs.gov/minerals-information-archives/articles/USGS-Mineral-Review-2022.pdf. Nevada's principal minerals are copper, gold, lime, silver, and stone (crushed). It is the largest gold producer in the USA. It is also a small oil producer. Arizona ranked first in this survey and Texas third. Both have a significant focus on cement and other construction minerals, which is the reason Nevada was chosen. Colorado ranked ninth.

production of certain types of hydrogen. Second, wind and solar farms will require investigation in relation to matters like the strength and reliability of the wind and the positioning of the rotors and panels but do not require the location and extraction of a mineral or petroleum resource. Exploration and development are, therefore, very different. Third, the mining and petroleum legislation does not apply. Renewable energy sources have only become mainstream in the last 30 years, and many jurisdictions do not have special legislation to regulate them. Access to land will be an issue and can often be negotiated with private landowners. Other legislation that can be applicable includes planning laws and laws regulating the production of electricity and connection to networks.

The meaning of principles and rules

1.33 The expressions 'rules' and 'regulations' are generally used in this book to mean legally binding rules which, following Dworkin's analysis, means that they lead to a particular legal consequence.[35] An example of a rule is a statutory provision to conduct operations safely under occupational health and safety legislation, breach of which could lead to a fine or criminal penalty such as imprisonment. A legal principle is somewhat broader in that it 'states a reason that argues in one direction, but does not necessitate a particular decision'.[36] According to Dworkin, a policy is 'that kind of standard that sets out a goal to be reached, generally an improvement in some economic, political, or social feature of the community'.[37] It is often the case that legislation of legal rules follows the development of a new policy or the revision of an existing one. Primarily, this is done by government, although frequently public consultation is involved. Policy is therefore often a precursor to the development of legal rules but can also be relevant to their interpretation, for example, guidelines developed by lower levels of government. As we will see, sustainability in minerals and energy is governed by a combination of policy, principles, and rules.

1.34 But we also need to take into account the increasing development in international law of the idea of 'soft law', which has various suggested meanings but is

---

35 R. Dworkin, *Taking Rights Seriously* (Duckworth, 1977), Chapter 2. There is an ongoing debate in legal philosophy between Dworkin's approach and that of H.L.A. Hart, whose view can be summarised as a law is a rule that comes from a source that can make laws. See H.L.A. Hart, *The Concept of Law* (3rd ed. 2012, Clarendon Law Series, Oxford University Press).

36 Ibid, 26. A principle is something like, 'No man may profit from his own wrong.' It can be the ground for a decision, as happened in *Riggs vs. Palmer* 115 N.Y. 506 (1889). In that case, a grandson did not inherit from his grandfather because he had murdered him. But there can be situations where someone can still profit from a wrongful act.

37 Ibid, 22.

usefully defined as 'a non-binding written instrument setting out international principles'.[38] The definition includes resolutions, declarations, rules, and codes of conduct which are not in a form that states agree are legally binding.[39] They can be highly influential and seem close in nature to Dworkin's idea of a legal principle but with the possible difference of a greater disposition to particular consequences.

A SNAPSHOT OF THE MINERALS AND ENERGY SECTOR

The purpose of this section is to illustrate the size and dimensions of the sector.

Minerals

The six countries with the largest production of minerals in 2021, excluding construction materials, and starting with the largest, are China, the USA, Russia, Saudi Arabia, Australia, and Canada.[40] Of China's production, which is in excess of US$900 billion, over US$600 billion was mineral fuels. Mineral fuels include coal, gas, petroleum, oil sands and shales, and uranium. The next largest component was non-ferrous metals, amounting to approximately US$100 billion. Over 90% of the production of minerals from the USA (with total production just over US$600 billion), Russia, and Saudi Arabia was mineral fuels. Australia's total production was a little over US$300 billion, with approximately US$100 billion from each of iron ore and mineral fuels. When looked at on a metric tonnage basis, the World Population Review comments on the 2021 figures: mineral fuels are the world's largest category, making up 4.1 billion of China's 4.6 billion-ton production. They similarly make up 2.1 billion of the United States' 2.2 billion tons and 1.6 billion of Russia's 1.7 billion tons. In fact, they make up the majority of almost every sizeable mineral-producing nation's output, except for Brazil, which mines 274.4 million tons of iron and ferro-alloys, compared with just 176.1 million tons of mineral fuels. That's enough to rank as the world's second largest iron producer, behind Australia's 575.2 million tons. China also mines a large amount of iron and ferro-alloys, 259.5 million tons.[41] 1.35

38 Stephen J Toope, 'Formality and Informality' in Daniel Bodansky, Jetta Brunnee, and Ellen Hey (eds), *The Oxford Handbook of International Environmental Law* (Oxford University Press, 2004) at 121.

39 Ibid.

40 Federal Ministry Republic of Austria and International Organising Committee for the World Mining Congresses, World Mining Data 2023 https://www.world-mining-data.info/wmd/downloads/PDF/WMD2023.pdf, 30.

41 World Population Review Mineral Production by country https://worldpopulationreview.com/country-rankings/mineral-production-by-country.

1.36 The eight largest mining companies in the world judged by market capitalisation, in order from the biggest, are BHP Group, Rio Tinto, China Shenhua Energy Co Ltd, Glencore Plc, Vale SA, Freeport-McMoRan Inc, Fortescue Ltd, and Newmont Corp.[42] BHP Group's total revenue in 2023 was US$53.817 billion with a profit after taxation from continuing operations of US$14.324 billion.[43] To indicate the contribution and size of the large mining companies, BHP Group's revenue represents in dollar terms very roughly 9% of total USA mineral production and 17% of Australian production.

Energy from fossil fuels and nuclear

1.37 The International Energy Agency's World Energy Outlook 2023 (IEA 2023 Outlook) has three scenarios, but the energy supply figures quoted next are taken from its Stated Policies Scenario (STEPS), which is based on what governments are actually doing, rather than what they say they are doing, and which is now associated with a temperature rise of 2.4°C in 2100 (with a 50% probability).[44] By 2030, it shows total renewable energy supply as 18% of the total energy supply (up from 12% in 2022).[45] Nuclear is at 6% (up from 5%), unabated natural gas is at 22% (in 2022, it was 23%), oil is at 29% (down from 30%) and unabated coal is at 22% (down from 27%). The main focus of this book in terms of fossil fuels is oil and gas. Coal is not given detailed coverage, although there are some references in relation to mining regulation. Nuclear has required its own specialised legislation and regulation and is not covered in this book for that reason. It is nevertheless an important part of the energy mix in some countries: France and the USA, for example.

1.38 The countries producing the largest amount of crude oil in the world in 2022, with their percentage of world production in brackets, were: the USA (14.7%), Saudi Arabia (13.2%), Russia (12.7%), Canada (5.6%), and Iraq (5.5%).[46] The eight largest producers of natural gas in 2022, starting with the largest, were the USA, Russia, Iran, China, Canada, Qatar, Australia, and Norway. Production ranged from 978.6 cubic metres in the USA and 618.40 cubic metres in Russia

42 As of 31 December 2022, Global Data https://www.globaldata.com/companies/top-companies-by-sector/mining/global-companies-by-market-cap/#.

43 BHP Group Annual Report 2023 https://www.bhp.com/-/media/documents/investors/annual-reports/2023/230822_bhpannualreport2023.pdf, 19.

44 IEA 2023 Outlook https://www.iea.org/reports/world-energy-outlook-2023, 91.

45 Ibid, 264.

46 US Energy Information, *Where our oil comes from* https://www.eia.gov/energyexplained/oil-and-petroleum-products/where-our-oil-comes-from.php.

to 122.8 cubic metres in Norway.[47] The USA has moved dramatically upwards in these league tables over the last few years as a result of its production of unconventional petroleum. Only a decade ago, the USA was apparently going to have to import large amounts of energy, and now it is exporting energy.

The eight largest oil and gas companies by market capitalisation are: Saudi Aramco, ExxonMobil, Chevron, PetroChina, Shell, TotalEnergies, ConocoPhillips, and Petrobras.[48] Using ExxonMobil as an example, its total revenues and other income in the 2022 annual report were US$413.68 billion. Net income after tax was US$55.74 billion.[49] That compares with the value of Canada's crude oil exports in 2019 of $84.3 billion, representing 14.1% of total Canadian exports.[50] **1.39**

Renewable energy

BP's Energy Outlook 2023 Edition (BP 2023 Outlook) also has three scenarios: Accelerated, Net Zero, and New Momentum. In the period to 2050, BP predicts that wind and solar installed capacity will increase by around 15-fold in the Accelerated and Net Zero scenarios and by 9-fold in the New Momentum scenario.[51] What that means is that by 2050, wind and solar 'account for around two-thirds of global power generation – and closer to 75% in the most advanced regions – in Accelerated and Net Zero. That share is around half by 2050 in New Momentum.'[52] According to BP, the growth in wind and power generation through to 2030 is dominated by China and the developed world, who together account for 80–85% of the growth, but that declines to 35–60% between 2030 and 2050 as the emerging markets, excluding China, experience strong growth. There is a growth in gas-fired power **1.40**

47 World Population Review, *Natural Gas by Country* https://worldpopulationreview.com/country-rankings/natural-gas-by-country.

48 Largest oil and gas companies by market cap https://companiesmarketcap.com/oil-gas/largest-oil-and-gas-companies-by-market-cap/. Statista produces a different result as of 31 December 2023, putting ExxonMobil as the largest and including BP at number 8. Reliance Industries from India is included at number 4, and PetroChina is 5th. Petrobras is 9th. https://www.statista.com/statistics/272709/top-10-oil-and-gas-companies-worldwide-based-on-market-value/.

49 ExxonMobil Annual Report 2022 https://d1io3yog0oux5.cloudfront.net/_c06c2f9e20ad0717841cebabefbe2aaf/exxonmobil/db/2301/22049/annual_report/2022-Annual-Report.pdf, 77.

50 Canada Energy Regulator, *Canadian Crude Oil Exports: A 30 year Review* https://www.cer-rec.gc.ca/en/data-analysis/energy-commodities/crude-oil-petroleum-products/report/canadian-crude-oil-exports-30-year-review/.

51 BP Energy Outlook 2023 Edition (n 2), 57.

52 Ibid, 65.

generation concentrated in those economies for the rest of the decade, but that and coal-fired generation both reduce after 2030.[53]

1.41 The International Renewable Energy Agency (IRENA) also produces useful data.[54] To get another perspective on the scale of renewable energy and its location, we can look at some of the country tables produced by IRENA. So, for solar in 2021, China was the largest generator of electricity using solar at in excess of 300,000 gigawatt hours (GWh), followed by the USA at 150 GWh, Japan at approximately 75 GWh, and India at 60 GWh.[55] China is the largest generator of electricity using wind energy at in excess of 600 GWh, followed by the USA at just under 400 GWh, and Germany at about 100 GWh.[56] They were followed by Brazil, the UK, India, and Spain, all at around 50 to 60 GWh. China and the USA are also the largest generators when all renewable sources are taken into account. In addition to wind and solar, renewable sources include bioenergy, geothermal energy, hydropower, marine energy, and pumped storage. China was about 2,500 GWh, the USA about 900,000 GWh, and Brazil and Canada ranked third and fourth at about 500,000 GWh.[57]

1.42 The largest renewable energy companies are headquartered in Spain and Denmark, but other large companies are based in China, the USA, and Canada. The biggest ones are General Electric Co, Iberdrola SA, Constellation Energy Corp, NextEra Energy, Vestas Wind Systems AS, Jinko Solar Holding Co. Ltd, Canadian Solar Inc, and Brookfield Renewable Corp.[58] As at January 2024, Iberdrola had a market capitalisation of $71.81 billion and previously reported revenue of $59 billion and net income of $4.9 billion. Iberdrola therefore has greater revenue than BHP Group.

---

53 Ibid, 57.

54 International Renewable Energy Agency (IRENA), https://www.irena.org/.

55 IRENA https://www.irena.org/Data/View-data-by-topic/Capacity-and-Generation/Country-Rankings, Solar.

56 Ibid, Wind.

57 Ibid, All renewable energy sources.

58 Matthew Johnston, '10 Biggest Renewable Energy Companies in the World' (Investopedia, 27 January 2024) https://www.investopedia.com/investing/top-alternative-energy-companies/.

COMPANY REPORTING OBLIGATIONS: ESG AND OTHER APPROACHES

Compulsory reporting of climate change and sustainability risks is increasing

Over the last 15 years, concern about the effects of climate change for investors and financial markets has led to an increase in compulsory disclosure of the financial impacts of climate change risks and opportunities. Rules on the disclosure of the financial impacts of climate change risks and opportunities were developed by the Task Force on Climate-related Financial Disclosures (TCFD), which was formed in 2015, and taken up by the IFRS Foundation in its International Financial Reporting Standards (IFRS) IFRS S1 and IFRS S2.[59] IFRS S1 deals with sustainability and IFRS S2 with climate change. IFRS S2 was published in June 2023. The European Union has taken things a stage further with its Corporate Sustainability Reporting Directive (CSRD), effective in January 2023, which uses a double materiality test that looks at sustainability and climate change impacts as well as financial impacts. **1.43**

Rules of the kind mentioned in 1.43 are causing a significant increase in the rigour of climate change and sustainability reporting. Up to their coming into force, which has only been in the last few years, companies had considerable flexibility in their ESG reporting. What can be said at this stage is that the rules generally have in common elements of the structure recommended by the TCFD, which involves the themes of governance, strategy, risk management, and setting metrics and targets. Those matters and the supporting policies have to be disclosed, which means that the applicable companies have to design them and report their progress. Companies have also followed the Global Reporting Initiative (GRI) framework discussed in the next paragraph.[60] It is possible too that the increasing rigour will cause a significant change in the approach of companies to sustainability in their operations. These are matters looked at in Chapters 8, 9, and 10. The public sector is also considering financial reporting based on IFRS through the work being done by the International Public Sector Accounting Standards Board (IPSASB). Chapter 3 will discuss the sustainability reporting obligations of government and semi-government bodies. **1.44**

We can obtain an overview of what large companies are doing from a report done by KPMG in 2022 – a survey of sustainability reporting called *Big Shifts* **1.45**

---

59 TCFD and IFRS S1 and IFRS S2. are outlined in Chapter 2, and the rules of IFRS S2 are examined in Chapter 9.

60 Global Reporting Initiative can be found at https://www.globalreporting.org.

Small Steps: Survey of Sustainability Reporting 2022 (KPMG 2022 Report).[61] That showed, amongst other things, that 96% of the 250 largest global companies (G250) report on sustainability or ESG matters and that a significant number use the GRI framework.

1.46 The G250 are all large companies with significant operations, and they produce detailed and lengthy sustainability reports.[62] In contrast, a small mining or oil and gas company at the exploration stage with just a few directors relying on services provided under contract by geologists and other relevant experts is not going to be able to afford to produce such a report and may be disinclined to do so. The natural starting point for such a company is likely to be meeting the minimum levels that the law requires. Chapter 9 contains a detailed comparison of the reporting regulations in Australia, Canada, the USA, and the European Union. An important question examined there for each jurisdiction is whether the reporting regulations apply to small companies such as our exploration company.

1.47 An example is provided by the USA, where the body responsible for securities regulation is the Securities and Exchange Commission (SEC). There, securities regulation is a federal jurisdiction, not a state one. The SEC has new climate disclosure rules that are being phased in from fiscal years starting in 2025 to apply to SEC registrants that generally include companies listed on a US securities exchange such as the New York Stock Exchange and Nasdaq.[63] The rules will require disclosure of material climate-related risks and activities to mitigate and adapt to such risks. Information on any climate-related targets or goals that are material to the company's business, results of operations, or financial condition must also be disclosed. As the rules apply to SEC registrants, the rules should not apply, for example, to companies not listed on a US securities exchange.

Other sources of rules and guidance

1.48 Companies need to be aware of three other sources of rules. The first is company law reporting requirements. They generally require the directors to prepare a report about the company's affairs going beyond a financial report to set out its prospects, including the environmental and similar risks it faces.

61 KPMG International, *Big Shifts, Small Steps: Survey of Sustainability Reporting 2022*, October 2022 (KPMG 2022 Report).

62 Nine are examined in Chapter 8, and the shortest is 73 pages.

63 The Climate Disclosure Rules are set out in a new Subpart 1500 of Regulation S-K and new Article 14 of Regulation S-X.

An example is the *Companies Act 2006 (UK)* section 414A that requires the directors to produce a strategic report. Under section 414C(2)(b), that report must contain a description of 'the principal risks and uncertainties facing the company'. That is further elaborated for a quoted company in section 414C(7)(b) that the report must contain information about 'environmental matters (including the impact of the company's business on the environment' and 'social, community and human rights issues'. There are equivalents in other jurisdictions.[64] The second is the rules of the securities regulators and stock exchanges. The SEC example has been given in 1.47. There are equivalents in other jurisdictions.[65] The third source is other regulatory requirements. Any project will have to comply with a significant number of statutes covering a range of government focus areas across transport, safety, imports and exports, and taxation, to name just a few. Some of these, such as occupational health and safety, have increased the level of care and liability required of company directors and officers. Another area of significant growth has been the regulation of areas associated with human rights, such as anti-discrimination and modern slavery legislation. To a considerable degree, as the examples of company reports in Chapter 8 show, companies treat human rights as falling within the social pillar of ESG reporting. However, it is important to sound a note of caution, as sustainability reports may not satisfy the requirements of that legislation. It is outside the scope of this book to deal with those requirements.

Other suggestions for structure and content are given by industry organisations **1.49**
providing guidance on the preparation of sustainability reports. That guidance is very useful: for example, Ipieca/API/IOGP *Sustainability Reporting Guidance for the Oil and Gas Industry* (4th edition 2020) (Ipieca Reporting Guidance).[66] The Ipieca Reporting Guidance points to the increasing desire of stakeholders such as the investment community and regulators for clear and transparent reporting, but also stresses the benefits to companies of having good sustainability reports.[67] The Ipieca Reporting Guidance has six steps: starting with (1) develop a reporting plan, followed by (2) engage stakeholders, (3) select your material issues for reporting, (4) develop the report, (5) develop

64 For example, in Australia under *Corporations Act 2001 (Cth)* s298.

65 For the Financial Conduct Authority in the UK and its listing rules, see the Corporate Reporting Authority's *TCFD and related reporting requirements* https://www.icaew.com/technical/corporate-reporting/non-financial-reporting/tcfd-and-related-uk-reporting-regulations#subheading-1b69cf8a-19c7-47be-8abd-bd58ba341dcd.

66 Ipieca/API/IOGP 2023 (Ipieca Reporting Guidance) available at https://www.ipieca.org/resources/sustainability-reporting-guidance. For more on Ipieca and its mining equivalent, the International Council of Metals and Mines (ICMM), see 2.019 and 2.022.

67 Ipieca Reporting Guidance 1.1.

report data, and (6) provide assurance.[68] The guidance has four modules: governance and business ethics; climate change and energy; environment, safety, health and security; and social. It indicates issues under each and discusses 42 indicators, starting with the governance approach.[69] ICMM also produces guidance in various areas.[70]

1.50 For any company that has not done it before, the first three steps mentioned by Ipieca are very important in determining the shape of the sustainability report and the work involved. Notwithstanding constraints on the structure and disclosures, there are areas where a company can make choices, for example in relation to targets, indicators, and data in general. These matters are explored in Chapter 8. Generally, the reports examined there covered the areas of environment, society, and governance, which are the classic areas of ESG.

1.51 There are some other important choices. One is the purpose of the report: is it aimed chiefly at disclosure and management of risks, or is it aimed at improving the sustainability of the company? Sustainability and ESG can be viewed differently. According to some views, ESG aimed more at disclosure. As one blog puts it, 'ESG reporting is the disclosure of environmental, social and corporate governance data. As with all disclosures, its purpose is to shed light on a company's ESG activities while improving investor transparency and inspiring other organizations to do the same.'[71] Some of the matters covered in the environmental part of ESG reports will be:

Environmental: What is an organisation doing to be a steward of the environment? The environmental umbrella covers:

- How a company is combating climate change;
- What a company is doing to reduce carbon emissions;
- How the company is preserving biodiversity, improving air and water quality, combating deforestation, or responsibly managing its waste;
- How the company is responsibly using resources and its supply chain;
- What the company is doing to reduce its emissions.[72]

---

68 Ipieca Reporting Guidance 1.7.

69 Ipieca Reporting Guidance 1.6.

70 This is under topics rather than general, for example, Social and Economic Reporting. See ICMM at https://www.icmm.com/en-gb/our-principles/validation/social-and-economic-reporting.

71 Fabrizio Tocchini and Grazia Cafagna, 'The ABCs of ESG reporting: What are ESG and sustainability reports, why are they important and what do CFOs need to know' (9 March 2022) https://www.wolterskluwer.com/en/expert-insights/the-abcs-of-esg-reporting.

72 Ibid.

Stewardship is potentially a very important concept when it comes to sustainability. It carries with it the idea of 'accepting the responsibility to shepherd and safeguard the valuables of others'.[73]

AGENDA AND CHAPTER OVERVIEW

Chapters 2 to 5 set the scene for the more detailed examination of the sustainability aspects of mining and energy in the second half of the book. Chapter 2 examines the organisations involved in the governance and administration of sustainability and their particular focus. These start with the United Nations (UN) and its offshoots and then extend to mining and energy organisations seeking to encourage best practices. Finally, there are the bodies dealing with standards and corporate and security regulation. Chapter 3 explains the principles of governance at the state and corporate level that apply to decisions by regulators and companies. Chapter 4 deals with sustainable development and the Sustainable Development Goals (SDGs), which are at the heart of UN policies and have been adopted by government regulators, public and private organisations, and companies. Chapter 5 explores the meaning of equity, and particularly equity between generations. **1.52**

The second half starts by examining the extent to which mining and energy regulators focus on sustainability. That examination commences in Chapters 6 and 7 by reviewing environmental and development approvals for projects and how they deal with sustainability and sustainability standards applicable to mining and energy. Chapters 8 and 9 examine how companies focus on sustainability. That examination commences in Chapter 8 with a review of nine company reports. Chapter 9 discusses the rules for company sustainability reporting. The last chapter, Chapter 10, examines the way forward and the future of sustainability.[74] **1.53**

Milestones in the advance of sustainability **1.54**

- 1872: Mining Law (USA)
- 1945: United Nations formed
- 1948: United Nations Universal Declaration of Human Rights
- 1963: Nuclear Test Ban Treaty
- 1972: UN Conference on the Human Environment (Stockholm)

73 John. A.P. Chandler, *Petroleum Resource Management: How Governments Manage Their Offshore Petroleum Resources* (Edward Elgar, 2018), 160.

74 This book does not cover nuclear energy or coal for the reasons mentioned above.

- 1987: World Commission on Environment and Development report: *Our Common Future* (Brundtland Report)
- 1988: Intergovernmental Panel on Climate Change (IPCC) was created
- 1992: UN Conference on Environment and Development (Rio)
- 1992: UN Framework Convention on Climate Change
- 1993: Convention on Biological Diversity
- 1994: United Nations Convention on the Law of the Sea (UNCLOS) comes into force
- 2000: UN Global Compact established
- 2000: Global Reporting Initiative (GRI) publishes its first sustainability reporting guidelines
- 2001: International Council of Mining and Metals (ICMM) founded
- 2007: First green bond launched by the European Investment Bank
- 2010: SEC issues guidance regarding disclosure related to climate change
- 2014: EU issues Non-financial Reporting Directive
- 2015: UN Climate Change Conference in Paris (COP 21) resulting in the Paris Agreement
- 2015: Sustainable Development Goals adopted
- 2015: Task Force on Climate-related Financial Disclosures formed
- 2016: Global Reporting Initiative (GRI) publishes guidelines as the first global framework for sustainability reporting
- 2018: SASB Standards published
- 2021: EU's Climate Law enters into force
- 2021: ICMA updates Green Bond Principles
- 2022: EFRAG issues EU's first European Sustainability Reporting Standards
- 2022: International Sustainability Standards Board (ISSB) of the IFRS Foundation assumes responsibility for the SASB standards
- 2023: ISSB issues sustainability and climate change standards IFRS S1 and IFRS S2
- 2024: SEC publishes new climate change disclosure rules

The list above sets out the years in which these milestone events occurred. Many more events could be selected, and the list combines a mixture of legislation, treaties, conferences, and standards. What is noticeable is the acceleration that occurred after 2015, the year of the Paris Agreement and the adoption of the SDGs.

REIMAGINING SUSTAINABILITY IN MINING AND ENERGY

1.55 The title of this book is *Sustainability Law in Mining and Energy*. It is clear that there is a developing body of what can be described as sustainability law relating to aspects of mining and energy which would meet Dworkin's test at 1.33 of a legally binding rule. First, there are laws regulating aspects of sustainability such as environmental, safety, and human rights matters which have penalties for non-compliance. Second, there are laws regulating the disclosure of sustainability risks and sustainability reporting which also have penalties for non-compliance. But it is difficult to argue currently that sustainability law has reached the level of a recognised legal subject like contract law or company law. Climate change law is perhaps closer to achieving that level of recognition.[75] Nevertheless, readers of this book will come across numerous instances of law on the regulation of sustainability, much of it affecting mining and energy companies and their operations. In due course, it is suggested that sustainability will be treated as a discrete area of law and one of particular relevance to mining and energy. At the core of that is the idea that all companies should operate in a sustainable manner, and governments too, and that the pressure on them to do so will continue to grow.

75 For a review of university courses in Australia, see John A.P. Chandler, 'How are Australian universities and law schools approaching sustainability in their curricula and what are the implications for legal education,' 2024 *Legal Education Review* 1. That said, at the time of writing, there were 38 law schools in Australia, and of these 21 offered a climate change option and 9 a unit dealing with sustainability.

2

SUSTAINABILITY ORGANISATIONS

INTRODUCTION 2.01
THE UNITED NATIONS 2.02
Conferences 2.02
UN Department of Economic and Social Affairs and Sustainable Development Solutions Network 2.04
The United Nations and human rights 2.05
United Nations Environment Programme 2.06
United Nations Development Programme 2.07
United Nations Educational, Scientific and Cultural Organization 2.08
OECD and World Bank 2.09
INTERGOVERNMENTAL BODIES 2.11
MINING AND ENERGY REGULATORS AND POLICY-SETTING 2.14
INDUSTRY BODIES IN MINING 2.19
INDUSTRY BODIES IN PETROLEUM AND ENERGY 2.21
REPORTING AND THE ESG LANDSCAPE 2.24
Overview 2.24
Global Reporting Initiative 2.26
Task Force on Climate-related Financial Disclosures 2.28
International Financial Reporting Standards 2.29
US GAAP and national accounting standards 2.30
Natural capital accounting 2.32
Sustainable finance 2.34
Rating and ranking 2.35
CORPORATE REGULATORS 2.36
SECURITIES EXCHANGES 2.37
CONCLUSIONS: GUIDANCE AND KEY PRINCIPLES 2.40
Checklist 2.43
Purpose of checklist 2.43

INTRODUCTION

2.01 The aim of this chapter is to provide an overview of the organisations that play a role in the governance of sustainability. We will begin with the United Nations, as it has been vital in setting the overall context through the SDGs and its action on climate change. That will be followed by the Organisation for Economic Co-operation and Development (OECD) and the World Bank, both of which have produced materials on responsible business conduct, regulation, and the mining and energy sectors. The next sections will examine the following: mining and energy regulators, the government and industry organisations that are advocates for particular industries and those which provide other support, such as data analysis and policy advice; organisations setting reporting standards and evaluating performance; and finally, those responsible for administering company law and securities exchanges. As we go through them, we should observe what is their role is it political or regulatory? Is it the provision of frameworks and standards to guide or measure performance? Is their role to provide guidance and support? Do they rate performance? Chapter 3 will explore governance and how some of the regimes that those organisations set up affect sustainability governance. Chapters 6 and 7 will examine environmental and development approvals. Chapters 8 and 9 will examine company sustainability reporting.

THE UNITED NATIONS

Conferences

The impact of UN conferences has already been mentioned in Chapter 1. The UN Framework Convention on Climate Change of 1992 continues to play a pivotal role in marshalling nations to take action on climate change. The Paris Agreement was adopted by 196 parties at the UN Climate Change Conference (COP21) in Paris on 12 December 2015, coming into force in 2016.[1] Its overarching goal is to hold the increase in the global average temperature to well below 2 degrees Celsius above pre-industrial levels and pursue efforts to limit the increase to 1.5 degrees Celsius above pre-industrial levels.[2] It also made it mandatory for parties to the agreement to submit nationally determined contributions, which set out their proposals to reduce emissions.[3] Those proposals are not binding. 2.02

Another important development occurred in relation to natural capital accounting in 2012 at the Rio+20 conference, when a number of countries expressed interest in developing it. The World Bank started the WAVES 50:50 Initiative to analyse the progress and next steps required for improving efforts to account for natural capital and enhance countries' sustainable decision-making capabilities. In simple terms, natural capital accounting is accounting for natural capital, which is 'the stock of renewable and non renewable resources (e.g., plants, animals, air, water, soils, minerals) that combine to yield a flow of benefits to people'.[4] Natural capital accounting is discussed further below. 2.03

---

1 *Paris Agreement to the United Nations Framework Convention on Climate Change*, 12 December 2015, T.I.A.S. No. 16 1104 (Paris Agreement).

2 Ibid, art 2.

3 Ibid, art 3.

4 A definition developed by the Natural Capital Coalition and referred to at the UN's Natural Capital and Ecosystem Services Project FAQ (Website) https://seea.un.org/content/natural-capital-and-ecosystem-services-faq.

UN Department of Economic and Social Affairs and Sustainable Development Solutions Network

2.04 The Division for Sustainable Development Goals (DSDG) in the United Nations Department of Economic and Social Affairs (UNDESA) acts as the Secretariat for the SDGs. DSDG plays a key role in the evaluation of implementation of the 2030 Agenda and in advocacy and outreach activities relating to the SDGs.[5] The Sustainable Development Solutions Network (SDSN) is another UN initiative under the auspices of the UN Secretary-General to mobilise the world's universities, think tanks, and national laboratories for action on the SDGs and the Paris Agreement.[6]

The United Nations and human rights

2.05 As a UN webpage says, 'one of the great achievements of the United Nations is the creation of a comprehensive body of human rights law'.[7] It goes on to say:

> The foundations of this body of law are the Charter of the United Nations and the Universal Declaration of Human Rights, adopted by the General Assembly in 1945 and 1948, respectively.[8] Since then, the United Nations has gradually expanded human rights law to encompass specific standards for women, children, persons with disabilities, minorities and other vulnerable groups, who now possess rights that protect them from discrimination that had long been common in many societies.

There are numerous treaties giving effect to those rights which countries have ratified.[9] Those in turn have given rise to reporting obligations and also led to legislation in related areas, an example of which is modern slavery legislation and bribery and corruption legislation.[10] It is outside the scope of this book to do a detailed treatment of those areas. There are a number of published works which do that.[11] The sustainability reports reviewed in Chapter 8 show that companies are reporting on human rights. The UN has a Human Rights

5 'DSDG Mission Statement,' *United Nations Division of Sustainable Development Growth* (Website) https://sdgs.un.org/about.

6 *SDSN* (Website) *About us* unsdsn.org.

7 United Nations Human Rights https://www.un.org/en/global-issues/human-rights.

8 UN General Assembly, Resolution 217A (III), Universal Declaration of Human Rights, A/RES/217(III) (December 10, 1948), https://www.un.org/en/about-us/universal-declaration-of-human-rights.

9 For example Australia has ratified seven, including those on the elimination of racial discrimination and discrimination against women. See https://www.ag.gov.au/rights-and-protections/human-rights-and-anti-discrimination/international-human-rights-system.

10 For example, the Modern Slavery Act 2015 (UK), the Modern Slavery Act 2018 (Cth), and the Foreign Corrupt Practices Act (USA).

11 For example, John Southalan, *Human Rights and Mining* (2015 Centro Politicas Publicas) and Sunil Rao, *Modern Slavery* (Routledge 2019).

Council and a United Nations Commissioner for Human Rights and has endorsed principles for reporting in the form of the UN Guiding Principles Reporting Framework.[12] The UN has also sought to mobilise companies to adopt a principles-based approach to human rights. The UN Global Compact was established in July 2000 by UN Secretary-General Kofi Annan to encourage companies to align their operations and strategies around ten universal principles in the areas of human rights, labour, the environment, and anti-corruption. The idea behind the Compact is that corporate sustainability starts with a principles-based approach to doing business, which means operating in ways that meet fundamental responsibilities in each of the four areas.[13]

United Nations Environment Programme

The United Nations Environment Programme (UNEP) regards itself as the leading global authority on the environment.[14] It unites 193 member states in an effort to find solutions to climate change, nature and biodiversity loss, and pollution and waste, collectively known as the triple planetary crisis. UNEP implementation focuses on three areas: scientific research, promoting global environmental legislation and accords, and advocacy through communication. The Emissions Gap Report is an example of the first. Examples of the third are global communications campaigns, such as Clean Seas and the UN Decade on Ecosystem Restoration. UNEP leads World Environment Day, a celebration of the natural world encouraging environmental action. **2.06**

United Nations Development Programme

The United Nations Development Programme (UNDP) is the UN's development agency. As such, it plays a critical role in helping countries achieve the SDGs. One of its projects with the Columbia Center on Sustainable Investment and others was the production of a white paper, *Mapping Mining to the Sustainable Development Goals: An Atlas*.[15] Core financial support from **2.07**

---

12 UN Guiding Principles Reporting Framework available at https://www.ungpreporting.org/.

13 United Nations Global Impact, *UN Global Compact Strategy 2021–2023*, https://ungc-communications-assets.s3.amazonaws.com/docs/about_the_gc/UN-GLOBAL-COMPACT-STRATEGY-2021-2023.pdf. 1. At p. 6, it says 'Corporate sustainability starts with a company's value system and a principles-based approach to doing business. This means operating in ways that, at a minimum, meet fundamental responsibilities in the areas of human rights, labour, environment and anti-corruption'.

14 For its website, see https://www.un.org/youthenvoy/2013/08/unep-united-nations-environment-programme/#:~:text=The%20United%20Nations%20Environment%20Programme,country%2C%20regional%20and%20global%20levels.

15 Columbia Center on Sustainable Investment, UNDP, World Economic Forum, Sustainable Solutions Network, *Mapping Mining to the Sustainable Development Goals: An Atlas* (July 2016).

countries is critical in allowing UNDP to fulfil its mission. The largest contributor in 2022 was the United States at $80.65 million, closely followed by Germany and Sweden.

United Nations Educational, Scientific and Cultural Organization

2.08 The purpose of the United Nations Educational, Scientific and Cultural Organization (UNESCO) is set out in Article 1 of its Constitution:

> The purpose of the Organization is to contribute to peace and security by promoting collaboration among the nations through education, science and culture in order to further universal respect for justice, for the rule of law and for the human rights and fundamental freedoms which are affirmed for the peoples of the world, without distinction of race, sex, language or religion, by the Charter of the United Nations.[16]

Its functions include collaborating 'in the work of advancing the mutual knowledge and understanding of peoples', giving 'fresh impulse to popular education and to the spread of culture' and 'maintaining, increasing and diffusing knowledge'.[17]

OECD and World Bank

2.09 The OECD is an international organisation with headquarters in Paris. It was founded in 1961 to stimulate economic progress and world trade. It has 38 member countries, most of which are high-income economies. It describes itself as working 'on establishing evidence-based international standards and finding solutions to a range of social, economic and environmental challenges'.[18] It produces guidelines on matters like responsible business conduct and the conduct of regulators, which are referred to in subsequent chapters.

2.10 The World Bank, founded in 1944, is an international financial institution that provides loans and grants to the governments of low- and middle-income countries for the purpose of pursuing capital projects. More recently, it has included non-government organisations and environmental groups in its loan portfolio. Its loan strategy is influenced by the United Nations' SDGs, as well as environmental and social safeguards.[19] The International Finance Corporation (IFC) arm of the World Bank Group involves sustainability in

16 *Constitution of the United Nations Educational, Scientific and Cultural Organization*, 16 November 1845, 4 UNTS 275 https://www.unesco.org/en/legal-affairs/constitution.

17 Ibid, art 1.

18 'Who we are', *OECD* (Website) https://www.oecd.org/about/.

19 For its publications, see 'Research', *World Bank* (Website) https://www.worldbank.org/en/research.

its review of projects it is financing. The IFC has eight performance standards that it expects to be met through the life of an investment by the IFC.[20] In project appraisal, the IFC uses the World Bank Group's Environmental, Health and Safety Guidelines as a technical source of information. If the levels and measures in host country regulations differ from those, then the IFC expects the project 'to achieve whichever is more stringent'.[21]

INTERGOVERNMENTAL BODIES

2.11 The International Energy Agency (IEA) is an autonomous intergovernmental organisation set up under the OECD. It provides policy recommendations, analysis, and data on the global energy sector. It is based in Paris and was established in 1974, following the 1973 oil crisis.[22] It has 31 member countries and 13 association countries, which represent 80% of global energy demand.[23] The IEA now covers the entire global energy system, including fossil fuels such as oil, gas, and coal, as well as renewable energy such as wind and solar. The IEA provides policy advice to its member states and association countries under its updated mandate 'to focus on a full range of energy issues, including climate change and decarbonisation, energy access and efficiency, investment and innovation, and ensuring reliable, affordable and sustainable energy systems'.[24] The IEA produces invaluable reports analysing data concerning energy demand, supply, trends, and usage.[25] It describes its data and reports as 'the gold standard in the energy world'.[26]

2.12 The International Renewable Energy Agency (IRENA) has a mission of 'supporting countries world-wide in their transition to a sustainable energy future'.[27] It has 169 members, including 168 countries and the European Union. Work on creating IRENA began in 2008, and it officially came into

20 International Finance Corporation, Performance Standard 6: Biodiversity Conservation and Sustainable Management of Living Natural Resources, IFC January 1, 2012, 1.

21 Ibid., ii.

22 'History', *IEA* (Website, last updated 24 January 2024) https://www.iea.org/about/history.

23 Ibid.

24 Ibid. The mandate was further expanded 'at the Ministerial Meeting of March 2022, to guide countries as they build net-zero emission energy systems to comply with internationally agreed climate goals, and to broaden the Agency's scope to include the critical minerals and metals needed to develop clean energy technologies' (ibid).

25 For example, the IEA's World Energy Outlook. For the 2023 Outlook, see https://www.iea.org/reports/world-energy-outlook-2023.

26 Ibid.

27 *IRENA* (Website) https://www.irena.org/.

being in 2011 following the entry into force of the IRENA statute in 2010.[28] Its permanent seat is in Abu Dhabi in the United Arab Emirates. It produces valuable data and reports.[29]

2.13 The main intergovernmental body concerning minerals outside the UN is the Intergovernmental Forum on Mining, Minerals, Metals and Sustainable Development (IGF). The IGF says that it 'supports governments to advance good mining governance for the betterment of communities, economies, and the environment'.[30] The IGF has 83 member countries that include all of North America and most of South America, southern Africa, the UK, France, Germany, Russia, and India. There are few members in south-east Asia, so China, Vietnam, Malaysia, the Philippines, Indonesia, Australia, and New Zealand are not members. The IGF also states that its 'cornerstone Mining Policy Framework represents the practices required for good environmental, social, and economic governance of the mining sector and the generation and equitable sharing of benefits to contribute to sustainable development'.[31] The IGF offers support in the form of technical assistance and capacity-building. Examples of its work are given on its website.[32] Another body is the World Business Council for Sustainable Development (WBCSD), which was established in 1995 as a platform for business to respond to sustainability challenges.[33] It has a large range of projects including matters like accountability, decarbonisation, hydrogen, and water.[34]

MINING AND ENERGY REGULATORS AND POLICY-SETTING

2.14 Table 2.1 sets out the main mining and petroleum statutes in Nevada, Western Australia, Saskatchewan, and the UK, together with the regulators for these areas. In those countries with a parliamentary system with an elected government and ministers responsible for specified portfolios – all of the above except Nevada – these areas are subject to ministerial responsibility and a government department responsible to the minister is often the regulator. Mining is

28 For the IRENA Statute and other important strategy and budget documents, see https://www.irena.org/About/Official-documents.

29 For example, its tables of different kinds of renewable energy production. See IRENA Country rankings, https://www.irena.org/Data/View-data-by-topic/Capacity-and-Generation/Country-Rankings.

30 *IGF* (Website) https://www.igfmining.org/.

31 'Mining and Policy Framework', *IGF* https://www.igfmining.org/resource/igf-mining-policy-framework/. See that URL for the *Mining and Policy Framework 2021*.

32 'Impact Stories', *IGF* https://www.igfmining.org/impactstory/.

33 *WBCSD* (Website) *About us* https://archive.wbcsd.org/Overview/About-us.

34 Ibid.

Table 2.1 Mining and petroleum statutes and regulators

Jurisdiction	USA Federal Lands in Nevada[a]	State of Nevada	Province of Saskatchewan	State of Western Australia	United Kingdom
Mining statute	General Mining Act 1872 (US)[b] Mineral Leasing Act 1920 (US)[c] Materials Act 1947 (US)[d]	Mining Regulations (N)[e]	Crown Minerals Act (S)[f] Mineral Tenure Registry Regulations 2012 (S) Subsurface Mineral Tenure Regulations 2015 (S)	Mining Act 1978 (WA)	Coal Industry Act 1994 (UK), Crown Estates Acts 1956 (UK) and 1961[g] The Mines and Quarries Act 1954 (UK)[h]
Mining regulator	Federal Bureau of Land Management (BLM)[i]	Nevada Department of Environmental Protection (NDEP) Bureau of Mining Regulation and Reclamation (BMRR)[j]	Ministry of Energy and Resources	Department of Energy, Mines, Industry Regulation and Safety (DMIRSWA)	The Coal Authority for coal and Crown Estate for gold and silver
Onshore petroleum statute	Mineral Leasing Act 1920	Nevada Revised Statutes Chapter 522 Oil and Gas[k]	Oil and Gas Conservation Act (S)[l]	Petroleum and Geothermal Energy Resources Act 1967 (WA) (PGERA)	Petroleum Act 1994 (UK)

Jurisdiction	USA Federal Lands in Nevada[a]	State of Nevada	Province of Saskatchewan	State of Western Australia	United Kingdom
Onshore petroleum regulator	Bureau of Land Management (BLM) Federal Energy Regulatory Commission (FERC)[m]	Nevada Division of Minerals[n]	Ministry of Energy and Resources	DMIRSWA	North Sea Transition Authority
Environmental protection statute	National Environmental Policy Act 1969 (US)[o]	Nevada Revised Statutes Chapter 445D Environmental Covenants	Mineral Industry Environmental Protection Regulations 1996 (S)	Environmental Protection Act 1986 (WA) (EPACTWA)	Environment Act 1956 (UK)
Environmental regulator	Environmental Protection Agency[p]	Division of Environmental Protection in the Department of Conservation and Natural Resources (NDCNR)[q]	Ministry of the Environment	Environmental Protection Authority (EPAWA)	Environment Agency[r]
Health and safety statute	Mine Safety and Health Act	Occupational Safety and Health Administration (OSHA) regulations	Occupational Health and Safety Regulations 2020	Work Health and Safety Act 2020 (WA)	Health and Safety at Work Act 1974 (UK)

Jurisdiction	USA Federal Lands in Nevada[a]	State of Nevada	Province of Saskatchewan	State of Western Australia	United Kingdom
Health and safety regulator	Department of Labor's Mines Safety and Health Administration (MSHA)	Nevada OSHA	Ministry of Labour Relations and Workplace Safety	Worksafe Commissioner	Health and Safety Executive

Notes:
[a] About 85% of the land open for mining in Nevada is federal land.
[b] 30 USC §22–42. Mining Law of 1872 (US), as amended, governs claims to so-called 'locatable minerals' that include gold, silver, copper, and other hard rock minerals. See the BLM's website at https://www.blm.gov/programs/energy-and-minerals/mining-and-minerals.
[c] The Mineral Leasing Acts cover leasable minerals, such as coal and a host of other commodities, https://minerals.nv.gov/Programs/OG/OG-FAQ/.
[d] The Materials Act 1947 (US) covers saleable minerals, such as sand and gravel that are essential to construction and road building.
[e] NDEP's Bureau of Mining Regulation and Reclamation (BMRR), in cooperation with other state, federal, and local agencies, regulates mining activities under regulations adopted in 1989. The Nevada Administrative Code (NAC) 445A.350–NAC 445A.447 and NAC 519A.010–NAC 519A.415 were developed to implement the requirements of the Nevada Revised Statutes (NRS) 445A.300–NRS 445A.730 and NRS 519A.010–NRS 519A.290.
[f] SS 1984–36, c C-50.2. The Act authorises the minister to issue Crown dispositions, which are rights granted by the Crown to explore for minerals and obtain an interest in Crown minerals. The Crown in Canada through the provinces like Saskatchewan generally owns most minerals.
[g] Owners of private land generally own minerals under it, with the exception of certain minerals in state ownership, such as gold, silver, and coal.
[h] The Mines and Quarries Act 1954 (UK) governs the management of mines and quarries.
[i] See the BLM's website at https://www.blm.gov/programs/energy-and-minerals/mining-and-minerals/about. At the federal level regulations include Surface Management rules (65 FR 70112) available at https://www.ecfr.gov/current/title-43/subtitle-B/chapter-II/subchapter-C/part-3800/subpart-3809.
[j] See the BMRR's webpage at https://www.ndep.nv.gov/land/mining. For the government departments involved in mining see https://minerals.nv.gov/uploadedFiles/mineralsnvgov/content/Programs/Mining/NVAgenciesInvolvedWithMining(2).pdf.
[k] Nevada Revised Statutes Chapter 522 Oil and Gas https://www.leg.state.nv.us/nrs/NRS-522.html.
[l] Chapter 0-2 of the Revised Statutes of Saskatchewan 1978.
[m] FERC regulates the interstate transmission and wholesale sale of gas and electricity.
[n] The Nevada Division of Minerals is the state's regulatory authority for all oil and gas wells drilled in Nevada. Oil and gas wells drilled within Nevada, on either private or federally managed lands, must be permitted by the Nevada Division of Minerals. See https://minerals.nv.gov/Programs/OG/OG/.
[o] National Environmental Policy Act 42 U.S.C. §4321 et seq. (1969).
[p] The website is epa.gov.
[q] The website is https://ndep.nv.gov/.
[r] The Environment Agency is the principal regulator for England. Under devolved powers there are separate agencies for Scotland, Wales, and Northern Ireland.

sometimes in a separate ministerial portfolio or department from petroleum. One of the reasons for ministerial responsibility is the economic and political significance of minerals and energy in countries like Australia and Canada. States in the USA have a political structure based on an elected governor. For example, in Nevada the governor of the state appoints the executive director of government departments that are cabinet level. There are other countries with significant mining or petroleum industries such as Brazil, Chile, Indonesia, and Qatar. The regulatory structure in those countries varies, but many have a minister with mining or energy in their portfolio.[35]

2.15 When it comes to mining and petroleum activities in the sea off a country's coast, there are generally specialist regulators for environmental and safety management. Australia has a complex structure as its offshore area is divided geographically between the states and territories, and decision-making is shared between the federal minister and state and territory ministers. Advice and day-to-day regulation of licensing and related activities are provided by the National Offshore Petroleum Titles Authority (NOPTA). The regulator for offshore environmental and safety matters is the National Offshore Petroleum Safety and Environmental Management Authority (NOPSEMA). The equivalent of these bodies in the UK is the North Sea Transition Authority (NSTA), formerly the Oil and Gas Authority (OGA), and the Offshore Safety Division within the Health and Safety Executive (HSE), which regulates workplace health, safety, and welfare. The regulator for environmental management is the Offshore Petroleum Regulator for Environment and Decommissioning (OPRED).[36] In the USA, revenue is collected by the Office of Natural Resources Revenue, and resource development and energy management is the responsibility of the Bureau of Ocean Energy Management. The Bureau of Safety and Environmental Enforcement enforces safety and environmental regulations. Australia has recently enacted offshore infrastructure legislation aimed at wind and other renewable energy supply. The regulator for that is the Offshore Infrastructure Regulator, whose activities are carried out to a large extent by NOPSEMA.

2.16 The role of ministers in those countries which have one is also to set policy. Most of the countries referred to have policy settings designed to attract new

---

35 Brazil has a Minister for Mines and Energy, Chile has a Minister of Mining and a Minister of Energy, Indonesia has a Ministry of Energy and Mineral Resources, and Qatar has a Minister of State for Energy Affairs.

36 https://www.gov.uk/government/organisations/offshore-petroleum-regulator-for-environment-and-decommissioning/about.

investment into exploration and the development of new projects. Each of them has a website intended to inform and attract possible investors.[37] There are also government departments producing mining and geological information.[38] At various times, governments may offer tax or other incentives to attract investment. When it comes to the supervision of operations by mining and industry regulators, most of those regulators generate detailed commentaries and guidance notes, which will be covered in Chapters 6 and 7. In some cases, these may refer to standards set by third parties. Common ones for the measurement of greenhouse gases are those from the Greenhouse Gas Protocol.[39] The International Organization for Standardization (ISO) has many standards, including one on greenhouse gas verification and others on sustainability.[40] There are standards bodies connected to the ISO in most countries, such as Standards Australia and the Standards Council of Canada. Other organisations develop standards for use in mining and energy. Examples include those for general industry use, such as the Norsok standards introduced by the Norwegian petroleum industry in 1994 to 'cut costs and improve competitiveness on the Norwegian continental shelf',[41] and those specific to particular areas such as tailings management in mining.[42]

Countries are also seeking to develop more renewable energy projects. The largest set of financial incentives is provided by the Inflation Reduction Act (IRA) (USA), which was signed into law by President Biden in 2022. The US Treasury is responsible for implementing major elements of the law, including tax incentives that spur investment in clean energy and manufacturing.[43] 2.17

---

37 For Canada, see 'Invest in Canada Mining', *Government of Canada* https://www.investcanada.ca/industries/mining, which says that Saskatchewan is the most attractive jurisdiction globally and that 90% of the world's leading mining companies operate in Canada. See also 'Mining and mineral resource development in Canada', *Government of Canada*, https://natural-resources.canada.ca/minerals-mining/mining-mineral-resource-development-canada. For Australia, see 'Mineral Facts', *Geoscience* Australia, which refers to state and territory information websites, https://www.ga.gov.au/education/classroom-resources/minerals-energy/australian-mineral-facts. See also 'Foreign Investment', *Australian Government Department of Foreign Affairs and Trade* https://www.ga.gov.au/education/minerals-energy/australian-mineral-facts.

38 For example, 'Australia's Identified Mineral Resources', *Geoscience Australia*, https://www.ga.gov.au/scientific-topics/minerals/mineral-resources-and-advice/aimr.

39 For the GHG Protocol website see https://ghgprotocol.org/#:~:text=Greenhouse%20Gas%20Protocol%20provides%20the,gas%20accounting%20standards%20for%20companies.&text=Greenhouse%20Gas%20Protocol%20provides%20standards,track%20progress%20toward%20climate%20goals.&text=In%202023%2C%2097%25%20of%20disclosing,to%20CDP%20using%20GHG%20Protocol.

40 ISO 14064-3 Standard – Greenhouse Gas Verification.

41 Norsok standards webpage https://standard.no/en/sectors/petroleum/norsok-standards/.

42 Global Industry Standard on Tailings Management https://globaltailingsreview.org/global-industry-standard/.

43 US Department of the Treasury (Website) https://home.treasury.gov/news/featured-stories/the-inflation-reduction-acts-benefits-and-costs.

The scale is enormous, with companies announcing more than $115 billion in manufacturing investments aimed at building the clean energy economy of the USA since President Biden took office.[44] The concern that other countries had was based on the fact that the IRA encouraged firms to set up operations in the USA, meaning that they would lose out. The European Union responded with its Green Deal aimed at creating a net-zero green economy by 2050,[45] enhancing manufacturing and digital capacity in crucial industries, and sustaining innovation leadership via scientific and technological investment.

2.18 Canada is in the process of introducing its own set of tax credits for renewable energy projects.[46] Australia's main policy mechanism is the Australian Renewable Energy Target (Australian RET). The target was 33,000 gigawatt hours of additional renewable electricity generation by 2020, and the same from 2020 to 2030. It arises under the *Renewable Energy (Electricity) Act 2000 (Cth)*, which in section 17 defines an 'eligible renewable energy source'. The definition has an extensive list including things like hydro, wave, solar, and wind, but excluding fossil fuels and their derivatives. Large-scale generation through renewable energy sources gives rise to Large-scale Generation Certificates (LGCs), which can be sold or transferred to retailers, liable entities, and traders. The *Renewable Energy (Electricity) (Large-scale Generation Shortfall Charge) Act 2000 (Cth)* imposes a charge on liable entities with respect of the shortfall of their renewable energy after deduction of LGCs.[47] Australia has a Clean Energy Regulator set up under the *Clean Energy Regulator Act 2011 (Cth)* to administer the Australian RET and greenhouse and energy reporting, among other things. Financial support is provided by entities like the Clean Energy Finance Corporation.[48] In Australia, renewable energy is currently in the portfolio of the federal Minister for Climate Change and Energy. The

---

44 US Treasury analysis 'demonstrates these announced investments in clean energy production, electric vehicles, and batteries are concentrated in communities with lower income, lower college graduation rates and lower employment rates'. US Department of the Treasury, Fact Sheet: *How the Inflation Reduction Act's Tax Incentives Are Ensuring All Americans Benefit from the Growth of the Clean Energy Economy* (22 October 2023) https://home.treasury.gov/news/press-releases/jy1830.

45 See 'EU Green Deal vs US Inflation Reduction Act' *KPMG* (15 September 2023) https://kpmg.com/ch/en/blogs/home/posts/2023/09/eu-green-deal-vs-us-inflation-reduction-act.html, which says: 'Achieving these goals shall be facilitated by an unprecedented high volume of non-tax incentives, including EU funds, national funds and the EU's Covid-specific NextGen Fund (depending on clearance by the European Commission, EC), which can be directly disbursed by member states without requiring EU consent.'

46 Zak Bentley, 'Desperate not to be "left behind" Canada enters renewables subsidy race', *Infrastructure Investor* (20 February 2024) https://www.infrastructureinvestor.com/desperate-not-to-be-left-behind-canada-enters-renewables-subsidy-race/.

47 See s 36 of the *Renewable Energy (Electricity) Act 2000 (Cth)* for the calculation method. There are also small-scale generation certificates.

48 See the home page of the *Clean Energy Finance Corporation* (Website) https://www.cefc.com.au/.

minister is responsible for the coordination and implementation of sustainable energy policies by the Australian Government.[49] Canada has a Minister for the Environment and Climate Change as well as a Minister for Energy and Resources.[50] Its energy policy was subject to a report by the International Energy Agency in 2022,[51] which sets out a broad range of incentives and support mechanisms. Canada has hydropower and nuclear in its energy mix, which contributes to the IEA's comments that it has one of the cleanest electricity systems in the world with over 83% of production from non-emitting sources.[52] According to the IEA, Canada ranked 10th in the world for renewable energy penetration in total energy consumption in 2019. The USA ranked 27th and Australia ranked 28th.[53] There are government bodies in these countries that support the development of renewable energy.[54]

INDUSTRY BODIES IN MINING

Countries with significant mineral and petroleum resources like Australia, Canada, and the USA have industry bodies, whose role is mainly advocacy for the industry. Examples include the Minerals Council of Australia,[55] the Mining Association of Canada,[56] and the Minerals Council South Africa.[57] There are also other bodies, sometimes state-based,[58] and others with a broader focus.[59] **2.19**

---

49 The responsible minister as of 10 May 2024 was the Honourable Chris Bowen, and the Department through which he administers his portfolios is the Department of Climate Change, Energy, the Environment, and Water (established on 1 July 2022).

50 As of 10 May 2024, the Minister for Environment and Climate Change is the Honourable Stephen Guilbeault, and the Minister for Energy and Resources is the Honourable Jonathan Wilkinson.

51 International Energy Agency Canada Energy Policy Review (2022) (IEA Canada Energy Policy 2022) https://iea.blob.core.windows.net/assets/7ec2467c-78b4-4c0c-a966-a42b8861ec5a/Canada2022.pdf.

52 Ibid, 13.

53 Ibid, 114.

54 For example, in Australia the Australian Renewable Energy Agency (ARENA) https://arena.gov.au/ and in the USA, the Office of Energy Efficiency and Renewable Energy https://www.energy.gov/eere/office energy-efficiency-and-renewable-energy.

55 Minerals Council of Australia describes itself as 'the leading advocate for Australia's minerals industry, promoting and enhancing sustainability, profitability and competitiveness'. *Minerals Council of Australia* (Website) https://minerals.org.au/about/.

56 *Mining Association of Canada* (Website) https://mining.ca/.

57 *Minerals Council South Africa* (Website) https://www.mineralscouncil.org.za/.

58 Such as chambers of mines: there is a Chamber of Minerals and Energy of Western Australia (CME) and equivalent bodies in South Australia and the Yukon. Other examples are the Colorado Mining Association and the Saskatchewan Mining Association.

59 For example, in Australia, the Association of Mining and Exploration Companies (AMEC).

2.20 At the international level, there is the International Council of Metals and Mines (ICMM). However, ICMM is different from the country-based advocacy bodies. It describes itself as follows:

> ICMM is a unique industry body. We exist not to serve the commercial interests of our members, as you might expect from a 'trade association'. Instead, we are a global leadership organisation for sustainable development, judging success by our contribution to creating a safe, just and sustainable world through responsibly produced metals and minerals.[60]

The list of its association members illustrates the significant number of country- or region-based bodies that exist throughout the world.[61] Forty-two are listed, and they range from country-based advocacy bodies to bodies representing particular minerals, like the World Gold Council and the International Lithium Organisation, to organisations representing a particular expertise group, like the Society for Mining, Metallurgy and Exploration and the Society of Mining Professors.[62] Some of these international association members of ICMM sponsor research and also organise conferences in their own right. Another organisation doing that is the World Mining Congress, whose 2023 conference was in Australia.[63]

INDUSTRY BODIES IN PETROLEUM AND ENERGY

2.21 The picture in petroleum is similar. In the USA, Canada, Australia, and the UK, the peak industry bodies are: US Oil and Gas Association (USOGA), Canadian Association of Petroleum Producers (CAPP), Australian Energy Producers (AEP) – until 2023 known as the Australian Petroleum Producers and Explorers Association (APPEA) – and UK Oil and Gas Industry Association Ltd (UK Oil and Gas). In the USA, the United States Energy Association (USEA) is not a lobbying organisation but has a mission to 'promote the sustainable supply and use of energy for the greatest benefit of all'.[64]

---

60 'Who we are', *ICMM* (Website)https://www.icmm.com/en-gb/our-story/who-we-are.

61 The association members are listed at https://www.icmm.com/en-gb/our-story/our-members.

62 Ibid.

63 'About', *World Mining Congress* (Website) https://wmc2023.org/about.

64 'About', *USEA* (Website) https://usea.org/about-usea.

As with minerals, there are other bodies.[65] Some are dedicated to specific areas such as gas, pipelines, and distribution systems,[66] and hydrogen.[67] There are also bodies associated with solar and wind energy. For example, in the USA there is the Solar Energy Industries Association.[68] For wind, there is the World Wind Energy Association.[69] **2.22**

At the international level in petroleum, there is Ipieca (formerly the International Petroleum Industry Environmental Conservation Association). Ipieca was founded at the request of the UNEP in 1974. Through its non-lobby and collaborative approach, Ipieca remains the industry's principal channel of engagement with the UN. Ipieca describes itself as the global oil and gas association dedicated to advancing environmental and social performance across the energy transition. It brings together members and stakeholders to lead in integrating sustainability by advancing climate action, environmental responsibility, and social performance across oil, gas, and renewables activities.[70] It has produced a number of important publications, which are referred to in the next chapter. They include: *Accelerating Action: an SDG Roadmap for the oil and gas sector*,[71] and *Sustainability reporting guidance for the oil and gas sector*.[72] **2.23**

---

65 Examples include: The Explorers and Producers Association of Canada (EPAC), founded in 1986 as the Small Explorers and Producers Association of Canada; the Independent Petroleum Association of America (IPAA), which represents independent oil and natural gas producers; and United Kingdom Onshore Oil and Gas (UKOOG).

66 For example, in Australia, the Australian Pipelines and Gas Association (APGA); in the USA, the Interstate Natural Gas Association of America (INGAA); and in Canada, the Canadian Gas Association (CGA).

67 For example, in Australia, the Australian Hydrogen Council and the Hydrogen Society of Australia; in Canada, the Canadian Hydrogen and Fuel Cell Association; and in the USA, the Fuel Cell and Hydrogen Energy Association (FCHEA).

68 For its website see https://seia.org/about/. Other bodies include the Clean Energy Council in Australia https://cleanenergycouncil.org.au and the Renewable Energy Association in Canada https://renewablesassociation.ca.

69 For its website see https://wwindea.org/. Other bodies include the Canadian Wind Energy Association https://tethys.pnnl.gov/organization/canadian-wind-energy-association-canwea and the Asia Wind Energy Association and its partner organisations, which include Australia https://www.asiawind.org/partner-organizations/australian-wind-alliance/.

70 'Who we are', *Ipieca* (Website) https://www.ipieca.org/about.

71 'Accelerating Action: An SDG Roadmap for the Oil and Gas Sector', *Ipieca*, (Ipieca and World Business Council for Sustainable Development, April 2021) https://www.ipieca.org/resources/sdg-roadmap.

72 'Sustainability reporting guidance for the oil and gas sector', *Ipieca* (Ipieca with API and IOGP, March 2020) https://www.ipieca.org/resources/sustainability-reporting-guidance.

REPORTING AND THE ESG LANDSCAPE

Overview

2.24 This section gives an overview of the organisations that have an influence on reporting and disclosure, including the applicable rules. Some have already been mentioned. They can be put into four groups: the developers of standards such as GRI, the developers of frameworks such as TCFD and TNFD, those that provide guidance such as Ipieca, and those that rate performance such as Bloomberg and MSCI. An excellent starting overview is provided by the KPMG Survey of Sustainability Reporting 2022 (KPMG 2022 Report). That identified that company reporting is often described as ESG reporting (environmental, social and governance) and that 96% of the 250 largest global companies (G250) report on sustainability or ESG matters.

2.25 The KPMG 2022 report also identified:

- There is a need for global consistency in reporting, but existing standards have increased in usage.
- The GRI (Global Reporting Initiative) remains the most dominant standard.
- Some regions have a clear preference for SASB (Sustainability Accounting Standards Board) or local stock exchange guidelines.
- While the GRI and SASB are voluntary, the likelihood is that we will move towards mandatory reporting.
- In Europe in 2012, the European Commission adopted a proposal for a Corporate Sustainability Reporting Directive (CSRD) to extend the non-financial reporting requirement in the EU. New European Sustainability Reporting Standards are aimed to apply to large companies' reports published in 2025.

Global Reporting Initiative

2.26 The Global Reporting Initiative (GRI) was founded in Boston (USA) in 1997 following the public outcry over the environmental damage of the Exxon Valdez oil spill eight years previously. Its aim was to create the first accountability mechanism to ensure companies adhere to responsible environmental conduct principles, which was then broadened to include social, economic, and governance issues. The first version of what was then the GRI Guidelines (G1) was published in 2000 and provided the first global framework for sustainability reporting. The following year, the GRI was established as an independent, non-profit institution. In 2002, the GRI's Secretariat relocated to Amsterdam. Updates to G1 were published in 2006 and 2013. Then, in 2016, the GRI transitioned from providing guidelines to setting the first global standards for sustainability reporting – the GRI Standards. Sector standards continue to be produced, including mining,[73] oil and gas, and renewable energy. GRI standards are aimed at meeting multi-stakeholder needs rather than just the needs of investors and financial markets.

In March 2022, the GRI and the IFRS Foundation,[74] discussed in a subsequent sub-section, signed a cooperation agreement, and their respective standard-setting boards, Global Sustainability Standards Board (GSSB) and the International Sustainability Standards Board (ISSB), will seek to coordinate their work programmes and standard-setting activities.[75] The objective is described in the following quote from the IFRS Foundation: **2.27**

> By working together, the IFRS Foundation and GRI provide two 'pillars' of international sustainability reporting—a first pillar representing investor-focused capital market standards of IFRS Sustainability Disclosure Standards developed by the ISSB, and a second pillar of GRI sustainability reporting requirements set by the GSSB, compatible with the first, designed to meet multi-stakeholder needs.[76]

Task Force on Climate-related Financial Disclosures

The Task Force on Climate-related Financial Disclosures (TCFD) was set up by the Financial Stability Board (FSB) in 2015 to improve and increase reporting of climate-related financial information. Following the release of the Task Force's 2023 Status Report, upon request of the FSB, the TCFD has been disbanded. Its final report of recommendations was published in 2017.[77] Its recommendations provide a highly influential framework that has been picked up by the IFRS and others. **2.28**

International Financial Reporting Standards

The International Financial Reporting Standards (IFRS) Foundation was founded in 2001. It also fits into the category of standard-setter. Its mission is 'to develop high-quality IFRS Standards that bring transparency, accountability **2.29**

73 The standards for mining and oil and gas can be found at https://www.globalreporting.org/standards/sector-program/.

74 IFRS stands for International Financial Reporting Standards.

75 'IFRS Foundation and GRI to align capital market and multi-stakeholder standards to create an interconnected approach for sustainability disclosures', *IFRS* https://www.ifrs.org/news-and-events/news/2022/03/ifrs-foundation-signs-agreement-with-gri/.

76 Ibid. The CEO of GRI puts it like this: 'Aligning GRI's established and widely adopted standards for sustainability impacts with the investor-focused standards being developed by the ISSB will benefit both companies and investors, as well as a wide range of stakeholders around the world.'

77 TCFD Final Report, *Recommendations of Task Force on Climate-related Financial Disclosure*, June 2017, https://assets.bbhub.io/company/sites/60/2021/10/FINAL-2017-TCFD-Report.pdf.

and efficiency to financial markets around the world'.[78] The rationale of its mission is that 'our work serves the public interest by fostering trust, growth and long-term financial stability in the global economy'.[79] The structure of the IFRS Foundation is such that it has two independent standard-setting boards of experts – the International Accounting Standards Board (IASB) and the International Sustainability Standards Board (ISSB), governed and overseen by trustees from around the world (IFRS Foundation Trustees) who, in turn, are accountable to a monitoring board of public authorities (IFRS Foundation Monitoring Board).[80] In 2021 the IFRS Foundation created the International Sustainability Standards Board (ISSB). The ISSB began developing IFRS Sustainability Disclosure Standard IFRS S1 that deals with sustainability and IFRS S2 with climate change, taking up TCFD recommendations. In August 2022, the ISSB assumed responsibility for the Sustainability Accounting Standards Board (SASB) Standards when the Value Reporting Foundation (VRF), a global non-profit organisation that previously maintained these standards, merged with the IFRS Foundation. Its website says: 'The SASB Standards help companies identify and disclose material information about sustainability-related risks and opportunities in the absence of specific IFRS Sustainability Disclosure Standards.'[81] SASB Standards have been commonly referred to by companies.[82] In 2023, the ISSB released IFRS S1 General Requirements for Disclosure of Sustainability-related Financial Information and IFRS S2 Climate-related Disclosures.[83] The IFRS is required to be used by public companies based in 167 jurisdictions, including all of the nations in the European Union as well as Canada, India, Russia, South Korea, South Africa, and Chile. Accordingly, IFRS S1 and IFRS S2 have the potential to have a significant impact on climate-related disclosures. For example, they have been largely adopted for the new Australian rules, which came into law in September 2024, and are discussed in Chapter 8. The USA and China each have their own systems.[84]

---

78 'Who we are', *IFRS* (Website) https://www.ifrs.org/about-us/who-we-are/.

79 Ibid.

80 Ibid.

81 See https://www.ifrs.org/issued-standards/sasb-standards/#:~:text=The%20SASB%20Standards%20are%20a,of%20Sustainability%2Drelated%20Financial%20Information.

82 See the chart in Chapter 8. On climate change risk, see the SASB Climate Risk Technical Bulletin 2023 Update. Table 1 on page 9 maps climate risk by industries according to whether they are physical, transitional, or regulatory https://sasb.ifrs.org/wp-content/uploads/2023/11/SASB-Climate-Risk-Technical-Bulletin-2023-0823.pdf.

83 For these, see the IFRS website at https://www.ifrs.org/issued-standards/ifrs-sustainability-standards-navigator/.

84 For IFRS's 2024 update on progress in corporate climate-related disclosures, see https://www.ifrs.org/news-and-events/news/2024/11/new-report-global-progress-corporate-climate-related-disclosures/.

US GAAP and national accounting standards

Public companies in the USA are required to use a rival system, the Generally 2.30
Accepted Accounting Principles (GAAP). The GAAP standards were developed by the Financial Accounting Standards Accounting Board (FASB) and the Governmental Accounting Standards Board (GASB). The Securities and Exchange Commission (SEC) in the USA has said it won't switch to International Financial Reporting Standards but will continue reviewing a proposal to allow IFRS information to supplement financial filings in the USA. Although GAAP and IFRS have the same ultimate objective of honesty in accounts, there are differences. For example, IFRS was designed as a standards-based approach that could be used internationally, whereas GAAP is a rules-based system used primarily in the USA.

Chinese companies do not use IFRS or GAAP. They use Chinese Accounting 2.31
Standards for Business Enterprises (ASBEs). Other jurisdictions have their own standard-setting bodies: for example, the Australian Accounting Standards Board (AASB) in Australia, the Canadian Accounting Standards Board (AcSB) in Canada, and the Financial Reporting Council (FRC) in the UK. Australian Standards incorporate the equivalents of IFRS standards issued by the IASB.[85] AcSB requires companies to use IFRS. The FRC produces a table of differences between UK standards and IFRS, which contains limited modifications to IFRS.[86]

Natural capital accounting

Natural capital accounting is described in one UN publication as: 2.32

> Natural capital accounting (NCA) is an umbrella term covering efforts to use an accounting framework to provide a systematic way to measure and report on stocks and flows of natural capital. Its underlying premise is that since the environment is important to society and the economy, it should be recognised as an asset that must be maintained and managed, and its contributions (services) be better integrated into commonly used frameworks like the System of National Accounts. NCA covers accounting for individual environmental assets or resources, both biotic and abiotic (such as water, minerals, energy,

85 See *IFRS Foundation* (Website) https://www.ifrs.org/use-around-the-world/use-of-ifrs-standards-by-jurisdiction/view-jurisdiction/australia/.

86 'Table of Differences', *FRC* https://www.frc.org.uk/library/standards-codes-policy/accounting-and-reporting/uk-accounting-standards/uk-accounting-standards-overview/differences-between-uk-and-ireland-financial-reporting-standards-and-ifrs-standards/. See also *IFRS Foundation* https://www.ifrs.org/use-around-the-world/use-of-ifrs-standards-by-jurisdiction/view-jurisdiction/united-kingdom/.

> timber, fish), as well as accounting for ecosystem assets (e.g., forests, wetlands), biodiversity and ecosystem services.[87]

It goes on to say that 'the System of Environmental Economic Accounting (SEEA) is the accepted international standard for environmental-economic accounting, providing a framework for organizing and presenting statistics on the environment and its relationship with the economy'.[88]

2.33 Ecosystem accounting in comparison is a framework 'for integrating measures of ecosystems and the flows of services from them with measures of economic and other human activity'.[89] Ecosystem accounting complements and builds on the accounting for environmental assets as described in the SEEA Central Framework (e.g., water resources, soil resources). In ecosystem accounting, as described in the SEEA Experimental Ecosystem Accounting (SEEA EEA), the accounting approach recognises that these individual resources function in combination within a broader system and within a given spatial area. It is an approach that can help answer what the contribution of ecosystems and their services is to the economy, social wellbeing, jobs, and livelihoods.

Sustainable finance

2.34 The interest of the IFC in referring to sustainability in its review of projects is mentioned at 2.10. It fits in the category of framework developer. Companies seeking to raise finance to develop mining and energy projects from banks and financial institutions are finding them increasingly interested in testing sustainability issues. There are a number of approaches that can be used. They include the Equator Principles, which describe themselves as 'a financial industry benchmark for determining, assessing and managing environmental and social risks in projects'.[90] The principles require an assessment of the environmental and social risks and an independent review.[91] The volume of green loans is increasing and with it securitisation, so how you test whether a loan qualifies is important. That depends on the jurisdictions that apply to it and the applicable criteria. The European Union, for example, has a taxonomy.[92]

---

87 UN's Natural Capital and Ecosystem Services Project FAQ https://seea.un.org/content/natural-capital-and-ecosystem-service. For SEEA see https://seea.un.org.

88 Ibid.

89 Ibid.

90 Equator Principles https://equator-principles.com.

91 Equator Principles EP 4 (July 2020) Principles 2 and 7 https://equator-principles.com/app/uploads/The-Equator-Principles_EP4_July2020.pdf.

92 EU taxonomy for sustainable activities https://finance.ec.europa.eu/sustainable-finance/tools-and-standards/eu-taxonomy-sustainable-activities_en. Other countries are also developing taxonomies; for example

Rating and ranking

2.35 There are a number of bodies involved in rating sustainability or ESG performance. Apparently there are over 140 ESG rating agencies in the USA alone.[93] Some of the most relevant are Bloomberg ESG Data, Dow Jones Sustainability Indexes, MSCI ESG Research, Sustainalytics, Refinitiv (Thomson Reuters) ESG Data, S&P Global, ISS-Ethix ESG, CDP Scores, Climetrics, Vigeo Eiris (Moody's), Corporate Knights Global 100, FTSE Russell ESG Scores, and Reprisk.[94] Some of them offer a free search tool.[95] So the problems here are the number of reporting agencies and that they use different methodologies. Finding a single source of accurate assessment is therefore challenging. The companies reviewed in Chapter 9 use a number of rating agencies.

CORPORATE REGULATORS

2.36 Countries which have laws regulating companies also tend to have a regulator whose job is to carry out activities like the registration of companies, but also to enforce the duties contained in the legislation. In the USA, every state has its own corporate law. For example, Delaware is a popular jurisdiction for companies to be incorporated in the USA. Its legislation is the *Delaware General Corporation Law*.[96] For Nevada, see Chapter 86 of the *Nevada Revised Statutes*.[97] Registration of companies in Delaware is dealt with by the Division of Corporations in the Delaware Secretary of State's office, and in Nevada, the Nevada Secretary of State's office. In Canada, corporations can be incorporated on a federal or provincial basis. The legislation in Saskatchewan is the *Business Corporations Act 2021 (S)*. In Australia, the federal legislation, the *Corporations Act 2001 (Cth)*, applies to all states and territories.[98] In the UK, the legislation is the *Companies Act 2006 (UK)*. Registration of all Australian companies is dealt with by the Australian Securities and Investments Commission (ASIC); the relevant body in the UK is Companies House.

Australia in relation to sustainable finance. See the Australian Sustainable Finance Institute https://www.asfi.org.au/about-taxonomy.

93 Adam Hayes, *How to tell if a company has high ESG scores*, Investopedia July 27 2023 https://www.investopedia.com/company-esg-score-7480372.

94 Ibid.

95 Such as MSCI ESG Research. See https://www.msci.com/sustainable-investing/esg-ratings.

96 Delaware General Corporation Law is Chapter 1 of Title 8 of the Delaware Code.

97 Nevada Revised Statutes, Chapter 86 Limited Liability Companies, https://www.leg.state.nv.us/NRS/NRS-086.html.

98 See *Corporations Act 2001 (Cth)* ss 3 to 5, which set out the constitutional basis of the Act resulting from the referral by states of corporations' powers to the Commonwealth of Australia.

SECURITIES EXCHANGES

2.37 Of the five largest stock exchanges in the world by market capitalisation, the two largest are in the USA: the New York Stock Exchange (NYSE) and the National Association of Securities Dealers Automated Quotations (Nasdaq). They are followed by Shanghai, Euronext in Europe, and the Tokyo Stock Exchange (TYO) in Japan. Toronto (TSE) ranks 10th, London (LSE) 11th, and Australia (ASX) 25th.[99] Toronto and Australia have a disproportionately large number of small mining and energy shares whose securities are quoted.

2.38 To achieve quotation on a stock exchange, a company has to seek admission, which involves compliance with the listing rules of the exchange. But for its securities to continue to be quoted requires ongoing compliance with those rules. The ones relevant to sustainability are discussed in the next chapter. A common element is the disclosure of certain key risks, such as risks associated with climate change.

2.39 A country may have additional laws that are applicable to securities. The Securities and Exchange Commission (SEC) in the USA is the regulator responsible for standards for trade in company shares found mainly in the *Securities Act 1933 (US)*, which regulates original issues of shares, and the *Securities and Exchange Act 1934 (US)*, which regulates secondary trading. These acts were amended by acts like the *Sarbanes-Oxley Act* 2002 *(US)*. So, for example, the SEC has a role in reviewing original offerings of securities to the public, which are required to be registered with it and required disclosures by listed companies.

CONCLUSIONS: GUIDANCE AND KEY PRINCIPLES

2.40 The basic conclusion from this chapter is that the significant number of organisations involved in mining and energy can roughly be put into the following groups:

- UN organisations providing support for the SDGs and other important areas such as the environment, development, and education (UNEP, UNDP, and UNESCO);

99 See *Statista* (Website) https://www.statista.com/statistics/270126/largest-stock-exchange-operators-by-market-capitalization-of-listed-companies/#:~:text=The%20New%20York%20Stock%20Exchange,and%20the%20Shanghai%20Stock%20Exchange.

- Those whose main role is to act as advocates or to provide research for a particular mineral or region (such as the World Gold Council, Minerals Councils and Associations in mining, USOGA, CAPP, AEP, UK Oil and Gas, and USEA in oil and gas, and solar and wind associations for renewable energy);[100]
- Those that provide research and policy advice (such as the IEA, Ipieca, and IRENA);
- Those dedicated to changing behaviour (such as the UN's Global Compact, IGF, and ICMM);
- Those that set standards in reporting and accounting (such as the GRI and IFRS);
- Those that will assess your performance (such as Bloomberg and MSCI);
- Regulators in a jurisdiction (such as mining and corporate regulators and those responsible for securities exchanges).

A distinction can be drawn between organisations which are very useful as a source of data and information (such as IEA and IRENA), those which act as advocates for mining or energy in a region (such as Mineral Councils) or for a mineral (such as the World Gold Council), those which seek to drive change (such as ICMM), and regulators who enforce the law and are supported by organisations setting standards (such as IFRS). **2.41**

Using or joining any of the first three groups is a matter of choice, which will depend on the needs and requirements of the entity doing the choosing. However, choices in relation to the last group – the regulators – are limited by the legal rules in which they operate. The checklist below can assist you in working through which organisations may be helpful to you. **2.42**

Checklist

Purpose of checklist

The purpose of this checklist is to guide you to organisations and their websites which may contain useful material. In due course, you may also wish to refer to Chapter 3 Governance and Chapter 9 Company sustainability reporting. The summary of your position in Part A below can be used for those as well. **2.43**

Part A – Your position

1. What is the focus of your organisation (for example, mining, oil and gas, or renewable energy company), service company (what kind of service), government department (specify area), or other organisation (specify area)?
2. Does your organisation currently track progress against any of the UN's Sustainable Development Goals (SDGs)?

---

100 See for example n 69.

3. Does your organisation produce environmental, social and governance (ESG) reports (specify whether published externally or not)?
4. Does your organisation produce sustainability reports (specify whether published externally or not)?
5. Is your organisation developing or revising a sustainability strategy?
6. Is your organisation seeking to reduce its greenhouse gas emissions by developing a renewable energy facility?

Part B – Mining focus

- For the SDGs, see the websites of UNDESA and UN Global Compact, and the mining industry bodies in your jurisdiction.
- For ESG and sustainability reports, see the websites of GRI, IFRS, SEEA (natural capital), WBCSD, the corporate regulator in your jurisdiction, and the rules of any securities exchange on which your securities are listed.
- Generally, see the websites of the World Bank and OECD.

Part C – Oil and gas focus

- For the SDGs, see the websites of Ipieca, UNDESA, and UN Global Compact, and the oil and gas industry bodies in your jurisdiction.
- For ESG and sustainability reports, see the websites of Ipieca, IEA, GRI, IFRS, SEEA (natural capital), WBCSD, the corporate regulator in your jurisdiction, and the rules of any securities exchange on which your securities are listed.
- Generally, see the websites of the World Bank and OECD.

Part D – Renewable energy focus

- For the SDGs, see the websites of IRENA, UNDESA, and UN Global Compact, and the oil and renewable energy bodies in your jurisdiction.
- For ESG and sustainability reports, see the websites of IRENA, IEA, GRI, IFRS, SEEA (natural capital), WBCSD, the corporate regulator in your jurisdiction, and the rules of any securities exchange on which your securities are listed.
- Generally, see the websites of the World Bank and OECD.

Part E – Government, regulator and policy focus

- For particular sectors, see the websites referred to in Parts B, C, and D.
- See the websites of the World Bank and OECD on regulatory matters.
- For accounting standards in the public sector, see the International Public Sector Accounting Standards Board website https://www.ipsasb.org/.

3

GOVERNANCE AND SUSTAINABILITY

INTRODUCTION 3.01
Cadbury Report: example of general governance principles – corporations 3.06
Corporate sustainability governance 3.08
Examples of general governance principles – government 3.12
The WFGW – the Welsh example of sustainability governance 3.18
The UN and sustainability governance 3.24
THE IMPORTANCE OF CULTURE AND REGULATION 3.26
Government policy on mining and energy operations 3.28
The focus of regulation where the state owns the resources 3.35
Public policy sustainability objectives and increased reporting requirements 3.39
Governance of renewable energy 3.40
COMPANY LAW 3.42
Outline 3.42
Duties to act within powers, in good faith, and in the interests of the corporation 3.44
Duty of care 3.46
Duty to report on financial and non-financial matters 3.50
SECURITIES EXCHANGES AND MARKET REGULATION 3.51
ACCOUNTING STANDARDS AND IFRS S1 SUSTAINABILITY FINANCIAL DISCLOSURE 3.57
Introduction 3.57
IFRS S1 and sustainability financial disclosure 3.59
CONCLUSIONS, GUIDANCE, AND KEY PRINCIPLES 3.62

INTRODUCTION

How sustainability is implemented in organisations will depend significantly on the governance arrangements. Therefore, governance is one of the key themes that a number of reporting regimes require companies to report on – for example, in recent times, the climate change disclosure regimes. Regimes are examined in this chapter and Chapter 9. Examples of company reports are given in Chapter 8. There are many definitions of governance, but the central idea is one of the system by which an organisation is directed and controlled. Of particular relevance will be who has oversight of the organisation and the duties of those people. Important questions are whether those duties extend to consider the long-term future of the organisation, its wider role in society, and of course its sustainability. This chapter will therefore start by examining general principles of governance to see if they deal with those matters, before looking at them in the following more focused regimes: government mining 3.01

and petroleum regimes, company law, securities exchanges, and accounting rules. Governance under the regimes will be guided by the structure and rules of the regime, including any legal duties imposed on those responsible for governance. With international organisations such as the United Nations, the document creating the organisation and setting its rules can often take the form of a treaty.[1]

3.02 The general principles of governance are based on two ideas. The first is that organisations, such as companies, statutory bodies, and non-government organisations, are inanimate, and therefore require human beings to steer them and manage their progress.[2] The second is that, commonly, there are three groups involved in any organisation: the board of directors, or other group responsible for governance; the executives, managers, or public servants who run the operations from day to day; and third, the group for whose benefit the organisation is being run. In the case of a company, that group is the shareholders, who are the ultimate owners of the company. In the case of a government organisation, department, or entity without actual members, it is broadly those who are supposed to benefit from the operations – that may be a section of the public or in the case of a government department, the inhabitants of the country as a whole. But giving a precise legal answer will depend on a number of factors, such as the statute creating the organisation and the constitution of the country.

3.03 Because of the separation between those responsible for governance, those responsible for day-to-day management, and the ultimate owners or beneficiaries, major themes of governance are directed at requiring those responsible for governance to act only for the ultimate owners and to do so with honesty and integrity. In the case of company boards, that principle is underpinned by the law in many jurisdictions, such as the United Kingdom (UK), Australia, and Canada, that the directors are in the position of trustees.[3] The legal concept of a trust arose in England as early as the 13th century – to impose duties

---

1 The constitutional document of the United Nations is the *United Nations Charter*, which sets out the powers and functions of the General Assembly and Security Council and creates the International Court of Justice. See, *Charter of the United Nations* https://www.un.org/en/about-us/un-charter. Contrast the International Whaling Commission, set up under Article III of the *International Convention for the Regulation of Whaling 1946* https://archive.iwc.int/pages/download.php?direct=1&noattach=true&ref=3607&ext=pdf&k=.

2 The word 'governance' comes from the Greek word 'Kybernan', to direct the course of a ship, or to steer the ship. The Romans borrowed the word as 'gubernare' and it found its way into English as 'Governor', a steersman or pilot.

3 Companies referred to in this book will generally be those incorporated under the companies legislation of the jurisdiction with limited liability and having a share capital. In many jurisdictions, there is also

on those holding property for others, where the person in the position of trustee held the legal title and the others held what became known as beneficial ownership.[4]

In relation to companies, although it has generally been possible for the shareholders, as owners of a company, to exercise control, particularly for a small family company, it was recognised early on that that control was not realistic or practical for larger companies. So, the first companies legislation, the *Joint Stock Companies Act 1844 (UK)*, said that directors were to be appointed 'for the conduct and superintendence of the affairs of the company'. That principle is one of general application in companies legislation throughout the world, and notwithstanding that different countries may have different board structures, for example, involving supervisory or advisory boards. A single board, sometimes called a unitary board, is common in companies legislation throughout the English-speaking world. **3.04**

The position with government is that the roles and responsibilities of the head of government, ministers, and government employees and officials are commonly set out in the country's constitutional documents and statutes. In democratic societies, the head of government is elected through popular elections, as are members of the parliament or other bodies containing representatives of electors. In some societies, such as the UK and Australia, government employees are employed on a long-term basis and do not change if a new government is elected. That is not the case with the federal system in the United States of America (USA), where an incoming president has, and usually exercises, a power of appointment over key federal positions, including the White House staff.[5] **3.05**

Cadbury Report: example of general governance principles – corporations

The 2012 *Report of the Committee on the Financial Aspects of Corporate Governance* (*Cadbury Report*) in the UK has been highly influential in setting guidelines **3.06**

---

legislation regulating charities, unincorporated and other non-corporate bodies. That legislation sometimes places duties on office-holders somewhat similar to the duties discussed below.

4 An early trust could arise if, for example, a landowner going to fight in a crusade in the Holy Land put his lands into the name of a neighbour. If the neighbour would not give them back when the landowner returned, the common law of the day did not have an available remedy. The practice grew of people like the landowner petitioning the King's Chancellor, who was usually a churchman, and who used his powers on a moral basis to require the neighbour to transfer back the land. Over time, this became known as part of the rules of equity and they came under the control of a separate court known in the UK as Chancery.

5 See, John Fairlie, 'The Administrative Powers of the President' (1903) 2 *Michigan Law Review* (3): 190–210.

for good governance in companies.[6] It defines corporate governance as 'the system by which companies are directed and controlled' and says that 'boards of directors are responsible for the governance of their companies'.[7] Its main output was a voluntary governance code with the following key principles of general application:

> 3.2 The principles on which the Code is based are those of openness, integrity and accountability. They go together. Openness on the part of companies, within the limits set by their competitive position, is the basis for the confidence which needs to exist between business and all those who have a stake in its success. An open approach to the disclosure of information contributes to the efficient working of the market economy, prompts boards to take effective action and allows shareholders and others to scrutinise companies more thoroughly.
>
> 3.3 Integrity means both straight forward dealing and completeness. What is required of financial reporting is that it should be honest and that it should present a balanced picture of the state of the company's affairs. The integrity of reports depends on the integrity of those who prepare and present them.
>
> 3.4 Boards of directors are accountable to their shareholders and both have to play their part in making that accountability effective. Boards of directors need to do so through the quality of the information which they provide to shareholders, and shareholders through their willingness to exercise their responsibilities as owners.[8]

3.07 These principles of openness, integrity and accountability echo in numerous writings about good governance.[9] They are also sometimes set out in codes (for example, the *UK Corporate Governance Code*).[10] The later section on securities exchanges examines the requirements of securities exchanges in relation to governance and the disclosure by companies of their corporate governance practices. What we will find resulting from the combined effect of corporate governance codes and the rules of securities exchanges is a focus on disclosure of the risks faced by the business, of which climate change risk has become

---

6 *Report of the Committee on The Financial Aspects of Corporate Governance* (1 December 2012) (*Cadbury Report*) https://www.icaew.com/-/media/corporate/files/library/subjects/corporate-governance/financial-aspects-of-corporate-governance.ashx?la=en.

7 Ibid. It goes on to say, 'The responsibilities of the board include setting the company's strategic aims, providing the leadership to put them into effect, supervising the management of the business and reporting to shareholders on their stewardship. The board's actions are subject to laws, regulations and the shareholders in general meeting.'

8 *Cadbury Report* (n 6) para 3.2.

9 For example, the opening chapters of the OECD's publication, *The Governance of Regulators (Best Practice Principles for Regulatory Policy* (OECD Publishing 2014) have titles as follows: Chapter 1 Role Clarity, Chapter 2 Preventing undue influence and maintaining trust, and Chapter 4 Accountability and transparency. See also the Evans Committee, n 24.

10 The latest version was issued in 2024, the Financial Reporting Council's *UK Corporate Governance Code 2024* (effective 2025) https://www.frc.org.uk/library/standards-codes-policy/corporate-governance/uk-corporate-governance-code/.

prominent in recent years. TCFD and the development of International Reporting Standards IFRS S1 and S2 were introduced in Chapter 1 from 1.43. There are variations in corporate governance between jurisdictions which depend on differences in requirements and emphasis, such as the importance placed on independence at the chairman or director level. That was well explained in a Canadian publication, which made the initial point that 'Canada's system of corporate governance is derived from the British common law model and strongly influenced by developments in the United States'.[11] It goes on to say:

> While corporate governance practices in the United Kingdom and the United States are similar in many respects, where there are differences, Canadian practice usually falls somewhere in between. For example, a Canadian corporation is more likely than a US corporation to have a chair who is not the CEO, and typically has fewer executives on the board than a UK corporation.[12]

What is clear is that the long-term future of the organisation, its wider role in society or its sustainability have not featured strongly in general corporate governance principles. To find references to those ideas, we will have to look at more specific disclosure rules, particularly recent ones, which are discussed in later sections of this chapter. The situation is much more fluid now as those rules are changing corporate governance practices.

Corporate sustainability governance

3.08 Companies are also focusing on sustainability issues to a much greater extent. It has become common for listed companies to have a sustainability committee. There is commentary on best practice in setting up such committees; a document entitled *Focus 15 Sustainability Committees: Structures and Practices* (*IFC Sustainability Practices*), published by the International Finance Corporation (IFC) arm of the World Bank Group, is a very useful guide.[13] It is apparent from that that sustainability is becoming more significant. The initial point of *IFC Sustainability Practices* is that sustainability is a very important issue for companies. It goes on to say that the board of directors is ultimately responsible for sustainability in a company. Delegating some activities to a board

11 Canadian Coalition for Good Governance, Corporate Governance in Canada https://www.ecgi.global/publications/codes/countries/corporate-governance-in-canada.

12 Ibid.

13 International Finance Corporation in partnership with the Finance Ministry of the Grand Duchy of Luxembourg, *Focus 15 Sustainability Committees: Structures and Practices* (Report, 16 June 2021) https://www.ifc.org/content/dam/ifc/doc/mgrt/focus-15-sustainability-committees.pdf (*IFC Sustainability Practices*).

sustainability committee or management sustainability committee does not remove that ultimate responsibility. So, an important initial question for a board is whether the whole board should deal with sustainability issues, or whether some or all of the activities should be delegated to a special committee. As we will discuss shortly, that will often be determined by the size of the company and its operations and their complexity. What we can note is that it is now very common for boards to have committees, of which the audit committee is the prime example.[14] In a small company, all the board members may sit on that committee. Usually a committee will have a charter or similar document setting out its responsibilities.

3.09 The definition of 'sustainability' adopted by *IFC Sustainability Practices* is 'the environmental and social factors that have an impact on the long-term performance of companies'.[15] It goes on to say that 'the economic contribution (effect) of the company, and how the broader economy affects it and its customer base, surrounding communities, and other stakeholders, are implied in the performance dimension'.[16] The rationale for the importance of sustainability in the view of the IFC lies in the performance aspect, that it is 'an imperative for long-term operational success'. That is because success is linked to three independent subsystems – the economy, society, and the natural environment.[17] At the same time, compliance is becoming increasingly important in line with more extensive sustainability reporting and other compliance obligations.

3.10 *IFC Sustainability Practices* says that companies on a sustainability journey fall into different categories. In a company with limited operations or with few sustainability issues, the board may take full responsibility for dealing with sustainability, without the support of management or board sustainability committees.[18] That assumes that the board has members who are sufficiently competent in the area. Companies at what the IFC describes as the intermediate level, which is a more advanced level than the first group, could initiate a more formal governance structure, which may include a management function or committee or a board committee to assist the board. Good international

---

14 In 2015, the author and Jared Clements did a survey of corporate governance practices of companies listed on the ASX as operating in the materials and energy sector. Of the companies surveyed, over 50% had an audit committee. Other committees included remuneration, nomination, risk, health and safety, sustainability, disclosure and project steering. See, John Chandler and Jared Clements, 'Corporate governance for Australian energy and resources companies', (2016) 34 *Company and Securities Law Journal* 175.

15 *IFC Sustainability Practices* (n 13) 2, quoting from IFC Toolkit for Disclosure and Transparency (2018), 5.

16 Ibid.

17 *IFC Sustainability Practices* (n 13) 4, quoting from Part 1 of King IV Report on Corporate Governance for South Africa (2016) https://www.iodsa.co.za/page/king-iv.

18 *IFC Sustainability Practices* (n 13) 9.

practice for companies at the advanced level, meaning that they have complex and high-impact operations, is to have both.[19] Figure 3.1 sets out important considerations and drivers in sustainability governance.

The considerations start with strategy, accountability, and culture at the top – those are affected by applicable laws which have been divided between company law on the left and other laws on the right. The box at the top then leads down to the processes used to implement the strategy, such as risk assessment. Supporting the structure is the box at the bottom: support and guidance. 3.11

Examples of general governance principles – government

Whether government sets sustainability objectives and accountability for the performance of those sustainability objectives are important issues in government sustainability governance. As the OECD principles of good regulation put it, 'The regulator exists to meet objectives deemed by the government and legislature to be in the public interest and operates within the powers attributed to it.'[20] The setting of clear objectives is therefore fundamental to good regulation. Accountability in fulfilling those objectives is also fundamental. In the context of this book, and indeed generally, accountability 'does not imply simply providing information or answering questions, but includes setting goals, providing and reporting on results and the visible consequences of getting things right or wrong including rewards or actions as appropriate'.[21] The main streams of accountability in a traditional sense are the duties of ministers and other government officials and the objectives set out in the statutes granting them powers. We will start by looking at those traditional streams before looking at a more modern stream: policy objectives of government departments concerning things like sustainability in procurement, there being a growing number of those policies and reporting rules requiring government departments to report on sustainability. 3.12

Dealing first with the duties of ministers and other government officials, there is no doubt that on first glance accountability in government is a complex matter. In an Australian context, which would apply equally to the UK and 3.13

19 Ibid.

20 For a discussion of regulators and regulation, see 3.27. In simple terms, regulators are public servants with designated administrative tasks. But the term 'regulators' has come into common use to describe them as regulation has taken on an increasingly important role. For the quotation, see OECD, *The Governance of Regulators* (Best Practice Principles for Regulatory Policy, OECD Publishing 2014) 81.

21 Australian Commonwealth Department of Prime Minister and Cabinet 1993, as quoted in Diana Nestorovska, 'Assessing the Effectiveness of ASIC's Accountability Framework' 34 *Company and Securities Law Journal* 193, 199.

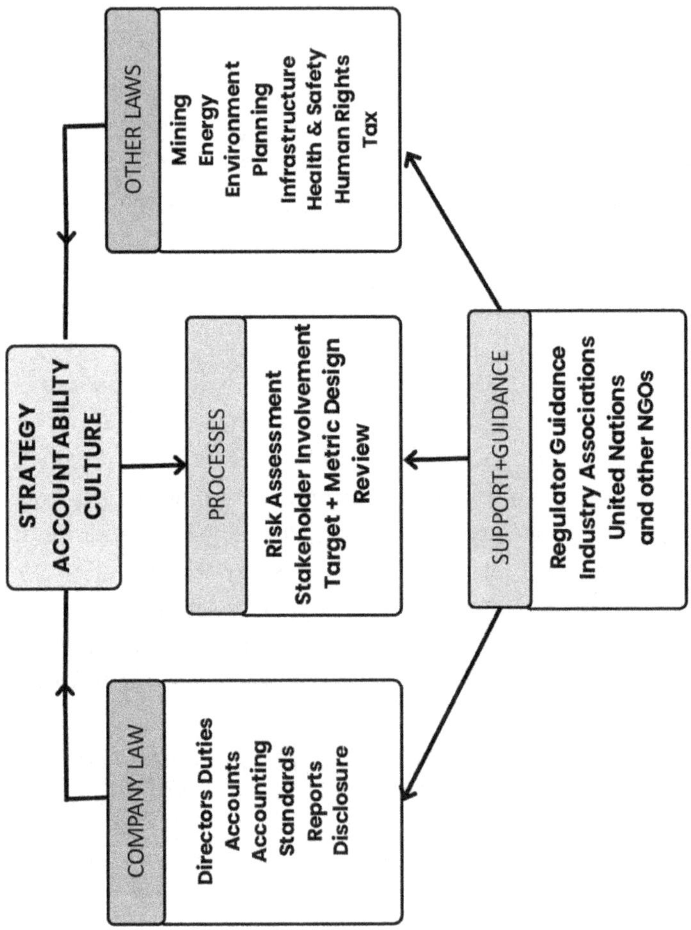

Source: Author's own.

Figure 3.1 Sustainability governance

Canada, that complexity arises because of the complexity in the relationships 'between the public service, the government, the parliament and Australia's citizens'.[22] There are a number of measures imposing accountability on the public service in most jurisdictions.[23] The last 30 years have seen an increased focus on ethics in government[24] and related matters.[25] There has been reinforcement of key principles of openness, integrity, and accountability.[26] There has been increased ethics regulation of public servants through the UK's Civil Service Commission and its equivalents in Australia.[27] But there are few indications of any rules that require a governance structure that would impose a duty to consider a long-term future or sustainability and set objectives in relation to them. The outstanding exception to that is the *Well-being of Future Generations (Wales) Act 2015* (*WFGW*), discussed in the next sub-section. But there is also a growing trend of setting objectives in statutes. Examples include the *Climate Change Act 2022 (Cth)*, which has a national emissions target and a requirement for the minister to review whether targets are being met, report to Parliament, and make adjustments; and the *Climate Change Act 2008 (UK)*.

To some degree the lack of objectives arises because of the way in which things have been done in the past. A starting point in understanding why that is the case is the oaths used by new office bearers, which do not include any precise duties. There is commonly a prescribed oath that executives, like the president 3.14

---

22 Australian Senate Select Committee on A Certain Maritime Incident, Report October 2002 https://www.aph.gov.au/Parliamentary_Business/Committees/Senate/Former_Committees/maritimeincident/report/c07 at 7.3. At 7.1, it said that discussions about considerations of accountability 'revealed forcefully what academic analysts have recently been asserting – that accountability is "a notoriously imprecise term", something that must be approached "as a problem with multiple levels and more than one possible meaning" and that balancing accountability with the need for flexibility of action is "the ongoing challenge of public policy in Australia"'.

23 So, in Australia at the federal level, legislative prescription for public service accountability is contained in the *Public Governance, Performance and Accountability Act 2013 (Cth)*.

24 In 1994, the UK government established a Committee on Standards in Public Life. The remit of the committee was to make recommendations to improve standards of behaviour in public life. It developed the Nolan principles, which, in addition to those mentioned by Cadbury, listed 'selflessness', 'objectivity', 'honesty', and 'leadership'. The Committee has continued its work and for its most recent report, see, *Upholding Standards in Public Life*, (Final Report of the Standards Matter 2 Review, November 2021) (*Evans Report*) https://www.gov.uk/government/publications/upholding-standards-in-public-life-published-report. In Australia, see the *Public Service Act 1999 (Cth)* and the Australian Public Service Commission document APS Values https://www.apsc.gov.au/working-aps/information-aps-employment/aps-values.

25 See the schedules to the *Evans Report* (n 24).

26 The Evans Committee (n 24) at 18 says, 'The Seven Principles of Public Life – selflessness, integrity, objectivity, accountability, openness, honesty and leadership – define the public service ethos of the United Kingdom. These ethical standards provide a common framework for the conduct of all those in public office, as well as those in the private sector providing public services'.

27 See *Evans Report* (n 24) 45.

of the USA and government ministers in countries having them, make upon taking office. Its wording varies between countries and not all countries require it for all offices. Commonly, its wording is fairly broad along the lines of, 'I will faithfully execute the Office of President,'[28] or 'I will truly serve the people of [insert country] in the office of [insert office].'[29] These forms of wording do not give much guidance as to the actual duties – for those, one has to turn to other materials such as the description of the office in any constitutional document.

3.15 The principles of ministerial responsibility in the Westminster system are similarly broad. There is a principle that says: 'In the event of departmental error, the principle requires that the minister accepts responsibility for the mistake and if possible, corrects it. If the departmental failure is sufficiently serious, the minister should resign.'[30] In 2006, an Australian Senate committee reviewing alleged breaches of a statute made the following observation in relation to the principle:

> 1.14 Over the past 30 years, as government departments have grown larger, more complex and diverse, new accountability mechanisms have been introduced to provide a necessary counterbalance to the growth of bureaucratic decision-making and its impact on the lives of ordinary people and businesses. Examples of accountability mechanisms which now apply to government departments include the Freedom of Information legislation, the Commonwealth Ombudsman, judicial review of decisions, and the Senate Estimates process.
>
> 1.15 As a result of the growth in public sector administration and accountability, the doctrine has been eroded. Ministers are accepting less direct responsibility for actions taken under their authority. Given the extremely broad range of issues that modern government departments deal with, it would be unreasonable for ministers to be expected to take responsibility for all of the actions of those under their authority. The principle in its contemporary form therefore does not cover situations beyond a Minister's knowledge, in which case the Departmental Secretary or some other senior official must take responsibility.

---

28 The Presidential oath in full is: 'I do solemnly swear (or affirm) that I will faithfully execute the Office of President of the United States, and will to the best of my Ability, preserve, protect and defend the Constitution of the United States', *Constitution of the United States of America* (ratified 1798) Article II Section 1 https://www.senate.gov/about/origins-foundations/senate-and-constitution/constitution.htm.

29 This is the Australian ministerial oath, which, in full, is along the lines of: 'I (name), do swear that I will well and truly serve the people of Australia in the office of (position) and that I will be faithful and bear true allegiance to His Majesty King Charles the Third, King of Australia. So help me God.' Parliament of Australia, *Oaths and affirmations made by the executive and members of federal parliament since 1901* (13 June 2013). The form of the oath is not set out in the Constitution of Australia and has had many variations over the years https://www.aph.gov.au/about_parliament/parliamentary_departments/parliamentary_library/pubs/rp/rp1314/oathsaffirmations#_Toc358025341.

30 References Committee of Australian Senate Standing Constitutional Committee on Legal and Constitutional Affairs, *Report on The Administration and Operation of the Migration Act 1958* (March 2006) Chapter 1.

The Prime Minister of Australia has also released guidelines on ministerial responsibilities entitled *A Guide on Key Elements of Ministerial Responsibility*. According to these guidelines:

> Ministers do … have overall responsibility for the administration of their portfolios and for carriage in the Parliament of their accountability obligations arising from that responsibility. They would properly be held to account for *matters for which they were personally responsible*, or where they were *aware of problems but had not acted to rectify them* [emphasis added].[31]

Canadian commentary on ministerial responsibility puts the matter differently from the principle set out at 3.15. It says in a message to ministers: **3.16**

> You are accountable to Parliament for the exercise of the powers, duties and functions with which you have been entrusted. This requires you to be present in Parliament to answer honestly and accurately about your areas of responsibility, to take corrective action as appropriate to address problems that may arise in your portfolios, to correct any inadvertent errors in answering to Parliament at the earliest opportunity, and to work with parliamentary colleagues of all political persuasions in a respectful and constructive manner.[32]

Notwithstanding these high-sounding words, there is a great temptation for politicians not to acknowledge mistakes and undertake to fix them – to the contrary, there are shocking examples of politicians not telling the truth about their behaviour. The application of the rule of law is one way of seeking a legal remedy. The way that the relevant legislation is framed is critical because under English and Australian law, executive power must be exercised for the purpose and within the boundaries for which it was conferred.[33] Those limits can be enforced through judicial review and in some cases through the prerogative **3.17**

---

31 Ibid.

32 Prime Minister of Canada Justin Trudeau, Message to Ministers in *Open and Accountable Government 2015* https://www.pm.gc.ca/en/news/backgrounders/2015/11/27/open-and-accountable-government. It also says in 1.1, 'Ministers are accountable to the Prime Minister: they are appointed by the Governor General on the advice of the Prime Minister and the Prime Minister may ask for their resignation at any time. Ministers are also accountable to Parliament. Most ministerial responsibilities are conferred on Ministers by Parliament through statutes that set out the powers, duties and functions for which the Minister is individually accountable. In addition, Ministers may also have other authorities in common law.'

33 In the Australian High Court, Brennan J expressed the position as follows: 'Judicial review is neither more nor less than the enforcement of the rule of law over executive action; it is the means by which executive action is prevented from exceeding the powers and functions assigned to the executive by law and the interests of the individual are protected accordingly.' *Church of Scientology v Woodward* [1982] HCA 78, (1982) 154 CLR 25, 70 (Brennan J).

writs. There are analogous principles in Canada, which are broadly similar to those in the UK, Australia,[34] and the USA.[35]

The WFGW – the Welsh example of sustainability governance

3.18 The *WFGW* is a unique piece of legislation, although others, such as Scotland, have shown interest in emulating it. There are four things about it that are very significant. First, it creates the position of Future Generations Commissioner for Wales, whose role includes promoting the interests of future generations. Second, it sets well-being objectives for Wales. These objectives go beyond economic growth targets and consider the quality of life of Welsh people and require public bodies to implement them. Third, the Commissioner facilitates improvements by public bodies in the way in which they implement sustainability principles. Fourth, public bodies are required to consider the long-term impact of their actions. Section 1 of the *WFGW* gives an overview of the Act and section 1(2) summarises the major operative provisions as follows:

1) Part 2 of this Act—
   a) explains what is meant by "sustainable development" and requires public bodies to carry out sustainable development (sections 2 and 3);
   b) requires the bodies to set well-being objectives that are to contribute to the achievement of well-being goals and to take steps to meet those objectives (section 3);
   c) requires the bodies to do those things in accordance with the sustainable development principle (section 3);
   d) explains what the well-being goals are and what it means to do things in accordance with the sustainable development principle (sections 4 and 5);
   e) requires indicators that measure progress towards achieving the well-being goals (section 10), and reports on future trends in the well-being of Wales (section 11), to be published by the Welsh Ministers;
   f) requires the bodies to report annually on their progress towards meeting their well-being objectives (sections 12 and 13 and Schedule 1);
   g) requires the Auditor General for Wales to carry out examinations into the extent to which public bodies set objectives and take steps to meet them in accordance with the sustainable development principle (section 15).

3.19 Part 3 establishes the office of Future Generations Commissioner for Wales (section 17 and Schedule 2) and provides for the Commissioner to promote

---

34 Thomas S. Kuttner, Zach Parrott and Andrew McIntosh, 'Administrative Law in Canada', *The Canadian Encyclopedia* (30 October 2020) https://development.thecanadianencyclopedia.ca/en/article/administrative-law.

35 So, in respect of federal administrative decisions, they are set out in *Administrative Procedure Act* (*APA*). There is also model legislation applicable to state decisions.

the needs of future generations by monitoring and reporting on the extent to which the public bodies are setting and seeking to meet their well-being objectives, in accordance with the sustainable development principle (section 18). Part 4 establishes a public services board for each local authority area in Wales and sets out with whom a board may work (Chapter 1). It requires boards to improve the well-being of their area by contributing to the well-being goals, which they are to do by assessing well-being in their area, setting local objectives designed to maximise the board's contribution (within its area) to the achievement of the well-being goals, and taking steps to meet those objectives (Chapter 2, section 36). It requires boards to do those things in accordance with the sustainable development principle (Chapter 2, section 36) and to publish local well-being plans: setting out their local objectives and how they propose to take steps to meet them (Chapter 2, section 39).

The sustainable development principle is defined in section 5(1), using the Brundtland Report wording, as requiring a public body to act 'in a manner which seeks to ensure that the needs of the present are met without compromising the ability of future generations to meet their own needs'. The temporal aspect is emphasised – but not detailed by allocation or decision-making rules – in section 5(2)(a), which requires a public body to take account of 'the importance of balancing short term needs with the need to safeguard the ability to meet long term needs, especially where things done to meet short term needs may have detrimental long-term effect'. 3.20

There are seven well-being goals set out in section 4: a prosperous Wales, a resilient Wales, a healthier Wales, a more equal Wales, a Wales of cohesive communities, a Wales of vibrant culture and thriving Welsh language, and a globally responsible Wales. Each of these comes with a description. A prosperous Wales is described as: 3.21

> An innovative, productive and low carbon society which recognises the limits of the global environment and therefore uses resources efficiently and proportionately (including acting on climate change); and which develops a skilled and well-educated population in an economy which generates wealth and provides employment opportunities, allowing people to take advantage of the wealth generated through securing decent work

A resilient Wales is 'a nation which maintains and enhances a biodiverse natural environment with healthy functioning ecosystems that support social, economic and ecological resilience and the capacity to adapt to change (for example climate change)'.

3.22 In order to act in accordance with the sustainability principle, a public body has to take into account the matters listed in section 5(2). They include section 5(2)(a) – 'the importance of balancing short term needs with the need to safeguard the ability to meet long term needs, especially where things done to meet short term needs may have detrimental long term effect', and section 5(2)(b) – the need to take an integrated approach by considering, for example, how 'the body's well-being objectives impact upon each other or upon other public bodies' objectives'.

3.23 The incoming Future Generations Commissioner, Derek Walker, had this to say in introducing himself in 2023:

> As Commissioner, my role is to be the guardian of future generations. This means helping public bodies and those who make policy in Wales to think about the long-term impact their decisions have.
>
> For example, if we know that around 35% of jobs in the UK may disappear as a result of robots, artificial intelligence or computers, what's that going to mean to you, your children and your grandchildren?[36]

The UN and sustainability governance

3.24 The UN has various initiatives to encourage and facilitate sustainability governance. These go back to at least 2002 and the UN's World Conference on Sustainable Development in Johannesburg, from which flowed the *Plan of Implementation of the World Summit on Sustainable Development.*[37] It points out:

> 4 Good governance within each country and at the international level is essential for sustainable development. At the domestic level, sound environmental, social and economic policies, democratic institutions responsive to the needs of the people, the rule of law, anti-corruption measures, gender equality and an enabling environment for investment are the basis for sustainable development.

It goes on to 'encourage relevant authorities at all levels to take sustainable development considerations into account in decision-making, including on national and local development planning, investment in infrastructure, business development and public procurement'.[38] That would include support for strategies and programmes and providing capacity-building and training.

---

36 Future Generations Commissioner for Wales (webpage) https://www.futuregenerations.wales/about-us/future-generations-commissioner/.

37 United Nations, *Plan of Implementation of the World Summit on Sustainable Development* (4 September 2002) UN Doc A/CONF.199/20 http://www.un-documents.net/jburgpln.htm.

38 Ibid, para 9.

In the UNEP 2020 report *Mineral Resource Governance in the 21st century*, there is a discussion of social licence to operate, following on from the ideas set forth in the Johannesburg Declaration. It is subtitled, 'Gearing extractive industries towards sustainable development', and shows that good governance is key to managing environmental and social impacts and unlocking the sector's potential as a catalyst of sustainable growth and development. At page 265, it argues for moving away from the amorphous and metaphorical nature of the social licence to operate and the sectorial and one-dimensional nature of existing governance instruments. Instead, it says that a much more holistic, integrated, and inclusive governance approach should be adopted, premised on the need for positive economic, social, and environmental outcomes, and appropriate governance mechanisms to achieve these. This framework is termed a 'Sustainable Development Licence to Operate' (SDLO). **3.25**

THE IMPORTANCE OF CULTURE AND REGULATION

It is all very well to have sound governance principles, but they are of little value if the practice of an organisation is to ignore them. That is why culture, which can be described as 'the way things are done in an organisation', is important. A more formal definition is 'the ways people in the organization behave and the attitudes and beliefs that inform those behaviours (i.e., "the way we do things around here") — including formal, stated norms as well as implicit ways people work and interact'.[39] That definition is important because it brings out the idea that the beliefs or principles that guide behaviour are a vital element of culture. They can be looked to as a compass which sets the direction for behaviour. It is tempting to describe it as a moral compass. It can certainly be a moral compass on some important questions. There are numerous examples in case law and Royal Commissions that illustrate that. What those cases also illustrate is that culture is of little value if it is not implemented effectively. That has become increasingly challenging as working conditions have changed, with many people working remotely and having greater job mobility. Having said that, there are certain areas where mining and energy companies have developed a strong culture – safety being the prime example. But extending culture out to include an embrace of sustainability principles is less common, although becoming more so.[40] **3.26**

39 Denise Lee Yohn, 'Company Culture is Everyone's Responsibility' (2021) *Harvard Business Review* https://hbr.org/2021/02/company-culture-is-everyones-responsibility.

40 See, for example, TotalEnergies, *TotalEnergies Sustainability and Climate Progress Report 2024*, 65 https://totalenergies.com/system/files/documents/2024-03/totalenergies_sustainability-climate-2024-progress

3.27 When it comes to governance and sustainability in government, the growth of public sector administration needs to be borne in mind. Much of the detailed administration of mining and energy is done by government officials who are often described as 'regulators'. The term 'regulator' is one of relatively recent origin. Regulators are simply government officials carrying out duties imposed on them by legislation. Their role and the rules they apply are generally set out in secondary, or subordinate, legislation supplemented by guidance documents they publish. Those are very common in oil and gas and mining. In recent decades their role has expanded so that they are 'now playing an increasingly important role in delivering economic and societal objectives as well as being tasked with *regulating* more complex situations'.[41] One of the drivers of that in mining and energy is the deregulation of the monopolies and state enterprises that controlled important infrastructure, such as rail, and energy markets and supply chains. Regulatory culture seeks to address the key attributes of government officials described at 3.12, such as integrity. A good example of how to develop a positive culture is the Welsh initiative under its future generations legislation – see 3.18 and the role of the Future Generations Commissioner in supporting progress and reporting on it.

Government policy on mining and energy operations

3.28 Table 2.1 in Chapter 2 gives the details of the principal regulators in some jurisdictions extensively involved in mining and energy. What that table shows is a functional separation of regulation in which, typically, the regulation of mining and energy operations is separate from environmental and occupational health and safety regulation. In addition, other activities can be regulated by other statutes and regulatory bodies. Examples include water, radiation and nuclear energy, electricity, road transport, sea transport, dangerous goods, and gas pipelines. To a considerable degree that separation mirrors the separation of the administration of these activities at government level in different ministries and departments, as they are packaged and repackaged into what seems to be continually changing groupings and the development of new areas.[42] As will be discussed in a later sub-section, a major focus of regulation in the jurisdictions where the state owns minerals and petroleum, such as Australia,

---

-report_2024_en_pdf.pdf.

41 *The Governance of Regulators* (n 20) 15.

42 For example, 20 years ago, there was no department or ministry in Australia, Canada, or the UK including the words 'climate change' in its title. The first appears to have been created in the UK in 2008 by Gordon Brown as 'the Department of Energy and Climate Change'. Starting in 2009, the White House in the USA had an Office of Energy and Climate Change Policy, but it is now defunct.

is the granting of rights to the private sector to commercialise the resource. That grant takes the form of authorisations allowing exploration, mining, and production, which bear various names like 'licence' or 'permit'.

The concerns of regulators have evolved over time. Mining has a long history in Europe. The early miners in Europe had an expectation that they would own what they found. That expectation went with them to the USA and Australia to feed the gold rushes there.[43] Miners in California used to 'stake a claim' to explore on public land. Codes were developed informally by mining camps to enforce rules about claims, which were eventually formalised in the federal *Mining Law* of 1872 in the USA.[44] An early preoccupation was the management of claims and operations. 3.29

Somewhat similar concerns arose in respect of petroleum, but for different reasons. Conventional petroleum is different from minerals because it can move in underground reservoirs to a well which penetrates the reservoir, and accordingly can cross property ownership boundaries on the surface.[45] The rule of capture was developed in the USA to provide clear title to a person extracting petroleum in his or her licence area, irrespective of where it comes from.[46] But that, when combined with the private ownership of petroleum, led to intense competition between drillers, small drilling titles being negotiated with landowners, and consequent wastage. As a result, conservation regulations were developed to focus on the spacing of drilling and other techniques to reduce wastage. 3.30

Over time most governments in countries with minerals and petroleum became interested in the economic growth, employment, and revenue that mining and energy projects create and have published strategies intended to achieve a strong pipeline of actual and potential projects. In more recent times, those strategies have extended to the development of renewable energy projects.[47] There has also been extensive commentary on the governance of regulators in 3.31

---

43 The Californian Gold Rush started in 1848. The first gold rushes in Australia started in New South Wales and Victoria in 1851 and the last occurred at Kalgoorlie in Western Australia in 1893.

44 The first mining law in Australia was the *Mining Act 1852* (Vic). From 1855, colonial parliaments in Australia legislated for ownership of minerals to be retained by the Crown in future grants of freehold title.

45 In this book 'conventional petroleum' refers to hydrocarbons in the form of oil and gas that can be extracted using traditional means, being wells. 'Unconventional petroleum' is located in harder rocks with smaller pore spaces and requires techniques like horizontal drilling and fracture stimulation, or fracking, to release the hydrocarbons.

46 On the rule of capture, see, Terence Daintith, *Finders Keepers? How the Law of Capture shaped the World Oil Industry* (Routledge, 2011).

47 See 3.39.

mining and energy matters, which has focused on how regulation has developed and how, generally speaking, safety and environmental matters have been separated off from the regulation of mining and petroleum operations.[48]

3.32 Leaving to one side for the moment environmental and safety approvals, controls over operations have evolved in three areas. The first is public consultation, which is a normal part of environmental impact assessment under environmental legislation. But this has been extended into petroleum and minerals legislation as part of approval processes for the grant of titles or development approval.

3.33 Next, there is works or development approval. For minerals, the regulatory approach is commonly to require the applicant to provide a plan of operations or mining plan for approval before any ground disturbance can occur.[49] In some petroleum legislation, approval of a field development plan is an important checkpoint before development can occur. The licensee provides detailed information to the regulator about the petroleum resource and means of extraction. These approvals will be discussed in more detail in Chapter 7, which deals with development approvals.

3.34 The third area is the resolution of potential competing uses of land. An example is Schedule 1 of the *New South Wales State Environmental Planning Policy (State and Regional Development) 2011* that says that any development for petroleum production, and any development for the purposes of mining that has a capital investment value of more than AUD30 million,[50] requires approval by the relevant consent authority before the Minister for Resources can grant a mining lease or petroleum production licence.[51] The Department's website notes that it has an integrated mining policy. Its aims include to 'improve the regulation and assessment of major mining projects' and to 'strike a balance between the significant benefits mining can bring to the economy and the potential impacts on communities and the environment'.[52] Part of the process is an

---

48 For a discussion of this separation in relation to offshore petroleum operations, but also the way in which regulation has developed in the 20th and 21st centuries more generally, see Terence Daintith and John Chandler, 'Offshore Petroleum Regulation: Theory and Disaster as Drivers for Institutional Change' (2017) 39 *Houston Journal of International Law* 331.

49 For an example, see Nevada from 6.24.

50 NSW Government, *State Environmental Planning Policy (State and Regional Development) 2011*, Schedule 1, cl 5(3)(b).

51 Ibid.

52 NSW Government, Department of Resources, *Integrated Mining Policy* https://www.planning.nsw.gov.au/about-us/policies#:~:text=The%20Integrated%20Mining%20Policy%20in,and%20social%20impacts%20of%20mining.

economic assessment, for which there are published guidelines for mining.[53] Here, we do find a focus on sustainability and consideration of the interests of future generations.[54]

The focus of regulation where the state owns the resources

The focus of mining and petroleum regulation will be determined at the outset by who owns the minerals and energy in the ground. As will be discussed shortly, renewable energy in the form of solar and wind power is different, because no one claims ownership of the sun or the wind, although they may own the land on which the facilities for their conversion to electricity are located. In much of the USA, other than federal lands, minerals and petroleum belong to the owner of the surface land. In many other jurisdictions, ownership of minerals is vested in the state by statute.[55] There are also statutes dealing with petroleum licensing that set out that confirmation.[56] In those jurisdictions, a function of the mining and petroleum legislation is to provide for the grant of titles to companies and individuals allowing them to explore for minerals or petroleum and then produce it. Titles are referred to by names like exploration licence or permit and mining licence or lease. Importantly, the legislation also provides for the transfer of property in minerals and petroleum from the state to the licence-holder upon their extraction. Commonly, the legislation also provides that it is an offence to conduct operations without the requisite licence. **3.35**

As 3.12 mentioned, a traditional stream of government accountability is objectives in the statutes granting powers to ministers and government officials. Statutory objectives are commonly set out in the objects clause in the statute. But many statutes do not contain one. The West Australian *Mining Act 1978 (WA)* is an example of a statute without an objects clause. The Court of Appeal considered it in the case of *Re Minister for Resources: Ex Parte Cazaly Iron Pty Ltd*.[57] The court referred with approval to the High Court's statement of its primary object being 'to encourage and promote the prospecting and exploration for, and mining of, mineral deposits in the state'.[58] Such a broad **3.36**

53 NSW Government, *Guidelines for the economic assessment of mining and coal seam gas proposals* (December 2015) https://www.planning.nsw.gov.au/sites/default/files/2023-03/guidelines-for-the-economic-assessment-of-mining-and-coal-seam-gas-proposals.pdf.

54 *Gloucester Resources Limited v Minister for Planning* [2019] NSWLEC 7.

55 See 6.21.

56 For Saskatchewan see 6.45, and for Western Australia see 6.50.

57 (2007) 37 WAR 403.

58 *Re Minister for Resources; Ex Parte Cazaly Iron Pty Ltd* (2007) 34 WAR 403, 426, [70] (Buss J.), citing *The Commonwealth of Australia v The State of Western Australia* (1999) 196 CLR 392, [172] (Kirby J).

formulation does not encourage governance requiring the regulator to consider economic or sustainability issues and be accountable for its performance in relation to them.

3.37 There are clear exceptions. We can begin with Norway's petroleum legislation.[59] The adoption by the UK of the objective of maximising the recovery of UK petroleum is another.[60] It also appears that there is an increasing trend for governments in the UK, Australia, and Canada to have clearer statutory objectives and accountability in relation to them. In part, that arises because regulation has become more oriented towards regulating risks – so public health regulation is now understood to be about regulating public health risks.[61] The same should apply to environmental and biodiversity risks. Risk management requires an analysis of the risks and then a plan to reduce them. Of its very nature, risk management of this kind lends itself to setting objectives and reporting outcomes.

3.38 But history suggests that without clear guidance in a relevant statute, there is little likelihood of courts implying a broader obligation for government to act in a sustainable manner. An example is provided by the public trust argument. That was illustrated by a 1970 article,[62] in which Professor Joseph Sax examined cases in the USA concerning the use of lands dedicated to the public interest, generally rivers, lakes, the sea and the seashore, and land in proximity to them.[63] None concerned minerals or petroleum. What the cases illustrated is that, although government is expected to actively manage resources it holds, under what can be called the public trust, the courts will view very suspiciously any significant disposal by government or limitation of its management, and, if the resource is one which the public uses, any significant limitation of that public use.[64] Professor Sax summarised the issue as 'what really seems to be at

59 See, the *Norwegian Petroleum Act 1996,* sections 1–2, that 'Resource management of petroleum resources shall be carried out in a long-term perspective for the benefit of the Norwegian society as a whole. In this regard the resource management shall provide revenues to the country and shall contribute to ensuring welfare, employment and an improved environment, as well as to the strengthening of Norwegian trade and industry and industrial development, and at the same time take due regard to regional and local policy considerations and other activities.'

60 *Energy Act 2016 (UK)* established the Oil and Gas Authority (OGA) and made it responsible for developing and applying the strategy. It is now the North Sea Transition Authority.

61 OECD The Governance of Regulators (n 20) 51.

62 Joseph Sax, 'The Public Trust Doctrine in Natural Resource Law: Effective Judicial Intervention' (1970) 68 *Michigan Law Review*, 471.

63 For example *Illinois Central Railroad Company v Illinois*, 146 U.S. 387 (1892); *Gould v Greylock Reservation Commission*, 350 Mass. 410, 215 N.E. 2d 144 (1966).

64 Joseph Sax, 'The Public Trust Doctrine in Natural Resource Law: Effective Judicial Intervention' (1970) 68 *Michigan Law Review*, 471.

stake, then, is the question whether the government can or should be viewed as having made any irrevocable commitments about the use of particular governmental resources'.[65] Absent such a commitment, the public trust does not extend to ensuring that government maximises the benefit it achieves from resources it is managing or making sure that they are managed sustainably. It should be noted, however, that there is an increasing interest in how the economic benefits from mining are shared, and this is a focus of the UN's Sustainable Development Goals as well as company reports. There are materials on how countries should account for various costs.[66]

Public policy sustainability objectives and increased reporting requirements

As was mentioned at 3.12, a more modern stream of government accountability is to be found in the increasing number of policy objectives of government departments concerning things like sustainability in procurement. One definition of sustainable procurement is that it is: **3.39**

> a process whereby organisations meet their needs for goods, services, works and utilities in a way that achieves value for money on a whole life basis in terms of generating benefits not only to the organisation, but also to society and the economy, whilst minimising damage to the environment.[67]

There are numerous examples of government sustainable procurement policies.[68] There are also other examples of government policies on sustainability, some of which involve reporting performance and setting targets.[69] Reporting requirements are also increasing. Apart from those attached to particular policies like procurement, the IPSASB has produced material on government sustainability reporting.[70]

---

65 Ibid, at 480.

66 In 2024, the IPSASB issued a new standard International Public Sector Accounting Standard 50, Exploration for and Evaluation of Mineral Resources and Stripping Costs in the Production Phase of a Surface Mine https://www.ipsasb.org/publications/ipsas-50-exploration-and-evaluation-mineral-resources.

67 UK Ministry of Justice Sustainable Procurement Policy, July 2019 https://assets.publishing.service.gov.uk/media/65116b8d2f404b000dc3d842/sustainable-procurement-policy.pdf.

68 For example, the Australian Government has an Environmentally Sustainable Procurement Policy with a reporting framework (Commonwealth of Australia 2024) https://www.dcceew.gov.au/environment/protection/waste/sustainable-procurement/environmentally-sustainable-procurement-policy and Canada has a policy on Green Procurement (Government of Canada 2022) https://www.tbs-sct.canada.ca/pol/doc-eng.aspx?id=32573.

69 For example, the UK Parliament has an Environmental Sustainability Policy Statement (UK Parliament 2023) https://www.parliament.uk/about/sustainability/environmental-policy/ and the Canadian National Arts Centre also has an Environmental Sustainability Policy https://nac-cna.ca/en/about/environmental-sustainability-policy.

70 See the IPSASB's website at https://www.ipsasb.org/focus-areas/sustainability-reporting.

Governance of renewable energy

3.40 A particular driving force for the development of renewable energy has been the desire of countries to reduce their greenhouse gas emissions. Therefore, many countries have legislation applicable to renewable energy projects and many offer economic incentives for their development.[71] The two main technologies that are growing fast are solar energy, using solar panels, and wind energy, using wind turbines. The latter can be situated onshore or offshore. In both cases, the energy output is initially in the form of electricity, although countries are also looking to develop products like hydrogen. Australia is a country doing that because its geographical isolation means that it is not economic to install the cables required to send electricity to its traditional markets in Asia. A similar issue led to the development of the liquefied natural gas industry in Australia. Liquefaction of methane gas reduces its volume and makes it more economical to ship.

3.41 In some jurisdictions, it is possible to negotiate the arrangements for access to land to install the panels or turbines with the private owners of land. In some jurisdictions, no government licence will be required for the development of a solar or wind facility. However, in some areas, an example being Australia's offshore waters, a government licence will be needed.[72] In any case, environmental and safety approvals are likely to be required. Some form of development approval may be required, such as under local town planning regulations. There is therefore some comparability with the regulatory oversight matters for minerals. These are matters explored in more detail in Chapters 6 and 7. In addition, there may be oversight over whether national renewable energy targets are being met and reporting under the renewable energy legislation.

COMPANY LAW

Outline

3.42 The main companies legislation in the UK, Western Australia, Saskatchewan, and Nevada is:

- UK: *Companies Act 2006 (UK)* (*CAUK*)
- Western Australia: *Corporations Act 2001(Cth)* (*CAWA*)

71 For a discussion of the incentives and also a list of legislation, see Penelope Crossley, *Alternative Energy: An International Assessment* (Cambridge University Press, 2019).

72 See, *Offshore Electricity Infrastructure Act 2021 (Cth).*

- Saskatchewan: *Business Corporations Act 2021 (S)* (*CASK*)
- Nevada: *Nevada Revised Statutes* – Chapter 78 Private Corporations (*CSN*)

The UK has one statute in the form of *CAUK* providing for the incorporation and regulation of limited liability companies. In Australia, there is uniform companies legislation that applies in all states and territories.[73] In the USA, companies can be incorporated at the state level, and in Canada at the province or federal level.[74] In this book, the state or province legislation is referred to – that is, *CAWA*, *CASK*, and *CSN*. The focus of this section is the provisions dealing with directors' duties, particularly as they relate to care. Our starting point is *CAUK* to set the scene for the other provisions. *CAUK* sections 171 to 177 are important provisions. They include a duty to act for proper purposes (section 171), a duty to promote the success of the company (section 172), a duty to exercise independent judgement (section 173), a duty of care, skill, and diligence (section 174), a duty to avoid conflicts of interest (section 175), a duty not to accept benefits from third parties (section 176), and a duty to declare interest in a proposed transaction (section 177). Also of importance are the provisions that require the directors to prepare a report about the company's affairs going beyond a financial report to set out its prospects, including the environmental and similar risks it faces (section 414A).

The provisions in the legislation of the other jurisdictions mentioned that are broadly equivalent are: **3.43**

Section 171 – *CAWA* section 181, *CSN* 78.138,[75] *CASK* 9-23(1)(a)[76]
Section 172 – *CAWA* section 181[77]

---

73 For Western Australia and the other states that is by reason of their referring corporations' powers to the Commonwealth of Australia. See the *Corporations (Commonwealth Powers) Act 2001 (WA)*.

74 This is put as follows in Canadian Coalition for Good Governance, Corporate Governance in Canada (n 11), 'Under Canada's Constitution, provincial governments have exclusive power over property and civil rights within the province. As a result, corporations may choose to incorporate under federal corporate law or under the corporate laws of any of the 10 provinces in Canada. In addition, securities law in Canada is regulated by securities administrators in Canada's 10 provinces and three territories. However, the federal governments and five provincial governments are collaborating on a cooperative capital markets regulatory system.'

75 Paragraph 1 says, 'The fiduciary duties of directors and officers are to exercise their respective powers in good faith and with a view to the interests of the corporation.'

76 *CASK* 9-23(1) reads: 'Every director and officer of a corporation in exercising the director's or officer's powers and discharging the director's or officer's duties shall: (a) act honestly and in good faith with a view to the best interests of the corporation; and (b) exercise the care, diligence and skill that a reasonably prudent person would exercise in comparable circumstances.

77 *CAWA* section 181 reads, '(1) A director or other officer of a corporation must exercise their powers and discharge their duties: (a) in good faith in the best interests of the corporation; and (b) for a proper purpose.'

Section 174 – *CAWA* section 180, *CSN* 78.138,[78] *CASK* 9-23(1)(b)[79]
Section 175 – *CAWA* sections 182 and 183,[80] *CSN* 78.140[81]
Section 176 – *CAWA* section 182
Section 177 – *CAWA* section 191, *CASK* 9-21[82]
Section 414A – *CAWA* section 298

What emerges from a comparison of these provisions is that there are some common themes, although the wording may differ. But, for example, not all the provisions in *CAUK* have an equivalent. The one that follows it most closely is *CAWA*, but that has differences as well. The following are the common themes, which also happen to be the most important areas for mining and energy governance.

Duties to act within powers, in good faith, and in the interests of the corporation

3.44 *CAUK* section 171 reads:

A director of a company must—

a) act in accordance with the company's constitution, and
b) only exercise powers for the purposes for which they are conferred.

3.45 *CAUK* section 172 reads:

1) A director of a company must act in the way he considers, in good faith, would be most likely to promote the success of the company for the benefit of its members as a whole, and in doing so have regard (amongst other matters) to—

---

78 Paragraph 3 says, 'Except as otherwise provided in subsection 1 of NRS 78.139, directors and officers, in deciding upon matters of business, are presumed to act in good faith, on an informed basis and with a view to the interests of the corporation. A director or officer is not individually liable for damages as a result of an act or failure to act in his or her capacity as a director or officer except as described in subsection 7.' Paragraphs 4 and 5 contain a list of matters that directors and officers can consider in exercising their respective powers with a view to the interests of the corporation, which may include '(3) The interests of the community or of society'.

79 See n 68.

80 *CAWA* section 182 says, '(1) A director, secretary, other officer or employee of a corporation must not improperly use their position to: (a) gain an advantage for themselves or someone else; or (b) cause detriment to the corporation.' *CAWA* section 183 deals with the misuse of information.

81 *CSN* 78.140 does not impose a duty to avoid conflicts of interest but provides for certain contracts and transactions not being voidable where a director has an interest.

82 *CASK* section 9-21(1) commences, 'A director or an officer of a corporation shall disclose to the corporation, in writing or by requesting to have it entered in the minutes of meetings of directors or of meetings of committees of directors, the nature and extent of any interest that the director or officer has in a material contract or material transaction, whether made or proposed, with the corporation…'. Under section 9-21(5), the director is then, with some exceptions, not to vote on a resolution approving the contract or transaction.

a) the likely consequences of any decision in the long term,
b) the interests of the company's employees,
c) the need to foster the company's business relationships with suppliers, customers and others,
d) the impact of the company's operations on the community and the environment,
e) the desirability of the company maintaining a reputation for high standards of business conduct, and
f) the need to act fairly as between members of the company.

2) Where or to the extent that the purposes of the company consist of or include purposes other than the benefit of its members, subsection (1) has effect as if the reference to promoting the success of the company for the benefit of its members were to achieving those purposes.
3) The duty imposed by this section has effect subject to any enactment or rule of law requiring directors, in certain circumstances, to consider or act in the interests of creditors of the company.

The ideas that resonate across all the jurisdictions are that directors must act in good faith and directors must act in the interests of the corporation. The latter is qualified in each jurisdiction with a list of things that the directors can consider.[83] The content of that list varies. Provisions like *CAUK* section 172 (2) are also important in allowing the directors to consider purposes other than the benefit of the members.

Duty of care

This is set out in *CAUK* section 174 as follows: **3.46**

1) A director of a company must exercise reasonable care, skill and diligence.
2) This means the care, skill and diligence that would be exercised by a reasonably diligent person with—
   a. the general knowledge, skill and experience that may reasonably be expected of a person carrying out the functions carried out by the director in relation to the company, and
   b. the general knowledge, skill and experience that the director has.

CAWA section 180 uses similar words in that directors 'must exercise their powers and discharge their duties with the degree of care and diligence that a reasonable person would', but then has different qualification from *CAUK*. Section 180 is qualified by 'the corporation's circumstances' and having 'the **3.47**

83 For example, *CASK* 9-23(2) says, 'When acting with a view to the best interests of the corporation pursuant to clause (1)(a), the directors and officers of the corporation may consider, but are not limited to, the following factors', and there follows a list of nine items which include governments and the environment.

same responsibilities within the corporation'. The duty of care is the duty that is most often considered in relation to sustainability, and particularly climate change, which was clearly illustrated by an opinion published in Australia in 2019 from two Australian barristers, Noel Hutley SC and Sebastian Hartford-Davis. They said:

> 14. Faced with the prospect that these well-documented risks may occur within 10 years unless "unprecedented" change occurs before then, it is our opinion that diligent company directors ought now to be assessing:
>
> 14.1 the impact on their business if concerted decarbonisation efforts (of the kind envisaged by the IPCC Report) do not occur. That is, what steps are necessary or appropriate to adapt to global warming of 1.50C (possibly within 5 years);
>
> 14.2 the impact on their business if concerted decarbonisation efforts do occur. That is, what steps are necessary or appropriate to seek to predict, influence and respond in the short to medium-term to the "unprecedented" transitions which will be required in order to avoid global warming of 1.50C, most particularly in the resource, energy, transport and industrial sectors; and
>
> 14.3 the impact on their business as a result of the escalating physical changes, which appear to be likely under either scenario.[84]

3.48 In their original 2016 opinion, Noel Hutley SC and Sebastian Hartford-Davis reiterated the trite law, that 'a director's duty is owed *to the company*, meaning the corporate entity itself'.[85] That is important because it dictates 'the perspective from which the directors must assess risks, including climate change risks'. In simple terms, in Australia, the directors do not owe a duty of care and diligence under company law to people affected by climate change or environmental damage. Arguably, that is also the case in those jurisdictions having a similar approach to the duty of care. People injured by a company's activities may have other causes of action against the company. What may also be relevant in jurisdictions other than Australia is the elaborations of the good faith principle (for example, *CAUK* section 172, *CASK* 9-23(2), and *CSN* 78.138) allowing directors to take other matters into account, such as the environment.

---

84 Noel Hutley SC and Sebastian Hartford Davis, 'Climate Change and Directors' Duties – Supplementary Memorandum of Opinion' (29 March 2019) *The Centre for Policy and Development*, https://cpd.org.au/wp-content/uploads/2019/03/Noel-Hutley-SC-and-Sebastian-Hartford-Davis-Opinion-2019-and-2016_pdf.pdf.

85 Noel Hutley SC and Sebastian Hartford Davis, 'Climate Change and Directors' Duties – Memorandum of Opinion' (7 October 2016) *The Centre for Policy Development and the Future Business School*, para 10 https://cpd.org.au/wp-content/uploads/2016/10/Legal-Opinion-on-Climate-Change-and-Directors-Duties.pdf.

The framework in which directors need to consider climate change and other sustainability issues will depend on how their duties are structured under the laws of the jurisdiction. Under UK and Australian law, that framework is one of assessing whether they represent risks that are material to the interests of the company,[86] but also ensuring the company is complying with its reporting and disclosure obligations. The perspective from which directors must assess risks, being the company to which they owe a duty, is critical and will limit their ability to act in the interests of others, notwithstanding provisions in the legislation allowing them to consider those interests – for example society in general.[87] The position would be different if directors are empowered to act to further those interests, for example under *CAUK* section 172(2). A further example is provided by the Delaware public benefit corporation. Its directors can act for the benefit of the interests specified.[88] **3.49**

Duty to report on financial and non-financial matters

It is generally a requirement both of companies legislation and stock exchange rules that companies prepare accounts.[89] It is a further requirement that those accounts comply with the specified accounting standards and regulations.[90] They were mentioned in Chapter 2. In addition, companies are required to prepare a directors' report. In many jurisdictions that includes a more extensive review. For example, the *Companies Act 2006 (UK)* section 414A requires the directors to produce a strategic report. Section 414C(2)(b) requires that report to contain a description 'of the principal risks and uncertainties facing the company'. That is further elaborated for a quoted company in section 414(C)(7)(b) that the report must contain information about 'environmental matters (including the impact of the company's business on the environment' and 'social, community and human rights issues'. The equivalent in Australia is called a review of operations.[91] One Australian publication explains that the review 'should complement the financial report.... The underlying drivers of the results and financial position should be explained, as well as risks, **3.50**

86 Ibid, para 3.3.

87 In this regard, see *CAUK* section 172(1)(d) (at 3.45) and *CSN* 78.138 (n 75) and *CASK* 9-23(2) (n 83).

88 See paragraph 365(a)–(c) of Subchapter XV of the Delaware General Corporation Law https://delcode.delaware.gov/title8/c001/sc15/ Paragraph 9(a) says, 'The board of directors shall manage or direct the business and affairs of the public benefit corporation in a manner that balances the pecuniary interests of the stockholders, the best interests of those materially affected by the corporation's conduct, and the specific public benefit or public benefits identified in its certificate of incorporation.'

89 *CAUK* Part 15, *CAWA* section 297.

90 Ibid. See also the UK's Financial Reporting Council's publication *FRS 100 Application of Financial Reporting Requirements (September 2024)*.

91 See, *CAWA* section 298.

management strategies and future prospects. Forward-looking information should have a reasonable basis and the market should be updated through continuous disclosure if circumstances change.'[92] Climate change risk is one of the things mentioned that could have a material impact on future prospects.[93]

SECURITIES EXCHANGES AND MARKET REGULATION

3.51 Companies wishing to raise money through the issue of securities generally have them listed on a recognised stock exchange to provide liquidity in the securities and enabling shareholders and others to buy and sell them. Listing enables the establishment of a market for the securities on which prices are quoted. Some of the more important markets are New York, London, and – for mining and energy companies – Toronto and the Australian Securities Exchange (ASX).[94] The exchange rules typically have rules applicable for having securities listed for the first time and ongoing obligations. Ongoing obligations include those requiring the market to be kept informed and those requiring compliance with corporate governance requirements. The exchange rules fit into a bigger picture of securities regulation, which in some jurisdictions is a federal rather than a state or province matter. For example, as noted at 2.37, in the USA it is a responsibility of the SEC, whose mission is 'protecting investors, maintaining fair, orderly, and efficient markets, and facilitating capital formation',[95] which goes back to its founding in 1934 at the height of the Great Depression and the introduction of securities laws.[96] These laws will generally apply to companies listed on the major exchanges in the USA, such as NYSE and Nasdaq. They require, amongst other things, the filing of information regarding companies and securities and the disclosure of information. Chapter 9 explores the SEC's rules on climate change disclosure in more detail. The equivalent of the SEC in the UK is the Financial Conduct Authority

92 ASIC, 'ASIC highlights focus areas for 31 December 2022 reporting' (Media release, 22-333MR, 1 December 2022' https://asic.gov.au/about-asic/news-centre/find-a-media-release/2022-releases/22-333mr-asic-highlights-focus-areas-for-31-december-2022-reporting/.

93 Ibid.

94 The New York Stock Exchange (NYSE) is the largest exchange in the world, followed by Nasdaq, as noted at 2.28. See, *Statista* (webpage) https://www.statista.com/statistics/270126/largest-stock-exchange-operators-by-market-capitalization-of-listed-companies/#:~:text=The%20New%20York%20Stock%20Exchange,and%20the%20Shanghai%20Stock%20Exchange.

95 See SEC Mission at https://www.sec.gov/about/mission.

96 These started with the *Securities Act 1933 (USA)* and the *Securities Exchange Act 1934 (USA)*. The federal securities laws are set out under Title 15 of the US Code – see https://www.govinfo.gov/content/pkg/USCODE-2019-title15/pdf/USCODE-2019-title15.pdf or https://www.law.cornell.edu/uscode/text/15.

(FCA), which regulates the financial services industry in the UK. The equivalents in Canada and Australia are the Canadian Securities Administrators (CSA) and the Australian Securities and Investments Commission (ASIC). All of these bodies have commentary or rules regarding climate change risk disclosure.

The way that disclosure is explained by the NYSE Company Listing Manual is as follows: **3.52**

> The Exchange's current form of listing agreement generally seeks to achieve the following objectives:
>
> - Ensure timely disclosure of information that may affect security values or influence investment decisions, and in which shareholders, the public and the Exchange have a warrantable interest.
> - Ensure frequent, regular and timely publication of financial reports prepared in accordance with generally accepted accounting principles.
> - Provide the Exchange with timely information to enable it to efficiently perform its function of maintaining an orderly market for the company's securities, to enable it to maintain necessary records and to allow it the opportunity to make comment as to certain matters before they become established facts.
> - Preclude certain business practices not generally considered sound.[97]

The first bullet point reflects a general principle across stock exchanges of ensuring the market is informed of all matters which could have a substantial impact on the price of a security. The sort of information that is considered necessary for the market to be aware of is described in UK Listing Rule 9.1 under the heading 'General obligation of disclosure for companies'. It requires a company to notify 'any major new developments in its sphere of activity which are not public knowledge', and which may 'by virtue of the effect of those developments on its assets and liabilities or financial position or on the general course of its business, lead to substantial movement in the price of its listed securities'.[98] **3.53**

97 *NYSE Listed Company Manual*, 201.00 Introduction https://nyseguide.srorules.com/listed-company-manual/09013e2c8503fca3.

98 *UK Listing Rules* (June 2024) rule 9.1 https://www.handbook.fca.org.uk/handbook/LR.pdf. See also, *Rules of the London Stock Exchange* (1 January 2021) rule 1400.1, requiring that member firms not 'do any act or engage in any course of conduct which creates or is likely to create a false or misleading impression as to the market in, or the price or value of, any security', https://www.londonstockexchange.com/resources/equities-trading-resources?tab=rules-and-regulations&accordionId=0-214789e7-908e-4ba2-8a26-d27bc26db67b&moduleId=block_content%3Ac058ff10-1e4d-4b37-819f-8ab73852f22d.

3.54 In some jurisdictions, such as Australia, the listing rules are also enforceable under company law against entities and their associates.[99]

3.55 In relation to corporate governance, the NYSE requires compliance with section 303A of the NYSE Company Listing Manual. Included in section 303A is sub-section 09, which says that 'Listed companies must adopt and disclose corporate governance guidelines'.[100] The London Stock Exchange Listing Rules L.R. 9.8.6(5) requires the annual financial accounts of UK incorporated companies to include a statement of how the listed company has applied the principles set out in the UK Corporate Governance Code 'in a manner that would enable shareholders to evaluate how the principles have been applied'.[101] The rules of the Toronto Stock Exchange require disclosure of specific matters, such as whether the chairman is independent, board committees, and related matters.[102]

3.56 The London Stock Exchange Listing Rules at LR9.8.6(6) set out the 'if not, why not' rule. So, a listed company has to disclose whether it has complied with the UK Corporate Governance Code principles and, if not, it needs to make disclosure in relation to those provisions it has not complied with. That disclosure 'in the case of provisions whose requirements are of a continuing nature' is of 'the period within which, if any, it did not comply with some or all of those provisions' and 'the company's reasons for non-compliance'.[103] In Australia, the ASX's Listing Rule 4.10.3 is similar in requiring each entity to include in its annual report (or separately publish on its website) a corporate governance statement that meets the requirements of the rule. In essence, that requires statements of whether the company is complying with the ASX Corporate Governance Council's Corporate Governance Principles and Recommendations and if not, why not.

---

99 See *CAWA* sections 793c and 1101.

100 *NYSE Listed Company Manual* (n 97).

101 *Financial Conduct Authority* (*FCA*) *Handbook* https://www.handbook.fca.org.uk/handbook/LR/9/8.html

102 Toronto Stock Exchange, 'TSX Guide to Good Disclosure for National Instrument' (58–10) https://www.tsx.com/listings/tsx-and-tsxv-issuer-resources/tsx-issuer-resources/corporate-governance.

103 See n 101.

ACCOUNTING STANDARDS AND IFRS S1 SUSTAINABILITY FINANCIAL DISCLOSURE

Introduction

It is trite to say that financial statements present the financial performance and position of an entity. They provide a basis for reviewing an entity's performance over time and comparing entities. The information in those statements about that performance and the entity's assets, liabilities, equity, income, and expenses is required by a range of interested users. The use of accounting standards in the preparation of financial statements is intended to ensure their quality, consistency, and comparability for those users. 3.57

It is outside the scope of this chapter to summarise the detailed workings of the standards. But what is relevant is how sustainability concepts affect, or are likely to affect, those standards and the preparation of financial statements and company reports. It needs to be borne in mind that accounting standards broadly fall into three groups: those related to particular transactions, those related to presentation and disclosure in accounts, and those related to particular industries. The point was made at 2.27 that the IFRS Foundation and the GRI provide two 'pillars' of international sustainability reporting: a first pillar, representing investor-focused capital market standards, of IFRS Sustainability Disclosure Standards developed by the ISSB; and a second pillar, designed to meet multi-stakeholder needs, of GRI sustainability reporting requirements set by the GSSB.[104] The issue in 2023 of the new IFRS standard 'IFRS S1 General Requirements for the Disclosure of Sustainability related Financial Information' (IFRS S1) was a significant development in the disclosure of sustainability issues in financial statements.[105] 3.58

IFRS S1 and sustainability financial disclosure

The objective of IFRS S1 is 'to require an entity to disclose information about its sustainability-related risks and opportunities that is useful to primary users 3.59

104 Ibid. The CEO of GRI put it like this: 'Aligning GRI's established and widely adopted standards for sustainability impacts with the investor focused standards being developed by the ISSB will benefit both companies and investors, as well as a wide range of stakeholders around the world.'

105 See 'IFRS S1 General Requirements for the Disclosure of Sustainability related Financial Information', (IFRS S1) see IFRS webpage https://www.ifrs.org/issued-standards/ifrs-sustainability-standards-navigator/ifrs-s1-general-requirements.html/content/dam/ifrs/publications/html-standards-issb/english/2023/issued/issbs1/.

of general purpose financial reports in making decisions relating to providing resources to the entity'.[106]

3.60 The definition of 'Sustainability Related Financial Disclosures' is critical, as there is no definition of 'sustainability'. That is as follows:

> A particular form of general purpose financial reports that provide information about the reporting entity's sustainability-related risks and opportunities that could reasonably be expected to affect the entity's cash flows, its access to finance or cost of capital over the short, medium or long term, including information about the entity's governance, strategy and risk management in relation to those risks and opportunities, and related metrics and targets.[107]

3.61 The core content of disclosures is governance, strategy, risk management, and metrics and targets.[108] The structure of the disclosure requirements is the same for all those areas, starting with an objective and then requiring more details. Using governance as an example, paragraph 26 says that 'the objective of sustainability-related financial disclosures on governance is to enable users of general purpose financial reports to understand the governance processes, controls and procedures an entity uses to monitor, manage and oversee sustainability-related risks and manage and oversee sustainability risks and opportunities'.[109] Paragraph 27 then requires more details. They include the responsible governance body or bodies, individual or individuals, the terms of reference, how appropriate skills and competencies are determined, how sustainability-related risks and opportunities are taken into account in overseeing strategy, the controls over those risks and opportunities, how targets are set, and how progress is monitored.

CONCLUSIONS, GUIDANCE, AND KEY PRINCIPLES

3.62 The basic conclusions from this chapter are:

- The directors of companies are ultimately responsible to the shareholders for the proper management of the company's affairs in their interests. To fulfil that responsibility, they require a governance system. Frequently, companies will have board committees as part of their governance system: audit and risk committees are common. Increasingly, companies, particularly large ones, have a committee of the board that has a focus on sustainability or ESG matters, or both.

---

106 Ibid.
107 IFRS S1 (n 105) para 25.
108 Ibid.
109 Ibid.

- Directors may also be required by company law or the rules of stock exchanges on which their securities are listed to make disclosures about the state of the company's affairs, including its compliance with corporate governance rules.
- Increasingly, company law, stock exchange rules, and accounting standards are requiring disclosure of important risks to the company's business, so shareholders, markets, and potential buyers of the company's securities are informed about those risks. Climate change risk is an example where the disclosure rules have become increasingly rigorous. It can be anticipated that that rigour will increase in relation to broader sustainability risks.
- It is also likely that the accounting standards will be strengthened over time to require more standardised reporting of sustainability issues.
- Companies will have to deal with activist groups promoting strong views about fossil fuels and decarbonisation, but also superannuation funds and lobbyists taking positions. Government will also promote its own views on decarbonisation.
- At the government level, there are fewer examples of an obligation to report on sustainability matters, except in relation to climate change. The outstanding example is the *Well-being of Future Generations (Wales) Act 2015*, which is recommended here as an excellent model because of its goal-setting approach to improving planning for the future and representation of the interests of future generations.
- Unsurprisingly, politicians want to retain flexibility to change tack in their policies according to where they are in the electoral cycle and to have flexibility to deal with unforeseen circumstances. But there is little doubt that public sector accountability is being increased through several measures – impact assessment of potential legislation, setting more detailed objectives in legislation, sustainability policies, and improved reporting and adjustment mechanisms to review progress regularly as a matter of course, rather than in response to major problems occurring.

The following ideas follow from these conclusions: **3.63**

- Directors need to be alert to the growing level of disclosure and compliance covering sustainability matters. There is currently a significant emphasis on climate change, but over time it is likely to cover other sustainability issues.
- A critical governance issue for directors is to ensure that they are continuously surveying the changing landscape of sustainability compliance. In that regard, a management sustainability function or a board sustainability committee, or both, will be invaluable.
- The environment in which mining and energy companies are operating is likely to become increasingly fractious, with various groups taking strong positions and the threat of litigation growing. Having a strong and defensible position on sustainability with appropriate public relations support will be essential.
- That will be a significant driver for companies to embrace sustainability more seriously and take their planning for the future of the company and future generations to a higher level.

- Government will gradually also have to respond to these pressures. Increasingly, sustainability objectives and accountability measures will find their way into the regulation of mining and energy industries.

GOVERNANCE CHECKLIST

Companies

1. Are your company's securities listed on a securities exchange, the rules applicable to which require your company to comply with rules covering governance structure and disclosure of risks, such as those associated with climate change or sustainability?
2. Are there any laws, such as company laws, applicable to the company or its directors and officers having a similar effect?
3. If the answer to question 1 or 2 is yes, what are your principal governance documents (for example a board charter, corporate strategy document, or statement of governance principles) that comply with those rules?
4. If the answer to question 1 or 2 is no, do you have any of those documents anyway?
5. Does your company produce ESG, sustainability, climate change, or risk reports?
6. Is your board interested in developing a strategy to advance ESG or sustainability in its operations, or improving an existing strategy?
7. If the answer to question 6 is yes, what do you consider the next step should be?

Government/regulators

1. What are the governance and policy documents relevant to your activities and do they contain sustainability objectives?
2. If the answer to question 1 is yes, is there anything you consider should be done to improve implementation?
3. If the answer to question 1 is no, is there any appetite and ability to introduce them and how would you start that process?
4. Do the guidelines and other documents you publish require those you regulate to conduct their operations in a sustainable manner?
5. Is there anything you would do to improve those documents and the sustainability of operations?
6. Are there any sustainability policies that apply to your activities that you should comply with such as those relating to procurement?

4

SUSTAINABLE DEVELOPMENT GOALS

INTRODUCTION	4.01	COUNTRY EXAMPLES	4.19
THE EARLY HISTORY AND SUSTAINABLE DEVELOPMENT	4.02	Canada	4.19
Early history and the UN	4.02	Philippines	4.22
The flexible nature of sustainable development	4.06	CORPORATE SDG REPORTING	4.25
The Sustainable Development Goals (SDGs)	4.10	Overview of mining	4.25
REPORTING ON THE SDGS – THE UN	4.12	Mining companies	4.29
The UN	4.12	Overview of oil and gas	4.33
UN high-level political forums and VNRs	4.18	Oil and gas companies	4.35
		Renewable energy companies	4.37
		CONCLUSIONS, GUIDANCE, AND KEY PRINCIPLES	4.38

INTRODUCTION

4.01 This chapter examines the concept of sustainable development and the United Nations (UN) Sustainable Development Goals (SDGs). The aim of the chapter is to explain how they influence decisions concerning mining and energy and the governance of mining and energy development more generally. Countries, institutions, and companies report their performance against the SDGs and this chapter will analyse some examples. There is no doubt that sustainable development is highly influential.[1] Yet, as Elliott and numerous other authors point out, the concept of sustainable development is contested, as is the case with the concept of sustainability, with different disciplines making different assumptions, but also setting different priorities when it comes to policies.[2] Those divergences make it challenging to find principles that are generally agreed upon, except of a very broad nature.[3] We will also find that although

1 See, for example, Jennifer Elliott, *An Introduction to Sustainable Development* (4th ed., Routledge 2013) (Elliott) 54.

2 Ibid 18.

3 Ibid.

many companies track their performance against SDGs, they are generally selective about which ones and the choice across companies is not consistent.

THE EARLY HISTORY AND SUSTAINABLE DEVELOPMENT

Early history and the UN

4.02 The United Nations was formed in 1947 after the Second World War, and conferences concerning the environment soon followed. The impetus for sustainable development can be traced back to the 1972 Stockholm Conference on the Human Environment. Principle 1 of the *Stockholm Declaration*'s 26 Principles expressed a general obligation to protect the environment for both present and future generations.[4] In 1980, the World Conservation Strategy (WCS) was produced by the International Union for Conservation of Nature and Natural Resources, which had been set up in 1948.[5] The WCS points to the ecological damage and harm to the rural poor that occur if conservation and development are not combined. Hence, 'the goal of the [WCS] is the integration of conservation and development to ensure that modifications to the planet do indeed secure the survival and wellbeing of all people'.[6] The WCS refers to sustainable development and the needs of future generations.[7]

4.03 The next major step occurred in 1987, with the report of the World Commission on Environment and Development (WCED), chaired by the Norwegian, Gro Harlem Brundtland, entitled *Our Common Future* (Brundtland Report).[8] The Brundtland Report defined the concept of sustainable development as 'development that meets the needs of the present without compromising the ability of future generations to meet their own needs'.[9] Its aim, similar to that of the WCS, was to encourage development to improve the position of poor nations, but in a way that did not further damage the environment. Segger and Khalfan suggest that sustainable development was a 'compromise term

---

4 *Report of the United Nations Conference on the Human Environment* (1972) UN Doc A/CONF.48/14.

5 International Union for Conservation of Nature and Natural Resources, *World Conservation Strategy* (1980) https://portals.iucn.org/library/sites/library/files/documents/WCS-004.pdf (*WCS*).

6 Ibid, Introduction para 12.

7 According to Klaus Bosselmann, *The Principle of Sustainability – Transforming Law and Governance* (Ashgate, 2008) ('Bosselmann Sustainability') 28, it was the first official reference to sustainable development.

8 World Commission on Environment and Development, *Our Common Future* (Oxford University Press, 1987); see also, World Commission on Environment and Development, *Report of the World Commission on Environment and Development*, UN Doc A/42/427 (4 August 1987) annex (*Brundtland Report*).

9 *Brundtland Report*, Chapter 2: Towards Sustainable Development, para 1.

for more environmentally sound natural resource exploitation, or to describe conservation policies in developing countries'.[10]

4.04 Subsequent UN conferences consolidated support for the idea of sustainable development.[11] At the United Nations Conference on Environment and Development (UNCED) in Rio de Janeiro in 1992, sometimes referred to as the Earth Summit, sustainable development received the approval of over 140 governments.[12] The General Assembly resolution calling for the conference clearly requires the integration of development and protection of the environment.[13] The first five principles from the Rio Declaration signal the tension that inevitably results from the attempted integration of these two ideas, which some might argue are diametrically opposed:

- Principle 1: 'Human beings are at the centre of concerns for sustainable development. They are entitled to a healthy and productive life in harmony with nature.'
- Principle 2: 'States have, in accordance with the Charter of the United Nations and the principles of international law, the sovereign right to exploit their own resources pursuant to their own environmental and developmental policies, and the responsibility to ensure that activities within their jurisdiction or control do not cause damage to the environment of other States or of areas beyond the limits of national jurisdiction.'
- Principle 3: 'The right to development must be fulfilled so as to equitably meet developmental and environmental needs of present and future generations.'
- Principle 4: 'In order to achieve sustainable development, environmental protection shall constitute an integral part of the development process and cannot be considered in isolation from it.'
- Principle 5: 'All States and all people shall cooperate in the essential task of eradicating poverty as an indispensable requirement for sustainable development, in order to decrease the disparities in standards of living and better meet the needs of the majority of the people of the world.'[14]

---

10 Mairie Claire Cordonnier Segger and Ashfaq Khalfan, *Sustainable Development Law: Principles, Practice & Prospects* (Oxford University Press, 2004) 15.

11 The UN Conference on Environment and Development in Rio de Janeiro in 1992 (Rio+20) and 2012 at the UN Conference on Sustainable Development (Earth Summit 2012). See also the Rio Declaration (United Nations, 1992) and the World Summit on Sustainable Development (United Nations, 2002).

12 *Report of the United Nations Conference on Environment and Development* (12 August 1992) UN Doc A/CONF.151/6/Rev1 (*Rio Declaration on Environment and Development*).

13 See, UN Resolution A/RES/44/228 (22 December 1989), para 15(c). Moving forward, this idea of integration is also reflected in paragraph 13 of UN Resolution A/RES/70/1 'Transforming Our World: The 2030 Agenda for Sustainable Development' (25 September 2015): 'Sustainable development recognizes that eradicating poverty in all its forms and dimensions, combating inequality within and among countries, preserving the planet, creating sustained, inclusive and sustainable economic growth and fostering social inclusion are linked to each other and are interdependent.'

14 *Rio Declaration on Environment and Development* (n 12).

The right of states to exploit their own resources is set out in resolutions of the UN as well as Principle 2.[15] A key output of UNCED was Agenda 21, which set out strategies and programmes to promote sustainable development and halt environmental degradation.[16]

4.05 There are several important ideas in the Rio Declaration that facilitate the protection of the environment. The first is embedding environmental protection in the development process (Principle 4) and requiring the enactment of effective environmental protection legislation (Principle 11). Second, 'the precautionary approach shall be widely applied by States according to their capabilities' (Principle 15).[17] Third and fourth, environmental costs should be internalised and the polluter should bear the cost of pollution (Principle 16).[18] Fifth, environmental impact assessment should also be embedded (Principle 17).[19] As we will see in Chapters 6 and 7, these ideas have generally been taken up in a combination of mining, energy, and environmental legislation.

The flexible nature of sustainable development

4.06 As already mentioned, the Brundtland Report produced the often-cited definition of sustainable development: 'development that meets the needs of the present without compromising the ability of future generations to meet their own needs'.[20] There are several reasons why it is flexible. They start with the use of expressions like 'needs', 'compromising', and 'future generations' without any further detail. There are no sub-principles to clarify these expressions, although commentators have done this. For example, Sands and Peel suggest that the following appear to comprise the legal elements of the concept

---

15 *Permanent Sovereignty over Natural Resources*, GA Res 1803 (XVII), UN Doc A/RES/1803(XVII) (14 December 1962); *Declaration on the Establishment of a New International Economic Order*, GA Res 3201 (S-VI), UN Doc A/RES/3201(S-VI) (1 May 1974); *Charter of Economic Rights and Duties of States*, GA Res 3281 (XXIX) (12 December 1974); *Declaration on the Right to Development*, GA Res 41/128, UN Doc A/RES/41/128 (4 December 1986).

16 United Nations Conference on Environment and Development, *Agenda 21* UN Doc A/CONF.151/26/Rev.1 (23 April 1992).

17 It goes on to explain the precautionary principle in terms that 'where there are threats of serious or irreversible damage, lack of full scientific certainty shall not be used as a reason for postponing cost-effective measures to prevent environmental degradation'. *Rio Declaration on Environment and Development* (n 12).

18 Ibid. Principle 16 says, 'National authorities should endeavour to promote the internalization of environmental costs and the use of economic instruments, taking into account the approach that the polluter should, in principle, bear the cost of pollution, with due regard to the public interest and without distorting international trade and investment.'

19 Ibid. Principle 17 says, 'Environmental impact assessment, as a national instrument, shall be undertaken for proposed activities that are likely to have a significant adverse impact on the environment and are subject to a decision of a competent national authority.'

20 *Brundtland Report*, Chapter 2: Towards Sustainable Development, para 1.

of sustainable development as reflected in international agreements on the basis that they are 'closely related and often used in combination (and [are] frequently interchangeably) which suggests that they do not yet have a well-established or agreed, legal definition, or status':

(1) the need to preserve the environment;
(2) reserve natural resources for the benefit of future generations (the principle of intergenerational equity);
(3) the aim of exploiting natural resources in a manner which is 'sustainable', 'prudent', 'wise', or 'appropriate' (the principle of sustainable use);
(4) the 'equitable use of natural resources', which implies that use by one state must take account of the needs of other states (the principle of equitable use, or intragenerational equity); and
(5) the need to ensure that environmental considerations are integrated into economic and other development plans, programmes, and projects, and that development needs are taken into account in applying environmental objectives (the principle of integration).[21]

As one commentator said, 'It is sufficiently flexible to allow a wide variety of policy decisions from a given set of facts. It combines environmental, social and economic concerns but does not prioritize them in case of conflict; it does not establish an environmental bottom line.'[22] That flexibility is not surprising given the international nature of the Brundtland Report and the need to find a formula acceptable to the different desires and positions of countries in different stages of development with different cultures and political views. **4.07**

A structural issue with the definition is that it links the needs of future generations with the needs of the present generation. To be sustainable, development must 'meet the needs of the present' but 'without compromising the ability of future generations to meet their own needs'.[23] Inevitably, the two conflict, and one of those groups, future generations, is in a far weaker position to defend its interests. Chapter 5, which deals with intergenerational equity, will examine that in more detail. **4.08**

Sustainable development has two conflicts built in: between intragenerational equity and intergenerational equity, and between development and **4.09**

---

21 Philippe Sands and Jacqueline Peel, with Adriana Fabra and Ruth MacKenzie, *Principles of International Environmental Law* (3rd ed., Cambridge University Press, 2012) 207.

22 B. Pardy, *Environmental Law: A Guide To Concepts* (1996) 267, quoted in Allan Ingelson, 'Sustainable Development and the Regulation of the Coal Bed Methane Industry in the United States', 20 *Journal of Natural Resources & Environmental Law* (2005–2006) 51, 54.

23 Brundtland Report (n 20).

environmental protection. As Bosselmann points out, the definition of sustainable development does not mention the importance of the environment and because of prevailing traditional social ethics, 'sustainable development is perceived as a balancing act between economic, social and environmental goals with trade-offs as a necessary outcome'.[24] He also points out that, while sustainable development may result in greater integration of policies, the danger is that the lack of guidance on ecological sustainability or the needs of future generations means that current unsustainable patterns of production and consumption will not change.[25] That danger is increased if the meaning of sustainability is linked exclusively to development, rather than as an independent term. For example, one UN webpage says that the Brundtland Report defined sustainability as 'meeting the needs of the present without compromising the ability of future generations to meet their own needs'.[26] That views sustainability through the lens of development, rather than promoting an examination of what sustainable means in its own right. It is suggested that it needs to be looked at differently for what is, for example, 'sustainable agriculture' or 'sustainable management of water', expressions used in SDGs 2 and 6, mentioned in the next section.

The Sustainable Development Goals (SDGs)

4.10 A major shift occurred when the Millennium Goals, which were due to expire at the end of 2015, were replaced by the SDGs as part of the 2030 Agenda for Sustainable Development.[27] Discussion and implementation of sustainable development have now focused on the 17 aspirational goals with targets that constitute the SDGs and seek to balance the economic, social, and environmental domains. For example, energy features in SDG 7: 'Ensure access to affordable, reliable, sustainable and modern energy for all'. The environment features in SDG 13: 'Take urgent action to combat climate change and its impacts'; and SDG 14: 'Conserve and sustainably use the oceans, seas and marine resources'.[28]

4.11 The Millennium Goals were focused on action by national governments. The SDGs are intended to be implemented through cooperation between national

24 Bosselmann Sustainability (n 7) 98.

25 Ibid.

26 'Sustainability', *United Nations* (webpage) https://www.un.org/en/academic-impact/sustainability.

27 For their history and the goals, see the UN's webpage on Sustainable Development Goals https://sdgs.un.org/goals#history. See also Erika Techera, *The Sustainable Development Goals in International Law and Policy*, (Routledge 2025).

28 Ibid.

governments, civil society, and the private sector. While the SDGs are not legally binding as a matter of international law, countries that commit to them are expected to establish a national framework to achieve them. The SDGs have been endorsed by many countries, although they have generally not been incorporated into domestic law.

REPORTING ON THE SDGS – THE UN

The UN

The 17 goals cover a diverse range of matters: **4.12**

- Goal 1: End poverty in all its forms everywhere.
- Goal 2: End hunger, improve food security and improved nutrition and promote sustainable agriculture.
- Goal 3: Ensure healthy lives and promote well-being for all at all ages.
- Goal 4: Ensure inclusive and equitable quality education and promote lifelong learning opportunities for all.
- Goal 5: Achieve gender equality and empower all women and girls.
- Goal 6: Ensure availability and sustainable management of water and sanitation for all.
- Goal 7: Ensure access to affordable, reliable, sustainable and modern energy for all.
- Goal 8: Promote sustained, inclusive and sustainable economic growth, full and productive employment and decent work for all.
- Goal 9: Build resilient infrastructure, promote inclusive and sustainable industrialization and foster innovation.
- Goal 10: Reduce inequality between and among countries.
- Goal 11: Make cities and human settlements inclusive, safe, resilient and sustainable.
- Goal 12: Ensure sustainable consumption and production patterns.
- Goal 13: Take urgent action to combat climate change and its impacts.
- Goal 14: Conserve and sustainably use the oceans, seas and marine resources for sustainable development.
- Goal 15: Protect, restore and promote sustainable use of terrestrial ecosystems, sustainably manage forests, combat desertification and halt and reverse land degradation and halt biodiversity loss.
- Goal 16: Promote peaceful and inclusive societies for sustainable development, provide access to justice for all and build effective, accountable and inclusive institutions at all levels.

- Goal 17: Strengthen the means of implementation and revitalize the Global Partnership for Sustainable Development.[29]

4.13 The commentary stresses that the goals are integrated and indivisible and balance the three dimensions of sustainable development: the economic, social, and environmental.[30] Each goal has targets. For example, Target 5 of Goal 15 is, 'Take urgent and significant action to reduce the degradation of natural habitats, halt the loss of biodiversity and, by 2020, protect and prevent the extinction of threatened species.' The indicator is the Red List Index.[31] Target 7 for Goal 4 says, 'By 2030, ensure that all learners acquire the knowledge and skill to promote sustainable development, including among others, through education for sustainable development and sustainable lifestyles, human rights, gender equality, promotion of a culture of peace and non-violence, global citizenship and appreciation of cultural diversity and of culture's contribution to sustainable development.'[32] The indicator is 'the extent to which (i) global citizenship education and (ii) education for sustainable development are mainstreamed in (a) national education policies; (b) curricula; (c) teacher education and (d) student assessment'.

4.14 The UN reports progress annually in its *United Nations Sustainable Development Goals Report*, a recent one being the *United Nations Sustainable Development Goals Report 2023 Special Edition* (UN SDG Report 2023).[33] That report reflects a severe situation. As the Secretary-General, Antonio Guterres, says in his foreword:

> Halfway to the deadline for the 2030 Agenda, the SDG Progress Report; Special Edition shows we are leaving more than half the world behind. Progress on more than 50 per cent of targets of the SDGs is weak and insufficient; on 30 per cent, it has stalled or gone into

---

29 United Nations, *Transforming Our World: The 2030 Agenda for Sustainable Development*, UN Doc A/RES/70/L.1 (22 September 2015).

30 Ibid, preamble https://sdgs.un.org/2030agenda.

31 See, United Nations Department of Economic and Social Affairs, 'Goal 15: Protect, restore and promote sustainable use of terrestrial ecosystems, sustainably manage forests, combat desertification, and halt and reverse land degradation and halt biodiversity loss', *Sustainable Development*, Targets and Indicators https://sdgs.un.org/goals/goal15#targets_and_indicators.

32 Ibid.

33 United Nations, *Sustainable Development Goals Report Special Edition* (Report, 2023) https://unstats.un.org/sdgs/report/2023/ (UN SDG Report 2023). See also the Global Indicator Framework, see UN Department of Economics and Social Affairs Statistics, 'Indicators', *Sustainable Development Goals* (webpage) https://unstats.un.org/sdgs/indicators/indicators-list/. For the 2023 results, see United Nations Economic and Social Council, *Progress Towards the Sustainable Development Goals: Report of the Secretary General, supplementary information*, UN Doc E/2023/6, annex https://unstats.un.org/sdgs/files/report/2023/E_2023_64_Statistical_Annex_I_and_II.pdf, also available at unstats.un.org/sdgs/.

reverse. These include key targets on poverty, hunger and climate. Unless we act now, the 2030 Agenda could become an epitaph for a world that might have been.[34]

The Secretary-General comments that an updated global financial architecture is required to ensure that the benefits of globalisation are shared and that there is a safety net for all countries in troubled times. He makes the powerful point that 'economic and financial decisions should prioritize the well-being of people and planet. Governments and the private sector should reorient their economies towards low-carbon, resilient patterns of growth.'[35] **4.15**

Let us take two specific examples from the UN SDG Report 2023. The comment made on Target 5 of Goal 15 was: **4.16**

> Plant and animal species are vital for our existence, from pollinating one third of global crops to providing medicines and economic opportunities. Yet, despite this importance, the world is currently facing the largest extinction event since the dinosaurs disappeared. Habitat destruction, invasive species, overexploitation, illegal wildlife trade, pollution and climate change are propelling this crisis. The Red List Index, which measures species' extinction risk across mammal, bird, amphibian, coral and cycad species, has deteriorated by about 11 per cent since 1993, with an accelerating decline each decade. Central and Southern Asia, Eastern and South-Eastern Asia, and Oceania have suffered the fastest declines.[36]

No specific comment was made in the 2023 report on Target 7 for Goal 4, but the picture presented was of poor progress on Goal 4 generally as COVID-19 caused learning losses in four out of five of the 104 countries studied. A general comment made was: **4.17**

> To deliver on Goal 4, education financing must become a national investment priority. Furthermore, measures such as making education free and compulsory, increasing the number of teachers, improving basic school infrastructure and embracing digital transformation are essential.[37]

---

34 Ibid 2. He notes, 'The COVID-19 pandemic and the triple crises of climate change, biodiversity loss and pollution are having a devastating and lasting impact. This has been amplified by Russia's invasion of Ukraine, which has driven increases in the prices of food and energy and in the cost of access to finance, creating a global cost-of-living crisis affecting billions of people. Developing countries are bearing the brunt of our collective failure to invest in the Sustainable Development Goals (SDGs). Many face a huge financing gap and are buried under a mountain of debt. One in three countries is a high risk of being unable to service their debt.'

35 Ibid.

36 Ibid 43.

37 Ibid.

UN high-level political forums and VNRs

4.18 In addition, the UN conducts an annual high-level political forum to review progress towards the SDGs. At that forum, countries produce voluntary national reviews (VNRs). The *2022 Voluntary National Reviews Synthesis Report* mentions that 187 countries out of 194 members of the forum presented a VNR since 2016.[38] The maximum number of times that countries had presented was four, and only three countries had done that.[39] The report noted that in 11 countries, 'the 2030 Agenda has been mainstreamed or aligned to their national development plans and framework'.[40]

COUNTRY EXAMPLES

Canada

4.19 Canada's most recent VNR is *Canada's 2023 Voluntary National Review* (Canada 2023 VNR).[41] Canada has a national strategy for implementing the SDGs in *Moving Forward Together: Canada's 2030 Agenda National Strategy*, which was released in 2021.[42] The Canada 2023 VNR comments that it reports on Canada's achievements and experiences to advance the 2030 Agenda since the baseline assessment in Canada's first VNR in 2018.[43] It goes on to say:

> Consistent with UN guidelines, Canada's second VNR describes how Canada established strong institutional mechanisms to implement the 2030 Agenda and built an enabling environment where dialogue and action on the 2030 Agenda converge and thrive across the country and internationally.[44] Progress is tracked against all 17 SDGs using the most current Canadian data available as of the end of April 2023 from the Global Indicator Framework and the Canadian Indicator Framework.[45]

---

38 United Nations Department of Economic and Social Affairs, *Voluntary National Reviews Synthesis* (Report, 2022) 6 https://hlpf.un.org/sites/default/files/2022-10/VNR%202022%20Synthesis%20Report.pdf.

39 Ibid 9. Those countries were Argentina, the Philippines, and Switzerland.

40 Ibid 11. The 11 countries were Cameroon, Ethiopia, Jamaica, Jordan, Ghana, Somalia, the Philippines, Suriname, Senegal, Liberia, and Togo.

41 Government of Canada, *Canada's 2023 Voluntary National Review* (2023), https://www.canada.ca/content/dam/canada/employment-social-development/programs/agenda-2030/voluntary-national-review/2023-report/VNR_Main%20Report_EN_August%202.pdf ('Canada's 2023 VNR').

42 Government of Canada, *Moving Forward Together: Canada's 2030 Agenda National Strategy* (2021) https://www.canada.ca/en/employment-social-development/programs/agenda-2030/moving-forward.html.

43 Government of Canada, *Canada's Implementation of the 2030 Agenda for Sustainable Development: Voluntary National Review* (2018) https://hlpf.un.org/sites/default/files/vnrs/2021/20312Canada_ENGLISH_18122_Canadas_Voluntary_National_ReviewENv7.pdf.

44 Canada 2023 VNR (n 41) 5.

45 For the Canadian Indicator Framework, see Statistics Canada, *The Canadian Indicator Framework for the Sustainable Development Goals* (webpage, 22 June 2021) https://www150.statcan.gc.ca/n1/pub/11-26

4.20 The Canada 2023 VNR says that Canada has a focus on five of the SDGs – No Poverty (SDG 1), Quality Education (SDG 4), Gender Equality (SDG 5), Climate Action (SDG 13), and Partnerships for the Goals (SDG 17) – because those SDGs are 'aligned with Canada's domestic and international priorities'.[46] Environmental sustainability is an important issue, and this is the subject of several Canadian ambitions in the Canadian Indicator Framework. For example, an ambition on Goal 15 is that 'Canada conserves and restores ecosystems and habitat' with a target of 'Conserve 25% of Canada's land by 2025, working towards 30% by 2030' and an indicator of 'the proportion of terrestrial (land and freshwater) areas conserved'.[47]

4.21 Also of note is the extent to which the SDGs have been taken up in broader Canadian policy-setting. There is a Federal Sustainable Development Strategy, which 'brings together the Government of Canada's sustainable development priorities'.[48] The SDGs have been included in Canada's parliamentary reporting by federal departments and agencies.[49] The tone of these VNRs is quite upbeat. So, to present a balanced picture, it is also necessary to mention that on a number of measures, Canada's environmental performance is poor.[50]

Philippines

4.22 The Philippines has produced three VNRs, the most recent being the *2022 Voluntary National Review of the Philippines* (*2022 Philippines VNR*).[51] There are some common themes with the Canadian approach. First, the Philippines did a baseline assessment in 2016 with its first VNR. It sets a

-0004/112600042021001-eng.htm. This contains what it describes as 'Canadian Ambition' for each goal. That for Goal 4 is 'Canadians have access to inclusive and quality education throughout their lives' with an indicator of 'High school completion rate'.

46 Canada 2023 VNR (n 41) 5.

47 Terms defined by reference to Canadian Environmental Sustainability Indicators 'Canada's conserved areas' contained in the Environment and Climate Change Canada. Canadian Protected and Conserved Areas Database. There are other databases such as that developed under the Canadian Environmental Sustainability Indicators Program (CESI) at https://www.canada.ca/en/environment-climate-change/services/environmental-indicators.html.

48 Canada 2023 VNR (n 41) 9. For the strategy, see Government of Canada, *Federal Sustainable Development Strategy* (webpage) https://www.fsds-sfdd.ca/en.

49 See Government of Canada, *Departmental Plans* (webpage) https://www.canada.ca/en/treasury-board-secretariat/services/planned-government-spending/reports-plans-priorities.html.

50 There are a number of comparisons of environmental performance. One is the Climate Change Performance Index, which rates Canada's performance as poor. See, 'Canada', *Climate Change Performance Index* (webpage) https://ccpi.org/country/can/.

51 *2022 Voluntary National Review of the Philippines* https://sdg.neda.gov.ph/2022-voluntary-national-review-of-the-philippines/#:~:text=The%20theme%20for%20the%202022,country's%20very%20first%20SDG%20Summit ('Philippines 2022 VNR').

long-term vision set in 2016 called AmBisyon Natin 2040, which guided the Philippines Development Plan (PDP), the medium-term development plan of the country.[52] Following the reversal suffered as a result of COVID-19, the Philippines updated its PDP, seeking to align all the goals to the SDGs 'while reshaping our short-term objective to building resilience'.[53] Elements for a long-term agenda mentioned in the report on progress contained in the *2022 Philippines VNR*, common with Canada, are building multi-stakeholder commitment, resource mobilisation, and clear assignment of responsibilities.[54] Another element is effective monitoring.

4.23 Like Canada, the Philippines focuses on particular SDGs. In its case, Goals 4, 5, 14, and 15, of which progress is discussed in four clusters – Health and Resiliency, Economic, Social, and Environment. It shares a focus on Goals 4 and 5 with Canada. Goals 14 and 15 relate to the ocean and terrestrial environments. Although the *2022 Philippine VNR* acknowledges the interconnectedness of all the goals and the importance of approaching them not in silos but as a whole; nevertheless, the Philippines has measured and reported progress through these clusters.

4.24 Environmental sustainability is also an important aspect of the *2022 Philippines VNR*, with its report on Goals 14 and 15 reporting progress on both.[55] On SDG 14, it reports that from 2016 to 2020, the coverage of protected marine areas increased from 1.41 million to 3.14 million hectares. On SDG 15, it reports that the country's forest cover has increased from 7.01 million hectares in 2010 to 7.18 million hectares in 2021. Also, the Red List Index increased from 0.48 to 0.59 between 2016 and 2022.[56] The Philippines Statistical Office maintains a monitoring service for SDGs called 'SDG Watch', which has a refined list of 131 indicators.[57]

---

52 Ibid 1.

53 Ibid 2.

54 Ibid, SDG Implementation 2016–2020.

55 Philippine 2022 VNR (n 51) 60.

56 See, 'SDG Watch', *Philippines Statistical Office* (webpage) https://psa.gov.ph/sdg/Philippines/baselinedata/life_on_land.

57 Ibid. The Philippines Statistical Office notes that the 2030 Agenda had 17 Goals and 169 Targets, and the Global Indicator Framework has 232 targets. It states that 'the Sustainable Development Goals (SDGs) and targets are integrated and indivisible, global in nature and universally applicable, and take into account different national realities, capacities and levels of development and respecting national policies and priorities. Each government is expected to take ownership and establish national frameworks, set nationally-owned targets guided by the global level of ambition but taking into account country-level circumstances for the achievement of the 17 goals. Countries will also decide how these aspirational and global targets should be incorporated in national planning processes, policies and strategies.'

CORPORATE SDG REPORTING

Overview of mining

4.25 In 2022, KPMG did a survey of sustainability reporting, *Big Shifts, Small Steps: Survey of Sustainability Reporting 2022* (*KPMG 2022 Report*).[58] It found that 96% of the 250 largest global companies (G250) report on sustainability on environmental, social, and governance (ESG) matters. According to KPMG, 74% of the G250 reported against the SDGs in 2022.[59] Germany had the highest reference rate to the SDGs with 100% of its G250 companies referring to them,[60] compared with the USA at 49%. Interestingly, the number of G250 companies in the industrials, manufacturing, and metals sector, which would include mining, reporting on the SDGs increased from 24% in 2017 to 63% in 2022.[61]

4.26 KPMG found that most companies communicated only the positive impacts they have on the SDGs, with one-third of G250 companies considering both positive and negative impacts.[62] Only 10% of the G250 reported on all 17 SDGs, with three SDGs being the most popular for reporting: SDG 8 (Decent Work and Economic Growth), SDG 12 (Responsible Consumption and Production), and SDG 13 (Climate Action). Few companies prioritised SDG 2 (Zero Hunger), SDG 14 (Life below Water), and SDG 15 (Life on Land).

4.27 Mining was considered specifically in two documents produced by the Columbia Center on Sustainable Investment (CCSI): *Mining and the SDGs: A 2020 Status Update* (*Mining SDG 2020 Update*), produced with the Responsible Mining Foundation (RMF),[63] and the earlier *Mapping Mining to the Sustainable Development Goals: An Atlas*,[64] which is a useful tool to assist companies with mapping their activities against the SDGs. In addition, the RMF

58 KPMG, *Big Shifts, Small Steps: Survey of Sustainability Reporting 2022* (2022) https://assets.kpmg.com/content/dam/kpmg/se/pdf/komm/2022/Global-Survey-of-Sustainability-Reporting-2022.pdf ('KPMG 2022 Report').

59 Ibid 57

60 Ibid 58.

61 Ibid 59.

62 Ibid 60.

63 The Columbia Center on Sustainable Investment and the Responsible Mining Foundation, *Mining and the SDGs: A 2020 Status Update* https://www.responsibleminingfoundation.org/app/uploads/RMF_CCSI_Mining_and_SDGs_EN_Sept2020.pdf (Mining SDG 2020 Update).

64 The Columbia Center on Sustainable Investment et al., *Mapping Mining to the Sustainable Development Goals: An Atlas* (July 2016) https://www.undp.org/sites/g/files/zskgke326/files/publications/Mapping_Mining_SDGs_An_Atlas_Executive_Summary_FINAL.pdf.

produced the *RMI Framework 2020*, presenting a comprehensive SDG-linked framework.[65] It also produced the *RMI Report 2020*. That report assessed the policies, practices, and mine-site-level actions of 38 geographically dispersed large-scale mining companies, which together accounted for around 28% of the global value of mining production.[66] Its report forms the basis of the conclusions in the *Mining SDG 2020 Update*. In summary, the *Mining SDG 2020 Update* concluded:

> Integrating and reporting on the SDGs, however, is still not the norm, though good practices are seen among a few companies. The results of this status update suggest that most mining companies still have considerable room for improvement in taking these strategic steps towards fulfilling their considerable potential to help deliver the SDGs.[67]

4.28 It commented specifically that 'good practices are seen among numerous companies on some SDG-supportive measures, showing models that other companies can follow. The sample of 38 mining companies shows relatively widespread action on SDG 4 (Quality Education) and SDG 17 (Partnerships for the Goals).'[68] It also said, 'There is very little evidence of action on SDG 3 (Good Health and Wellbeing), SDG 5 (Gender Equality), SDG 6 (Clean Water and Sanitation) and SDG 14 (Life Below Water).'[69]

Mining companies

4.29 Among the companies reported on in the RMI Report 2020 are many of the big mining companies. As mentioned in Chapter 1, the eight largest mining companies in the world, judged by market capitalisation in order from the biggest, are BHP Group, Rio Tinto, China Shenhua Energy Co Ltd, Glencore Plc, Vale SA, Freeport-McMoRan Inc, Fortescue Ltd, and Newmont Corp.[70] We will use BHP, Rio Tinto, and AngloGold Ashanti as examples in this section.

---

65 Responsible Mining Foundation, *RMI Framework 2020* https://www.responsibleminingfoundation.org/rmi-framework-2020/.

66 Responsible Mining Foundation, *RMI Report 2020* https://www.responsibleminingfoundation.org/rmi-report-2020/.

67 Mining and the SDGs 2020 (n 63) 6.

68 Ibid.

69 Ibid.

70 As at 31 December 2022, 'Top 10 Mining Companies in the World by Market Cap', *Global Data* (webpage) https://www.globaldata.com/companies/top-companies-by-sector/mining/global-companies-by-market-cap/#.

BHP refers to 10 SDGs in its sustainability approach in the following groupings and sub-groupings:[71] Decarbonisation (climate change SDGs 7 and 13), Healthy Environment (Biodiversity and land management SDGs 11 and 16, and Water SDG 6), Indigenous partnerships (Indigenous people SDG 8), Safe, inclusive and future-ready workforce (Safety SDG 8, People SDGs 5 and 10, and Health SDGs 3 and 8), Thriving Empowered Communities (Community SDG 8), and Other (Ethics and Business Conduct SDG 16).[72] BHP sets objectives, an example of which is gender balance, where in 2016 BHP aspired 'to achieve gender balance within our employee workforce globally by the end of FY2025, which we define as a minimum 40 per cent women and 40 per cent men'.[73] In its 2024 Annual Report, it produced a social value scorecard which showed female participation at 37.1%.[74] **4.30**

Rio Tinto's approach is also selective of particular SDGs. Its initial comment is 'our approach to sustainability aligns with the United Nations Sustainable Development Goals (UN SDGs), which are recognised as the global blueprint for a sustainable future'.[75] It then goes on to say: **4.31**

> Our sustainability framework focuses on the two lead goals that we feel are most relevant to operating our business responsibly and where we can have the biggest impact: responsible consumption and production (SDG 12) and decent work and economic growth (SDG 8).
>
> Our business operations also contribute to eight supporting SDGs (3, 4, 5, 6, 9, 10, 13, 15), while partnerships for the goals (SDG 17) reflects our approach to sustainability and is fundamental to the way we run our business.

AngloGold Ashanti is an example of a company that appears in the RMI Report 2020 that has selected nine SDGs, which it says are core to its **4.32**

---

71 BHP 2024 Annual Report *Material topics and impacts for sustainability reporting* https://www.bhp.com/investors/annual-reporting/annual-report-2024 33.

72 Ibid.

73 BHP 2024 Annual Report *Gender Balance* https://www.bhp.com/investors/annual-reporting/annual-report-2024 36. This goes further than the Targets and Goals published by the UN, the closest being Target 5.5: 'Ensure women's full and effective participation and equal opportunities for leadership at all levels of decision-making in political, economic and public life,' with an indicator 5.5.2: 'Proportion of women in managerial positions'.

74 BHP 2024 Annual Report *Social value scorecard* https://www.bhp.com/investors/annual-reporting/annual report 2024 35.

75 'Our Sustainability', *Rio Tinto* (webpage), Alignment with the United Nations Sustainable Development Goals https://www.riotinto.com/en/sustainability/our-approach. Before that, it describes its approach as follows: 'Our sustainability framework describes how we manage the ESG issues that are important to us and our stakeholders, and how we contribute to the United Nations Sustainable Development Goals (UN SDGs). This includes providing people and communities with economic opportunities; safeguarding and promoting the health, wellbeing and human rights of people and communities; combatting climate change; and becoming trusted stewards of the natural resources entrusted to us.'

sustainability strategy and where it can make a positive contribution.[76] It also mentions six that are not core to its business where it can have an impact.[77] It is worth noting that there are significant differences in the SDGs selected by the three companies, as well as some common SDGs.

Overview of oil and gas

4.33 The *KPMG 2022 Report* found that between 2017 and 2022, the percentage of G250 companies in the oil and gas sector reporting on the SDGs increased from 39% to 83%.[78] That is a higher percentage than for mining. As with mining, there are tools to assist companies in mapping areas of SDG impact and reporting on their contribution. In the case of the oil and gas industry, Ipieca, UNDP, and the IFC published *Mapping the oil and gas industry to the Sustainable Development Goals: an Atlas* in 2017.[79] That was followed in 2018 by the SDG Roadmap Guidelines, developed by the World Business Council for Sustainable Development (WBCSD),[80] and in 2021 by the joint Ipieca and WBCSD publication, *Accelerating action: An SDG Roadmap for the oil and gas sector* (*Oil and Gas SDG Roadmap 2021*).[81]

4.34 The *Oil and Gas SDG Roadmap 2021* commented that although the oil and gas industry has the potential to advance all 17 goals, 10 SDGs were identified for the purpose of the roadmap, where the sector 'has the most influence or ability to respond to societal needs by driving innovation and impact in its own operations and across the value chain'.[82] Those SDGs were 3 (Good health and wellbeing), 6 (Clean water and sanitation), 7 (Affordable and clean energy), 8 (Decent work and economic growth), 9 (Industry, innovation and infrastructure), 12 (Responsible consumption and production), 13 (Climate action), 14 (Life below water), 15 (Life on land), and 16 (Peace, justice and strong institutions). It also comments that 'SDG 17 "Partnerships for the Goals"

76 AngloGold Ashanti, *Sustainability Report* 202, 20 https://reports.anglogoldashanti.com/22/wp-content/uploads/2023/04/AGA-SR22.pdf. The nine SDGs are 3, 5, 7, 8, 9, 11, 12, 13, and 17.

77 Ibid. The six are 1, 4, 6, 10, 15, and 16.

78 KPMG Report 2022 (n 58) 59.

79 Ipieca, UNDP and IFC, *Mapping the oil and gas industry to the Sustainable Development Goals: an Atlas* (August 14, 2017) https://www.undp.org/publications/mapping-oil-and-gas-industry-sdgs-atlas. Compare the equivalent for mining at n 64.

80 WBCSD, *SDG Roadmap Guidelines* (10 June 2021) https://www.wbcsd.org/Programs/People-and-Society/Sustainable-Development-Goals/SDG-Sector-Roadmaps/Resources/SDG-Sector-Roadmaps-Guidelines.

81 IPIECA and WBCSD, *Accelerating action An SDG Roadmap for the oil and gas sector* (1 May 2021) https://www.ipieca.org/resources/sdg-roadmap/accelerating-action-an-sdg-roadmap-for-the-oil-and-gas-sector-infographic-overview ('Oil and Gas SDG Roadmap 2021').

82 Oil and Gas SDG Roadmap 202 (n 80) 4.

was identified as a cross-cutting goal essential to all impact opportunities'.[83] The three-step framework used by the *Oil and Gas SDG Roadmap 2021* has a first step of mapping the oil and gas sector's current level of SDG impact in its operations and supply chain and identifying priority SDGs for the sector. What that first step shows is that the sector makes a significant contribution to the SDGs. The important point here, which is applicable across all sectors, is that many are contributing to the SDGs without realising that they are doing so. Hence, there are significant opportunities to analyse that contribution and report on it, without doing more.

Oil and gas companies

The author did an analysis of the strategies of the eight largest international oil and gas companies for a book published in 2018 to see what they had to say about climate change and sustainability.[84] That analysis looked at published annual and sustainability reports, generally for 2016 and 2017. It is clear that the position of several of these companies has advanced significantly on sustainability, including on reporting on the SDGs. That is not surprising, given that the SDGs came into existence in 2015. Total (now TotalEnergies) is a good example. Like BHP and RioTinto, it also takes a selective approach to the SDGs, introducing its approach as: 'TotalEnergies involves its employees in identifying the SDGs on which it can have the greatest impact, in connection with its ambition to reach carbon neutrality (net zero emissions) by 2050, together with society.'[85] **4.35**

TotalEnergies has built its sustainability approach on four areas of action and has identified three levels of impact: core contributions through its mission,[86] direct contributions through its responsible business approach,[87] and indirect contributions through its responsible business approach.[88] In addition, SDG 17 is cross-cutting and is considered an enabler to deliver the company's sustainability strategy. As a member of the Global Compact's Reporting on the SDG's Action Platform,[89] TotalEnergies based its reporting on the Global **4.36**

---

83 Ibid.

84 John A.P. Chandler, *Petroleum Resource Management: How Governments Manage Their Offshore Petroleum Resources* (Edward Elgar, 2018) Chapter 4.

85 'Reporting Standards', *TotalEnergies* (webpage) https://totalenergies.com/sustainability/reports-and-indicators/reporting-standards/sustainable-development-goals.

86 SDGs 7, 8, 9, and 13.

87 SDGs 3, 4, 5, 10, 12, 14, 15, and 16.

88 SDGs 1, 2, 6, and 11.

89 'Reporting on the SDGs', *UN Global Compact Action Platform* (webpage) https://unglobalcompact.org/take-action/action-platforms/sdg-reporting. See also, Global Reporting Initiative United Nations

Compact's publication *An Analysis of the Goals and Targets*.[90] It also produces its own TotalEnergies SDG reports.[91]

Renewable energy companies

4.37 Renewable energy companies also track their progress against the SDGs on a selective basis. Iberdrola says that the SDGs are part of its business strategy with its main focus being on SDG 7 and 13, commenting that it makes a direct contribution to 6, 9, 15, and 17.[92] It says that it makes an indirect contribution to all other SDGs.[93] Vestas Wind focuses on five of the SDGs: 12, 7, 13, 8, and 17.[94] It groups them under headings: 'where we can reduce the negative impacts of our operations' (SDG 12), 'where we can create positive impacts with our customers and value chain' (SDGs 7, 13, and 8) and 'where we can influence society at large' (SDG 17). Canadian Solar lists 13 SDGs to which it contributes: 1, 2, 3, 4, 5, 7, 9, 10, 11, 13, 15, 16, and 17.[95] It then lists individual SDGs against particular areas – for example SDG 12 is mentioned in the context of the circular economy.

CONCLUSIONS, GUIDANCE, AND KEY PRINCIPLES

4.38 The basic conclusions from this chapter are:

- The SDGs have become the dominant paradigm when it comes to sustainability, particularly at the country level. They represent 'a global blueprint for a sustainable future'.[96] Bear in mind that they came into being only in 2015.
- The SDGs are a classic example of 'soft law', meaning that they are not legally binding as a matter of international law, and compliance with them has generally not been incorporated into domestic law.

Global Compact, *Integrating the SDGs into corporate reporting: A practical guide* (August 2018) (https://unglobalcompact.org/library/5628).

90 See, UN Global Compact, *An Analysis of the Goals and Targets* (2022) https://unglobalcompact.org/library/5361.

91 TotalEnergies, *SDG Report 2021–2022*. https://totalenergies.com/sites/g/files/nytnzq121/files/documents/2022-11/SDG_Report_2021-2022.pdf.

92 Iberdrola *Committed to the SDGs* https://www.iberdrola.com/sustainability/committed-sustainable-development-goals.

93 Ibid.

94 Vestas Sustainability Report 2023, https://www.vestas.com/content/dam/vestas-com/global/en/investor/reports-and-presentations/financial/2023/2023-annual-report/Sustainability%20Report%202023.pdf.coredownload.inline.pdf 72.

95 Canadian Solar Sustainability Report 2023 https://investors.canadiansolar.com/news-releases/news-release-details/canadian-solar-releases-2023-corporate-sustainability-report from 5.

96 See n 75.

- Nevertheless, nearly all members of the UN have produced voluntary national reviews, in which they take stock and assess progress and challenges in the implementation of the SDGs. Many have internal mechanisms to track their performance.
- Companies are increasingly referring to the SDGs in their published reports. In some jurisdictions (for example, Germany), this is the norm for large companies. The number reporting has increased each year since 2015.[97]
- There are 17 SDGs, which are described as 'integrated and indivisible'.[98]
- Countries, organisations, and companies often focus on selected SDGs because they align with other priorities.[99]
- Organisations and companies often make contributions to the SDGs which they are not aware of, simply because they have not devoted resources to analysing their contribution.

The following ideas follow from those conclusions: **4.39**

- A stocktaking exercise reviewing contributions to the SDGs will provide useful information on where an organisation or company is already making an impact.
- Two important questions can follow. The first is what the sustainability priorities of the organisation are and, where a contribution is being made, whether they relate to the SDGs. The second is whether reporting performance against the SDGs is valuable for the organisation. That can be the case where there is some independent ranking of performance which will assist the organisation.[100]
- Focusing on selected SDGs because they align with an organisation's other priorities can cause impacts, sometimes negative, on other SDGs. If a selective approach is taken, it is important to ensure that no harm is being done.[101]

SDG CHECKLIST

Companies

1. If you are a mining company, have you looked at the mapping guides (referred to at n 63 to n 65)?
2. If you are an oil and gas company, have you looked at the mapping guides (referred to at n 79 to n 81)?

---

97 See n 61.

98 See n 29.

99 See n 45 relating to Canada, which says its focus SDGs are 'aligned with Canada's domestic and international priorities'

100 For universities, that ranking exists in the form of the *Times Higher Education Impact Rankings* https://www.timeshighereducation.com/impactrankings.

101 Nina Weitz et al., *SDGs and the Environment in the EU: A systems view to improve coherence* (Report commissioned by the European Environment Agency, October 2019, Stockholm Environment Institute) https://sdgs.un.org/sites/default/files/2023-01/sei-2019-pr-weitz-sdg-synergies-eu-env.pdf.

3. If you are a renewable energy or service company, have you looked at these or other mapping guides?
4. Do your company's sustainability priorities relate to SDGs where a contribution is being made? Do you consider that reporting performance against the SDGs will be valuable for the organisation?
5. If the answer is yes to both questions in question 4, what do you consider the next step should be? Will you undertake a stocktaking exercise?

Government/regulators

1. Are there any reports or mapping guides relevant to you, for example, voluntary national reports or reports for your government or department?
2. Do these provide any requirements for you to report against specified SDGs and guidance for you to do so?
3. If the answer to question 1 is yes, is there a clear path for you to follow? If not, how will you obtain clarification?
4. If the answer to question 1 is no, do you consider that reporting performance against the SDGs will be of value? If so, how will you implement it?

5

INTERGENERATIONAL AND INTRAGENERATIONAL EQUITY AND MINING AND ENERGY

INTRODUCTION 5.01
Equity 5.03
CONCEPTUAL AND LEGAL DIFFICULTIES IN INTERGENERATIONAL EQUITY 5.06
Defining needs 5.06
Valuation and apportionment 5.07
CONCEPTUAL AND LEGAL DIFFICULTIES IN INTRAGENERATIONAL EQUITY 5.08
Distributional equity and energy justice 5.08
Analysis of costs and benefits 5.10
ACHIEVING THE FAIR DISTRIBUTION OF COSTS AND BENEFITS 5.13
Making fair decisions 5.13
The growing importance of soft law 5.14
CREEPING INTERGENERATIONALISATION AND ENERGY JUSTICE IN INTERNATIONAL AND DOMESTIC LAWS 5.16
Lack of treaties requiring intergenerational equity 5.16
The International Court of Justice 5.18
CONCLUSIONS, GUIDANCE, AND KEY PRINCIPLES 5.24

INTRODUCTION

The first question we need to examine is why there is a chapter on intergenerational equity and intragenerational equity. The second question is how it helps the reader solve sustainability problems. First, many of the difficult questions in relation to mining and energy involve conflicts of interest between different groups of people: for example, us compared with our grandchildren, the inhabitants of wealthy countries compared with the inhabitants of poor countries, and poor people within a country compared with wealthy people in that country. Second, principles of equity provide the means to resolve those conflicts. Intergenerational and intragenerational equity also constitute moral and ethical principles that underpin environmental protection and sustainable development. In many cases, they are the thread that provides the answer to difficult questions of the fair distribution of benefits and burdens of mineral and energy development and production. Those questions underpin the approach of a company or regulator to the contribution it wants to make to 5.01

society and how it will measure its performance. Hence, it is important to understand both intergenerational equity and intragenerational equity.

5.02 The relevant dictionary definitions of the word 'equity' often say it means 'fairness'.[1] There are only short steps to say that it is an important tool in addressing disadvantage and also to link it to the word 'justice'. We can elaborate the importance of fairness and the points made in the previous paragraph by referring to the element of sustainable development, variously described as 'social inclusion', 'societal development', 'society', or even 'equity'.[2] A number of the SDGs address social issues, for example, Goal 5 – 'Achieve gender equality and empower all women and girls', Goal 6 – 'Ensure availability and sustainable management of water and sanitation for all', Goal 7 – 'Ensure access to affordable, reliable, sustainable and modern energy for all', Goal 8 – 'Promote sustained, inclusive and sustainable economic growth, full and productive employment and decent work for all', and Goal 16 – 'Promote peaceful and inclusive societies for sustainable development, provide access to justice for all and build effective, accountable and inclusive institutions at all levels'. All of these require improvement in the position of particular groups in a society, such as women, or of a whole society, for example, a country with insufficient energy. They therefore require a distribution of resources to those groups or societies. A number of these ideas are picked up by companies in measuring their performance against the SDGs or their performance generally on ESG matters. Examples are gender balance, usually described by reference to the percentage of women employed or in leadership roles, providing full and productive employment, and water quality. Chapters 8 and 9 will look at company reporting in detail.

Equity

5.03 The two categories of equity described here, intergenerational equity and intragenerational equity, are both fundamental to sustainable development. The Brundtland Report's definition of sustainable development refers to intergenerational equity by requiring development to meet the needs of the present 'without compromising the ability of future generations to meet their own needs'.[3] It also indirectly refers to intragenerational equity because it requires

---

1 The Shorter Oxford English Dictionary, Definition 1: 'The quality of being equal or fair; impartiality; even-handed dealing' and Definition 2: 'That which is fair or right' (Clarendon Press, Oxford 3rd ed., 1973).

2 See 1.13.

3 Brundtland Report, Chapter 2: Towards Sustainable Development, para 1.

'the needs of the present' to be met. It is particularly focused on one large disadvantaged group, the poor nations. As Chapter 1 explains, intragenerational equity requires that part of the population is not disadvantaged in its ability to get energy or to get it at prices comparable with the rest of the population.[4]

Intergenerational equity came to prominence soon after the Brundtland Report through Edith Brown Weiss's 1988 book, *In Fairness to Future Generations: International Law, Common Patrimony and Intergenerational Equity* (*Brown Weiss IFFG*).[5] Her book contains one of the most quoted expressions of intergenerational equity applicable to natural resources, that 'we, as a species, hold the natural and cultural environment of our planet in common, both with other members of the present generation and with other generations, past and future'.[6] **5.04**

Brown Weiss IFFG was written in the 1980s while the Brundtland Report was in consideration and soon after the *World Conservation Strategy* was published in 1980.[7] The context for her book was one in which issues like concern for the environment and concern for the position of poor nations were coming to the fore. The idea of intergenerational equity reflects a desire to find an ethical and philosophical foundation for the treatment of the environment and natural resources. Without that, the world could just see unfettered development. As Brown Weiss notes, 'intergenerational equity arises in the context of fairness among all generations'.[8] That is the basis of it. **5.05**

---

4 At 1.10.

5 Edith Brown Weiss, *In Fairness to Future Generations: International Law, Common Patrimony and Intergenerational Equity* (United Nations University Tokyo and Transnational Publishers, 1988).

6 Ibid 7. This is sometimes shortened along the lines that 'every generation holds the Earth in common with members of the present generation and with other generations, past and future', see, e.g. Edith Brown Weiss, 'Intergenerational Equity', *Oxford Public International Law* (Max Planck Encyclopedia of Public International Law, February 2013), para 1 https://opil.ouplaw.com/view/10.1093/law:epil/9780199231690/law-9780199231690-e1421.

7 International Union for the Conservation of Nature and Natural Resources, *World Conservation Strategy: Living Resource Conservation for Sustainable Development* (1980).

8 Brown Weiss IFFG (n 5) 21. Beckerman and others acknowledge that the current generation can owe moral obligations to future generations. Wilfred Beckerman, 'The impossibility of a theory of intergenerational justice' in Joerg Chet Tremmel (ed.), *Handbook of Intergenerational Justice* (Edward Elgar, 2006) 53, 68.

CONCEPTUAL AND LEGAL DIFFICULTIES IN INTERGENERATIONAL EQUITY

Defining needs

5.06 There are conceptual and legal difficulties in creating rights for future generations. They are set out here for illustrative purposes only. This chapter suggests that the reader should not be distracted by them because the underlying principles are clear and a green thread to lead through them is set out at 5.13. The difficulties start with defining the needs of future generations because we cannot predict the future and their circumstances.[9] This also makes it difficult to define the obligations of the present generation. If it is intended to create legal rights for future generations, how many generations should be considered?[10] Then, how should a legal system confer rights on people who do not exist and provide for the enforcement of those rights?[11]

Valuation and apportionment

5.07 How the benefits and burdens are to be valued and apportioned is by no means clear. For example, how are plants or resources critical to human survival to be valued, or should they just be regarded as sacrosanct? This is just a brief illustration of some of the difficulties. They lead Fitzmaurice, who in 2008 did a thorough review of the arguments, and Brown Weiss's proposal of intergenerational equity, to the conclusion that 'the issue of the existence of the rights of future generations is not at all clear and remains an unsettled question both in philosophy and international law'.[12] In relation to intergenerational equity, she thought that 'from a legal point of view, doubts remain whether such a theory is a workable and practical proposition'.[13]

---

9 Beckerman (n 8) 66.

10 See, L.B. Solum, 'To Our Children's Children's Children: The Problems of Intergenerational Ethics' (2021) 35 *Loyola Los Angeles Law Review* 163, 169.

11 See Vaughan Lowe, 'Sustainable Development and Unsustainable Arguments' in Alan Boyle and David Freestone (eds), *International Law and Sustainable Development Past Achievements and Future Challenges* (Oxford University Press, 1999) 19, 31, and Wilfred Beckerman (n 8) 66.

12 Malgosia Fitzmaurice, 'Intergenerational Equity Revisited' in James Crawford, et al. (eds), *International Law between Universalism and Fragmentation* (Brill, 2008) 195, 229. The conceptual difficulties highlighted come through in the UN Secretary-General's 2013 report, *Intergenerational solidarity and the needs of future generations*, UN Doc A/68/322 (5 August 2013) ('*UN Intergenerational solidarity report*') 5–21, which discusses some of the underlying concepts like the meaning of future generations and whether they have rights.

13 Ibid.

CONCEPTUAL AND LEGAL DIFFICULTIES IN INTRAGENERATIONAL EQUITY

Distributional equity and energy justice

Distributional equity, or justice, has been examined by a number of writers, such as Rawls.[14] It has developed into a specific area of energy justice in recent years.[15] Sovacool, Heffron, and others defined it in a 2014 article as: **5.08**

> a global energy system that fairly disseminates both the benefits and costs of energy services, and one that contributes to more representative and impartial energy decision-making.[16]

The components of energy justice combine the essence of distributional and procedural justice with the older ideas of equity and fairness in a world in which 'one-quarter of humanity has no access to cleaner forms of cooking or electricity, and another quarter has less than one-tenth of what those in industrializing countries had a decade ago'.[17] The article goes on to say: **5.09**

> It challenges us not only to coldly calculate costs and benefits, but to determine how these are distributed. It asks that we decide whether it is fair to deplete hundreds of millions of years of energy resources in a few generations, or to reap the benefits corresponding to greenhouse gas emissions today, such as economic development, at the expense of those not yet born tomorrow.[18]

Analysis of costs and benefits

That snapshot of energy justice highlights the difficult areas of calculating costs and benefits and then how to distribute them. Those difficulties are brought out in the following quote from Justice Preston, the Chief Judge of the Land and Environment Court of New South Wales. Because the environmental legislation of New South Wales has a public interest test which requires consideration of sustainable development, defined to include intergenerational equity, the Land and Environment Court of New South Wales has frequently considered sustainability and equity issues in relation to both intergenerational and intragenerational equity. Justice Preston has considered the fair distribution of benefits and burdens, and in so doing he elaborates on **5.10**

---

14 Distributive justice builds on the work of John Rawls, *A Theory of Justice* (Harvard University Press, 1971).

15 See, Raphael Heffron and Darren McCauley, 'The concept of energy justice across the disciplines' (2017) 105 *Energy Policy* 658.

16 Benjamin Sovacool, et al., 'Energy decisions reframed as justice and ethical concerns' (2016) 1(5) *Nature Energy* 1, 4. It goes on to say that the key elements are distribution of costs, distribution of benefits, and 'procedures, or ensuring that energy decision-making respects due process and representation'.

17 Ibid.

18 Ibid.

the equity component using the expression 'distributive justice'. Justice Preston explains it in the following way in relation to the environment:

> Distributive justice concerns the just distribution of environmental benefits and environmental burdens of economic activity. Distributive justice is promoted by giving substantive rights to members of the community of justice to share in environmental benefits (such as clean air, water and land, a quiet acoustic environment, scenic landscapes and a healthy ecology) and to prevent, mitigate, remediate or be compensated for environmental burdens (such as air, water, land and noise pollution and loss of amenity, scenic landscapes, biological diversity or ecological integrity). Issues of distributive justice not only apply within generations (intra-generational equity) but also extend across generations (inter-generational equity).[19]

5.11 Although it might seem challenging to do so, the case of *Gloucester Resources Limited v Minister for Planning* [2019] NSWLEC 7 (*Gloucester Resources*) demonstrates that it is possible to value benefits and burdens of this kind and then work out whether a suggested distribution is fair. Justice Preston heard an appeal by Gloucester Resources Limited (GRL), which had unsuccessfully applied to the Minister for Planning for development consent for the Rocky Hill Coal Project in the Gloucester Valley in New South Wales. The role of the court amounted to a merits review circumscribed by what the minister had to consider. Development applications for coal mines in New South Wales are covered by detailed legislation and policies. This meant that the court gave detailed consideration to the visual, amenity, and social impacts of the proposed mine, which Justice Preston found were incompatible with the existing, approved, and likely preferred uses in the vicinity.[20]

5.12 Section 4.15(1) of the *Environmental Planning and Assessment Act 1979* (NSW) requires the relevant authority, in determining a development application, to take the public interest into consideration, which in turn has been found to include the principles of ecologically sustainable development.[21] The discussion of public interest in *Gloucester Resources* involved whether the public benefits of the development outweigh its costs to the members of a community and whether they outweigh the public benefits of other land uses. New South Wales has guidelines for the economic assessment of mining and coal seam gas proposals. The court in *Gloucester Resources* considered a cost–benefit analysis and estimates of tax payable and employment benefits. Justice Preston found that the economic benefits of the project were uncertain and overstated.[22] He

19 *Gloucester Resources Limited v Minister for Planning* [2019] NSWLEC 7, 88 [398].

20 Ibid 22 [86].

21 Ibid 111 [498].

22 Ibid 142 [664].

also found that there was distributive inequity in the project.[23] Justice Preston found that the negative impacts outweighed the benefits of the project, and accordingly, that it was not in the public interest and that the development application should be approved.[24]

ACHIEVING THE FAIR DISTRIBUTION OF COSTS AND BENEFITS

Making fair decisions

The central problem that companies and regulators face in making resource allocation decisions in relation to different interest groups is to make decisions that are fair. A starting point is to assess the costs and benefits associated with a particular decision. That should not be difficult where a benefit is provided to a particular group, such as improved water quality or reduced flaring of gas, without detriment to any other group. It becomes more difficult where one group derives a benefit, but a cost is borne by another group. That was the basis of *Gloucester Resources*, where Justice Preston found that the current generation would enjoy economic benefits from the mine development, but future generations would experience environmental costs. The principle that companies can follow is to assess costs and benefits before making resource allocation decisions in favour of any group. If another group will suffer a significant cost or detriment, that will be a strong indication of lack of equity – an indication of unfairness. **5.13**

The growing importance of soft law

There is now plenty of support for the guiding principle of fairness, notwithstanding a lack of legally enforceable rules applying it. That support lies in what is described as 'soft law' – non-binding rules such as guidelines or treaties not yet in force reflective of an important principle that should be followed. This is exemplified by arguments of Decleris and others that sustainable development 'consists primarily of general principles and directives which will allow the shaping of statutes and behaviour'.[25] That analysis is supported by de Sadeleer's examination of the increasing importance of soft law as environmental law **5.14**

23 For future generations, this was because there were 'groups within the current generation receiving economic benefits but future generations experiencing environmental costs (Economic Assessment Guidelines, p19)', Ibid 143 [669].

24 Ibid [688].

25 Michael Decleris, *The Law of Sustainable Development: General Principles* Report produced for the European Commission (Luxembourg 2020) 5.

moves into the post-modern era.[26] An example of such a principle in sustainable development is not 'compromising the ability of future generations to meet their own needs'. The SDGs themselves contain more examples of general principles, such as SDG 5 and 6.

5.15 It is suggested, therefore, that the conceptual and legal difficulties in implementing intergenerational and intragenerational equity should not guide decisions. This is a situation where the law is gradually catching up with the correct moral position. As the next section illustrates, there is a gradual increase in the recognition of the rights of both future generations and the disadvantaged groups in the current generation as law moves into the post-modern era.[27] This is supported by the contributions that many companies are making to the SDGs and to the preservation of the environment. Increasingly, companies will have to consider the impact of their activities on the communities in which they operate, as well as future generations. They will have to ensure their planning processes consider not only how developing risks are managed, but also how to produce benefits for their shareholders, present and future and others they are legally required to benefit and also those on whom the success of the business depends, like the communities where they operate. The same ideas apply to regulators.

CREEPING INTERGENERATIONALISATION AND ENERGY JUSTICE IN INTERNATIONAL AND DOMESTIC LAWS

Lack of treaties requiring intergenerational equity

5.16 There is no treaty conferring legal rights on future generations or requiring intergenerational equity, notwithstanding some notable efforts.[28] Attempts to give a voice to future generations at the international level, for example through an ombudsperson or commissioner for future generations, have failed so far.[29] The international conferences and the declarations and other docu-

26 Nicolas de Sadeleer, *Environmental Principles From Political Slogans to Legal Rules* (Oxford University Press, 2002).

27 Ibid.

28 For example, Jacques Cousteau launched a Bill of Rights for Future Generations in the 1990s. A redrafted version was approved by the general conference of UNESCO on 12 November 1997, but it never became law internationally. See further the Cousteau Society https://www.cousteau.org/right-of-future-generations/#:~:text=Launched%20by%20Captain%20Cousteau%20in,human%20history%2C%20of%20culture%2C%20and.

29 See Jane Anstee-Wedderburn, 'Giving a Voice to Future Generations: Intergenerational Equity, Representatives of Generations to Come and the Challenge of Planetary Rights' (2014) 1(1) *Australian Journal of Environmental Law* 37, 54–60.

ments produced from them concerning the environment, including sustainable development and future generations, have generally remained as soft law. Nevertheless, Redgwell, writing in 1999, was able to identify a steady shift towards the recognition of the interests of future generations that she described as a 'creeping intergenerationalisation'.[30]

There are treaties referring to the interests of future generations, usually in the preamble, as background to the measures dealing with specific issues such as whaling, endangered species, etc.[31] However, a major source of recognition of future generations and also disadvantaged groups in the present generation has been the development of soft law relating to sustainable development and its focus on future generations as well as the present. At the United Nations Conference on Environment and Development (UNCED) in Rio de Janeiro in 1992, support for sustainable development crystallised in the Rio Declaration.[32] The initial principles from the Rio Declaration recognised in Principle 1 that human beings 'are entitled to a healthy and productive life in harmony with nature' and in Principle 3 that 'the right to development must be fulfilled so as to equitably meet developmental and environmental needs of present and future generations'.[33] That then led to the Millennium Goals and the SDGs. **5.17**

The International Court of Justice

There is currently no binding decision of the International Court of Justice setting out rules of intergenerational equity. It seems, therefore, that it has not yet reached the point of being a generally accepted international practice or principle of law accepted by civilised nations.[34] The court did not acknowledge it as international law in the *Case Concerning the Gabcikovo-Nagymaros* **5.18**

---

30 Catherine Redgwell, *Intergenerational Trusts and Environmental Protection* (Juris Publishing, 1999) 126.

31 For example, the preamble to the *International Convention for the Regulation of Whaling*, 161 UNTS 75 (1946) (*ICRW*) refers to 'the interest of the nations of the world in safeguarding for future generations the great natural resources represented by the whale stocks'.

32 'Rio Declaration on Environment and Development', *Report of the United Nations Conference on Environment and Development*, UN Doc A/CONF.151/6/Rev1 (Vol. I) (12 August 1992).

33 Ibid

34 One way for this to occur is if a relevant dispute comes before the court and international law has evolved to the point that intergenerational equity should be allowed for. This happened with environmental impact assessment in the *Case Concerning Pulp Mills on the River Uruguay (Argentina v Uruguay)* [2010] ICJ Rep 14. The court found 'that it may now be considered a requirement under general international law to undertake an environmental impact assessment where there is a risk that the proposed industrial activity may have a significant adverse impact in a transboundary context, in particular, on a shared resource' at p 83 [204].

Dam (Hungary/Slovakia).[35] This case is perhaps best known for the minority Separate Opinion of former Vice-President of the International Court of Justice, Christopher Weeramantry, who found the principle of sustainable development to be one of customary international law on the basis of its worldwide acceptance across a wide range of treaties, declarations, and documents.[36] In his review, Judge Weeramantry did not suggest any rules of intergenerational equity.

5.19 A primary concern of environmental law is conservation or preservation of the environment. There are a number of treaties which refer to preserving the environment, including threatened species and ecological systems. That can mean preserving it for the future or for current inhabitants of the planet.[37]

5.20 Brown Weiss was able to refer in 2019 to the significant increase in constitutional provisions in domestic law relating to future generations, but these can also have an impact on the present generation,[38] for example, a requirement for the government to protect the natural environment. That was illustrated by the *Minors Oposa* case.[39] This is regularly cited because the court found that the parents had the right to apply on behalf of their children.[40]

---

35 [1997] ICJ Rep 7, 88. Judge Weeramantry mentioned intergenerational equity earlier in *Legality of the Threat or Use of Nuclear Weapons, Advisory Opinion* [1996] ICJ Rep 226, 455 in which he remarked on the abundant juristic opinion concerning the rights of future generations. He was not alone amongst the judges on the International Court of Justice in considering it important. Judge Antonio Cancado Trindade reviewed its history and importance in *Whaling in the Antarctic (Australia v Japan: New Zealand Intervening)* [2014] ICJ Rep 262, 362–7 [41]–[47]. His concluding remarks in the case included the statement that 'the formation of international law in domains of public or common interest, such as that of conservation and sustainable use of living marine resources, is a much wider process than the formulation of its "formal sources", above all in seeking the legitimacy of norms to govern international life' (ibid 381 [89]).

36 Ibid 97 and 110.

37 See *ICRW* (n 31). There are many other treaties concerning the environment, ecosystems, and nature: for example, the *Convention on Long-range Transboundary Air Pollution* (1979) and the *United Nations Framework Convention on Climate Change* (1992).

38 Edith Brown Weiss, 'Intergenerational Equity in a Kaleidoscopic World' (2019) 49(1) *Environmental Policy and Law* 3, 3. She refers to the number of these provisions increasing from 12 to 55 between 1990 and 2016. In 1988, she was able to refer to 34; Brown Weiss IFFG 107.

39 *Oposa v Factoran* (1994) 33 ILM 173.

40 Section 16, Article II of the *1987 Constitution of the Philippines* requires the state to 'protect and advance the right of the people to a balanced and healthful ecology in accord with the rhythm and harmony of nature'. In the *Minors Oposa* case, minors represented by their parents used this provision to seek an order that the government in the Philippines discontinue existing and future timber licence agreements on the basis that deforestation was causing environmental damage.

There are provisions that give a right to a healthy environment.[41] Some states 5.21
have human rights legislation giving a right to a certain quality of life.[42] These provisions have been deployed to take action on climate change and there is a growing body of case law.[43]

While not currently recognised in international law as a human right,[44] 5.22
whether the right to the supply of electricity has the potential to be a human right is the subject of academic discussion.[45] SDG 7 provides, 'Ensure access to affordable, reliable, sustainable and modern energy for all'. Providing universal access to electricity is considered in some jurisdictions.[46] That is likely to become more common as electricity becomes more important as an energy source.

The *Well-being of Future Generations (Wales) Act 2015* (*WFGW*) has already 5.23
been discussed in Chapter 3 in relation to governance. It is an important development as it requires public bodies in Wales to not only act in accordance with the sustainable development principle, but also to set and publish objectives designed to maximise their contribution to specified well-being goals.[47] The sustainable development principle is defined in section 5(1) as requiring a public body to act 'in a manner which seeks to ensure that the needs of the present are met without compromising the ability of future generations to meet

---

41 So, Article 112 of the *Norwegian Constitution* provides that 'Every person has the right to an environment that is conducive to health and to a natural environment whose productivity and diversity are maintained. Natural resources shall be managed on the basis of comprehensive long-term considerations which will safeguard this right for future generations as well'. https://www.stortinget.no/globalassets/pdf/english/constitutionenglish.pdf.

42 See, *State of the Netherlands v Urgenda* [2019] ECLI:NL:GHDHA:2018:2591 (Supreme Court of the Netherlands) https://uitspraken.rechtspraak.nl/inziendocument?id=ECLI:NL:HR:2019:2006 ('*State of the Netherlands v Urgenda*'), which was based on obligations under the European Convention on Human Rights and *Waratah Coal Pty Ltd v Youth Verdict Ltd & Ors* (No 6) [2022] QLC 21.

43 See, *Foreningen Greenpeace Norden and others v The Government of Norway*, case number 16-1666741TVI-OTIR/06 (Norwegian Supreme Court). It can be compared with *State of the Netherlands v Urgenda* (n 42). See also, the Hague District Court Decision in *Vereniging Milieudefensie and Others v Royal Dutch Shell PLC* [2021] ECLI:NL: RBDHA:2021:5339, case number/09/571932/HA 19-379 (English version), currently subject to appeal, and *R (application of Finch on behalf of the Weald Action Group) v Surrey County Council and Others* [2024] UKSC 20.

44 Adrian J Bradbrook and Judith G Gardam, 'Placing the Access to Energy Services Within a Human Rights Framework' (2006) *Human Rights Quarterly* 389.

45 Lars Lofquist, 'Is there a universal human right to electricity' (2020) 24 *Journal of Human Rights* 711; Raphael Heffron and Louis De Fontenelle, 'Implementing energy justice through a new social contract' (2023) 41 *Journal of Energy and Natural Resources Law* 141.

46 For example, in the European Union. See, 'Access to and Use of Energy Services' *Your Europe* (webpage) https://europa.eu/youreurope/citizens/consumers/energy-supply/access-use-energy-services/index_en.htm, which says, 'In the EU you have the right to have your home connected to the local electricity network and be supplied with electricity.'

47 *Well-being of Future Generations (Wales) Act 2015*, s 3.

their own needs'. So here again, the broad formula of the Brundtland Report is used. The temporal aspect is emphasised, but not detailed by allocation or decision-making rules, in section 5(2)(a), which requires a public body to take account of 'the importance of balancing short term needs with the need to safeguard the ability to meet long term needs, especially where things done to meet short term needs may have detrimental long term effect'.

CONCLUSIONS, GUIDANCE, AND KEY PRINCIPLES

5.24 Some of the basic conclusions from this chapter are:

- Sustainable development 'consists primarily of general principles and directives which will allow the shaping of statutes and behaviour';[48] for example, not 'compromising the ability of future generations to meet their own needs'. Those general principles now have significant weight behind them, for example through the SDGs, notwithstanding a lack of binding legal rules.
- The main legal problems have been to accurately define the rights of future generations and disadvantaged groups in the present generation and then implement redress. Companies and regulators can use cost–benefit analysis to gauge whether a resource allocation decision (including a new mining or energy operation) is disadvantaging a group or causing it loss. If a group will suffer a significant cost or detriment without a matching benefit, that will be strong indication of lack of equity – an indication of unfairness.
- When it comes to intragenerational equity, there are many problems associated with giving poor people or people in remote areas access to energy. SDG 7 creates a goal to do that. While there is currently no human right to energy, we can anticipate a continuing focus on this area and the continuing growth of ideas of energy justice.
- A number of processes exist that require planning for the future, such as environmental impact assessments or the disclosure of risks such as climate change risk.

5.25 The following ideas follow from those conclusions:

- One lesson from climate change is that companies need to think about the future and ensure their planning processes consider not only how developing risks are managed, but also how to produce benefits for their stakeholders, including future stakeholders.

48 Decleris (n 25).

- Another is the growing body of court decisions (some are mentioned at n 42 and following) making it clear that the producers of hydrocarbons are responsible for the environmental damage caused by greenhouse gases.
- Organisations should have a rigorous mechanism for testing whether their operations will cause harm to any group, whether existing or in the future, and develop strategies to prevent that harm.

6

ENVIRONMENTAL APPROVALS IN MINING AND ENERGY

INTRODUCTION 6.01

REVIEW OF PROJECTS LIKELY TO HAVE A SIGNIFICANT ENVIRONMENTAL IMPACT 6.03

Two streams of environmental approvals 6.03

Federal approval in the USA for major federal actions significantly affecting the quality of the human environment 6.04

Federal review in Canada of designated projects 6.05

Review at the Saskatchewan province level of developments 6.08

Federal review in Australia of significant impacts on matters of national environmental significance 6.10

Review at the Western Australian state level of proposals likely to have a significant effect on the environment 6.14

Other offences 6.15

Environmental impact assessment, the public interest, and sustainability 6.16

MINING ENVIRONMENTAL APPROVALS 6.21

Introductory comments about Nevada, Saskatchewan, and Western Australia 6.21

Nevada mining 6.24

Saskatchewan mining 6.30

Western Australia mining 6.36

OIL AND GAS ENVIRONMENTAL APPROVALS 6.40

Introductory comments 6.40

Nevada oil and gas 6.42

Saskatchewan oil and gas 6.45

Western Australia oil and gas 6.50

RENEWABLE ENERGY ENVIRONMENTAL APPROVALS 6.54

Introductory comments 6.54

Renewable energy in Nevada 6.56

Renewable energy in Saskatchewan 6.59

Renewable energy in Western Australia 6.61

CONCLUSIONS, GUIDANCE, AND KEY PRINCIPLES 6.64

INTRODUCTION

6.01 This chapter will start with a brief outline of environmental protection, looking specifically at the USA, Canada, and Australia, before taking a more detailed look at environmental approvals for mining, oil and gas, and renewable energy in Nevada, Saskatchewan, and Western Australia. In all these jurisdictions, an environmental approval is required either before a project can proceed or before exploration, mining, or oil and gas operations can commence, or both. It is those environmental approvals that are the focus of this chapter. Questions to be examined in this chapter are:

- Do the environmental regulations contain sustainability tests? If the expression 'sustainability' is not used, how do the regulations approach matters that underpin sustainability, and what are they?
- Do the environmental regulations have a particular focus, such as minimising environmental risks, and what are the main tools used?
- Are the environmental regulations supported by other regulatory approvals and how are they coordinated?
- Are there any processes or approaches that are commonly used?

We can then look at the implications for companies and regulators for their own activities.

The other regulatory approvals mentioned in the penultimate bullet point in **6.02** 6.01 that are examined in this chapter will not include the non-environmental approvals of the mining or energy regulator. As mentioned in 3.33, mining regulations in many jurisdictions require the mining company to provide a mining or operations plan for approval before any ground disturbance can occur.[1] There are similar processes in oil and gas before development – development being the stage at which production facilities for a commercial discovery are designed and constructed. They are examined in Chapter 7. But, as the next paragraph explains, the mining and energy regulators also issue environmental approvals for projects.

REVIEW OF PROJECTS LIKELY TO HAVE A SIGNIFICANT ENVIRONMENTAL IMPACT

Two streams of environmental approvals

There are commonly two streams of environmental approvals: one dealing **6.03** with significant projects because of their potential impact on the environment; and the second at the level of the mining or energy regulator dealing specifically with proposed mining or energy projects. In countries with a federal structure, which include the USA, Canada, and Australia, jurisdiction over the environment may be divided or shared between federal and state/provincial government, meaning there is often a federal body responsible for general environmental protection, which deals with significant projects that have effects within federal jurisdiction. A state or province body may also review significant projects. A matter that has to be resolved in each case is whether those bodies duplicate their work or work together, and how they work with

1 There can be requirements for additional materials, such as mineralisation reports.

regulators with specific responsibilities. There is usually some level of communication between federal and state or province bodies, but the degree of formality varies. There are examples of red-tape reduction, for example, where the federal body agrees to accept the state or province's assessment as satisfying its requirements. The legislative structure varies between the USA, Canada, and Australia, but there are two common themes at the federal level that go to the second question being examined in this chapter. First, they focus on assessing reasonably significant potential environmental effects. Second, the main tool they use is environmental impact assessment.

Federal approval in the USA for major federal actions significantly affecting the quality of the human environment

6.04 In the USA, the body charged with national environmental protection is the Environmental Protection Agency (EPAUSA), operating under the *National Environmental Policy Act 1969 (US)* (*NEPA*).[2] The operation of *NEPA* depends on there being a proposal for federal legislation or a major federal action significantly affecting the quality of the human environment.[3] In that case, the agency concerned is required to provide an environmental document in the form of an environmental impact statement (EIS) or an environmental assessment (EA).[4] An EIS is required where the proposed action will have 'a reasonably foreseeable significant effect on the human environment',[5] and an EA where there is a finding of no significant effect.[6] A federal action is the trigger necessary for a mining or energy activity to require an EIS or EA. The review of a plan of operations for a mining or processing activity will act as a trigger. Section 102 of *NEPA* places obligations on the agency concerned in relation

2 National Environmental Policy Act 42 U.S.C. §4321 et seq. (1969). Section 101 of the *NEPA* has a national policy 'to use all practicable means and measures, including financial and technical assistance, in a manner calculated to foster and promote the general welfare, to create and maintain conditions under which man and nature can exist in productive harmony, and fulfill the social, economic, and other requirements of present and future generations of Americans.' 42 U.S.C. §4331(a).

3 *NEPA* section 102.

4 In that case, *NEPA* section 102 requires the responsible official to prepare a detailed statement on: (1) reasonably foreseeable environmental effects of the proposed agency action; (2) any reasonably foreseeable adverse effects that cannot be avoided; (3) alternatives to the proposed action; (4) the relationship between local short-term uses of man's environment and the maintenance and enhancement of long-term productivity; and (5) any irreversible and irretrievable commitments of resources that would be involved in the proposed action. 42 U.S.C. §4332(2)(C).

5 *NEPA* section 106(b)(1).

6 *NEPA* section 106(b)(2) says that 'such environmental assessment shall be a concise public document prepared by a Federal agency to set forth the basis of such agency's finding of no significant impact or determination that an environmental impact statement is necessary'.

to the rigour applied to the statement.[7] The considerations are purely about the environment and do not include social, economic, or broader public interest considerations. An EIS is required to be available for public comment.[8] EPAUSA monitors the steps in the process, and they are required to be filed on its register.[9] In his previous administration, US President Donald Trump restricted the activities of EPAUSA and it is widely anticipated that he will do the same again when he takes office at the start of 2025.

Federal review in Canada of designated projects

Environmental impact assessment in Canada, where it is referred to simply as impact assessment, is triggered differently – by a proposal for a designated project under the federal legislation, or a development under the Saskatchewan provincial legislation. The Canadian federal *Impact Assessment Act 2019 (C)* (*CIAA*) and its regulations establish the legislative basis for federal environmental impact assessment in Canada. Under this Act, a 'designated project' that may have adverse effects on an area within federal jurisdiction requires assessment. Projects are designated either by the regulations, or at the discretion of the responsible minister (*CIAA* section 9). The designated project list in the regulations includes a project to construct or operate a new mine with a daily ore production of the specified amount.[10] The Act also contains a purpose of fostering sustainability.[11] The *CIAA* replaced the former *Environmental Assessment Act 2012 (C)*. We should note here that the constitutionality of the *CIAA* was thrown into doubt by a reference decision of the Supreme Court of Canada in October 2023 on the basis that it overreached in relation to areas **6.05**

7 *NEPA* section 102(d) to 'ensure the professional integrity, including scientific integrity, of the discussion and analysis in an environmental document; and (e) make use of reliable data and resources in carrying out this Act'.

8 *NEPA* section 107(c).

9 See EPAUSA, *Environmental Impact Statement Filing Guidance* https://www.epa.gov/nepa/environmental-impact-statement-filing-guidance.

10 Designated projects are those involving a physical activity listed in the Regulations Designating Physical Activities (SOR/2012-147) https://laws-lois.justice.gc.ca/eng/regulations/SOR-2012-147/index.html. See para 16, which says that a metal mine must have an ore production capacity of 3000 t/day or more and a rare earth element or gold mine an ore production capacity of 600 t/day or more.

11 *CIAA* section 6(1)(a). Sustainability is defined in section 2 as 'sustainability means the ability to protect the environment, contribute to the social and economic well-being of the people of Canada and preserve their health in a manner that benefits present and future generations'.

of provincial authority.[12] The Canadian government amended the *CIAA* in 2024 to deal with those matters.[13]

6.06 Under the *CIAA*, a company or organisation, described in the legislation as 'a proponent', is prohibited from taking any step in relation to a designated project[14] unless the Impact Assessment Agency gives notice that no impact assessment is required, or the proponent complies with the conditions in the minister's decision statement issued under *CIAA* section 65.[15] The impact assessment will generally be conducted by the Impact Assessment Agency or a review panel, consisting of a group of independent and impartial experts appointed by the minister. The *CIAA* provides for meaningful public participation[16] and the consideration of indigenous knowledge.[17] There is provision in the legislation for cooperation with the government of a province or an agency of a province which also has powers, duties, or functions in relation to the assessment of environmental effects of the designated project (*CIAA* section 21), which may include substitution of the provincial process.[18]

6.07 In coming to a determination as to whether the designated project should proceed, and on what conditions, the minister or Governor in Council must consider a public interest test, which is set out in *CIAA* section 63. The test starts in paragraph (a) with consideration of 'the impacts that are likely to be

---

12 Supreme Court of Canada *Reference re Impact Assessment Act* [2023] SCC 23 https://decisions.scc-csc.ca/scc-csc/scc-csc/en/item/20102/index.do.

13 —Government of Canada, Amended Impact Assessment Act now in force, 21 June October 2024, Amended Impact Assessment Act now in force — https://www.canada.ca/en/impact-assessment-agency/news/media-room/amended-impact-assessment-act-now-in-force.html.

14 *CIAA* section 7(1) says that 'the proponent of a designated project must not do any act or thing in connection with the carrying out of the designated project, in whole or in part, if that act or thing causes a specified effect, such as a change to the environment on federal lands'.

15 *CIA* section 7(3). *CIAA* section 60(1)(a) says, 'after taking into account the report with respect to the impact assessment of a designated project that is submitted to the Minister under subsection 28(2) or at the end of the assessment under the process approved under section 31, the Minister must (a) determine whether the adverse effects within federal jurisdiction — and the adverse direct or incidental effects — that are indicated in the report are, in light of the factors referred to in section 63 and the extent to which those effects are significant, in the public interest.' The Minister must issue a decision statement under section 65 which sets out any conditions.

16 *CIAA* section 99; Government of Canada, Fact Sheet on *Public Participation in Impact Assessment*, which sets out principles for meaningful public participation https://www.canada.ca/en/impact-assessment-agency/services/policy-guidance/public-participation-impact-assessment-fact-sheet.html#; and the Guidance at https://www.canada.ca/en/impact-assessment-agency/services/policy-guidance/practitioners-guide-impact-assessment-act/guidance-public-particaption-impact.html.

17 *CIA* section 102(2) provides that 'subject to section 119, the report must set out how the Agency or committee, as the case may be, took into account and used any Indigenous knowledge provided with respect to the assessment'.

18 *CIA* section 31. For the *Environmental Management and Protection Act 2010 (S)*, see 6.31. Also, there is the facility to involve the Canada Energy Regulator or the Canadian Nuclear Safety Commission.

caused by carrying out the project on indigenous peoples of Canada and their constitutionally recognised rights (b) the effects of carrying out the project on Canada's ability to meet its environmental obligations and commitments in relation to climate change and (c) the extent to which the effects are likely to be caused by carrying out the project'.

Review at the Saskatchewan province level of developments

At the provincial level, Saskatchewan has the *Environmental Assessment Act 1980 (S)* (*EAASAS*) and the *Environmental Management and Protection Act 2010 (S)*.[19] Under *EAASAS* section 8, a development cannot proceed without ministerial approval. If an activity constitutes a development, then an environmental impact assessment will be required[20] and the proponent must prepare a statement for the minister concerning the development,[21] which the minister reviews. The statement and the minister's review are then published.[22] There are requirements for public consultation and consultation with First Nations peoples.[23] The *EAASAS* applies predominantly to non-federal land in Saskatchewan, but there are situations where federal and provincial regulations overlap. Saskatchewan provincial publications suggest that there is no formal arrangement for the province's processes to satisfy the *CIAA*.[24] **6.08**

---

19 For the legislation, see the Ministry of the Environment at https://www.saskatchewan.ca/environment #legislation.

20 Development is widely defined (*EAASAS* section 2) to include 'any project, operation or activity or any alteration or expansion of any project, operation or activity which is likely to: (i) have an effect on any unique, rare or endangered feature of the environment; (ii) substantially utilize any provincial resource and in so doing pre-empt the use, or potential use, of that resource for any other purpose; (iii) cause the emission of any pollutants or create by-products, residual or waste products which require handling and disposal in a manner that is not regulated by any other Act or regulation; (iv) cause widespread public concern because of potential environmental changes; (v) involve a new technology that is concerned with resource utilization and that may induce significant environmental change; or (vi) have a significant impact on the environment or necessitate a further development which is likely to have a significant impact on the environment.'

21 *EAASAS* section 9.

22 *EAASAS* section 11.

23 See, Government of Saskatchewan fact sheet on Public Participation https://www.saskatchewan.ca/business/environmental-protection-and-sustainability/environmental-assessment/how-the-public-can-participate.

24 The Government of Saskatchewan publication describing the Environmental Assessment Process has this to say: 'For projects that are subject to both a provincial and federal EA, the ministry will co-ordinate with our federal counterparts to ensure information is being shared. The ministry works with federal agencies to reduce regulatory duplication where possible while ensuring environmental impacts are minimized through a fulsome process'. https://www.saskatchewan.ca/business/environmental-protection-and-sustainability/environmental-assessment/environmental-assessment-process. And see *CIAA* section 21 and n 18 above.

6.09 Decisions of the minister under the *EAASAS* are not expressly focused on the public interest, but on compliance with the Act. So, if the minister is satisfied that the proponent has met all its requirements, he or she shall approve the development proceeding.[25] Those requirements include the conduct of the impact assessment. As one government publication puts it:

> The Minister must decide whether there will be adequate safeguards and protection to the environment as the development proceeds. The decision is based on safeguards provided through the design of the development, the proponent's measures to mitigate likely impacts, the constraints that may be placed on the development through subsequent regulatory requirements or the Minister's ability to constrain the project through conditions of approval.[26]

Federal review in Australia of significant impacts on matters of national environmental significance

6.10 The federal environmental legislation in Australia is the *Environmental Protection and Biodiversity Conservation Act 1999 (Cth)* (*EPBCA*), which contains a different approach again. That approach focuses on matters of national environmental significance (MNESs). MNESs are itemised in *EPBCA* Part 3 and include world heritage, wetlands of international importance, migratory species protected under international agreements, the Commonwealth marine environment, and the Great Barrier Reef Marine Park – generally areas subject to protection under international treaties to which Australia is a party. It is those international commitments and the national significance of the matters dealt with that provide the constitutional basis for the legislation. A person must not take an action which will or is likely to have a significant impact on an MNES, and it is an offence to do so.[27] It is an exception if the minister approves the action under Part 9.

6.11 The objects of the *EPBCA* set out in section 3 start in paragraph (a) with protecting the environment, especially MNESs, and then include in paragraph (b) 'to promote ecologically sustainable development through the conservation and ecologically sustainable use of natural resources'. The principles of ecologically sustainable development (ESD) are set out in *EPBCA* section 3A. They include the precautionary principle and intergenerational equity. Those principles have been picked up in a number of state statutes and are the subject

---

25 *EAASAS* section 15. Note also the extended definition of environment in *EAASAS* section 2.

26 The Government of Saskatchewan, High Level Overview of the Environmental Assessment Process, June 2014, at https://www.saskatchewan.ca/business/environmental-protection-and-sustainability/environmental-assessment/environmental-assessment-process 9.

27 For example, in relation to listed threatened species under *EPBCA* section 18.

of extensive case law, particularly in the Land and Environment Court of New South Wales.[28]

The principles of ESD are based on work done by the Hawke Labor government in the 1990s, which saw the development of a national policy for ESD.[29] The principles are: 6.12

(a) decision-making processes should effectively integrate both long-term and short-term economic, environmental, social and equitable considerations;
(b) if there are threats of serious or irreversible environmental damage, lack of full scientific certainty should not be used as a reason for postponing measures to prevent environmental degradation;
(c) the principle of inter-generational equity—that the present generation should ensure that the health, diversity and productivity of the environment is maintained or enhanced for the benefit of future generations;
(d) the conservation of biological diversity and ecological integrity should be a fundamental consideration in decision making;
(e) improved valuation, pricing and incentive mechanisms should be promoted.[30]

It is noteworthy that the principles are not prioritised.[31]

The approval processes under the *EPBCA* start with an application for referral. That is then assessed to determine whether the action requires assessment by the minister, described as a 'controlled action', because it poses a significant risk to an MNES. There are several possible means of assessment that include assessment on the referral information, a public environment report, and an environmental impact statement. If the action does not pose a significant risk, it is described as an 'uncontrolled action' and will not require further assessment. The minister has the power under *EPBCA* section 133 to approve or decline a controlled action. He or she must consider a range of matters including the assessment material, the principles of ESD mentioned above, and a number of special matters for individual MNESs, such as applicable international treaties. Given that the *EPBCA* is limited to MNESs, the state-based environmental legislation is important. 6.13

28 See *Walker v Minister for Planning* [2007] NSWLEC 741, reversed by *Minister for Planning v Walker* [2008] NSWCA 224.

29 For an overview, see https://documents.parliament.qld.gov.au/TableOffice/TabledPapers/2016/5516T2036.pdf.

30 *EPBCA* section 3A.

31 The Chief Judge of the Land and Environment Court in New South Wales, Justice Brian Preston, has written numerous papers extrajudicially on ESD as well as analysing it in his judgments and has argued that the principles work together and that there is an environmental bottom line. For a listing of his recent speeches and papers, see the Land and Environment Court website https://lec.nsw.gov.au/publications-and-resources/judicial-speeches-and-papers.html.

Review at the Western Australian state level of proposals likely to have a significant effect on the environment

6.14 The state environmental protection legislation in Western Australia is the *Environmental Protection Act 1986 (WA)* (*WAenvpAct1986*). The Act provides that a proposal likely, if implemented, to have a significant effect on the environment can be referred by any person to the Environment Protection Authority set up under the statute (EPAWA). The EPAWA must then decide whether to assess the proposal,[32] and, if it does, can require further steps be taken such as the conduct of an environmental review by the proponent, or a public enquiry.[33] It then prepares an assessment report for the minister.[34] The EPAWA has a consultation hub which stresses the importance of public consultation and on which all documents available for public comment are published.[35] The minister's decision appears to be similar to that of the minister in Saskatchewan outlined at 6.09 in that he or she issues a statement of decision under *WAenvpAct1986* section 45, which is based on the matters set out in section 44,[36] after consulting with other interested ministers and relevant decision-making bodies.

Other offences

6.15 In addition to the assessment mechanisms, there are offences for polluting the environment. Examples in the USA include offences under the *Clean Water Act*.[37] In Canada, the *Environmental Protection Act 1999 (C)* regulates the management and control of toxic substances and hazardous waste. The *Environmental Enforcement Act* enforces most Canadian federal environmental legislation, including the *Environmental Protection Act*. In Australia, the *EPBCA* contains various offences in relation to MNESs but does not directly mention pollution. Examples of pollution offences are to be found in state legislation, for example, *WAenvpAct1986* section 49(3), which has an offence of causing pollution. Pollution is defined in section 3A to mean 'direct or indirect alteration of the environment (a) to its detriment or degradation; or (b)

---

32 *WAenvAct1986* section 38G.

33 Ibid section 40 (2).

34 Ibid section 44(1). Section 44(2) says that the assessment report must set out '(a) what the Authority considers to be the key environmental factors identified in the course of the assessment; and (b) the Authority's recommendations as to whether or not the proposal may be implemented and, if it recommends that implementation be allowed, as to the conditions and procedures, if any, to which implementation should be subject'.

35 EPAWA consultation hub at https://consultation.epa.wa.gov.au.

36 See n 29.

37 *Clean Water Act 33 U.S.C. §§ 131.*

to the detriment of an environmental value; or (c) of a prescribed kind, that involves an emission'.[38] There are also numerous other statutes that protect specific animals, habitats, ecosystems, and processes and which require specific approvals.[39]

Environmental impact assessment, the public interest, and sustainability

6.16 The USA was the first country to adopt environmental impact assessment. Many other countries followed, including Canada and Australia in 1973 and 1974. The European Union followed in 1985. Environmental impact assessment processes have generally been aimed at 'moving away from correcting environmental problems *ex post facto*, towards preventing them from occurring *ab initio* or, at least, assuring that they are contained at tolerable levels'.[40] The purpose of the assessment is to ensure that decision-makers consider the environmental impacts when deciding whether or not to proceed with a project. It is one of the primary initiatives taken by government to reconcile economic development with environmental preservation.[41] It is also possible to apply the process to a plan or programme when it is generally called strategic environmental assessment (SEA). Two things are noticeable, however. The first is the limited use of cost–benefit analysis to assess the total long-term costs of a project and the extent to which they result in intergenerational inequity because a future generation will bear the costs but not derive benefits.[42] The second is that environmental impact assessment is focused on the impact of a specified project, but it is not always clear that the cumulative effects of projects or mining or energy activity must be considered. The overall impact of greenhouse gas emissions on the climate is an example where courts are beginning to require cumulative effects to be considered.[43]

---

38 The equivalent in Saskatchewan is the *Environmental Management and Protection Act 2010 (S)* section 8.

39 For example, see 6.18, 6.24, and 6.28.

40 *Labrador Inuit Association v Newfoundland (Minister of Environment and Labour)*, 1997 CanLII 14612 (NL CA) [9]. Also discussed at 5.07.

41 Ibid [2] to [8]. In discussing the Canadian and Newfoundland environmental assessment legislation of the time, the court said, 'If the rights of future generations to the protection of the present integrity of the natural world are to be taken seriously, and not to be regarded as mere empty rhetoric, care must be taken in the interpretation and application of the legislation. Environmental laws must be construed against their commitment to future generations and against a recognition that, in addressing environmental issues, we often have imperfect knowledge as to the potential impact of activities on the environment. One must also be alert to the fact that governments themselves, even strongly pro-environment ones, are subject to many countervailing social and economic forces, sometimes legitimate and sometimes not. Their agendas are often influenced by non-environmental considerations.'

42 For an example where the regulations in New South Wales require cost–benefit analysis for a development, see *Gloucester Resources Limited v Minister for Planning* [2019] NSWLEC 7.

43 See *R (on the application of Finch on behalf of the Weald Action Group) v Surrey County Council and others* [2024] UKSC 20 and *Waratah Coal Pty Ltd v Youth Verdict Ltd & Ors (No 6)* [2022] QLC 21.

6.17 There is a contrast in the environmental regulations examined so far between those (such as the Saskatchewan *EAASAS*) that are focused only on the environmental impact of a project and those that take broader public interest considerations into account, such as social and economic issues. Most of the legislation referred to falls into the first group. In each case, a regulator or minister has to make decisions concerning the assessment, which can also include public interest questions in jurisdictions requiring a consideration of the public interest. In most jurisdictions, there is a significant amount of case law, often based on judicial review, considering whether decision-making powers have been properly exercised. It is outside the scope of this book to go into those decisions. They are dealt with in the leading texts on environmental law. The point here is merely to indicate the broad nature of the decision being made by the minister.

6.18 The Canadian *CIAA* is the only statute mentioned in this section that has a purpose of fostering sustainability. Sustainability is defined as mentioned at 6.05, but there are no sustainability-based criteria for assessments.[44] The published guidance about its implementation was updated in 2021.[45] The answer to the first question posed at 6.01 is that the CIAA does not contain sustainability tests, although it has a purpose of fostering sustainability. The *EPBCA* falls into the second group to some extent because of the width of the principles of ESD. But the principles of ESD are not prioritised. The first principle, 'the integration principle', means that there is a balancing act between environmental, social, and economic considerations.

6.19 The overall conclusion is that neither the *CIAA* nor the *EPBCA* puts the long-term preservation of the environment or the quality of human life above other considerations. In his most recent review of the *EPBCA* in 2020, Graeme Samuel highlighted the need for clearer outcomes through legally enforceable national environmental standards; otherwise, the state of Australia's environment would continue to decline.[46]

---

44 On this, see Robert B. Gibson, 'An initial evaluation of Canada's new sustainability-based *Impact Assessment Act*,' (2020) 33(1) *Journal of Environmental Law and Policy* 1, 10.

45 Ibid. Commenting on the 2019 interim guidance, since updated in Government of Canada, *Guidance: Considering the extent to which a project contributes to sustainability*, 6 December 2021 https://www.canada.ca/en/impact-assessment-agency/services/policy-guidance/practitioners-guide-impact-assessment-act/guidance-considering-extent-project-contributes-sustainability.html.

46 Graeme Samuel, Independent Review of the EPBC Act – Final Report (Commonwealth of Australia, October 2020) https://www.dcceew.gov.au/sites/default/files/documents/epbc-act-review-final-report-october-2020.pdf ii.

There are some processes that all the regulations share, such as the publication of assessments and reports. Two processes of growing importance, both mentioned in the mining, oil and gas, and renewable energy approvals below, are public consultation and the involvement of indigenous people and their knowledge. Interviews conducted for this book suggested that those processes in Australia were becoming increasingly time-consuming and expensive because of 'consultation fatigue' in possible stakeholders, the limited number of those stakeholders and of indigenous people with relevant knowledge, the agendas of those prepared to be consulted, which are often against any development at all, and the fact that mining companies have to pay people to be consulted. 6.20

MINING ENVIRONMENTAL APPROVALS

Introductory comments about Nevada, Saskatchewan, and Western Australia

Highlighting some of the main features of these jurisdictions helps in understanding the detail of the environmental approvals for mining that we look at next. Those features start with the extent of federal ownership. Much of the land open for mining in Nevada is owned or controlled by the federal government and, therefore, rights to mine are subject to federal control. That is perhaps counterintuitive, as in many places in the USA mineral rights are owned by the private owner of the surface of the land. In both Western Australia and Saskatchewan, the Crown reserved ownership of minerals to itself, but not immediately. So, there are limited examples of private ownership of minerals in Western Australia, mainly relating to the grant of title to land in the southwest of the state by the Crown in the 19th century before it reserved ownership of minerals. 6.21

In Canada, there is some private ownership of minerals,[47] but otherwise, it rests with the Crown in right of the provinces.[48] Saskatchewan became a province in 1905 and began to follow the practice in other provinces of reserving or excepting minerals from Crown grants of title to land. Prior to 1905, that practice was not necessarily followed by the relevant regulators, such as those under the Dominion of Canada – for example, in relation to the purchase of homestead properties from the Dominion prior to 1887. Saskatchewan's control of its mineral resources was passed over to it from the federal government 6.22

47 Railway companies acquired significant amounts of land privately. See *Borys v Canadian Pacific Railway Co* [1953] D.L.R. 65.

48 *Constitution Act 1867 (U.K.)* s 109 and *Constitution Act 1982 (U.K.)* ss 50, 51, 92A, being Schedule B to the *Canada Act 1982 (U.K.)* c 11.

in 1930.[49] The rights of First Nations peoples have to be borne in mind as they can own mineral rights under the special arrangements applicable to them.[50] It is difficult to come up with a precise assessment of the extent of ownership other than by the province of Saskatchewan, but it seems to be around 22%.[51] The private owners of minerals in Saskatchewan grant the rights to mine over them. But the grant of rights to mine in Western Australia and Saskatchewan is predominantly under the control of the state. The federal government in Canada and Australia can interfere on limited matters of national interest, relevantly including some environmental ones. The same is true in Nevada, but the emphasis is slightly different because the majority of the land is under federal control, so the question is rather the extent to which the federal government gives powers to the state of Nevada. In each jurisdiction, there are special rights given to indigenous peoples, which are the subject of special legislation or treaties. Their rights are generally not covered in this chapter because of their specialised nature. Australia was late in recognising the rights of indigenous peoples, and they are subject to what is called 'native title', which has its own regulatory regime.[52]

6.23 Western Australia has a wide variety of minerals, including gold, iron ore, lithium, and rare earths. The mining legislation does not distinguish between them by granting rights specific to any particular kind of mineral or form of mining. There is only one form of exploration permit and one form of mining lease. The idea of separate authorisation for exploration and mining is common to all three jurisdictions. But there are some differences in terminology, particularly in guidance provided by the regulators. In the USA, the expression 'locatable minerals' is used to describe minerals such as gold that are located and can be made subject to a claim giving a right to mine. It is used in the *Mining Law of 1872 (US)* in which the USA gave rights to mine those minerals on public lands.[53] In Nevada and Saskatchewan, placer mining is referred to. That is mining of heavily eroded minerals like gold by separating them from

---

49 Section 1 of the *Saskatchewan Natural Resources Act (C), RSC 1930, c 41* says that minerals (precious and base) belong to the province. They had previously been owned by the government of Canada pursuant to the *Saskatchewan Act 1905 (U.K.)* section 21.

50 For a comprehensive review, see P. Dawn Mills, 'A systematic review of the *Indian Mining Regulations* in comparison to Saskatchewan mining law where the First Nations holds mineral title' (2018) 56 *Alberta Law Review* 231.

51 Those non-province owners include private individuals, corporations, First Nations Peoples, and the Canadian federal government: Stefania A. Fortugno, *When the Oilpatch comes to your backyard: a citizen's guide to protecting your rights* (Saskatchewan Environmental Society, 2004) http://www.saskoil.org/landowners 3.

52 Under the *Native Title Act 1993 (Cth).*

53 *30 USC §29 the Mining Law of 1872 (US)* para 22. It is defined in 43 CFR Part 3830 Subpart C.

sand or gravel, often using water.[54] It contrasts with mining a lode consisting of minerals embedded in fissures or as separate veins in rock – hence requiring hardrock mining.[55] Gold is mined in all three jurisdictions, with gold production being significant in Nevada and Western Australia. Saskatchewan has significant amounts of uranium and potash. Potash is mined either by conventional underground mining or by solution mining, which involves injecting water underground and then processing the resulting brine.

Nevada mining

There is limited oil and gas activity in Nevada, but extensive mining activity, much of it taking place on federal land, of which roughly 85% is owned or controlled by the federal government through the federal Bureau of Land Management (BLM), the Forestry Service, the Department of Energy, or the Department of Defense.[56] Much of the land controlled by the BLM and the Forestry Service is open for prospecting and claims. Minerals that are 'locatable', such as gold, silver, and copper, can be disposed of by the BLM pursuant to the *Mining Law of 1872 (US)*,[57] and the process for asserting those rights involves making a mining claim, recording it, and locating a discovery.[58] The BLM regulations require that a notice be submitted to the appropriate field office for exploration activities in which five acres or less are proposed for disturbance.[59] **6.24**

A plan of operations is needed for all mining and processing activities, plus all activities exceeding five acres of proposed disturbance or bulk sampling involving the removal of 1,000 or more tons of presumed ore.[60] But in addition, state permits are required, which are administered in Nevada by the Bureau of Mining Regulation and Reclamation (BMRR) within the Division **6.25**

54 The word 'placer' is thought to be of Catalan and Spanish origin, meaning a shoal or sandbar.

55 Both are referred to in the USA claim regulations 43 CFR Part 3832.

56 K.G. Papke, D.A. Ross et al., *Mining claim procedures for Nevada prospectors and miners* (The University of Nevada, Reno, 2019, sixth ed.), Nevada Bureau of Mines and Geology Special Publication 6, 9. On a website, the Bureau of Land Management says that '67% of Nevada – 48 million acres belong to the American people' BLM Nevada webpage https://www.blm.gov/nevada.

57 *30 USC §29 the Mining Law of 1872 (US)* para 22 says that 'all valuable mineral deposits in lands belonging to the United States, both surveyed and unsurveyed, shall be free and open to exploration and purchase, and the lands in which they are found to occupation and purchase, by citizens of the United States'.

58 There are regulations for claims set out in 43 Code of Federal Regulations 3833.

59 For BLM offices, see BLM Nevada webpage (n 56). For the requirements for claims, see 43 CFR Part 3832.

60 See n 54, 11.

of Environmental Protection (NDEP) in the Department of Conservation and Natural Resources (NDCNR).[61]

6.26 As one commentator, Jim Butler, explains:

> BLM's review of the plan of operations requires compliance with the National Environmental Policy Act; this usually means the preparation of an Environmental Assessment or Environmental Impact Statement to be circulated for public comment. The plan of operations also becomes the means for demonstrating compliance with other federal laws, such as the Endangered Species Act and the National Historic Preservation Act. The plan of operations is typically a large compilation of site-specific plans for mining; management of waste rock and tailings; control of storm water and erosion; monitoring of air and water; and reclamation. BLM and NDEP coordinate their review of mine and reclamation plans, along with reviewing and accepting financial assurances, also required by the BLM. Mining on BLM land cannot begin until the operator has obtained BLM approval along with the necessary permits from the state of Nevada or other agencies.[62]

6.27 The BLM has to comply with NEPA at the plan of operations stage, so that will require an EA or EIS. As discussed above, NEPA does not contain any references to sustainability, nor do the regulations governing the plan of operations. But the plan of operations is used to demonstrate compliance with other federal laws governing matters like endangered species. Also, aspects of the plan will cover environmental areas such as tailings, water, and reclamation. So, we can answer the question: as the expression 'sustainability' is not used, how do the regulations approach matters that underpin sustainability, and what are they? The answer lies in the site-specific plans in the plan of operations that cover those matters like tailings, water, and reclamation. There are a number of aspects of those matters that underpin sustainability – for example, reducing water usage, appropriate treatment of wastewater, good tailings management, and so on. To support that idea, we can also refer to the sustainability performance indicators used by companies in their sustainability reports, which cover these areas – for example, complying with applicable tailings management standards or protocols.[63] What those reports also show is that there are a number of standards and protocols, the use of which varies between countries. It is a reasonable assumption that in most cases it will be

61 The website is ndep.nv.gov.

62 Jim Butler, 'Environmental Regulation of Nevada's Mining Industry' (April 2013) *Nevada Lawyer*, https://www.nvbar.org/wp-content/uploads/NevLawyer_April_2013_Environmental_Regulation.pdf 8.

63 For example, Barrick uses the Mining Association of Canada's Towards Sustainable Mining Tailings Management Protocol. See 8.18.

up to the mining company to demonstrate that it is approaching a task, say tailings management, to an appropriate level of risk management.

The third question posed in 6.01 was whether the environmental regulations are supported by other regulatory approvals and how are they coordinated? Here, we find that EPAUSA also sets standards on drinking water and air quality under the authority of the *Clean Air Act (US)*,[64] the *Clean Water Act*, and the *Safe Drinking Water Act (US)*.[65] In most cases, EPAUSA allows states to develop and implement the regulations necessary to meet federal standards. In a few areas, EPAUSA's regulatory role is more direct. For example, EPAUSA sets rules on things like emissions.[66] As part of its permitting processes, EPAUSA can require an EIS. EPAUSA has regional offices, and EPAUSA's Pacific Southwest (Region 9) office implements and enforces federal environmental laws in Arizona, California, Hawaii, Nevada, the Pacific Islands, and 148 tribal nations.[67] Areas used in the past for nuclear testing are subject to special arrangements between the US federal Department of Energy and the State of Nevada acting through the Nevada Division of Environmental Protection's Bureau of Federal Facilities (BFF).[68] 6.28

Also at the Nevada state level, BMRR rules cover various aspects of mining operations.[69] The BMRR has published guidance on matters like the preparation of operating plans for mining facilities.[70] That guidance requires detailed plans covering the circuits, monitoring, and closure, but standards are not referred to.[71] Water Pollution Control Permits (WPCPs) are issued to an operator prior to the construction of any mining, milling, or other beneficiation process activity.[72] There is a published list of required approvals.[73] Those 6.29

64 *Clean Air Act 1970 (US)* 42 U.S.C. §7401 et seq. (1970).

65 *Clean Water Act 1972 (US)* 33 U.S.C. §1251 et seq. (1972).

66 U.S. Environmental Protection Agency. https://www.epa.gov/regulatory-information-sector/oil-and-gas-extraction-sector-naics-211.

67 EPA South West https://www.epa.gov/aboutepa/epa-region-9-pacific-southwest.

68 Nevada Division of Environmental Protection's (NDEP) Bureau of Federal Facilities (BFF) webpage https://ndep.nv.gov/land/department-of-energy-oversight.

69 Bureau of Land Management – Surface Management of Locatable Minerals https://www.blm.gov/programs/energy-and-minerals/mining-and-minerals/locatable-materials/surface-management and Bureau of Land Management – Oil and Gas: Regulations, Onshore Orders and Notices to Lessees https://www.blm.gov/programs/energy-and-minerals/oil-and-gas/operations-and-production/regs-notices-to-lessees.

70 Nevada Bureau of Mining Regulation and Reclamation, *Guidance Note on Preparation of Operating Plans for Mining Facilities* https://ndep.nv.gov/uploads/land-mining-regs-guidance-docs/20220113_Guidnce_PrepOperPlans_MiningFacilities_ADA.pdf.

71 Ibid.

72 See Regulation Branch webpage https://ndep.nv.gov/land/mining/regulation.

73 Nevada Bureau of Mines and Geology Special Publication L-6, *State and Federal Permits required in Nevada before Mining or Milling can begin* (updated February 2024) https://minerals.nv.gov/uploadedFiles

approvals involve different regulators, chiefly bureaus within the NDEP but also others like the Department of Wildlife and federal regulators, including the BLM.

Saskatchewan mining

6.30 As mentioned in 6.05, the *CIAA* establishes the legislative basis for federal environmental assessment in most regions of Canada. But importantly, at the provincial level under *EAASAS* section 8, a development cannot proceed without ministerial approval. If there appears to be development or there is some uncertainty about it, Saskatchewan's Ministry of Environment will screen the proposed project to determine whether an environmental impact assessment is required.[74] There are several guidance documents, including guidance on the technical proposal that must be submitted at the screening stage and will form the basis of the initial screening review.[75] If an environmental impact assessment is required, the proponent prepares draft terms of reference setting out the studies to be undertaken, which are reviewed by the ministry. The proponent also prepares a draft EIS. Copies of these documents for developments and ministerial approvals are published. A number of these cover mining developments.[76]

6.31 The *Environmental Management and Protection Act 2010 (S)* also gives the relevant provincial minister in Saskatchewan specified responsibilities in relation to the state of the environment and sets out offences, including discharge into the environment without authorisation of substances that may cause an adverse effect.[77] The *Mineral Industry Environmental Protection Regulations 1996 (S)* set out requirements for the conduct of mineral exploration commencing from regulation 23, with regulation 24 requiring a notice to the minister before drilling, trenching, or hydraulic removal of overburden can commence.[78] But

/mineralsnvgov/content/Programs/Mining/SPL6_StAndFedPermitsRequired_202402.pdf.

74 See the Guidelines for Environmental Assessment webpage https://www.saskatchewan.ca/business/environmental-protection-and-sustainability/environmental-assessment/does-my-project-need-an-environmental-assessment.

75 See the webpage at n 26. The Technical Proposal Guidelines can also be found at https://pubsaskdev.blob.core.windows.net/pubsask-prod/137589/Technical-Proposal-Guidelines%252B25Oct22.pdf.

76 For example, the EIS for the McIlvenna Bay Project https://publications.saskatchewan.ca/#/products/121166.

77 *Environmental Management and Protection Act 2010 (S)* section 8. There is also an Environmental Management Code that sets out standards and requirements https://publications.saskatchewan.ca/#/categories/69.

78 For the guidelines and other relevant material, see Saskatchewan Mining Permits https://www.saskatchewan.ca/business/agriculture-natural-resources-and-industry/mineral-exploration-and-mining/mining-permits.

because the definition of 'pollution control facility' in regulation 2 includes 'any equipment used in exploration', approvals are also required for the construction or installation of equipment and other processes in relation to exploration.

Therefore at the provincial level under the *EAASAS*, there is the potential for the development of a mine to have an environmental impact assessment. The fact sheet describing the process says: 6.32

> The process is designed to systematically evaluate the ecological, socio-economic and cultural aspects of a development within a single framework, so that the real costs and trade-offs of a proposed project can be fully understood.[79]

The definition of 'environment' in *EAASAS* section 2 includes 'the social, economic and cultural conditions that influence the life of man or a community' insofar as they are related to the matters previously listed like land, air, water, and plants. As mentioned at 6.09, the main focus of the legislation is the environment and, in particular, ensuring that an impact assessment process is conducted. Unlike the federal *CIAA*, the *EAASAS* does not refer to sustainability.

Mining in Saskatchewan is regulated by the *Energy and Mines Act (S)*,[80] *Crown Minerals Act (S)* (*CMASAS*),[81] *Mineral Resources Act 1985 (S)*,[82] *Mineral Taxation Act 1983 (S)*,[83] and their regulations. The *Energy and Mines Act* creates the ministry, minister, and staff that manage Crown minerals. *CMASAS* section 4 authorises the minister to issue Crown dispositions, which are rights granted by the Crown to explore for minerals and obtain an interest in Crown minerals. Permits giving a right to explore were regulated under the *Mineral Disposition Regulations 1986*, which have been replaced by the *Mineral Tenure Registry Regulations 2012* (*MTRAC*). Mineral dispositions are kept on an electronic registry, the Mineral Administration Registry Saskatchewan (MARS). Under *MTRAC* regulations 32 and 35, following an application for lands which the minister has designated as available, the minister can grant a permit giving the holder the exclusive right to explore Crown minerals that are the subject of the regulations. Under *MTRAC* regulation 38, the holder of a permit in good standing can convert it to a claim, which under regulation 6.33

79 Saskatchewan Environmental Assessment Fact Sheet https://www.saskatchewan.ca/business/environmental-protection-and-sustainability/environmental-assessment/environmental-assessment-process
80 Sections 1982–83, c E-9.10001. See also the Mineral Exploration Incentive Regulations, RRS c E-9.10001, Reg 1.
81 Sections 1984–86, c C-50.2. There are also other regulations such as the Coal Disposition Regulations, RRS c C-50.2, Reg 3.
82 Sections 1984–86, c M-16.1. See also the Mineral Exploration Tax Credit Regulations, RRS c M-16.1.
83 Sections 1983–84, c M-17.1 and various regulations covering sodium chloride, potash, and coal.

40 grants the holder the exclusive right to explore and convert the claim to a lease. The maximum size of a claim is 6,000 hectares.[84] In order to mine, a lease must be obtained under Part VII of the *MTRAC*. These have a term of 10 years and can be renewed.[85]

6.34 In order to conduct mineral exploration activities on Crown land within Saskatchewan, surface disturbance permits are required from the Ministry of Environment before any work can be started.[86] An application must be submitted to a Ministry of Environment Ecological Protection Specialist.[87] The permits include Forest Product, Aquatic Habitat Protection, Work Authorisation, and/or Temporary Work Camp permits. There are a number of best management practices (BMPs) that are referred to.[88] Extensive information is required under the Saskatchewan Mineral Exploration and Government Advisory Committee, *Mineral Exploration Guidelines for Saskatchewan* (2016) (*Mineral Exploration Guidelines (S)*).[89] A decommissioning and reclamation plan will have to be developed starting at the environmental impact assessment stage.[90] In addition, an underground mine has to submit a mine plan.[91] Saskatchewan also has an Environmental Code which contains approved standards, none of which appear to be specific to mining.[92]

6.35 Saskatchewan is different from Nevada in that the plan of operations does not play a central role. Instead, the role of the initial environmental impact assessment seems critical as it will require the proponent to illustrate how it is going to deal with environmental risks. Then, as the development proceeds, permits will be required at the provincial level to disturb the surface of the land, remove overburden, and construct plant. These are the other regulatory approvals that support the initial approval of the development following the

---

84 *MTRAC* regulation 41(2)(b).

85 *MTRAC* regulations 51 and 52.

86 Saskatchewan Mineral Exploration and Government Advisory Committee, Mineral Exploration Guidelines for Saskatchewan (2016) https://www.saskatchewan.ca/business/agriculture-natural-resources-and-industry/mineral-exploration-and-mining/mining-permits (Mineral Exploration Guidelines (S)) 13.

87 Ibid.

88 Ibid 20 – for example, BMP 001 Grassroots Exploration.

89 See n 82.

90 Northern Mine Decommissioning and Reclamation Guidelines (Government of Saskatchewan, 2008) https://library.usask.ca/gp/sk/en/epb381nov2008.pdf.

91 Government of Saskatchewan https://www.saskatchewan.ca/business/agriculture-natural-resources-and-industry/mineral-exploration-and-mining/mineral-tenure/submit-a-yearly-mine-plan#:~:text=Regulations%20require%20that%20a%20yearly,railways%2C%20power%20lines%2C%20etc.

92 Saskatchewan Environmental Code https://www.saskatchewan.ca/business/environmental-protection-and-sustainability/environmental-code.

conduct of the impact assessment. At the exploration stage, the Ministry of Environment Ecological Protection Specialist is the main focus of the review of the permits.

Western Australia mining

The Western Australian state environmental legislation is the *WAenvpAct1986* supplemented by regulations.[93] That creates the Environmental Protection Authority (EPAWA). *WAenvAct1986* section 4A says that the object of the Act is to protect the environment of the state, having regard to the principles set out in the section. Those principles reflect, with some variations, the principles of ecologically sustainable development that are set out in *EPBCA* section 3A.[94] Western Australia has a *Mining Act 1972 (WA)* (*MAWA*), which regulates mining for all minerals with exclusions for substances the recovery of which is governed by the petroleum legislation, meaning oil and gas, soil, and some forms of sand, gravel, and similar substances.[95] Land in Western Australia is divided between Crown land and private land. In principle, both are open for mining, although there are more restrictions on mining on private land. For example, mining on land on which there is a substantial improvement is prohibited unless the owner consents.[96] But in order to conduct exploration and mining activities, a miner will have to be granted the appropriate mining tenement under the *MAWA* – for exploration an exploration licence and for mining a mining lease.[97] **6.36**

Importantly, the *MAWA* says that it shall be read and construed subject to the *WAenvpAct1986* to the extent that if a provision of the *MAWA* is inconsistent with a provision of the *WAenvpAct1986*, the *MAWA* provision 'shall, to the extent of the inconsistency, be deemed to be inoperative'.[98] Under *WAenvpAct1986* section 38(1), any person may refer a significant proposal to the the EPAWA. A 'significant proposal' means a proposal likely, if implemented, to have a significant effect on the environment and includes a significant amendment of an approved proposal. As outlined at 6.07, if a referral is made and the EPAWA decides to assess it, then further steps will follow, such **6.37**

93 *Environmental Protection Regulations 1987 (WA)* (*WAenvpRegs*).

94 See 6.06.

95 *MAWA* section 8 defines 'minerals' as 'naturally occurring substances obtained or obtainable from any land by mining operations carried out on or under the surface of the land'.

96 *MAWA* section 27.

97 *MAWA* section 66 authorises the holder of an exploration licence to conduct exploration. Section 85 authorises the holder of a mining lease to mine and extract minerals.

98 *MAWA* section 6(1).

as environmental review, which culminates in a report to the minister from the EPAWA. Guidance from the EPAWA suggests that mining exploration on a small scale or the construction of a small mine is unlikely to be regarded as significant.

6.38 The *MAWA* has no express environmental or sustainability objective. The Environmental Objectives Policy for Mining of March 2020 says:

> Resource industry activities are designed, operated, closed, decommissioned and rehabilitated in an ecologically sustainable manner, consistent with agreed environmental outcomes and post-mining land-uses without unacceptable liability to the State.

A mining proposal is required under *MAWA* section 74(1). The Statutory Mining Proposal Guidance published by the Department of Energy, Mines, Industry Regulation and Safety (DMIRSWA) contains specific requirements for stakeholder engagements (internal and external).[99] There is a focus on risk assessment and identification, environmental outcomes, and an obligation to have an environmental management system.[100] A permit is required under Part V of *WAenvpAct1986* to clear native vegetation. The process under Part V is to deal with clearing having very low environmental impact. If the impact was significant, then the procedure in Part IV would apply.[101] A permit is also required pursuant to *WAenvpAct1986* for mine dewatering, if the quantity is sufficient, and for some works.[102]

6.39 The position with mining in Western Australia is that matters that underpin sustainability are secured through the mining proposal, the specified outcomes, and the environmental management system. The DMIRSWA is the department responsible. Specific permits are required from other departments for some matters like mine dewatering and clearing native vegetation, but the DMIRSWA provides the majority of the approvals.

---

99 Government of Western Australia, Department of Energy, Mines, Industry Regulation and Safety, *The Statutory Mining Proposal Guidance* is available at https://www.wa.gov.au/organisation/department-of-energy-mines-industry-regulation-and-safety/mining-proposal. See section 7 for stakeholder engagements.

100 Ibid sections 9 and 11.

101 Government of Western Australia, Department of Water and Environmental Regulation, *Guideline Native Vegetation Clearance Referrals (October 2021)* https://www.wa.gov.au/system/files/2021-10/Guideline_Native_vegetation_clearing_referrals.pdf.

102 See Government of Western Australia Water Protection Guideline No 11 (2000) https://www.wa.gov.au/system/files/2022-04/WQPG-11-Mine-dewatering.pdf and Department of Water and Environmental Regulation, *Licence and works approval applications* (updated 1 November 2024) https://www.wa.gov.au/service/environment/environment-information-services/licences-and-works-approvals-prescribed-premises.

OIL AND GAS ENVIRONMENTAL APPROVALS

Introductory comments

There are broad similarities in the approval processes for oil and gas and mining in the sense that an EIS or EA under the *NEPA* in the USA and an approval by the EPAUSA, BMRR, ESAAS, and EPAWA may be required. In addition, the approval of other state or province regulators will be required on environmental aspects. 6.40

In the USA, the private sector can get access to oil and gas on public land only through a lease under federal legislation. In Saskatchewan and Western Australia, the authorisations for oil and gas operations are issued at the province or state level, and there are separate permits for exploration as opposed to production. In Nevada and Saskatchewan, the regulatory bodies for oil and gas at the state or province level are different from those regulating mining. In Western Australia, the DMIRSWA does both. 6.41

Nevada oil and gas

The overall structure for oil and gas activities in areas controlled by the federal government is broadly the same as that for mining, as the two main federal bodies involved are the BLM and the EPAUSA. An important difference is that oil and gas on federal lands have to be leased by the BLM pursuant to the *Mineral Leasing Act 1920*.[103] The BLM has recently revised its oil and gas leasing arrangements, which are set out in *43 Code of Federal Regulations* (*CFR*) Part 3100 and described under the heading Fluid Mineral Leases and Leasing Process.[104] Part 3160 contains rules concerning the drilling of wells, safety, disposition of production, and royalties. Drilling a well requires an Application for Permit to Drill which will, in turn, trigger the *NEPA* EIS or EA process that is discussed above at 6.03.[105] 6.42

The Nevada Division of Minerals oversees all oil and gas operations in Nevada. It describes its role as: 6.43

---

103 31 USC 181.

104 For a BLM Fact Sheet of April 2024 outlining the major changes, see https://www.blm.gov/sites/default/files/docs/2024-04/BLM-Final-Onshore-Oil-and-Gas-Leasing-Rule-General-Fact-sheet.pdf. A lessee's rights are set out in 43 CFR para 3101.12.

105 Under *43 CFR* para 3162.5.1, before an authorised officer approves the application or other plan requiring approval, 'the authorized officer shall prepare an environmental record of review or an environmental assessment, as appropriate. These environmental documents will be used in determining whether or not an environmental impact statement is required and in determining any appropriate terms and conditions of approval of the submitted plan.'

> The Nevada Division of Minerals is the state's regulatory authority for all oil and gas wells drilled in Nevada. Oil and gas wells drilled within Nevada, on either private or federally managed lands, must be permitted by the Nevada Division of Minerals. The associated drilling and completion programs must be approved by the Division before either program is implemented. The Division oversees the drilling and subsequent completion operations through daily reporting to the Division by the operator, as well as inspect the wells after they are completed. The Division must also approve all maintenance and workover operations during the life of the well, as well as the final plugging and abandonment of a well at the end of its useful life. Oil and gas production and injection information is submitted to the Division on a monthly basis, where the information is tabulated both monthly and annually.[106]

6.44 There are also detailed rules set out in Nevada statutes Chapter 522 on Oil and Gas and in the Nevada Administrative Code 522 on Oil and Gas.[107] For example, there is a requirement under Nevada Revised Statute (NRS) 522.050 for a permit to drill a well, which is separate from the BLM permit mentioned at 6.42. There are detailed reporting requirements to both BLM and the Nevada Division of Minerals, and they both have requirements concerning operations and processing facilities.[108] What can be noted here is that sustainability is not mentioned as a requirement, although some of the requirements address sustainability issues, such as reducing waste and emissions.[109] There does not appear to be a separate environmental approval required at the Nevada state level to drill a well.[110] As noted at 6.43, the Nevada Division of Minerals has the principal role in overseeing operations.

Saskatchewan oil and gas

6.45 The *CMASAS* sets out the province of Saskatchewan's ownership of minerals, which include oil and gas. The *Oil and Gas Tenure Registry Regulations (S)* (*OGTRR*) set out the permitting and licensing rules. Under the *OGTRR*, the minister can grant special exploration permits, exploration licences, and leases. The first two give exploration rights,[111] and the third rights to drill for

---

106 Nevada Division of Minerals webpage https://minerals.nv.gov/Programs/OG/OG/.

107 For Nevada Revised Statutes Chapter 522 – Oil and Gas, see https://www.leg.state.nv.us/NRS/NRS-522.html. For the Nevada Administrative Code Chapter 522 Oil and Gas, see https://www.leg.state.nv.us/NAC/NAC-522.html.

108 For Nevada Division of Minerals, see https://minerals.nv.gov/Programs/OG/OGForms/. For the BLM, see https://www.blm.gov/programs/energy-and-minerals/oil-and-gas/operations-and-production/onshore-orders. There are also standards that are commonly used, such as American Petroleum Institute standards.

109 For restrictions on flaring and venting gas, which also constitute waste, see https://www.energy.gov/sites/default/files/2022-06/Nevada-state-profile.pdf.

110 For the approvals required, see the matrix supplied at https://minerals.nv.gov/Programs/OG/OGForms/.

111 *OGTRR* regulation 6-6 (rights to explore granted by special exploration permit) and *OGTRR* regulation 8-4 (rights to explore granted by exploration licence).

oil and gas and produce and sell it.[112] Oil and gas permits, licences, and leases are applied for and recorded on the Integrated Resource Information System (IRIS).

The *Oil and Gas Conservation Act 1978 (S)* (*OGCASAS*) and regulations set out rules for the production of oil and gas. *OGCASAS* section 3 sets out the purposes of the Act that include minimising waste and preventing wasteful operations, regulating production with a view to achieving maximum ultimate recovery, and protecting 'the environment, property and the safety of the public with respect to the operations of the oil and gas industry'. Under *OGCASAS* section 8, a licence is required to drill a well. The application may be reviewed by the Saskatchewan Department of the Environment.[113] The *Oil and Gas Conservation Regulations 2012 (S)* (*OGRS*) contain detailed rules on matters concerning licences, operations, and reporting. There are matters which support sustainability, such as restrictions on flaring and venting and prevention of blowouts.[114] But neither the *OGCASAS* nor the *OGRS* mentions sustainability. The Ministry of Energy and Resources is responsible for the regulation of oil and gas in Saskatchewan.[115] It produces directives and guidelines on a broad range of operational matters.[116] Two examples are the *Directive PNG001 Facility Licence Requirements* and *Directive PNG018 Detailed Site Assessment Requirements*.[117] The former expands on the licensing requirements of the *OGCASAS* and the *OGRS* for a facility, examples of which are facilities for treating and disposing of water and gas plants.[118] The latter sets out details of what is required in terms of reclamation for a company to comply with its abandonment and decommissioning obligations under the *OGRS*. **6.46**

As discussed from 6.05, under the *CIAA*, a 'designated project' that may have adverse effects on an area within federal jurisdiction requires assessment. Projects are designated either by the regulations, or at the discretion of the responsible minister (*CIAA* section 9 IAA). The designated project list in the regulations for an onshore oil and gas activity requires a facility or pipeline **6.47**

112 *OGTRR* regulation 9-4 setting out rights granted to holder and conditions of lease.

113 See Well Licence Approvals at https://www.saskatchewan.ca/business/agriculture-natural-resources-and-industry/oil-and-gas/oil-and-gas-licensing-operations-and-requirements/oil-and-gas-drilling-and-operations/licence-to-drill-a-well.

114 *OGRS* regulations 51 and 70.

115 Ministry of Energy and Resources website https://www.saskatchewan.ca/government/government-structure/ministries/energy-and-resources.

116 For directives, see https://publications.saskatchewan.ca/#/categories/5568 and for guidelines see https://publications.saskatchewan.ca/#/categories/5569.

117 Ibid.

118 *Directive PNG001 Facility Licence Requirements 3.1.*

in a wildlife area or migratory bird sanctuary,[119] a pipeline of more than 40 kilometres or certain kinds of storage or other facilities – not a simple well.[120] Designated projects for oil and gas are mainly directed towards offshore activities. There are numerous federal directives and guidelines concerning the means of production and also emissions.

6.48 Also, development in Saskatchewan cannot proceed without ministerial approval at the provincial level under *EAASAS* section 8. The Saskatchewan Ministry of the Environment has published guidance on environmental review for oil and gas, *Environmental Review Guidelines for Oil and Gas Activities* (*Oil and Gas ER Guidelines (S)*).[121] An oil and gas project proposal must be submitted by the project proponent.[122] The approach is:

> The OGP must provide comprehensive project information, identify potential environmental impacts associated with the project and summarize proposed mitigation measures. This will allow the ministry to conduct a detailed screening of the project and confirm whether or not the project has the potential to cause significant environmental impacts.[123]

Proposals for oil and gas projects with no, or relatively minor, environmental impacts are reviewed by the Fish, Wildlife and Lands Unit. Higher-risk projects with the potential for significant environmental impacts are reviewed by the Environmental Assessment and Stewardship Branch.[124]

6.49 The position for oil and gas in Saskatchewan is broadly similar to that of mining summarised at 6.34. Following approval by the minister under *EAASAS* section 8, permitting is largely focused on the *OGCASAS* and the *OGRS*, which, as elaborated by directives and guidelines, contain detailed requirements on matters that underpin sustainability, such as requirements concerning wells, facilities, water, waste, and reclamation.

Western Australia oil and gas

6.50 Oil and gas in the state of Western Australia are owned by the state and regulated by the *Petroleum and Geothermal Energy and Resources Act 1967* (*PGERA*). Other regulations apply offshore, which are divided between state waters for

119 Ibid schedule 1 para 1.
120 Ibid schedule 1 paras 15, 44, and 46.
121 Environmental Review Guidelines for Oil and Gas Activities (Government of Saskatchewan, September 2022).
122 Ibid 6.
123 Ibid.
124 Ibid ii.

the first three nautical miles and then Commonwealth waters.[125] It is an offence to carry out oil and gas operations in the state without the appropriate authority, and the state issues permits for exploration and production licences to enable production. There are three sets of regulations under the *PGERA*, dealing respectively with resource management and administration,[126] the environment, and safety.[127]

Oil and gas operations onshore are often likely to have potentially significant impact on the environment and therefore may be subject to review by the EPAWA, as set out in 6.14. In addition, an environment plan will have to be submitted under the *Petroleum and Geothermal Energy Resources (Environment) Regulations 2012* (*PGERAER*) and approved by the minister before an activity is commenced.[128] The requirements for an environment plan are set out in *PGERAER* regulation 14 and include the environmental risks being reduced to as low as reasonably practicable, known as the ALARP test, and providing for 'appropriate environmental performance objectives, environmental performance standards and measurement criteria'. **6.51**

Sustainability is not mentioned in the *PGERA* nor the *PGERAER*, but ESD is. The objects of the *PGERAER* in regulation 3 include ensuring that any petroleum activity in the state is carried out in accordance with the principles of ESD. The other object is that the activity should be carried out in accordance with an environment plan which fulfils the requirements of the ALARP test, has appropriate environmental performance objectives, and appropriate measurement criteria to judge whether they have been met. ESD is not defined in the *PGERA* or the regulations but is clarified in guidance which refers to the seven principles of ESD described in the 1992 federal government strategy.[129] The guidance emphasises that operators should carefully consider the principles of ESD in developing their plans and also that 'the principles of **6.52**

125 The state legislation is the *Petroleum Submerged Lands Act 1982 (WA)*, and the federal legislation is the *Offshore Petroleum and Greenhouse Gas Storage Act 2006 (Cth)*.

126 *Petroleum and Geothermal Energy Resources (Resource Management and Administration) Regulations 2014* (*PGERRMA*).

127 The environment regulations are the *Petroleum and Geothermal Energy Resources (Environment) Regulations 2012* (*PGERAER*) and the safety regulations are the *Petroleum and Geothermal Energy Resources (Management of Safety) Regulations 2010* (*PGERASR*).

128 *PGERAER* regulation 7. The Minister is responsible for mines and petroleum and is supported by the DMIRS.

129 Government of Western Australia draft *Guideline for the Development of Petroleum Geothermal and Pipeline Environment Plans in Western Australia* (July 2021) https://www.dmirs.wa.gov.au/sites/default/files/atoms/files/draft-guideline_for_the_development_of_petroleum_geothermal_pipeline_env_plans_in_wa.. See Table 2 for the seven principles.

ESD should also be considered in demonstrating that the levels of environmental risks and impacts are of an acceptable level'.[130]

6.53 The emphasis in the oil and gas regulation is on the principles of ESD. Matters underpinning sustainability are supported by the environment plan and the ALARP test. Environment plans are generally comprehensive and cover matters like wells, water, waste, and decommissioning. Other approvals are required under the *PGERA* and the *Petroleum and Geothermal Energy Resources (Resource Management and Administration) Regulations 2014* (*PGERRMA*) for drilling wells and constructing facilities. The DMIRSWA has the principal role in overseeing oil and gas activities.

RENEWABLE ENERGY ENVIRONMENTAL APPROVALS

Introductory comments

6.54 The renewable energy dealt with here is solar and wind. Solar and wind developments tend to cover large areas and change the environment and are therefore subject to the environmental approvals mentioned in the section on significant projects starting at 6.03. In Nevada, there is regulation of public utilities. But otherwise, Nevada, Saskatchewan, and Western Australia do not have legislation specific to solar or wind requiring a licence or permit to construct or operate them. Accordingly, unless a renewable energy project is a significant project as described from 6.03, there is little regulation of sustainability or matters that underpin it.

6.55 Regulatory approvals will be required from the local government under planning or zoning regulations. Obtaining access to land to construct the facility is an important initial consideration in all three jurisdictions. The energy produced through solar and wind is in the form of electricity. If the solar or wind facility is to be connected to the network or involves the sale of electricity, then approvals and permits will be required. Other regulations, such as occupational health and safety regulations, will also apply.

Renewable energy in Nevada

6.56 Nevada has a state agency, the Public Utilities Commission of Nevada (PUCN), that regulates public utilities in specified services, including electricity and

130 That is a requirement for approval of an environment plan under *PGERAER* regulation 11(1)(c).

natural gas, and ensures compliance with Nevada's laws.[131] Amongst these is Nevada's Renewable Portfolio Standard, which requires a certain percentage of electricity sold by each electric utility to its customers to come from renewable energy.[132] The PUCN reviews filings by utilities to ensure they are complying. In addition, NRS 704.865 provides that a person, other than a local government, constructing a utility facility in Nevada must obtain a *Utility Environmental Protection Act* (*UEPA*) permit from the Commission. The process balances the potential environmental impact of a proposed utility with the public interest served by such a facility. Facilities include renewable energy power plants rated over 70 megawatts (nameplate) and electric transmission facilities rated over 200 kilovolts.

The PUCN has published a guide for *UEPA* permit applicants.[133] Under NRS 740.870, an application for a *UEPA* permit must contain specified information, including details of environmental impact assessments. One of the things the Commission will consider is whether the need for the facility balances any adverse effects on the environment. NRS 740.870 sets out the procedure to be followed should a federal environmental approval also be required: in summary, this requires an amended application after the federal approval when the appropriate federal agency has issued its EA or EIS.[134] **6.57**

Obtaining access to land for the facility will be an important step. In Nevada, that can involve negotiation with the BLM or private owners. In early 2024, the BLM was considering a number of renewable energy projects, mainly solar.[135] The BLM can issue leases of land for solar development.[136] Seven Nevada solar projects are proposed that 'collectively would cover nearly 90,000 acres — equivalent to 140 square miles, or double the size of Washington — and generate an estimated 8,850 MW of electricity, which is enough to power more than 2 million homes'.[137] Next will be obtaining any zoning approvals.[138] **6.58**

---

131 The enabling legislation is contained in Nevada Revised Statutes Chapters 703 and 704.

132 See Nevada Administrative Code (NAC) 704.8831 to 704.8899.

133 PUCN, *UEPA Guide for Applicants – Electric Facilities*, October 2015, https://puc.nv.gov/uploadedFiles/pucnvgov/Content/Utilities/UEPA_Guide_Electric.pdf.

134 As explained on the PUCN webpage on General UEPA information https://puc.nv.gov/Utilities/Construction_Permits/General_UEPA/.

135 See BLM, *Active Renewable Energy Projects* https://www.blm.gov/programs/energy-and-minerals/renewable-energy/active-renewable-projects and Scott Streeter, 'BLM's new mission: protect landscape in West's "sea of solar"' (1 January 2024) E&E News by *Politico* https://www.eenews.net/articles/blms-new-mission-protect-landscape-in-wests-sea-of-solar/.

136 For example, see the Dry Lake Solar Energy Zone https://blmsolar.anl.gov/solar-peis/sez/nv/dry-lake/.

137 See Streeter (n 135).

138 NRS 278.02077 and 278.028 relate to zoning. They prevent governing bodies from adopting ordinances or regulations that prohibit or reasonably restrict property owners from obtaining wind or solar energy on

Renewable energy in Saskatchewan

6.59 In 2015 the Government of Saskatchewan committed to increasing its target for renewable energy generating capacity from 25% to 50% by 2030.[139] The goal will include increased reliance on wind, solar, geothermal, biomass, and other sources. Saskatchewan's primary electricity supplier is SaskPower. By 2030, SaskPower is expecting to have developed 300 megawatts of electricity through solar and 1,800 megawatts through wind.[140] Development will mainly occur through independent power producers.[141]

6.60 Environmental approval for wind and solar projects in Saskatchewan under the *EAASAS* will depend on whether there is a designated project or development, which are discussed at 6.05 and 6.08. At the provincial level, a project proponent will submit a Technical Project Proposal to the Environmental Assessment and Sustainability Branch of the ministry for screening of whether the project is a development. If it is, an environmental impact assessment and environmental statement will be prepared. For wind, there are sensitivities for the impact on bird life, and there is guidance on adaptive management.[142] There are a number of published examples of proposals for wind and solar projects on the ministry's website.[143]

Renewable energy in Western Australia

6.61 Access to privately owned land for wind or solar facilities can be negotiated with the owner. Access to Crown land can be negotiated with the government of Western Australia and is usually in the form of a lease. Diversification leases were introduced in 2023 as Part 6A of the *Land Administration Act 1967*

---

their property. The provision relating to wind was amended in 2017 to provide that the governing body of a city or county may deny an installation permit for obtaining wind energy if the size, height, or configuration of the system (1) represents a danger to the health, safety, or welfare of the public or (2) is not compatible with the character of the area in which the system is located.

139 The federal government in Canada has committed to requiring all generation of electricity to be net zero by 2035 through the enactment of a Clean Energy Standard under the Canadian Environmental Protection Act, expanding renewable energy development, and connecting regions to clean power. However, the provincial government in Saskatchewan does not agree with this target: Pratyush Dayal, 'Sask Premier says federal net zero electricity would double power rates' (16 August 2023) *CBC News*.

140 Saskatchewan Chamber of Commerce, 'Current State of Renewable Energy in Saskatchewan' (February 2019) https://saskchamber.com/assets/2019/04/state-of-renewable-energy-in-saskatchewan.pdf.

141 Ibid.

142 Adaptive Management Guidelines for Saskatchewan Wind Projects https://www.saskatchewan.ca/business/environmental-protection-and-sustainability/environmental-assessment/does-my-project-need-an-environmental-assessment.

143 For example the EIS for the Outlaw Trail Wind Energy Project https://publications.saskatchewan.ca/#/products/114764.

(WA) to facilitate development. These leases are 'for the conduct of single, or multiple, land uses on a large area of Crown land, where the proposed lease purpose(s) can coexist with other land uses'.[144] The other initial major considerations are dealing with any native title issues, environmental approval, and planning approval under planning legislation.

The Government of Western Australia has an Energy Transformation Strategy. Stage 2 was announced in 2021 and extends to 2025.[145] It has identified a number of renewable energy zones that it considers suitable to harness renewable energy resources: they include the Goldfields for solar and Geraldton and the Mid-West for wind.[146] The Western Australian Planning Commission published a position statement on renewable energy facilities in March 2020, intended to promote renewable energy facilities and indicating that local governments should address renewable energy facilities in their local planning framework.[147] It says that an environmental review of the site should be conducted prior to design.[148] Development Assessment Panel rules were updated in 2024 to streamline planning approvals.[149] However, in one recent instance, the project proponent resorted to making an application to the Western Australian Planning Commission where a project spanned two local government areas, one represented by a regional joint development assessment panel.[150] **6.62**

As discussed at 6.14, the *WAenvpAct1986* provides that a proposal likely, if implemented, to have a significant effect on the environment can be referred by any person to the EPAWA. There are examples of both solar and wind projects being referred. **6.63**

144 Government of Western Australia, *Leasing Crown Land (Crown leases)*, https://www.wa.gov.au/organisation/department-of-planning-lands-and-heritage/leasing-crown-land-crown-leases.

145 Government of Western Australia, *Energy Transformation Strategy Stage 2: 2021–2025* (July 2021) https://www.wa.gov.au/system/files/2021-07/Energy-Transformation-Strategy-Stage2-July2021.pdf.

146 The West Australian REZs are not listed in the Australian Energy Market Operator's listing of REZs. See Appendix 3 to the Operator's 2024 Integrated System Plan for the National Energy Market https://aemo.com.au/energy-systems/major-publications/integrated-system-plan-isp/2024-integrated-system-plan-isp.

147 Western Australian Planning Commission, *Position Statement: Renewable Energy Facilities* (March 2020) https://www.wa.gov.au/system/files/2021-07/POS-Renewable-energy-facilities-position-statement.pdf.

148 Ibid 3.

149 See Government of Western Australia, *How Development Assessment Panels Work* https://www.planning.wa.gov.au/development-assessment-panels/how-development-assessment-panels-work.

150 Enel Green Power's Flat Rocks wind farm was given the green light by the WA Planning Commission on 1 April 2024. Sophie Vorrath, 'Wind firm gets state planning approval months after concrete poured and first wind turbines erected' (20 August 2024) *Renew Economy* https://reneweconomy.com.au/wind-farm-gets-state-planning-approval-months-after-concrete-poured-and-first-turbines-erected.

CONCLUSIONS, GUIDANCE, AND KEY PRINCIPLES

6.64 The basic conclusions from this chapter are:

- At the start of this chapter, four question areas were posed:
  - Do the environmental regulations contain sustainability tests? If the expression 'sustainability' is not used, how do the regulations approach matters that underpin sustainability, and what are they?
  - Do the environmental regulations have a particular focus, such as minimising environmental risks, and what are the main tools used?
  - Are the environmental regulations supported by other regulatory approvals and how are they coordinated?
  - Are there any processes or approaches that are commonly used?
- The answers can be summarised as follows, starting with there being limited references to sustainability in the environmental regulation of mining and energy in Nevada, Saskatchewan, and Western Australia. It is referred to in the Canadian federal impact assessment legislation, the *CIAA*, but not fleshed out with detailed principles or performance measures. The equivalent in Australian and Western Australian legislation are the principles of ecologically sustainable development, or ESD. They are also not accompanied by detailed performance measures.
- The main focus of the environmental approvals is the environment. There is much less focus on the social and economic aspects of development. However, in some jurisdictions, such as Saskatchewan, the definition of the environment includes related socioeconomic and cultural matters. The regulations focus on the protection of the environment and strategies to manage and minimise risks of harm to the environment. The main process used is environmental assessment before a project commences.
- On federal land in Nevada, it is the government agency triggering the review that conducts the environmental assessment. In Canada and Australia, it is the proponent of the project, usually the company owning and developing it, that carries out the assessment work. Public consultation is required, and the material will be reviewed by the regulator.
- The conduct of a mining or energy operation requires numerous approvals, including approvals of individual processes such as drilling, the transport of dangerous materials, and the use of radioactive substances.
- The mining and oil and gas regulations all have processes that underpin sustainability. Although the terminology varies, they generally require a plan of operations, proposal, or licence application which set out how operations will be conducted in some detail. They are accompanied by details of the approach to the management of matters like drilling, waste, water, tailings, decommissioning, and reclamation. The regulations are also supported by detailed requirements on these matters, whether in the form of regulations, directives, or guidance. A number of those detailed requirements are reflected in sustainability indicators and targets used by companies for measuring their sustainability.
- Interviews suggested that the environmental assessment reports and statements produced by project proponents in Canada and Australia are becoming longer

and more detailed. There are requirements for public consultation and consultation with traditional owners that are becoming increasingly rigorous, difficult, and expensive. Companies are having to deal with people in those processes who do not want a constructive dialogue about development.

- The environmental approval processes for wind and solar are less developed in Saskatchewan and Western Australia because only significant projects will be examined by the environment minister or the EPAWA. There is no specific regulator for solar or wind projects and no legislation conferring rights or titles on the project developer; therefore, no separate environmental plan or approval is required at that level.
- Two common gaps in environmental legislation are the absence of a requirement for a full analysis of the costs and benefits of a project and a requirement to consider the cumulative effects of mining and energy activities, for example, on the climate. Decided cases are indicating that the latter position is changing as courts are beginning to insist that emissions from the use of products by customers (called Scope 3) must be considered by regulators.

The following ideas follow from these conclusions: 6.65

- In developing their sustainability plans and performance measures, companies can derive a lot of information about environmental benchmarks from the environmental assessments of their projects. There is much less relevant information on the social and economic aspects of development.
- Companies that have a sustainability strategy and performance measures should ensure that any environmental assessments they conduct align with them.

ENVIRONMENT CHECKLIST

Companies

1. Do you summarise the key points of any environmental assessments you conduct and any approvals and approval conditions flowing from them and provide them to the persons responsible for sustainability in your company? Are they compared with your sustainability strategy, performance measures, and reporting requirements?
2. Do you have a process for capturing the lessons learned from the processes mentioned in question 1 so you can improve future performance?
3. Do you have a system for recording important performance measures and reportable matters on individual projects so you can analyse them and produce reports as required in a timely fashion?
4. Do you produce an analysis of the long-term (20 years or more) costs and benefits of your projects?
5. Do you have a strategy for engagement with communities and traditional owners with whom you may consult in the future or who are stakeholders in existing projects?

6. Is there anything you would do based on your reading of this chapter to improve the sustainability of your company?

Government/regulators

1. Are your activities subject to environmental review processes? If so, or if you have to comply with an analogous process, consider whether any of questions 1 to 4 for companies (above) apply to your organisation or could be useful for a broader purpose.
2. If the answer to question 1 is no, is your organisation responsible for assisting or participating in environmental reviews or giving feedback on environmental matters? If so, have you developed procedures for how you will conduct them?
3. Do you analyse the costs and benefits of your programmes in a holistic manner so you can assess whether they benefit society in the long run (say 20 years or more)?
4. If the answer to question 2 is also no, are there any lessons to be learned from this chapter about the management of your organisation's activities to improve the sustainability of your organisation or any other organisation or section of society in your area of responsibility?
5. Is there anything you would do based on your answer to question 3 or 4 to improve the sustainability of your operations?

7

PROJECT DEVELOPMENT APPROVALS AND SUSTAINABILITY STANDARDS

INTRODUCTION	7.01
What are development approvals?	7.01
Questions on development	7.02
BACKGROUND TO APPROVALS FOR DEVELOPMENT	7.04
MINING DEVELOPMENT APPROVALS	7.09
Mining in Nevada	7.09
Saskatchewan mining	7.12
Western Australia mining	7.16
OIL AND GAS DEVELOPMENT APPROVALS	7.18
Introduction	7.18
Nevada oil and gas	7.19
Saskatchewan oil and gas	7.22
Western Australia oil and gas	7.24
RENEWABLE ENERGY DEVELOPMENT APPROVALS	7.30
Introduction	7.30
Renewable energy in Nevada	7.31
Renewable energy in Saskatchewan	7.32
Renewable energy in Western Australia	7.33
DEVELOPMENT FINANCE	7.35
CONCLUSIONS, GUIDANCE, AND KEY PRINCIPLES	7.37

INTRODUCTION

What are development approvals?

This chapter will start with a brief outline of the history of development approvals in mining and energy, looking specifically at the USA, Canada, and Australia, before taking a more detailed look at approvals for mining, oil and gas, and renewable energy in Nevada, Saskatchewan, and Western Australia. In all these jurisdictions, an approval from a mining or energy regulator is required either before exploration for minerals or oil and gas or before production can commence, or both. Exploration approvals were examined in Chapter 6, and it is development and production approvals that are the focus of this chapter. Generally speaking, it is a specialist mining or oil and gas regulator that gives that approval. With limited exceptions, renewable energy in the form of wind and solar does not have a specialist regulator. The terminology concerning development and production approval varies, and the expression used in this chapter is development approval. What is of interest is not just the regulator's approval to produce, but the elements it may have to approve as part of that – the strategy for extracting the resource, the extraction method 7.01

(which will be very different for a gold mine as opposed to an oil well), the required production and processing facilities, the ancillary facilities (such as accommodation for workers), other required infrastructure and services (such as transport, storage and energy supply), and environmental processes for the treatment of waste, tailings, and rehabilitation. All of these elements need to be managed appropriately for the operation to be sustainable. By way of example, what is approved for mining in Nevada is a plan of operations and in Western Australia a mining proposal. For oil and gas in Western Australia, it is a field development plan. All of these are comprehensive documents.

Questions on development

7.02 The broad question examined in this section is why governments have an interest in approving development and what the objectives of development regulation are. Development approval is important because it is at that stage that the mining or energy regulator can assess how the project will produce and whether it will do so in an optimal way in the long term without causing environmental damage. Those matters are at the heart of sustainability. Of interest here is whether the regulator's objectives include sustainability and what companies and regulators can learn from those objectives and the development approval process.

7.03 Questions to be examined in this chapter, similar to those examined in Chapter 6, are:

- Do the regulations concerning development and production approvals by the mining and energy regulator contain sustainability tests? If the expression 'sustainability' is not used, how do the regulations approach matters that underpin sustainability, and what are they?
- Do the regulations have a particular focus, and what are the main tools used?
- Are the regulations supported by other regulatory approvals, and how are they coordinated?
- Are there any processes or approaches that are commonly used?

BACKGROUND TO APPROVALS FOR DEVELOPMENT

7.04 Chapter 6 explained that minerals and oil and gas on public lands in the USA are controlled by the federal government because it never parted with the mineral or oil and gas rights. Public lands are lands owned by the federal government since they became part of the USA and not dedicated to a specific use. Much of the land in Nevada is owned by the federal government and constitutes public lands. In the *Mining Law of 1872 (US)*, the federal government of the USA gave rights to mine minerals on public lands.[1] But oil and gas on public lands have to be leased pursuant to the *Mineral Leasing Act 1920 (US)*.[2] In both Saskatchewan and Western Australia, the Crown acting through the province of Saskatchewan and the state of Western Australia reserved ownership of minerals to itself. As mentioned in 6.21, in Saskatchewan, areas were allocated to private owners before that occurred, and those owners own the mineral and oil and gas rights and therefore grant rights over them. That also happened to a small extent in relation to minerals in Western Australia, but all hydrocarbons were brought into state ownership by the petroleum legislation.[3] In each jurisdiction, there are special rights given to indigenous peoples, which are generally not covered in this chapter because of their specialised nature.

7.05 In each of Nevada, Saskatchewan, and Western Australia, there are regulations specific to mining and oil and gas. Significant mining activities started in the USA, Canada, and Australia with the gold rushes in the middle of the 19th century.[4] Early miners in those countries believed that they had a right to enter land and mine. This right, sometimes called 'free mining' or 'free entry', was an ancient concept that was significant in medieval Europe and became the customary law in the stannary districts of the United Kingdom,[5] predominantly in Devon and Cornwall.[6] The right was 'independent of the rights of the owner of the surface of the land, outside the constraints of the feudal system, and free from interference from local courts and authorities'.[7] The stannaries in the United Kingdom had developed rules about work commitments, marking boundaries, prohibitions on mining on cultivated land, payment of royalties, and enforcement through the stannary courts, all of which resonate with modern mining law.[8] But in the 19th-century gold rushes in the USA, Canada, and Australia, where there was competition between miners to explore and produce, the miners themselves organised their own rules to establish claims. They took these rules with them to new mining areas as they were established.

---

1 30 USC §29 the Mining Law of 1872, para 22. It is defined in 43 CFR Part 3830 Subpart C.

2 31 USC §181.

3 Currently, Petroleum and Geothermal Energy and Resources Act 1967 (WA) (PGERA) section 9.

4 The California gold rush began in 1848 with a discovery at Sutter's Mill. The Queen Charlotte gold rush in British Columbia started in 1850, and there was a subsequent rush there in 1858. Australian gold rushes started in 1851 in New South Wales and Victoria. The last was the Klondike gold rush in Canada in 1897

5 The word 'stannary' is derived from the medieval Latin word 'stannaria', meaning a tin mine. Stannary towns were established in Cornwall by King John around 1200. Tin could not be sold until it was coined in a stannary town, which was how tax was collected.

6 Barry J. Barton, *Canadian Law of Mining* (Canadian Institute of Resources Law, Calgary 1993) 115.

7 Ibid.

8 Ibid.

Gradually, governments felt the need to formalise these rules, which was done in the early mining acts.[9]

7.06 Government interest in regulating mining operations more closely developed slowly and was often associated with a desire to ensure that the government was not left with an environmental problem as a result of mining. As mentioned in Chapter 6, environmental laws increased following the Second World War, and a common theme in modern environmental or mining legislation is a requirement for a mine closure plan to be approved by the regulator. It was also after the Second World War that regulators took an interest in making production more efficient and ensuring it was viable. An early example from British Columbia in the 1970s was the introduction of regulations that the minister had to approve a production plan 'providing for the best possible method of producing the minerals and achieving the best possible results from production' and considering 'environmental and socio-economic issues'.[10] That ministerial control was 'greatly disliked by the mining industry' and was removed soon after.[11] We can conclude that development approval is a relatively recent regulatory process in mining. How that process works and the terms used vary between jurisdictions.

7.07 Commercial oil and gas production only started in the USA in the late 19th century. Because of the importance of oil, governments in Australia and Canada brought it under state ownership,[12] something that was not done in the USA in relation to oil and gas on privately owned land. The federal government owned minerals, including oil and gas, on public lands. The early petroleum legislation in Canada and Australia that had to be introduced to confer exploration and production rights on the private sector was fairly basic and owed much conceptually to mining law.[13]

7.08 It was not until later in the 20th century that governments began to take an interest in making oil and gas production more efficient and reducing waste. Waste was particularly noticeable in relation to oil and gas in the USA, with multiple wells being drilled in close proximity as producers competed

9 An early example was the Gold Fields Act of British Columbia, which came into force in 1859 and was largely based on the New Zealand mining laws. Barton (n 6) 119.

10 Barton (n 6) 125.

11 Ibid 126.

12 In Western Australia, that was done by the *Petroleum Act 1936 (WA)* section 9.

13 For example, Alberta introduced its first petroleum regulation in the 1930s, soon after it obtained control of minerals from the federal government. Western Australia's first Petroleum Act was the *Petroleum Act 1936 (WA)*. Some permits could be issued before that under the *Mining Act 1904 (WA)* to conduct mining of minerals.

to produce quickly to get the most benefit from reservoir pressure that was strongest at the start of operations. The result was the passing of what was described as conservation legislation accompanied by rules dealing with the spacing of wells and the rate of production.[14] Generally reporting of exploration and production activities and results was not detailed.[15] Regulators had limited power to give directions to the operator except in relation to preventing waste.[16]

MINING DEVELOPMENT APPROVALS

Mining in Nevada

As explained at 6.23, the federal Bureau of Land Management (BLM) controls the disposal of minerals on public lands that are 'locatable', such as gold, silver, and copper, pursuant to the federal *Mining Law of 1872 (US)*.[17] Obtaining exploration or production rights over those minerals involves making a mining claim, recording it, and locating a discovery, matters regulated by the BLM.[18] The conduct of mining operations will also require permits from the state government of Nevada. They are administered by the Bureau of Mining Regulation and Reclamation (BMRR) within the Division of Environmental Protection (NDEP) in the Department of Conservation and Natural Resources (NDCNR).[19] The Nevada state government publishes a comprehensive list of federal and state permits required for mining and milling.[20] **7.09**

The role of development approval is fulfilled by the approval of a plan of operations by both the BLM and NDEP. This is required for all mining and processing activities, plus all activities exceeding five acres of proposed disturbance or **7.10**

14 The first Saskatchewan Oil and Gas Conservation Act was passed in 1952 following consultations in the USA on the Interstate Compact to Conserve Oil and Gas. The compact was a 1935 agreement between states in the USA to limit physical waste of oil and gas, and the participating states agreed to pass conservation legislation to give effect to it. A Commission was set up to make recommendations to reduce physical waste.

15 For an example, see the *Petroleum Act 1958 (Vic)* section 34.

16 Ibid section 47

17 30 USC §29 of the *Mining Law of 1872 (US)*, para 22 says that 'all valuable mineral deposits in lands belonging to the United States, both surveyed and unsurveyed, shall be free and open to exploration and purchase, and the lands in which they are found to occupation and purchase, by citizens of the United States'.

18 There are regulations for claims set out in 43 Code of Federal Regulations 3833.

19 The website is ndep.nv.gov.

20 Nevada Bureau of Mines and Geology Special Publication L-6, *State and Federal Permits Required in Nevada Before Mining or Milling Can Begin* (updated February 2024) https://minerals.nv.gov/uploadedFiles/mineralsnvgov/content/Programs/Mining/SPL6_StAndFedPermitsRequired_202402.pdf.

bulk sampling involving the removal of 1,000 or more tons of presumed ore. The plan of operations is typically a large compilation of site-specific plans for mining, management of waste rock and tailings, control of storm water and erosion, monitoring of air and water, and reclamation. The BLM and NDEP coordinate their review of mine and reclamation plans, along with reviewing and accepting financial assurances, also required by the BLM.[21] A plan of operations will also require the BLM to complete an environmental impact statement or environmental assessment, as discussed at 6.03.[22]

7.11 The BLM's webpage on Surface Management of Locatable Minerals explains that exploration, mining, and mineral processing activities involving locatable minerals on BLM-administered land are controlled by the regulations at 43 CFR Subparts 3715 and 3809 and in Wilderness Study Areas, 43 CFR Subpart 3802.[23] 43 CFR Subpart 3809.420 sets out performance standards that apply to a plan of operations. They begin in paragraph (a) with general performance standards that cover matters like technology, sequence of operations, land-use planning, and mitigation. For example, the sequence of operations says 'you must avoid unnecessary impacts and facilitate reclamation by following a reasonable and customary mineral exploration, development, mining and reclamation sequence'.[24] Paragraph (b) contains specific standards that deal with matters like access routes, mining wastes, reclamation,[25] air quality, water quality, fire, and leaching operations and impoundments.[26] For example, that of water quality says 'all operators shall comply with applicable Federal

21 Jim Butler, 'Environmental Regulation of Nevada's Mining Industry', *Nevada Lawyer*, April 2013 https://www.nvbar.org/wp-content/uploads/NevLawyer_April_2013_Environmental_Regulation.pdf 8.

22 Under 43 CFR para 3162.5.1, before an authorised officer approves the application or other plan requiring approval, 'the authorized officer shall prepare an environmental record of review or an environmental assessment, as appropriate. These environmental documents will be used in determining whether or not an environmental impact statement is required and in determining any appropriate terms and conditions of approval of the submitted plan.'

23 Bureau of Land Management – Surface Management of Locatable Minerals https://www.blm.gov/programs/energy-and-minerals/mining-and-minerals/locatable-materials/surface-management.

24 43 CFR 3809.420(a)(2).

25 Reclamation is given an extensive definition in 43 CFR 3809.420(b)(3)(ii) to include, but not be limited to:
'(A) Saving of topsoil for final application after reshaping of disturbed areas have been completed;
(B) Measures to control erosion, landslides, and water runoff;
(C) Measures to isolate, remove, or control toxic materials;
(D) Reshaping the area disturbed, application of the topsoil, and revegetation of disturbed areas, where reasonably practicable; and
(E) Rehabilitation of fisheries and wildlife habitat.'

26 Leaching operations and impoundments in 43 CFR 3809.420(b)(12) contain a number of detailed rules including (iii) 'You must design, construct, and operate cyanide or other leaching facilities and impoundments to contain precipitation from the local 100-year, 24-hour storm event in addition to the maximum process solution inventory. Your design must also include allowances for snowmelt events and draindown from heaps during power outages in the design.'

and state water quality standards, including the Federal Water Pollution Control Act, as amended'.[27] The BLM has produced a *Handbook on Surface Management* which contains detailed commentary on the standards and highlights approaches to achieve them.[28] For example, on water quality, it says 'the BLM must analyze potential impacts to water quality in the environmental analysis document prepared for the Plan of Operations'.[29] It goes on to say:

> The best approach to ensure that operators meet water quality standards is to include the corresponding state or Federal water quality permitting agency in the review and/or approval process for the Notice or Plan of Operations. This approach allows the BLM to evaluate potential pollution sources and controls in the mine plan simultaneously with treatment options and effluent limits in order to verify that the applicable agency has determined that the operator is meeting the water quality standards. Alternatively, certification from the state or Federal water quality permitting authority can serve as evidence that the proposed operation is expected to comply with applicable water quality standards.[30]

On the design and operations of leaching operations and impoundments, it says:

> The operator must design, construct, and operate all leach pads, tailings impoundments, ponds, and solutions-holding facilities according to standard engineering practices so as to achieve and maintain stability and facilitate reclamation.
>
> One method to ensure this standard is met is for the operator to have the facility designed by a licensed professional engineer, with construction oversight and verification by an engineering firm using standard quality assurance procedures. A stability analysis should be performed as part of the design evaluation using acceptable engineering standards for structures in that particular seismic region.[31]

The BMRR has published guidance on matters like the preparation of operating plans for mining facilities.[32] The guidance on operating plans comments:

> The plan should serve as a practical guide to the facility operator and provide useful information for both routine and unusual circumstances. Well-planned operation of a facility will optimize process efficiency and minimize the potential to degrade waters of the State.[33]

27 43 CFR 3809.420(b)(5).

28 BLM Handbook H 3809 1 https://www.blm.gov/sites/blm.gov/files/H-3809-1.pdf.

29 Ibid 5-15.

30 Ibid 5-16.

31 Ibid 5-23.

32 Nevada Bureau of Mining Regulation and Reclamation *Guidance Note on Preparation of Operating Plans for Mining Facilities* https://ndep.nv.gov/uploads/land-mining-regs-guidance-docs/20220113_Guidnce_PrepOperPlans_MiningFacilities_ADA.pdf.

33 Ibid 1.

Water Pollution Control Permits (WPCP) are issued to an operator prior to the construction of any mining, milling, or other beneficiation process activity.[34]

Saskatchewan mining

7.12 As 7.04 explained, in Canada, ownership of minerals mainly rests with the Crown in right of the provinces. Saskatchewan gained control of those mineral resources in 1930.[35]

7.13 6.33 explains that section 4 of the *Crown Minerals Act (S)* (CMASAS) authorises the minister to issue Crown dispositions, which are rights granted by the Crown to explore for minerals and obtain an interest in Crown minerals.[36] The rules for making a claim and obtaining a lease are set out in the *Mineral Tenure Registry Regulations 2012 (S)* (MTRAC). Mineral dispositions are kept in an electronic registry, the Mineral Administration Registry Saskatchewan (MARS). In order to mine, a lease must be obtained under Part VII of MTRAC. These have a term of 10 years and can be renewed.[37] Where mineral salts for minerals like boron, lithium, and potassium are more than 60 metres below the surface, they will be subject to a separate disposition under the *Subsurface Mineral Tenure Regulations 2015 (S)*, which contains broadly similar provisions regarding permits, claims, and leases to MTRAC.[38] Where minerals are privately owned, it is the owner who will grant rights to mine.

7.14 There is no equivalent requirement under MTRAC to a plan of operations, mining proposal, or development approval. An assessment report is required for work to count towards an expenditure requirement,[39] and it seems that it has no other purpose. However, the report must 'describe and interpret the results obtained from the assessment work'.[40] A yearly mine plan will have to be submitted for underground operations of an operating mine.[41]

7.15 As discussed in Chapter 6 from 6.33, a number of permits are required in order to conduct mineral exploration or production activities on Crown land within

34 See Regulation Branch webpage https://ndep.nv.gov/land/mining/regulation.

35 Section 1 of *Saskatchewan Natural Resources Act, RSC 1930, c 41* says that minerals (precious and base) belong to the province. They had previously been owned by the government of Canada pursuant to the Saskatchewan Act 1905 (U.K.) section 21.

36 SS 1984–86, c C-50.2.

37 MTRAC regulation 48.

38 *Subsurface Mineral Tenure Regulations 2015 (SAS) Chapter* C-50.2 Reg 30 (effective March 26, 2015).

39 MTRAC regulation 60.

40 MTRAC regulation 62.

41 See https://www.saskatchewan.ca/business/agriculture-natural-resources-and-industry/mineral-exploration-and-mining/mineral-tenure/submit-a-yearly-mine-plan.

Saskatchewan, generally from the Ministry of the Environment. These include surface disturbance permits before any exploration work can be started,[42] and also Forest Product, Aquatic Habitat Protection, Work Authorization, and/or Temporary Work Camp permits. As discussed at 6.08, at the provincial level under the *Environmental Assessment Act 1980* (EAASAS) section 8, a development cannot proceed without ministerial approval. The *Mineral Industry Environmental Protection Regulations 1996 (S)* set out requirements for the conduct of mineral exploration commencing from regulation 23, with regulation 24 requiring notice to the minister before drilling, trenching, or hydraulic removal of overburden can commence.[43] But because the definition of 'pollution control facility' in regulation 2 includes 'any equipment used in exploration', approvals are also required for the construction or installation of equipment and other processes in relation to exploration.

Western Australia mining

Western Australia has a *Mining Act 1972 (WA)* (MAWA) which regulates mining for all minerals with exclusions for substances the recovery of which is governed by the petroleum legislation, meaning oil and gas, and soil and some forms of sand, gravel, and similar substances.[44] In order to conduct exploration and mining activities, a miner will have to be granted the appropriate mining tenement under MAWA; for exploration, an exploration licence, and for mining a mining lease.[45] As discussed at 6.36, MAWA says that it shall be read and construed subject to the *Environmental Protection Act 1986 (WA)* (WAenvpAct1986). As outlined at 6.14, if a referral of a significant proposal is made to the Environment Protection Authority (EPAWA) and EPAWA decides to assess it, then further steps will follow, such as environmental review, which culminates in a report to the minister from EPAWA. 7.16

MAWA has no express environmental or sustainability objective. The Environmental Objectives Policy for Mining of March 2020 says: 7.17

42 Saskatchewan Mineral Exploration and Government Advisory Committee, Mineral Exploration Guidelines for Saskatchewan (2016) https://www.saskatchewan.ca/business/agriculture-natural resources-and-industry/mineral-exploration-and-mining/mining-permits 13.

43 For the guidelines and other relevant material, see Saskatchewan Mining Permits https://www.saskatchewan.ca/business/agriculture-natural-resources-and-industry/mineral-exploration-and-mining/mining-permits.

44 MAWA section 8 defines 'minerals' as 'naturally occurring substances obtained or obtainable from any land by mining operations carried out on or under the surface of the land'.

45 MAWA section 66 authorises the holder of an exploration licence to conduct exploration. Section 85 authorises the holder of a mining lease to mine and extract minerals.

> Resource industry activities are designed, operated, closed, decommissioned and rehabilitated in an ecologically sustainable manner, consistent with agreed environmental outcomes and post-mining land-uses without unacceptable liability to the State.

A mining proposal is required under MAWA section 74(1). The Statutory Mining Proposal Guidance published by the Department of Energy, Mines, Industry Regulation and Safety (DMIRSWA) requires details of the proposed mining operations, details of the site, plant and tailings, and environmental baseline data.[46] The Guidance contains specific requirements for stakeholder engagements (internal and external), risk assessment and identification, environmental outcomes, and an environmental management system.[47] Sustainability is not mentioned.

OIL AND GAS DEVELOPMENT APPROVALS

Introduction

7.18 In the USA, the private sector can get access to oil and gas on public lands only through a lease from the BLM under the *Mineral Leasing Act 1920 (US)*.[48] In Saskatchewan and Western Australia, the authorisations for oil and gas operations are issued at the province or state level, and there are separate permits for exploration as opposed to production. In Nevada and Saskatchewan, the regulatory bodies for oil and gas at the state or province level are different from those regulating mining. In Western Australia, the DMIRSWA does both.

Nevada oil and gas

7.19 The BLM has recently revised its oil and gas leasing arrangements, which are set out in 43 Code of Federal Regulations (CFR) Part 3100 and described under the heading Fluid Mineral Leases and Leasing Process.[49] Part 3160 contains rules concerning the drilling of wells, safety, disposition of production, and royalties. Drilling a well requires an Application for Permit to Drill which

---

46 Government of Western Australia, Department of Energy, Mines, Industry Regulation and Safety, *The Statutory Mining Proposal Guidance* is available at https://www.wa.gov.au/government/publications/statutory-guidelines-mining-proposals-0. See section 7 for stakeholder engagements.

47 Ibid sections 9 and 11.

48 31 USC 181.

49 For a BLM Factsheet of April 2024 outlining the major changes, see https://www.blm.gov/sites/default/files/docs/2024-04/BLM-Final-Onshore-Oil-and-Gas-Leasing-Rule-General-Fact-sheet.pdf. A lessee's rights are set out in 43 CFR para 3101.12.

will, in turn, trigger the environmental impact statement or environmental assessment process that is discussed at 6.04.[50]

As 6.43 explains, the Nevada Division of Minerals oversees all oil and gas operations in Nevada, and there are also detailed rules set out in Nevada statutes Chapter 522 on Oil and Gas and in the Nevada Administrative Code 522 on Oil and Gas.[51] There is a requirement under NRS 522.050 for a permit to drill a well, which is separate from the BLM permit mentioned at 7.19. There are detailed reporting requirements to both the BLM and the Nevada Division of Minerals, and they both have requirements concerning operations and processing facilities.[52] **7.20**

The position is the same as that expressed in 6.44 in relation to environmental approvals, which is that sustainability is not mentioned as a requirement, although some of the requirements address sustainability issues, such as reducing waste and emissions.[53] There are applicable standards, such as those of the American Petroleum Institute. An example is under NAC 522.234 in relation to 'well control and safety; equipment for prevention of blowout'.[54] The American Petroleum Institute's webpage on sustainability comments: **7.21**

> API members are actively working together to track and improve their sustainability performance while striving for increased transparency with stakeholders. API remains committed to building tools and platforms to support these efforts, as well as helping members

50 Under 43 CFR para 3162.5.1, before an authorised officer approves the application or other plan requiring approval, 'the authorized officer shall prepare an environmental record of review or an environmental assessment, as appropriate. These environmental documents will be used in determining whether or not an environmental impact statement is required and in determining any appropriate terms and conditions of approval of the submitted plan.'

51 For Nevada Revised Statutes Chapter 522 – Oil and Gas, see https://www.leg.state.nv.us/NRS/NRS-522.html. For the Nevada Administrative Code Chapter 522 – Oil and Gas see https://www.leg.state.nv.us/NAC/NAC-522.html.

52 For Nevada Division of Minerals, see https://minerals.nv.gov/Programs/OG/OGForms/. For BLM, see Bureau of Land Management https://www.blm.gov/programs/energy-and-minerals/oil-and-gas/operations-and-production/regs-notices-to-lessees#main-content.

53 For restrictions on flaring and venting gas, which also constitute waste, see https://www.energy.gov/sites/default/files/2022-06/Nevada-state-profile.pdf.

54 Which says, 'well control and wellhead assemblies used in an oil or gas well must meet the minimum specifications for assemblies prescribed by the American Petroleum Institute in Standard 53, "Blowout Prevention Equipment Systems for Drilling Wells, Fourth Edition," or by its successor organization, or as may be otherwise prescribed by the Administrator.' Another example in relation to the operator's duties in relation to casing under NAC 522:232 is that 'casing installed in the well meets the minimum specifications for casing prescribed by the American Petroleum Institute in Specification 5CT, "Specification for Casing and Tubing, Ninth Edition."'

> engage with stakeholders to meet expectations for the many opportunities and challenges that lie ahead.[55]

It then gives a number of examples of focus areas, including greenhouse gas emissions, biodiversity, and discharges to water.

Saskatchewan oil and gas

7.22 The *CMASAS* sets out the province of Saskatchewan's ownership of minerals, which include oil and gas. The *Oil and Gas Tenure Registry Regulations (S)* (*OGTRR*) set out the permitting and licensing rules. Under the OGTRR, the minister can grant special exploration permits, exploration licences, and leases. The first two give exploration rights,[56] and the third grants rights to drill for oil and gas and produce and sell it.[57] Oil and gas permits, licences, and leases are applied for and recorded on the Integrated Resource Information System (IRIS). Where oil and gas is privately owned, the owner will grant rights, usually through a lease.

7.23 The *Oil and Gas Conservation Act (S)* (*OGCASAS*) and regulations set out rules for the production of oil and gas.[58] *OGCASAS* section 3 sets out the purposes of the Act, including minimising waste and preventing wasteful operations, regulating production with a view to achieving maximum ultimate recovery, and protecting 'the environment, property and the safety of the public with respect to the operations of the oil and gas industry'. Under *OGCASAS* section 8, a licence is required to drill a well. The application may be reviewed by the Saskatchewan Department of the Environment.[59] Development cannot proceed without ministerial approval at the provincial level under *EAASAS* section 8. The Saskatchewan Ministry of the Environment has published guidance on environmental review for oil and gas.[60] An oil and gas project

---

55 The American Petroleum Institute *The Natural Gas and Oil Industry's Commitment to Sustainability* https://www.api.org/news-policy-and-issues/sustainability#:~:text=API%20helps%20the%20industry%20enhance,for%20increased%20transparency%20with%20stakeholders.

56 OGTRR regulation 6-6 (rights to explore granted by special exploration permit) and OGTRR regulation 8-4 (rights to explore granted by exploration licence).

57 OGTRR regulation 9-4 setting out rights granted to the holder and conditions of the lease.

58 The first version of the Act was passed in 1952. It has been amended several times since.

59 See Well Licence Approvals at https://www.saskatchewan.ca/business/agriculture-natural-resources-and-industry/oil-and-gas/oil-and-gas-licensing-operations-and-requirements/oil-and-gas-drilling-and-operations/licence-to-drill-a-well.

60 Environmental Review Guidelines for Oil and Gas Activities, September 2022 https://publications.saskatchewan.ca/#/products/78871.

proposal must be submitted by the project proponent.[61] However, sustainability is not mentioned.

Western Australia oil and gas

Oil and gas in the State of Western Australia, which are the focus of this section, are owned by the state and regulated by the *Petroleum and Geothermal Energy and Resources Act 1967 (WA)* (*PGERA*). Other regulations apply offshore, which are divided between state waters for the first three nautical miles and then Commonwealth waters.[62] It is an offence to carry out oil and gas operations in the state without the appropriate authority, and the state issues permits for exploration and production licences to enable production. There are three sets of regulations under *PGERA* dealing respectively with resource management and administration,[63] the environment, and safety.[64] The regulations most relevant to development are the *Petroleum and Geothermal Energy Resources (Resource Management and Administration) Regulations 2015 (WA) (PGERRMA)*. 7.24

Oil and gas operations onshore are often likely to have a potentially significant impact on the environment and therefore may be subject to review by EPAWA, as set out in 6.14. In addition, an environment plan will have to be submitted under the *Petroleum and Geothermal Energy Resources (Environment) Regulations 2012* (*PGERAER*) before an activity is commenced.[65] The requirements for an environment plan are set out in *PGERAER* regulation 14 and include the environmental risks being reduced to as low as reasonably practicable, known as the ALARP test, and providing for 'appropriate environmental performance objectives, environmental performance standards and measurement criteria'. 7.25

Sustainability is not mentioned in *PGERA* or *PGERRMA*. The objects of *PGERRMA* include in regulation 3(a) that operations will be: 7.26

---

61 Ibid 6.

62 The state legislation is the *Petroleum Submerged Lands Act 1982 (WA)*, and the federal legislation is the *Offshore Petroleum and Greenhouse Gas Storage Act 2006 (Cth)*.

63 Petroleum and Geothermal Energy Resources (Resource Management and Administration) Regulations 2015 (*PGERRMA*).

64 The environment regulations are the *Petroleum and Geothermal Energy Resources (Environment) Regulations 2012* (*PGERAER*) and the safety regulations are the *Petroleum and Geothermal Energy Resources (Management of Safety) Regulations 2010* (*PGERASR*).

65 *PGERAER* regulation 7.

(i) carried out in a proper and workmanlike manner and, in the case of operations relating to the exploration for or recovery of petroleum, in accordance with good oil-field practice; and
(ii) compatible with the optimum long-term recovery of petroleum and geothermal energy; and
(iii) carried out in a way that reduces the risk of aquifer contamination.

7.27 *PGERRMA* requires approved plans before certain activities are conducted – these are a well management plan and a field management plan. Under *PGERRMA* regulation 47, the minister must approve a field management plan if it contains the required information and the plan demonstrates that the applicant will manage the field:

(i) in accordance with sound engineering principles, codes, standards and specifications; and
(ii) in a manner that is consistent with good oil-field practice and compatible with optimum long-term recovery of the petroleum.

7.28 Schedule 3 sets out the required information, which includes a range of matters affecting production such as the strategy for development of the field (Item 4), but also matters affecting the environment, such as how waste is dealt with (Item 14) and flaring (Item 15). Item 17 requires the applicant to list 'the principal Australian and international standards that apply in relation to the applicant's operations and plant used in connection with those operations'.[66]

7.29 In addition various assessment reports are required, such as an annual assessment report that records matters like production, a production forecast, and flaring as well as potential exploration.

66 The 2015 Guidelines on the PGERRMA say at 4.16.9.7 on page 28, 'This item requires a list of the particular standards that the titleholder is going to apply to their field management, for example, AS2885 series: Pipelines – Gas and Liquid Petroleum. It is possible that a title holder might apply their own standard. This case would necessarily include more detail than just the name of the standard, as would occur with a commonly known and accepted standard. The standard would then be examined to see if it was equivalent to and consistent with a commonly known and accepted standard.' https://www.dmp.wa.gov.au/Documents/Petroleum/REC-PC-159D.pdf. There is also a guideline on how to prepare a Field Management Plan on the DMIRS website, but this does not say anything further about standards. See https://www.dmp.wa.gov.au/Documents/Petroleum/REC-PC-159D.pdf.

RENEWABLE ENERGY DEVELOPMENT APPROVALS

Introduction

The renewable energy dealt with here is solar and wind. In Nevada, there is regulation of public utilities. But otherwise, Nevada, Saskatchewan, and Western Australia do not have legislation specific to solar or wind requiring a licence or permit to construct or operate them. Regulatory approvals will be required from local government under planning or zoning regulations, but these do not generally deal with sustainability. **7.30**

Renewable energy in Nevada

Nevada has a state agency, the Public Utilities Commission of Nevada (PUCN), that regulates public utilities in specified services, including electricity and natural gas, and ensures compliance with Nevada's laws.[67] In early 2024, the BLM was considering a number of renewable energy projects, mainly solar.[68] The BLM can issue leases of land for solar development.[69] Zoning approvals will have to be obtained in some cases.[70] **7.31**

Renewable energy in Saskatchewan

Environmental approval for wind and solar projects in Saskatchewan under the EAASAS will depend on whether there is a development, a matter discussed at 6.05 and 6.13. A project proponent will submit a Technical Project Proposal to the Environmental Assessment and Sustainability Branch of the ministry for screening of whether the project is a development. If it is, an environmental impact assessment and environmental impact statement will be prepared. For wind, there are sensitivities for the impact on bird life and there is guidance on adaptive management.[71] There are published examples of **7.32**

---

67 The enabling legislation is contained in Nevada Revised Statutes Chapters 703 and 704.

68 See BLM *Active Renewable Energy Projects* https://www.blm.gov/programs/energy-and-minerals/renewable-energy/active-renewable-projects and Scott Streeter, 'BLM's new mission: protect landscape in West's "sea of solar"', E&E News by Politico 1 January 2024, https://www.eenews.net/articles/blms-new-mission-protect-landscape-in-wests-sea-of-solar/.

69 For an example, see the Dry Lake Solar Energy Zone https://blmsolar.anl.gov/solar-peis/sez/nv/dry-lake/.

70 NRS 278.02077 and 278.028 relate to zoning. They prevent governing bodies from adopting ordinances or regulations that prohibit or reasonably restrict property owners from obtaining wind or solar energy on their property. The provision relating to wind was amended in 2017 to provide that the governing body of a city or county may deny an installation permit for obtaining wind energy if the size, height, or configuration of the system (1) represents a danger to the health, safety, or welfare of the public or (2) is not compatible with the character of the areas in which the system is located.

71 Adaptive Management Guidelines for Saskatchewan Wind Projects https://publications.saskatchewan.ca/#/products/90235.

proposals for wind and solar projects on the ministry's website.[72] These provide examples of permits required across a number of pieces of legislation focusing on wildlife protection and particular environmental issues, such as weed control.[73] Municipalities can address development and land use issues under the *Planning and Development Act 2007 (S)* if they have a zoning bylaw and community plan in place.[74]

Renewable energy in Western Australia

7.33 The Western Australian Planning Commission published a position statement on renewable energy facilities in March 2020, intended to promote renewable energy facilities and indicating that local governments should address renewable energy facilities in their local planning framework.[75] Some have introduced policies that deal with environmental impacts generally, as well as visual impact and noise,[76] and have raised questions about whether the State of Western Australia needs more detailed regulation.[77]

7.34 As discussed at 6.05, the *WAenvpAct1986* provides that a proposal likely, if implemented, to have a significant effect on the environment can be referred by any person to the EPAWA. There are examples of both solar and wind projects being referred.

DEVELOPMENT FINANCE

7.35 So far this chapter has few references to sustainability in the legislation. If a company wishes to obtain finance for a development, it is likely to find that financiers take a closer interest in sustainability issues. There are a number of approaches to sustainable finance or green loans. The International Finance Corporation (IFC) arm of the World Bank Group makes it clear that it takes a keen interest in sustainability aspects of projects it is financing. Its publication Focus 15 Sustainability Committees: Structures and Practices (IFC

---

72 For example, the EIS for the Outlaw Trail Wind Energy Project https://publications.saskatchewan.ca/#/categories/2135.

73 Ibid 6.

74 Ibid 7.

75 Western Australian Planning Commission, *Position Statement: Renewable energy facilities*, March 2020, https://www.wa.gov.au/system/files/2021-07/POS-Renewable-energy-facilities-position-statement.pdf.

76 Shire of Narrogin, D11 – Local Planning Policy – Wind Farm Turbines www.narrogin.wa.gov.au/documents/1516/draft-local-planning-policy-wind-farm-turbines.

77 Andrew Chounding, WA government's wind farm development policy lagging behind, councils say (ABC August 2024) https://www.abc.net.au/news/2024-08-05/wa-great-southern-to-become-renewable-energy-hub/104174530.

Sustainability Practices), which was mentioned at 1.09, defines 'sustainability' as: 'The environmental and social factors that have an impact on the long-term performance of companies'.[78] The IFC has eight performance standards that it expects to be met through the life of an investment by the IFC.[79] In project appraisal, the IFC uses the World Bank Group's Environmental, Health and Safety Guidelines as a technical source of information. If the levels and measures in host-country regulations differ from those, then the IFC expects the project 'to achieve whichever is more stringent'.[80]

The Equator Principles (EPs) were set up 'to serve as a common baseline and risk management framework for financial institutions to identify, assess and manage environmental and social risks when financing projects'.[81] The latest version is EP4, issued in 2020.[82] **7.36**

CONCLUSIONS, GUIDANCE, AND KEY PRINCIPLES

The basic conclusions from this chapter are that: **7.37**

- In answer to the first question posed at 7.02, which is whether the regulations concerning development and production approvals by the mining and energy regulator contain sustainability tests, is that the expression 'sustainability' is not used in mining and oil and gas regulations to test the adequacy of proposed operations.
- The conduct of a mining or oil and gas operation requires numerous approvals, including approvals of individual processes such as drilling. These are granted by a range of government bodies, but certain bodies play a central role: the BLM and BMRR in Nevada, the Department of the Environment in Saskatchewan, and DMIRSWA in Western Australia.
- Some of the regulations have detailed requirements (for example, under the Nevada Administrative Code) and refer to standards such as those of the American Petroleum Institute. However, these generally do not refer to sustainability. The regulations deal with matters that underpin sustainability, particularly potential harm to the environment.

78 IFC Sustainability Practices 2, quoting from IFC Toolkit for Disclosure and Transparency, 2018, 5. It goes on to say that 'the economic contribution (effect) of the company, and how the broader economy affects it and its customer base, surrounding communities, and other stakeholders, are implied in the performance dimension'.

79 International Finance Corporation, Performance Standard 6: Biodiversity Conservation and Sustainable Management of Living Natural Resources, IFC, January 1 2012, 1.

80 Ibid, ii.

81 Webpage *About the Equator Principles* https://equator-principles.com/about-the-equator-principles/.

82 Equator Principles EP 4 (July 2020) Ibid.

- In Nevada a plan of operations and in Western Australia a mining proposal for mining and a field development plan for oil and gas contain extensive details about the proposed development and are the main tools used in development approval. The main focus is on the manner in which operations will be conducted, which includes areas such as tailings and water management and rehabilitation. There is much less focus on the social and economic aspects of development. Those matters are focused on in project finance if the financing group follows the Equator Principles or other similar principles.
- There is no specific regulator for solar or wind projects and no legislation conferring rights or titles on the project developer, and therefore no development plan or approval is required at that level. Development approval can be required through environmental legislation and also through local planning and zoning requirements.

7.38 The following ideas follow from these conclusions:

- In developing their sustainability plans and performance measures, companies should ensure that important documents like development approvals, environmental proposals, and plans of operations are consistent and contain metrics and targets aligned with their sustainability strategy and performance measures.
- Social and economic aspects of development are of limited interest to mining and energy regulators, but companies need to consider these for their sustainability strategies and reports.

DEVELOPMENT CHECKLIST

Companies

1. Similar to the Chapter 6 checklist, do you maintain a comprehensive list of the approvals required for your projects, including any required at critical points like development, and do you have a process to keep it up to date and monitor compliance?
2. Do you summarise the key points of any development approvals you obtain and any approval conditions flowing from them, and provide them to the persons responsible for sustainability in your company? Are they compared with your sustainability strategy, performance measures, and reporting requirements?
3. Do you have a process for capturing the lessons learned from the processes mentioned in question 1 so you can improve future performance?
4. Do you have a system for recording important performance measures and reportable matters on individual projects so you can analyse them and produce reports as required by development approvals in a timely fashion?
5. Do you produce an analysis of the long-term (20 years or more) costs and benefits of your projects?
6. Is there anything you would do based on your reading of this chapter to improve the sustainability of your company when it comes to development?

Government/regulators

1. Are your activities subject to approvals? If so, or if you have to comply with an analogous process, consider whether any of questions 1 to 4 for companies (above) apply to your organisation or could be useful for a broader purpose.
2. If the answer to question 1 is no, is your organisation responsible for assisting or participating in development reviews or giving feedback on development matters? If so, have you developed procedures for how you will conduct them?
3. Do you analyse the costs and benefits of your programmes in a holistic manner so you can assess whether they benefit society in the long run (say 20 years or more)?
4. If the answer to question 2 is also no, are there any lessons to be learned from this chapter about the management of your organisation's activities to improve the sustainability of your organisation or any other organisation or section of society in your area of responsibility?
5. Is there anything you would do based on your answer to question 3 or 4 to improve the sustainability of your operations?

8

EXAMPLES OF COMPANY SUSTAINABILITY REPORTING

INTRODUCTION	8.01
The nine companies	8.01
Reporting required by law	8.03
Process and guidance for reporting	8.04
Common features of the reports examined	8.07
THE MINING COMPANIES	8.12
Introduction	8.12
Barrick	8.13
Cameco	8.17
MinRes	8.20
THE OIL AND GAS COMPANIES	8.23
Introduction	8.23
TotalEnergies	8.24
Conoco	8.31
Cenovus	8.35
THE RENEWABLE ENERGY COMPANIES	8.39
Introduction	8.39
Iberdrola	8.40
Vestas	8.46
CSI	8.48
FLEXIBLE OPTIONS AND BEST PRACTICE	8.53
Flexible options	8.53
Guidance on best practice	8.54
CONCLUSIONS, GUIDANCE, AND KEY PRINCIPLES	8.56

INTRODUCTION

The nine companies

8.01 Nine companies will be compared to analyse the distinguishing features of their approaches to sustainability reporting, with three each from mining, oil and gas, and renewable energy. Their reports were for either 2023 or 2024, and the most recent available at the time of writing is referred to. As the reader will see from this chapter, there are significant differences in structure, style, and approach. The reasons for the comparison are to provide examples for those interested and to analyse the differences and the reasons for them to help those developing their own reports.

8.02 The nine companies are:

Mining
Barrick Gold Corp (Barrick)
Cameco Corp (Cameco)
Mineral Resources Limited (MinRes)

Oil and gas
TotalEnergies SE (TotalEnergies)
ConocoPhillips Inc (Conoco)
Cenovus Energy Inc (Cenovus)
Renewable energy
Iberdrola SA (Iberdrola)
Vestas Wind Systems AS (Vestas)
Canadian Solar Inc (CSI)[1]

Reporting required by law

All these companies produce reports that cover environment, social, and governance – the classic areas of ESG. Their reports are generally called sustainability reports. The length and quality of the reports reflect the fact that they are large producing companies. They have been chosen because their reports provide a range of good examples of different aspects and options. As discussed in Chapter 1 from 1.44, the natural starting point for a small mining or oil and gas company at the exploration stage with just a few directors is likely to be what it is legally required to report. As mentioned there, those legal requirements have two main sources: company laws requiring directors to report on non-financial matters,[2] and laws of stock exchanges or market regulators requiring disclosure of matters like material climate-related risks.[3] Generally directors of companies which do not have securities listed on a securities exchange will only have to comply with the first of these. Also if, as will often be the case with a small company, it only has limited activities, that should limit the extent of its sustainability reporting. In many jurisdictions, disclosure will also apply to environmental, social, and governance risks. There will, of course, be variations in the details between jurisdictions. Chapter 9 contains a more detailed comparison of the regulations in Australia, Canada, the USA, and the European Union. **8.03**

Process and guidance for reporting

There is very useful guidance on how a company should prepare a sustainability report: for example, Ipieca/API/IOGP *Sustainability reporting guidance* **8.04**

1 These are among the 10 largest renewable energy companies. Matthew Johnston, '10 Biggest Renewable Energy Companies in the World' (Investopedia, 27 January 2024) https://www.investopedia.com/investing/top-alternative-energy-companies/.
2 For example, *Companies Act 2006 (UK)* section 414A.
3 For example, the SEC's new climate disclosure rules will be phased in from fiscal years starting in 2025 and will apply to companies listed on NYSE and Nasdaq. The Climate Disclosure Rules are set out in a new Subpart 1500 of Regulation S-K and new Article 14 of Regulation S-X.

for the oil and gas industry (4th edition, 2020) (Ipieca Reporting Guidance).[4] The Ipieca Reporting Guidance has six steps: (1) develop a reporting plan; followed by (2) engage stakeholders; (3) select your material issues for reporting; (4) develop report; (5) develop report data; and (6) provide assurance.[5] The guidance has five modules in addition to the first module on the reporting process: governance and business ethics; climate change and energy; environment; safety, health, and security; and, finally, social. It indicates issues under each and a discussion of 42 indicators, starting with governance approach.[6]

8.05 The first three steps are very important for any company embarking on preparing a report. There will be other important choices, such as which frameworks to apply, as they can have a bearing on the structure of the report and important issues like judging materiality.[7] For example, the Global Reporting Initiative (GRI), which all the companies reviewed in this chapter comply with to some degree, requires compliance with its standards. A simple example is GRI 2: General Disclosures 2021.[8] That has 29 required disclosures covering a range of general matters, such as sustainable reporting practices, information about the organisation and its practices, its governance structure, its sustainable development strategy, and stakeholder engagement. That standard makes clear that 'an organization reporting in accordance with the GRI Standards is required to report all disclosures in this Standard'.[9] There are many other relevant GRI Standards. It is clear too that many companies follow the recommendations of the Task Force for Climate Related Financial Disclosure (TCFD).[10] In its final report of June 2017, *Recommendations of the Task Force for Climate Related Financial Disclosure* (TCFD Final Report),[11] it says that it 'structured its recommendations around four thematic areas that represent core elements of how organizations operate: governance, strategy, risk management, and metrics and targets'.[12] Those thematic areas are found

---

4 Ipieca/API/IOGP 2023 (Ipieca Reporting Guidance). See 1.49.

5 Ibid 1.7.

6 Ibid 1.6.

7 The Ipieca Reporting Guidance defines 'materiality' as 'a principle and management process that determines which issues should be covered and their priority within a report' (Ipieca Reporting Guidance 1.3).

8 GRI 2: General Disclosures 2021, 6. See https://www.globalreporting.org.

9 Ibid.

10 GRI and TCFD were two of the frameworks most commonly used by Ipieca members to guide their reporting in 2019 – Ipieca Reporting Guidance 1.39. Others included the UNGC, the UN Guiding Principles on Business and Human Rights, and the SDGs.

11 Task Force on Climate-related Financial Disclosures, Final Report Recommendations of the Task Force for Climate Related Financial Disclosure, June 2017 (TCFD Final Report) https://assets.bbhub.io/company/sites/60/2021/10/FINAL-2017-TCFD-Report.pdf.

12 TCFD Final Report iv.

in all the reports examined in this chapter, but their placement and treatment vary.

Other issues will flow from the nature of the company's business, its strategic plan, governance structure, and engaging with stakeholders. The company should also consider its position on sustainability more broadly, on the SDGs, and on the energy transition. These are discussed in succeeding paragraphs. The Ipieca Reporting Guidance points not only to the increasing desire of stakeholders, such as the investment community and regulators, for clear and transparent reporting, but also to the benefits to companies of having good sustainability reports,[13] which could be expressed as making improvements through embracing sustainability. **8.06**

Common features of the reports examined

Some of the common features in the reports examined in this chapter are: **8.07**

- A structure starting with an opening statement from the chief executive officer or a director, followed by an introduction to the company, its current operations, and its approach to the report and sustainability. That may be followed by a discussion of its material issues, a report of its successes and failures, and a section on climate change and/or energy transition. There then follow sections on environment, social, and governance. But there is no consistent approach to the naming of those sections or how they are broken up. For example, all of the companies cover safety, but some treat it as a separate area. The treatment of human rights, energy transition, and emissions also varies. The last sections contain data such as performance metrics.
- The reports contain performance metrics against the indicators specified.
- All the companies set targets, for example, in relation to their level of emissions. But their approaches vary. Some have a comprehensive list of targets. Those that have such a list make it a feature of their report structure. But even those companies that do not have a comprehensive list set out targets or objectives in selected areas – emissions is a very common area.
- There are some broad goals that all the companies share (these will be referred to as Commonly Used Goals), although the targets or metrics may vary, and there are some variations:[14]
  - Each has a net zero ambition in relation to Scope 1 and 2 emissions.
  - Each is seeking to improve the efficiency of its water use.
  - Each measures injuries using measures like the total recordable injury rate (TRIR) and is seeking to bring it close to zero.

13 Ipieca Reporting Guidance 1.1.

14 Some companies use TRIFR rather than TRIR, and there are variations in relation to the numerical base they use, for example, injuries per million employee hours. But they all measure an injury rate.

  - Each is seeking to increase female representation in its workforce and/or at the board level.
  - Each is seeking to benefit the communities in which they have operations through initiatives like employing local people.
- In their reports, the companies all have regard to some or all of the standards of the Sustainability Accounting Standards Board (SASB),[15] the GRI and the SDGs. Companies subject to European Union directives also comply with those, for example, the Corporate Sustainability Reporting Directive (CSRD).[16] The reports also refer to a diverse range of other frameworks.
- They all have some form of assurance in their reports, commonly but not exclusively, from an independent accounting firm.

8.08 It is an interesting question whether any of the matters referred to in the previous paragraph are either essential core elements or required by reporting and disclosure rules. That will be examined in the next chapter. Many of the accounting standards are moving towards adopting principles developed by the international accounting standards boards. Many of the companies examined in this chapter track their performance against selected SDGs, and that in turn informs their goals and indicators.[17] So, an important matter for a company considering a sustainability report is deciding whether it will track its performance against the SDGs and which ones.[18]

8.09 It is suggested that there are two other important initial matters: deciding its approach to sustainability more broadly as a business objective and then deciding its strategy in relation to the energy transition. Two approaches to sustainability can be distinguished in the reports reviewed in this chapter – one focused on the disclosure, management, and minimisation of sustainability risks, and the other on improving sustainability performance. Although risk management is important, the first approach seems largely driven by

---

15 In 2022, the Trustees of the IFRS Foundation formed the International Sustainable Standards Board (ISSB) and consolidated the Climate Disclosure Standards Board (CDSB) and the Value Reporting Foundation (which housed the SASB Standards). The website says that 'the ISSB encourages companies and investors to continue to support and use the SASB Standards until they are replaced by IFRS Sustainability Disclosure Standards' https://sasb.ifrs.org/blog/answering-your-top-five-questions-about-the-issb-and-sasb-standards/.

16 Corporate Sustainability Reporting Directive (CSRD) and Directive (EU) 2022/2464 of the European Parliament and of the Council of 14 December 2022 amending Regulation (EU) No 537/2014, Directive 2004/109/EC, Directive 2006/43/EC and Directive 2013/34/EU https://eur-lex.europa.eu/legal-content/EN/TXT/?uri=CELEX:32022L2464.

17 The only exception is Conoco, although Conoco does mention the SDGs on its website in relation to global giving. See https://www.conocophillips.com/sustainability/creating-shared-value/global-giving/global-giving-overview/.

18 GRI 2: General Disclosures 2021 35 Disclosure 2-22 requires a statement on sustainable development 'about the relevance of sustainable development to the organization and its strategy for contributing to sustainable development'. For more on sustainable development, see Chapter 4 from 4.25.

ensuring markets are informed about a company's prospects. As already noted, that approach is mandated by disclosure rules. If those rules mandate the use of a particular standard, that will influence the structure and content of the report. The second approach is aimed at improving the company's business. It tends to use targets to align corporate and employee performance on achieving improvements. Combining the two approaches is a challenge because disclosing and managing risk, although it should reduce risks, will not necessarily make broader improvements to the business. So, a very important question that will set the tone of the sustainability report is which should dominate. The question that should be asked is why the company is preparing the report. Is it because the company wants to be more sustainable and has to make appropriate disclosures? Or is it because the company wants to comply with the legal requirements for disclosures? Another factor that is informing statements made in sustainability reports is the move from aspirational statements (making a better business) to now having directors' duties attached to the statements with significant consequences. It will mean that companies are less likely to make statements about intended business improvements unless they are an absolute certainty.[19]

A unifying factor is that the nature of the company's business lies at the heart of the risks it faces and its sustainability issues. It also has a significant bearing on its enthusiasms and approach. For example, the renewable energy companies reviewed in this chapter emphasise the importance of energy transition and their role in it. But mining and oil and gas companies may do the same, depending on their business focus. Climate change and the energy transition are major issues of our time. A company can take various positions. One position might be that the company will keep doing what it has always done for as long as it can maximise shareholder return by doing that and, while disclosing its material risks, take a minimalist position on mitigating them. An important question for directors is whether they are under any legal duty to mitigate material risks if they are fully disclosed.[20] Another position might be to embrace the energy transition and move to refocus the company's business to prosper in the changed economic conditions. You will see examples of these positions in the reports reviewed in this chapter and some intermediate positions as well. **8.10**

19 Industry interview, January 2025.

20 For directors' duties, see Chapter 3 from 3.41.

8.11 Table 8.1 sets out brief details of the companies whose reports are reviewed and the structure of their reports.

THE MINING COMPANIES

Introduction

8.12 All three mining companies produced sustainability reports. Various factors play a part in causing differences in their reports. Those factors include the countries in which they are headquartered, where their operations are located, the minerals they produce, and size. Barrick and Cameco have their headquarters in Canada, and MinRes in Australia. All have their securities listed on a stock exchange.[21] The largest in terms of market capitalisation is Barrick at US$35.11 billion,[22] followed by Cameco at US$17.46 billion, and third, MinRes at US$5.078 billion (7.43 billion Australian dollars).[23] Barrick has operations in about 12 countries, Cameco in three, and MinRes only in Australia. Barrick is principally a gold and copper miner, Cameco mines uranium, and MinRes mines iron ore and lithium and also has an energy focus.

Barrick

8.13 Although each report covers the environment, social, and governance to some degree, there are considerable variations in how they approach them, the targets they set, and the key performance measures they use. Starting with Barrick, the Barrick 2023 Sustainability Report (Barrick 2023 SR), which has data up to 31 December 2023, highlights the special nature of Barrick's business, which in turn is a significant driver of its sustainability reporting. Although Barrick has substantial operations in Nevada, what is special about its business is that it has the most international operations of the three companies, operating in around a dozen countries across South America, Africa, the Middle East, and Asia. A key theme is that Barrick says that to deliver value, it needs to be 'the partner of choice for the countries and communities in which we operate', and many of its strategies flow from how it implements partnership.[24] The report is broken down into an Introduction, followed by sections on Community and People, Workplace Safety and Health, Respecting Human

---

21 The securities of Barrick and Cameco are quoted on the New York Stock Exchange (NYSE). MinRes's securities are quoted on the Australian Stock Exchange (ASX).

22 The market capitalisation of Barrick and Cameco is at 19 September 2024.

23 The market capitalisation is also at 19 September 2024, and the conversion to USD is as at that date.

24 Barrick 2023 SR, 4.

Table 8.1 Snapshot of sustainability reports

Name	Barrick	Cameco	MinRes	TotalEnergies	Conoco	Cenovus	Iberdrola	Vestas Wind	Canadian Solar
Focus	Gold and copper – global operations	Uranium – mainly Canada	Iron ore and energy – Australia	Oil and gas and renewables – global operations	Oil and gas – global operations	Oil and gas – Canada	Renewable energy – global operations	Wind energy – global operations	Solar energy – global operations
Sustainability report	Sustainability Report 2023[a] (Barrick 2023 SR) 112 pages	2023 Sustainability Report (Cameco 2023 SR) 114 pages	2024 Sustainability Report (MinRes 2024 SR) 227 pages	Sustainability and Climate Progress Report 2024[b] (TotalEnergies 2024 SR) 110 pages	2023 Sustainability Report (Conoco 2023 SR) 101 pages	2023 Corporate Social Sustainability Report (Cenovus 2023 SR) 69 pages	Statement of Non-Financial Information. Sustainability Report Financial Year 2023[c] (Iberdrola 2023 SR) 375 pages	2023 Sustainability Report (Vestas 2023 SR) 73 pages	2023 Sustainability Report (CSI 2023 SR) 83 pages
Refers to GRI, SASB, and SDGs	Yes	SASB, SDGs – also TCFD	Yes	Yes – also EU rules	SDGs on webpage, otherwise Yes	SASB and SDGs	Yes – also EU rules	SASB and SDGs – also TCFD and EU rules	Yes – also IFRS 2
Report assurance	Yes	Yes	Yes	Yes	Yes	Yes	Yes	Yes	Yes

Notes:
[a] Barrick Sustainability Report 2023 (Barrick 2023 SR) http://q4live.s25.clientfiles.s3-website-us-east-1.amazonaws.com/322814910/files/doc_downloads/sustainability/Barrick_Sustainability_Report_2023.pdf.
[b] TotalEnergies Sustainability and Climate Progress Report 2024 (TotalEnergies 2024 SR) https://totalenergies.com/system/files/documents/2024-03/totalenergies_sustainability-climate-2024-progress-report_2024_en_pdf.pdf.
[c] Statement of Non-Financial Information. Sustainability Report Financial Year 2023 (Iberdrola 2023 SR) https://www.iberdrola.com/documents/20125/42388/IB_Sustainability_Report.pdf.

Rights, Natural Capital, and Governance. The introductory section contains an introductory letter from the President/CEO, a sustainability vision, and a materiality assessment. At the end of the report are sections concerning managing risk and governance. Throughout the document are explanations, scorecards, and case studies.

8.14 In its report, Barrick provides a strong endorsement of the Sustainable Development Goals (SDGs) and the importance of mining because it 'has a critical role to play in delivering socio-economic upliftment and a fairer future'.[25] Implementing its partnership approach leads to some of its key performance indicators being directed at socioeconomic benefits, such as the extent to which its workforce is made up of host nationals and economic value staying in the host country.[26] That international emphasis is not present in the Cameco and MinRes reports, which instead focus on native or indigenous peoples in Canada and Australia. The unifying factor between all three is a focus on the communities in which they operate.

8.15 Barrick 2023 SR makes clear that Barrick is serious in its approach to sustainability performance and has evolved its thinking and disclosures over time.[27] It characterises its approach as:

> Our approach to disclosure and frameworks is that we will use them wherever they deliver value to our business and our stakeholders, particularly those communities closest to our operations.[28]

It sounds a note of caution about the development of ESG frameworks, saying:

> While we very much welcome a focus on aspects beyond the bottom line we believe the 'ESG industry' is now at risk of missing the point. It risks becoming more than a race to compliance, with too much emphasis on contextless box-ticking, ranking exercises and competition to be 'first on paper'. In short, ESG has lost sight of what it means to be sustainable. Real world progress and situational complexities are sometimes missed with a new form of short-termism emerging'.[29]

8.16 The structure of the Barrick 2023 SR is not to set out a comprehensive list of targets in one place. For example, it adopts the Commonly Used Goals mentioned at 8.07, but they appear throughout the report in relevant places where they are explained. Barrick 2023 SR also has a scorecard for each of the

25 Ibid 7.
26 See the Social and Economic Development Scorecard in Ibid 14.
27 Ibid 7.
28 Ibid.
29 Ibid.

four pillars to enable it to rate and benchmark its sustainability performance against its peers and its own past performance. Those four pillars are 'contributing to the social and economic development of our host countries and communities, protecting the safety and health of our people, respecting human rights and minimizing our impact on the natural environment'.[30] It has what it describes as an Independent Assurance Schedule, which tracks its performance against the Responsible Gold Mining Principles and relevant ICMM performance expectations.[31] That leads to statements like that on diversity, that 'we will implement policies and practices to promote diversity at all levels of the Company and, especially, the representation of women, and will report on our progress'.[32] Barrick 2023 SR has also been prepared with reference to the SDGs, the GRI Universal Standards, and the TCFD.[33]

Cameco

The Cameco 2023 Sustainability Report (Cameco 2023 SR), which has data up to 31 December 2023, highlights the main distinguishing feature of its business, which is that it produces uranium. It is therefore an advocate for nuclear power as a response to climate change, saying that nuclear power is 'a central part of the clean energy transition'.[34] Cameco's vision is 'Energizing a clean-air world', guided by four key values: safety and environment, people, integrity, and excellence. The report starts with a letter from the CEO and 2023 sustainability highlights. There follow sections on 'Providing the uranium fuel the world needs', 'Supporting global climate action', 'Demonstrating environmental stewardship', 'Building a strong workforce and resilient communities', 'Leading with our values', and Appendices. The Appendices contain a performance table, SASB index, a mine tailings disclosure schedule, and a limited assurance report. The report has also been prepared with reference to SASB and TCFD recommendations.[35] **8.17**

Cameco also adopts the Commonly Used Goals mentioned at 8.07 and they appear throughout the report. In addition, there is a performance table with **8.18**

30 Barrick 2023 SR, 4.
31 Ibid from 102.
32 Ibid 107. That compares with ICMM 3.8, which says, 'Implement policies and practices to respect the rights and interests of women that reflect gender-informed approaches to work practices and job design, and that protect against all forms of discrimination and harassment, and behaviours that adversely impact on women's successful participation in the workplace'. See https://www.icmm.com/website/publications/pdfs/mining-principles/mining-principles.pdf?cb=83767.
33 Barrick 2023 SR, 8.
34 Cameco 2023 SR, 6.
35 Cameco 2023 SR, 16.

the categories environment, social, and governance, which also provides details in relation to things like water usage.[36] Cameco sets out its scorecard for its 2023 targets. Except in the environmental area where the focus on effluent discharge, groundwater, and tailings management is coloured to some degree by the radioactive nature of uranium, its targets are not dissimilar to MinRes.

8.19 In relation to the environment, it reported those targets as:

> **Net-Zero ambition**
> Develop tailored decarbonization pathways for operationally controlled sites.
> **Climate-related**
> Refine the calculations necessary to quantify our Scope 3 GHG emissions profile.
> Engage a third-party expert to conduct physical risk assessments of our Fuel Services Division's operations.
> **Environmental performance**
> Improve effluent discharge management at our Saskatchewan and Ontario operations by maintaining quality within regulatory limits and action levels, predicted environmental effects, and achieving historic benchmarks.
> Progress groundwater restoration at our US operations by: Advancing two specified mine units into the stability monitoring stage; Developing and submitting to regulatory authorities Alternate Concentration Limits (ACL) for one mine unit; and Achieving clean evaluations for 134 production wells.
> **Tailings Management**
> Achieve Level A for all our tailings facilities in all indicators of Mining Association of Canada's Towards Sustainable Mining Tailings Management Protocol by the end of 2023.

MinRes

8.20 The MinRes 2024 Sustainability Report (MinRes 2024 SR) starts with a letter from the sustainability committee chair and deals with its 2024 performance, information about the company, and its sustainability approach. MinRes 2024 SR covers the 12 months ending on 30 June 2024. There follow sections on governance, social, and environment. At the end are an index of tables and figures and a limited assurance statement. MinRes 2024 SR comments that 'Following a period of transformational growth, MinRes has refreshed its vision and values to better reflect our company's aspirations and culture.'[37] Its vision, as set out in MinRes 2024 SR, says that 'MinRes will be the global

36 Cameco 2023 SR, 96.

37 MinRes 2024 Sustainability Report (MinRes 2024 SR) at https://reports.mineralresources.com.au/2024-sustainability-report/ 16. It covers the 12 months to 30 June 2024.

leader in innovative resources project design, delivery and operation'.[38] It has also amended its sustainability approach. The current version is set out in the MinRes 2024 SR, starting with a Sustainability Pathway:

> MinRes is committed to improving our sustainability performance while we continue providing the metals and minerals the world needs to transition to a low-carbon future. We strive to make an impact through our innovation and leadership in mining services and operations, encouraging responsible business practices, whilst recognising the importance of sustainability, and acting in a manner that maintains our social licence to operate. We aim to create long-term value for all stakeholders through the incorporation of responsible mining principles into our decision-making, strategic planning and risk management processes.
>
> Since our inaugural sustainability report in FY18, we have continued to embed sustainability within the business, ensuring compliance with relevant legislation and regulations and strengthening our governance frameworks. This has enabled a deepening in transparency and reliability of our reporting, with continued alignment to several internationally recognised reporting frameworks and an improved external assurance program. Refer to our website to view our sustainability pathway, which showcases our progress and achievements from FY18 to FY24, as well as our future commitments.[39]

Its approach in MinRes 2023 SR was different.[40]

The importance that MinRes places on sustainability comes out in comments **8.21** such as: 'MinRes would not have a business without sustainability – it defines everything that MinRes does.'[41] Its report has detailed performance data,[42] some of which has been subject to independent assurance.[43] It also has targets and reports its performance.[44] MinRes also adopts the Commonly Used Goals mentioned at 8.07 and they appear throughout the report. MinRes's 2024 targets for the Environment were:

Managing environmental impact
90 per cent of actions progressed in our Biodiversity Action Plan (that are relevant to this FY)
Develop an implementation plan to meet the Global Industry Standard on Tailings Management (GISTM)

---

38 MinRes 2024 SR 16. In the MinRes 2023 Sustainability Report (MinRes 2023 SR) its vision was 'to be recognised as a great Australian company and a leading provider of innovative and sustainable mining services and operations' (MinRes 2023 SR, 1).

39 MinRes 2024 SR, 20

40 It was 'we strive to generate shareholder value and maintain our social licence to operate by supporting the wellbeing of our people, protecting the environment and making a positive contribution to the communities in which we operate' (MinRes 2023 SR, 1).

41 Industry Interview, August 2024.

42 The tables are spread throughout the report. For a listing, see MinRes 2024 SR, 209.

43 See MinRes 2024 SR, 212.

44 See Ibid 33.

Develop Water Management Plans across all operational sites
Climate change
Net zero operational emissions by 2050
50% reduction in operational emissions on existing operations by 2035 from baseline FY 22[45]

MinRes has set targets for 2025.[46] It says that its reporting is guided by the following initiatives: the GRI, SASB Metals and Mining Standard, UNGC, 12 of the SDGs,[47] and the TCFD.[48] It says that in the future it intends to report in accordance with Australian Accounting Standards Board (AASB)'s S1 and S2 Standards and the Taskforce on Nature-related Financial Disclosure Framework.[49]

8.22 The targets in 8.16 and 8.21 are set out to provide examples. For both Cameco and MinRes, some involve planning (e.g., develop decarbonisation pathways or develop biodiversity strategy), some are task-oriented (e.g., advance mine units to the stability monitoring stage or complete onsite water efficiency audits), and some are numerical or require an independent standard to be met (e.g., achieve Level A for all our tailings facilities or net zero operational emissions by 2050). It can be anticipated that companies or organisations on a sustainability journey will need different kinds of targets depending on the scope of their activities and how they are progressing. The targets will vary across areas. There are other subtleties that are beyond the scope of this book and with which industry professionals will be familiar. For example, all the companies want to improve safety and so track historical data like TRIFR. But they also commonly use leading indicators such as near misses or the level of training.

THE OIL AND GAS COMPANIES

Introduction

8.23 All three oil and gas companies produced sustainability reports. Various factors play a part in causing differences in their reports. Similar to mining, these factors start with the countries in which they are headquartered and where

45 MinRes 2024 SR, 13.
46 MinRes 2024 SR, 24.
47 SDG 3, 4, 5, 6, 7, 8, 10, 11, 12, 13, 15, and 17. It reports its progress in the Sustainability Data Tables. See https://www.mineralresources.com.au/investor-centre/annual-reporting-suite/ under 2024 Sustainability Report.
48 MinRes 2024 SR, 20.
49 MinRes 2024 SR, 21.

their operations are located, what they produce, and size. TotalEnergies has its headquarters in France, Conoco in the USA, and Cenovus in Canada. All have their securities listed on a stock exchange.[50] The market capitalisation of TotalEnergies is US$158.89 billion (143.6 billion euros),[51] Conoco is US$127.901 billion, and Cenovus US$31.52 billion.[52] TotalEnergies and Conoco have operations in numerous countries, while Cenovus has operations in Canada.

TotalEnergies

TotalEnergies Sustainability and Climate 2024 Progress Report *More Energy Less Emissions* (TotalEnergies 2024 SR) starts with an Introduction with a message from the chairman and CEO and then deals with governance and climate-related risks. There is then a section on TotalEnergies' ambition and progress. TotalEnergies 2024 SR covers the 12 months ending on 30 June 2024. There follow sections on 'Energy and climate: our orderly energy transition' and 'Our Actions for a just transition'. The latter has sub-sections on 'Acting for the well-being of our employees', 'Caring for the environment', and 'Having a positive impact for stakeholders', as well as a final sub-section of 'Performance indicators'. At the end are an index of tables and figures and a limited assurance statement. TotalEnergies 2024 SR is the first report dealt with in this chapter which follows the EU Taxonomy,[53] so there are detailed tables reporting on sustainability.[54] TotalEnergies is present in about 120 countries and produces hydrocarbons or explores for them in 50.[55] It has operations in the Americas, Africa, the Middle East, and Asia. Its operations are diverse and becoming increasingly so as they encompass upstream and downstream oil and gas, carbon capture and storage, production of biogas and aircraft fuel, renewable energy production, electricity storage, and development of electric charging sites for motor vehicles. By 2030, TotalEnergies aims to be one of the top five producers of wind and solar energy in the world outside China.[56] 8.24

50 TotalEnergies securities are quoted on Euronext and on the NYSE. Conoco's are quoted on the NYSE. Cenovus's are quoted on the Toronto Stock Exchange and the NYSE.
51 As of 2 October 2024 for TotalEnergies and Conoco.
52 Also as of 2 October 2024.
53 TotalEnergies 2024 SR, 25.
54 Ibid from 99.
55 Total Energies Universal Registration Document 2023, including the Annual Financial Report, 14 https://totalenergies.com/system/files/documents/2024-03/totalenergies_universal-registration-document-2023_2023_en_pdf.pdf.
56 TotalEnergies 2024 SR, 47.

8.25 TotalEnergies puts climate change and the energy transition at the centre of its strategy and approach to sustainability. TotalEnergies 2024 SR says at the start that its purpose is 'to provide as many people as possible with energy that is more reliable, more affordable, and more sustainable' and its ambition is 'to be a major player in the energy transition, on the road to Net Zero by 2050, together with society'. TotalEnergies 2024 SR is clear in its support for agreements reached in Dubai as part of COP28 as part of 'transitioning away from fossil fuels in a just, orderly and equitable manner'.[57] It comments:

> TotalEnergies supports the objectives of tripling the amount of renewable energy and doubling energy efficiency by 2030, as well as slashing methane emissions within that time frame. These objectives are at the heart of TotalEnergies roadmap for 2030.[58]

TotalEnergies sees its primary responsibility as a producer of fossil fuels to 'substantially reduce emissions on our facilities'.[59]

8.26 The scope of the change that TotalEnergies is planning in its business is significant. According to Chairman and CEO Patrick Pouyanné, its transition strategy is:

> anchored on two pillars, the responsible production and sales of Oil & Gas, and electricity, notably renewables. TotalEnergies supports the objectives of tripling renewable energies (and aims to do more at its own level) and doubling energy efficiency by 2030, as well as slashing methane emissions within that time frame *("aiming for zero methane").*[60]

That involves a significant investment in renewables,[61] but also growing oil and gas production by 2–3% over the next five years, 'predominantly from LNG, thanks to its rich low cost, low emission Upstream portfolio'.[62] The overall result is that by 2050 about 50% of its energy will be in the form of electricity, including storage, about 25% of its energy will be in the form of biogas, hydrogen, or synthetic liquid fuels from circular reactions, and around 1 million boe per day of oil and gas, which would be about one quarter of the production in 2030.[63] TotalEnergies has a significant part of its refining and marketing activities in Europe and therefore has to respond to the initiatives that the European Union has on climate change and sustainability. Among those are

57 Ibid 12.

58 Ibid.

59 Ibid 30.

60 Ibid 4.

61 Ibid, where it says 'the Company aims to grow its power generation to more than 100 TWh by 2030, investing on average $4 billion per year'.

62 Ibid 1.

63 TotalEnergies 2024 SR, 14.

the European Union's Green Deal and 'Fit for 55' regulatory package along with its 'ambition to be the first carbon-neutral continent by 2050'.[64] There are also significant regulatory requirements, such as the Corporate Sustainability Reporting Directive (CSRD),[65] the Directive on Corporate Sustainability Due Diligence (CSDD),[66] and the EU Taxonomy for Sustainable Activities (EU Taxonomy).[67]

TotalEnergies 2024 SR stresses the importance of the SDGs, saying that 'energy is at the heart of the most daunting challenges of the 21st century, defined in the U.N.'s 2030 Agenda in the form of its 17 Sustainable Development Goals (SDGs)'. It goes on to say: **8.27**

> As part of its transition strategy to achieve its 2050 Net Zero Ambition, together with society, the Company affirms its purpose: to provide as many people as possible with energy that is more reliable, more affordable and more sustainable, and has placed Sustainability at the heart of its strategy, its projects and its operations.
>
> Our commitment is based on the values defined in our Code of Conduct and our approach to sustainability is structured around 4 axes:
>
> - climate and sustainable energy,
> - caring for the environment,
> - acting for the well-being of employees,
> - having a positive impact for stakeholders.

TotalEnergies has a 'Just Transition Plan' which, among the companies reviewed in this chapter, is one of the most philosophically supportive of the least developed countries. Having said that, it is interesting to compare it with Barrick's 'partner of choice' approach. Also, all of the companies reviewed track progress against the SDGs, and a number of them have particular transition initiatives. But TotalEnergies raises the critical question of how 'we can move to a sustainable development model that meets the vital needs of the planet's 8 billion current inhabitants today… without compromising the ability of future generations to meet their own needs'.[68] It says: **8.28**

> This transition process must be just if it is to succeed. It must provide the least developed countries with the clean, reliable and affordable energy they need for their growing

64 Ibid 43.

65 Corporate Sustainability Reporting Directive, EU Directive 2022/2464.

66 Directive on corporate sustainability due diligence (CSDD) EU Directive 2024/1760 that came into force on 25 July 2024 https://eur-lex.europa.eu/eli/dir/2024/1760/oj.

67 EU Taxonomy for Sustainable Activities, Regulation 2020/852/EU (EU Taxonomy), came into force on 12 July 2020 https://eur-lex.europa.eu/legal-content/EN/TXT/?uri=CELEX:32020R0852.

68 TotalEnergies 2024 SR, 55.

populations aspiring to a higher standard of living. The most developed countries, in turn, will need to assist those who could be adversely affected by the transition.[69]

8.29 TotalEnergies also has a sustainability programme called 'Sustainab'All' that involved employees taking part in workshops in 2022 to develop 10 objectives and indicators aligned with the SDGs. In 2023, every site, business unit, and affiliate adopted an action plan with targets to be met by 2025. The 10 key performance indicators are:

TotalEnergies becoming a global player in Sustainable Energy

- Low-carbon energy produced, or low carbon energy sold (in energy unit)
- Energy consumption (in energy unit) and low-carbon consumption (in energy unit)
- Number of suppliers with local sales over $10,000 with a climate commitment, i.e. having a plan with climate goals (in number and in % total number of suppliers)
- Number of innovative solutions that help us use less and better energy, or produce and sell more low-carbon energy

Thanks to our commitment to a just transition for our people

- The level of employee engagement measures once a year via TotalEnergies engagement index
- Number of hours of training per employee per year
- Share of women among NP14 (in %) and share of international staff among NP15+ (in %)

TotalEnergies saves natural resources

- Sum of weight of recycled waste and recycled feedstock (in tons)
- Number of biodiversity plans being developed

TotalEnergies creates shared value

- Share of spending with local stakeholders as a % of total spending = local wages + local spend + societal spend/opex + capex (in %)

Each has SDGs listed against it to which the target contributes. These indicators provide an example of targeting, but targeting directed at employees.

8.30 TotalEnergies 2024 SR sets out numerous performance metrics that cover emissions (including methane), water use, biodiversity, hydrocarbon spills, waste, safety, economic contribution, its workforce, human rights, and governance.[70] The metrics generally cover each year going back to 2019 so it is

69 Ibid.

70 Ibid starting at 98.

possible to compare performance over time. A number of the extra financial indicators used in the metrics were subject to an assurance conclusion by an independent third party.[71] TotalEnergies also adopts the Commonly Used Goals, and they appear throughout the report.

Conoco

Conoco produced a 2023 Sustainability Report (Conoco 2023 SR).[72] Conoco 2023 SR starts with a message from the chairman and CEO and then has a section on 'Governance and our approach' that deals with governance and climate-related risks. Conoco 2023 SR covers the 12 months ending on 31 December 2023. There follow sections on 'Climate', 'Nature', 'Social', 'Our people', 'Safety, health and security', and, finally, 'Performance'. Conoco has operations in 12 countries. It makes the point initially that the 'energy transition will be complex and will continue to evolve, with oil and natural gas projected to remain essential parts of the energy supply mix for decades across a broad range of transition scenarios'.[73] Conoco intends to play a valued part in the transition by executing on its triple mandate: 'meeting transition pathway energy demand, delivering competitive returns to shareholders and driving accountability for emissions within our control'.[74] Meeting demand requires a 'focus on delivering production that will best compete in any transition scenario'.[75] That production will be delivered 'from a diverse portfolio of resources with a competitive cost of supply and low greenhouse gas (GHG) emissions intensity'.[76] It says that Conoco demonstrates its commitment to sustainability through: **8.31**

- Planning for the net zero energy transition and managing climate-related risks
- Proactively implementing mitigation actions and conservation efforts related to nature-related risks, impacts, dependencies and opportunities
- Ensuring safe operations and creating shared value for neighbouring communities
- Attracting and retaining a world-class workforce
- Prioritizing the safety, health and security of our workforce and the communities where we operate

71 The third party was EY & Associates. See TotalEnergies SR, 97.

72 ConocoPhillips 2023 Sustainability Report (Conoco 2023 SR) https://static.conocophillips.com/files/resources/conocophillips-2023-sustainability-report.pdf.

73 Ibid 2.

74 Ibid 5.

75 Ibid 2.

76 Ibid.

> We continue to be guided by our Triple Mandate to reliably and responsibly meet demand, deliver competitive returns on and of capital and achieve our net operational emissions ambition (Scope 1 and 2 emissions on a net equity and gross operated basis).[77]

8.32 Conoco 2024 SR sets out numerous performance metrics that cover the same areas as are mentioned in relation to TotalEnergies at 8.30. There are variations in that Conoco separately expresses metrics for flaring and energy use.[78] The metrics generally cover each year going back to 2019 and specify the applicable GRI, Ipieca, and SASB references. Conoco also follows the AXPC ESG metrics template.[79] Conoco adopts the Commonly Used Goals mentioned at 8.07 and they appear throughout the report. Generally, in each performance area of its report, such as GHG emissions, Conoco reports on performance and target progress.

8.33 Conoco 2023 SR has an emphasis on how it manages risks. For example, it emphasises the importance of its analysis of climate-related risk scenarios.[80] Clear targets are set for emissions, although targets in other areas are harder to find. Emissions targets are as follows:

- Ambition to reach net-zero emissions for Scope 1 and 2 emissions by 2050.
- Reduce GHG emissions intensity to 50–60% by 2030 on both a gross operated and net equity basis from a 2016 baseline.
- Achieve near-zero methane emissions intensity by 2030.
- Reduce methane emissions intensity by 10% by 2025 from a 2020 baseline.
- Achieve a target of zero routine flaring by the end of 2025, five years sooner than the World Bank initiative's goal of 2030.[81]

8.34 While Conoco does not set targets in a number of areas such as biodiversity, its report contains performance metrics on biodiversity and also comments on Conoco's activities. For example, in relation to nature-related risks and impacts, it makes the point that the evolution in nature-related disclosures led by the Task Force on Nature-related Financial Disclosures (TNFD) underscores increasing disclosure expectations. Accordingly, Conoco's approach is 'to assess how its business impacts nature, identify ecosystem services we rely on and implement risk reduction and transformative opportunities'.[82] It then sets out five areas where it is seeking to minimise, restore, or offset impacts:

---

77 Ibid 5. For a discussion of the implications of maintaining a competitive cost of supply, see page 19.

78 Ibid starting at 85.

79 Ibid 9 and starting at 93.

80 Ibid 8.

81 Ibid 23.

82 Ibid 42.

land, freshwater or ocean-use change, resource use, invasive species, pollution, and climate change.[83] Using water as an example, the performance metrics set out extensive data going back to 2019 of water usage, consumption, and recycling. Another example is pollution, where there is also extensive data on spills which shows that total spills in 2023 are considerably less than previous years. On the other hand, GHG emissions increased in 2023 over 2022 by 9%, but Conoco explains why that is the case.[84]

Cenovus

Cenovus produced a 2023 Corporate Social Sustainability Report (Cenovus 2023 SR).[85] It covers the 12 months ending on 31 December 2023. Cenovus 2023 SR explains that it differs from previous reports in not commenting on environmental performance, which it attributes to changes in Canada's competition laws.[86] Cenovus is a Canadian integrated oil and gas company. It has five environmental, social, and governance (ESG) focus areas: climate and greenhouse gas (GHG) emissions, water stewardship, biodiversity, indigenous reconciliation, and inclusion and diversity, which are contained in its sustainability policy updated in 2021.[87] 8.35

Following on from the previous paragraph that Cenovus 2023 SR does not comment on environmental performance, environmental matters and emissions are not covered in its performance indicators.[88] So while Cenovus adopts the Commonly Used Goals in the non-environmental areas and has objectives broadly aligned with those relating to emissions and water, there is no current information on the environmental goals and what its position is on Scope 1 and 2 emissions. The indicators published in Cenovus 2023 SR cover the areas of safety and asset integrity, financial indicators, indigenous and community engagement, our people, and business ethics. The report is broken down into an executive summary with a message from the President/CEO and a progress 8.36

---

83 Ibid.

84 Conoco 2023 SR 25 mentions, among other things, improved and corrected data and increased activity in two places.

85 Cenovus 2023 Corporate Social Sustainability Report (Cenovus 2023 SR) https://mc-3405db07-6660-4b4e-8bc8-1763-cdn-endpoint.azureedge.net/-/media/Project/WWW/docs/sustainability/2023/2023-corporate-social-responsibility-report.pdf?rev=ed1cc9eef4934bea9e2d4a8564d551a3&sc_lang=en&hash=5DA62A7E1A074F5C940E1B6A3275EA7B.

86 Ibid 4.

87 Ibid. These are also set out in Cenovus's sustainability policy, last updated 28 July 2021 https://mc-3405db07-6660-4b4e-8bc8-1763-cdn-endpoint.azureedge.net/-/media/Project/WWW/docs/our-company/sustainability.pdf?rev=4a357afd2fcc4d18aeb81de0f3e26bec&sc_lang=en&hash=7B883EDE2536AEDB9281989C78E3EA1B.

88 Starting at Cenovus 2023 SR, 59.

report. It is followed by sections on 'Our safety culture', 'Indigenous reconciliation', 'Inclusion and diversity', and 'Governance', with sub-sections on risk, strategy, and governance. The last section contains data. Throughout the document are explanations and scorecards.

8.37 By way of example, the metrics for indigenous engagement set out what is described as the 'indigenous spend' for each year going back to 2019. But social targets are also set as follows:

> **Indigenous reconciliation**
> Achieve a minimum of $1.2 billion of spending with Indigenous businesses between 2019 and year-end 2025.
> Attain Gold Partnership Accreditation in Indigenous Relations certification from the Canadian Council for Indigenous Business by year-end 2025.
> **Inclusion & diversity**
> Increase women in leadership roles to 30% by year-end 2030.
> Aspire to have at least 40% representation from designated groups among non-management directors.
> Including at least 30% women, by year-end 2025.

The first and the last two were met by 2023. Gold Partnership Accreditation was not achieved. The women in leadership level was 26% in 2023, just short of the target.

8.38 The report aligns with some SASB standards such as the Extractives and Mineral Processing – Oil and Gas – Exploration and Production (E & P) Standard and uses the Ipieca guidance when there is no SASB guidance.[89] A table of SASB accounting metrics and relevant indexes is provided, and Cenovus compliance noted.[90] Independent assurance of nine indicators used in the report was carried out.[91]

THE RENEWABLE ENERGY COMPANIES

Introduction

8.39 The renewable energy companies selected are Iberdrola SA (Iberdrola), Vestas Wind (Vestas), and Canadian Solar Inc (CSI). All have their securities listed on a securities exchange.[92] Iberdrola is a major producer and supplier of

---

89 Ibid 63.

90 Ibid 66.

91 By PWC. See Cenovus 2023 SR, 69.

92 Iberdrola is listed on Euronext. Vestas is listed on Nasdaq Copenhagen. CSI is listed on Nasdaq.

electricity from wind and solar. Vestas describes itself as the market leader in onshore wind, becoming significant in offshore wind as well. CSI is a leading manufacturer of solar photovoltaic modules, provider of solar energy and battery energy storage solutions, and developer of utility-scale solar power and battery energy storage projects.

Iberdrola

8.40 Iberdrola produced a Non-financial Information Statement Sustainability Report covering the 12 months to 31 December 2023 (Iberdrola 2023 SR). Its report is subject to the rules of the EU.[93] So there are detailed tables reporting on sustainability in accordance with the EU Taxonomy.[94] In addition to the GRI and SASB,[95] the report follows the recommendations of the TCFD and complies with UNGC.[96] Iberdrola 2023 SR starts with a letter from the chairman and CEO and then sets out 'Recognitions/Awards and ratings'. There follow major sections entitled 'Iberdrola: the utility of the future', 'Environmental', 'Social', 'Governance', 'Financial', 'About this report', and 'Annexes'. The first five have sub-sections, with the first having sub-sections entitled 'About Iberdrola', 'Governance and Sustainability System', 'Climate action and TCFD', and 'Our ESG + F Proposal'. Iberdrola carries on business in 25 countries. Its activities include the production, transmission, supply, and sale of electricity from conventional as well as renewable sources.[97] Its corporate purpose, which it says is in line with the SDGs and 'mirrors the main social trends and addresses major economic, social and environmental challenges, reflecting the expectations of Stakeholders and defining Iberdrola's role as an agent of social change and transformation in the energy sector', is expressed as follows: 'To continue building together each day a healthier, more accessible energy model, based on electricity.'[98]

93 Iberdrola Non-financial Information Statement Sustainability Report (Iberdrola 2023 SR). Iberdrola's Annual Financial Information for 2023 is at 2023 https://www.iberdrola.com/documents/20125/42388/IB_Annual_Financial_Information.pdf (Iberdrola 2023 FI) and Integrated Report of April 2024 at https://www.iberdrola.com/documents/20125/42388/IB_Integrated_Report.pdf. In their Independent Assurance Report at the start of Iberdrola 2023 SR, KPMG note that it was prepared in accordance with the Sustainability Reporting Standard of the GRI and the indicators of SASB for the 'Electric Utilities & Power Generators Sectors'.

94 Iberdrola 2023 SR from 276.

95 Iberdrola SR 298 and n 93.

96 Iberdrola 2023 SR, 298.

97 Iberdrola 2023 FI, 11.

98 Iberdrola 2023 SR, 13.

8.41 To attain this purpose, the Iberdrola group has condensed its corporate values into the following three concepts:

- **Sustainable energy**: the group seeks to always be a model of inspiration, creating economic, social and environmental value in all of its surroundings, and with the future in mind.
- **Integrating force**: the group works with strength and responsibility, combining talents, for a Purpose that is to be achieved by all and for all.
- **Driving force**: the Iberdrola group brings about small and large changes in order to make people's lives easier, always seeking to improve, and to do so efficiently and with high self- imposed standards.[99]

8.42 Iberdrola has declared its ambition to achieve CO2eq neutrality by 2030 for Scopes 1 and 2, with an ultimate goal to achieve net zero emissions by 2040.[100] The four main levers for actions to achieve these ambitions are 100% renewables (investment in renewables), 100% smart grids (development of robust grids), green solutions for its customers (by, for example, contributing to their electrification and decarbonisation as well as promoting initiatives such as green hydrogen), and green purchases (the use of renewables in its business and development of green products).[101] Iberdrola's business plan to 2026 indicates it plans to allocate €15.5 billion to renewable business to grow selectively in flexible technologies and storage. More than half of this amount is focused on offshore wind in the United States, the United Kingdom, France, and Germany, with 28% on onshore wind and 18% on solar.[102]

8.43 In the sub-section of the report titled 'ESG + F Goals: the sustainability roadmap', Iberdrola explains how ESG factors are integrated into its strategic plan and operations. It says that integration is rooted in three factors: 'the corporate purpose that structures the company's positioning, stakeholders' expectations, and finally the demands of the capital markets, represented by the ESG indices and ratings, voting policies, and institutional investor alliances',[103] all of which are included in its materiality analysis.[104] It makes the point that 'Iberdrola's commitment to sustainable development, the social dividend, and the generation of value shared with all stakeholders is reflected in multiple indicators that

99 Ibid.
100 Ibid 42.
101 Ibid 43.
102 About Iberdrola World leader in renewable energy https://www.iberdrola.com/about-us/our-company/renewable-energies.
103 Iberdrola 2023 SR, 70.
104 Ibid chapter VI.2.

make it possible to measure the positive impact generated by the group'.[105] Its value generation is crystallised in its Sustainable Development Plan 2020–2022, *Energy to Advance*, 'a roadmap with goals defined around the group's environmental, social and governance priorities'.

The report goes on to explain the balance between indicators and targets: **8.44**

> In the current market context, our Stakeholders are asking for more ESG information from the company, which, coupled with increasingly demanding regulations, requires us to review these targets, align them with best market practices and ensure that they are sufficiently ambitious to anticipate their demands and ensure that Iberdrola maintains its current leadership position.[106]

It summarises its targeting in the other ESG areas as:

- In environmental terms, the goal is to continue to contribute to the creation of an energy system that is positive for nature, facing the threefold environmental challenge of the fight against climate change, the preservation of biodiversity, and the circularity of resources.
- In social terms, the company continues to focus on maximising its positive impact through the generation of quality jobs, focusing on diversity, safety, health and education; on improving the products and services offered to our customers; on creating a responsible value chain; and on developing the communities in which we do business.
- In terms of governance, the goal is to maintain robust corporate governance and compliance standards, continually revised and assessed to ensure that best practices, adapted to the context of operations and regulation, are applied at all times.

Iberdrola has 39 objectives across the areas of Environmental, Social, Governance, and Sustainable Finance.[107] Iberdrola adopts the Commonly Used Goals. So, for example, under Environmental, it has a target of 'Net Zero in scopes 1, 2 and 3 before 2024'. The metric is 'Achieve before 2040' (progress towards 2030 target). Progress in 2023 was 45%. SDGs 7 and 13 are listed against it. **8.45**

105 Ibid 70.

106 Ibid. At 297, it explains, 'This document forms part of the *Management report of Iberdrola, S.A.* and of the *Management report of Iberdrola, S.A.* consolidated with its subsidiaries for financial year 2023, and is subject to the same approval, deposit and publication standards as said reports.'

107 Set out from Ibid 71.

Vestas

8.46 With more than 40 years in the wind industry, Vestas says that it has more experience than anyone else in making wind work,[108] having installed more than 181 GW of wind power capacity (including more than 10 GW offshore), and its turbines have been installed in 88 countries.[109] Vestas' 2023 Sustainability Report (Vestas 2023 SR) starts with an Executive Statement and then sets out details of 'Expected emissions avoided' and 'Sustainability strategy and performance'. Then, there is a 'General' section followed by sections entitled 'Environment', 'Social', 'Governance', and 'Sustainability data'. The report covers the 12 months to 31 December 2023. In Vestas 2023 SR, Vestas says that it is committed to 'advancing the global green energy transition', investing €500 million in green energy research and development in 2023.[110] Vestas was recognised in the Corporate Knights Global 100 ranking as the most sustainable company in the entire energy industry for the third year running.[111] Two matters of importance that it stresses in its report are, first, the large areas that wind farms take up and, therefore, the need for spatial planning and appropriate environmental impact assessment.[112] Second, as a producer of wind turbines, the majority of its emissions come from its supply chain and that its turbines have to be disposed of at the end of their economic life.[113] These ideas guide its sustainability strategy, 'Sustainability in Everything We Do', which has four pillars: carbon neutrality in its own operations and a 45% reduction in supply chain emissions by 2030, production of zero-waste wind turbines by 2040, being the safest, most inclusive socially responsible company in the energy industry, and leading the transition to a world powered by renewable energy.

8.47 Vestas adopts the Commonly Used Goals. In its report, it sets out what it describes as sustainability key data, which deals with the areas that are the subject of the Commonly Used Goals, amongst others.[114] Targets are spread throughout the report. The report is Vestas' mandatory annual sustainability report for the purposes of the Danish Financial Statements Act and the

108 Vestas track record https://www.vestas.com/en/energy-solutions/track-record.
109 Ibid.
110 Vestas 2023 SR 4.
111 Ibid.
112 Ibid 25.
113 Ibid 4 and 19.
114 Ibid 57.

EU Sustainable Finance Taxonomy.[115] It also reports in relation to selected SDGs.[116] Its metrics align with SASB and TCFD recommendations.[117]

CSI

CSI has two business segments: CSI Solar is a manufacturer and provider of solar photovoltaic modules and solar energy and battery energy storage solutions; Recurrent Energy is a developer of utility-scale solar power and battery energy storage projects.[118] Its 2023 Sustainability Report (CSI 2023 SR) covers the 12 months to 31 December 2023. It starts with a message from the CEO and then sets out highlights. There follow sections entitled 'About Canadian Solar', 'Environmental Metrics and Targets', 'Social Responsibility', 'Responsible Supply Chain', 'Governance', and 'About this Report' and 'Annexes'. There is an appendix dealing with Global Reporting Frameworks, SASB Index, IFRS Disclosures, and GRI Metrics. CSI 2023 SR says that CSI powered 32 million households, employing 22,000 people worldwide.[119] It also says: **8.48**

> Canadian Solar is committed to powering the world with solar energy and creating a cleaner earth for future generations. At Canadian Solar, we are committed to improving our practices to ensure long-term sustainability by integrating Environmental, Social, and Governance (ESG) considerations into our business and strategic decisions.[120]

CSI describes its position on each of the three ESG areas as: Environmental – Working sustainably within our planetary boundaries; Social – Committing to socially responsible and equitable outcomes; and Governance – Demonstrating responsible conduct.[121] It has a number of policies in each of these areas – for example, an Environmental, Occupational Health, and Safety policy.[122] **8.49**

Under 'Environmental' it mentions the following: **8.50**

- GHG emissions and manufacturing energy intensity
- Commitment to 100% renewable energy before 2030
- Solar PV system carbon payback time of 1 year

115 Ibid 2.
116 Ibid 67.
117 Ibid 2.
118 Canadian Solar, About Us https://www.canadiansolar.com/aboutus/#rwjs; 2023 Sustainability Report (CSI 2023 SR), 8 https://www.canadiansolar.com/2023-esg-sustainability-report/.
119 CSI 2023 SR 4.
120 Ibid 9.
121 Ibid.
122 At https://investors.canadiansolar.com/static-files/2c79f247-ad03-48aa-918b-d430b9385b42.

- Water intensity management
- Material use, waste, and circularity
- Environmental stewardship in project development
- Assessing climate risks and opportunities[123]

8.51 Under 'Social' it mentions the following:

- Human rights
- Equal opportunity employer
- Equity, diversity, and inclusion
- Talent strategy, training, and development
- Freedom of association and collective bargaining
- Occupational health and safety
- Community commitments and partnerships[124]

8.52 CSI's sustainability report reflects the nature of its business, which involves manufacturing, and so a significant portion of its Scope 1 and 2 emissions come from electricity consumption in manufacturing. While it has some targets in line with the Commonly Used Goals, there are variations because of the nature of its business. So on emissions, it targets 'powering global operations with 100% renewable energy before 2030' as well as 'from 2023 to 2028 targeting 22% decrease in GHG emission intensity'.[125] It emphasises the circular economy and under that reported a '72% decrease in water intensity between 2017 and 2023'.[126]

FLEXIBLE OPTIONS AND BEST PRACTICE

Flexible options

8.53 The legal requirements set out the parameters of what a sustainability report must contain in a jurisdiction. But in addition, frameworks like the GRI and SASB will 'have a significant impact on the structure of their reports in this Standard'.[127] So a question for many companies is what choices remain after the GRI and SASB standards are complied with. There are choices. These start with the actual wording of the GRI Standards and gaps in them. To give one example from section 3 of GRI 2: General Disclosures 2021 dealing with

123 CSI 2023 SR 9.
124 Ibid.
125 Ibid 22.
126 Ibid 5 and 30.
127 GRI 2: General Disclosures 2021, 6.

governance. That requires information about the highest governing body and its structure and the role of it and senior executives in 'developing, approving and updating its goals for sustainable development'.[128] What it does not do is mandate a particular structure, such as a sustainability committee of the board. So a company can choose whether to have one or not. In certain areas, there are detailed requirements for data – the make-up of employees is one.[129] But that does not impose requirements in relation to the make-up of the workforce – the number of full-time workers or their diversity, for example. Some of the ICMM documents have a useful analysis of gaps that can assist in making choices.[130]

Guidance on best practice

The best place to look for guidance on best practices in sustainability reporting is the guidance provided by organisations like Ipieca and the ICMM.[131] For example, Ipieca is non-judgemental about what frameworks to use. It comments on frameworks: 'you may wish to consider the additional recommendations within these frameworks, in the light of your material issues'.[132] It gives examples of indicators that can be used across all the relevant areas and these are detailed in areas like emissions and safety, to name but two. Copious references are provided to inform indicators like safety indicators. At the same time, its overall position on indicators is: **8.54**

> Once you have identified your material issues, you will need to select indicators that support your narrative and provide evidence of performance. The Guidance offers information on a range of typical issues relevant to many oil and gas companies, along with indicators that demonstrate how the issues are being addressed.[133]

Determining best practice in sustainability reports is difficult. Clearly, there are criteria that can be used to assess the completeness of a report and whether it complies with relevant frameworks. But that is not necessarily the same as making significant progress in achieving sustainability, which involves assessing actual performance. One way to assess whether a report meets best practice requirements is to look for an independent assessment. There are bodies **8.55**

---

128 Disclosure 2-12 GRI 2: General Disclosures 2021.

129 Ibid, Disclosure 2-7.

130 For example, *Framework and Guidance on Social and Economic Reporting* https://www.icmm.com/website/publications/pdfs/social-performance/2022/guidance_social-and-economic-reporting.pdf.

131 For example, ICMM (n 130) and Ipieca, *Sustainability reporting guidance for the oil and gas industry* (4th edition, 2020).

132 Ibid 1.38.

133 Ibid 1.20.

that do ESG rating, and companies reviewed in this chapter have received various awards.[134] That is not to say that there aren't problems with those assessments.[135] What the reader can do is examine the targets set by companies, assess how relevant and challenging they are, and form a conclusion as to which are the best. What can be said about all the companies reviewed in this chapter is that they have made a very serious attempt to set out their sustainability strategy and intentions and that those intentions appear genuine. That is not the same as evaluating whether their reports comply with the relevant rules or whether they represent best practice.

CONCLUSIONS, GUIDANCE, AND KEY PRINCIPLES

8.56 The basic conclusions from this chapter are:

- A conclusion from Chapter 3 was that increasingly, company law, stock exchange and securities rules, and accounting standards are requiring disclosure of important risks to the company's business so that shareholders, markets, and potential buyers of the company's securities are informed about those risks. Climate change risk is an example where the disclosure rules have become increasingly rigorous. It can be anticipated that that rigour will increase in relation to broader sustainability risks. Companies need to be mindful of sanctions, particularly those relating to making misleading statements.
- The legal requirements for reporting will depend on the rules that apply. In many jurisdictions, the rules will require directors to disclose climate-related risks that are material and also actions taken to mitigate them. The companies producing the reports reviewed in this chapter all had an assessment process to decide what issues are material to their business and how risks are managed. However, their reports were extensive, going well beyond climate risks. They generally covered climate change risk (for a good example, see Conoco), but in other cases covered sustainability issues more broadly (for a good example, see MinRes). Their sustainability reports disclosed the risks and the management of them. The reports contained data tables with relevant metrics so a reader could see how the company had performed. Given the increasing number of reporting regimes and their

134 For example, Ecovadis does sustainability ratings. The following are just a few examples of awards. Conoco received the Oil and Gas Methane Partnership 2.0 Gold Standard Pathway designation in recognition of its multiyear measurement-based reporting plan (Conoco 2023 SR 2). Iberdrola received numerous awards (Iberdrola 2023 SR 10), such as being in the Top 5% S&P Global ESG Score, Classified as Prime in the Global 100, and AAA in the MSCI ESG Ratings. It received a Gold Ecovadis medal in 2023. CSI received the following: Ecovadis Silver Sustainability Rating (2024) and ISS ESG Prime Rating, Industry Top 5% (2024).

135 Kenneth P. Pucker, 'Overselling Sustainability Reporting' (2021) *Harvard Business Review* https://hbr.org/2021/05/overselling-sustainability-reporting.

requirements, a significant challenge for writers of reports is making them readable and informative in the important areas.
- There are some important threshold matters for a company considering a sustainability report. These include deciding whether it will track its performance against the SDGs and which ones, deciding its approach to sustainability more broadly as a business objective, and then deciding its strategy in relation to the energy transition.
- The starting point in structuring a report involves deciding the ambit of the materiality assessment, the process for concluding it, and the setting of indicators for which data will be retained to verify outcomes.
- In their reporting, the companies generally had regard to relevant GRI and/or SASB standards. A number of additional frameworks were used. Of note here for companies to which European Union rules apply were the European Union's rules.
- The companies had some independent assurance of aspects of their reports, for example, from an independent firm of accountants.

CHECKLIST

1. Which country's laws apply to the directors of your company and on which securities exchange, if any, are its securities listed? The laws applicable to your directors and your securities will determine whether you need to produce a sustainability report and what the rules are.
2. If you are already required to produce a sustainability report, you should check that it meets the legal requirements and also review the next chapter for possible changes.
3. If the answer is that you are not required to produce a sustainability report currently, perhaps because your securities are not listed, but you will have to produce one, perhaps because you are about to list, then you should check the legal requirements.
4. If you are preparing a sustainability report for the first time, have you considered whether you will track performance against the SDGs and which ones, your approach to sustainability more broadly as a business objective, and your strategy in relation to the energy transition?
5. In reviewing this chapter, have you come across any examples in the reports that you can learn from or emulate?
6. Do the sections on 'Flexible Options' and 'Best Practice' raise any questions for you on your current approach to sustainability?

SCHEDULE (OTHER FRAMEWORKS REFERRED TO IN REPORTS)

Mining

- WGC Responsible Gold Mining Principles (RGMP)
- ICMM Mining Principles Performance Expectations (ICMMPE)

- Global Industry Standard for Tailings Management (GISTM)
- Mining Association of Canada's Towards Sustainable Mining Standard
- TheCopperMark
- Mining Association of Canada's Towards Sustainable Mining Tailings Management Protocol

Oil and gas

- API Template for GHG Reporting
- AXPC ESG Metrics

GENERAL

- Bloomberg Gender Equity Framework
- Science Based Targets Initiative (SBTi)
- United Nations Guiding Principles on Business and Human Rights (UNGPs)
- OECD Guidelines for Multinational Enterprises

9

REGULATION OF COMPANY SUSTAINABILITY REPORTING

INTRODUCTION	9.01
Regulation of disclosure	9.01
Australia, USA, Canada, and the European Union examined	9.02
AUSTRALIA	9.04
IFRS and Australia's new climate disclosure rules	9.04
The Australian climate-related disclosure legislation	9.05
Amendments to Australian companies legislation	9.06
Other reporting obligations of directors	9.10
The structure of AASB S2	9.11
Main requirements of AASB S2	9.12
The focus of IFRS S2 and AASB S2	9.13
USA	9.18
The SEC	9.18
The SEC's new climate disclosure rules	9.19
CANADA AND SASKATCHEWAN	9.27
Canadian Securities Administrators	9.27
Canadian federal regulation	9.28
The Canadian Finance Taxonomy and Sustainability Standards	9.29
Saskatchewan	9.31
THE EUROPEAN UNION AND THE CSRD	9.32
CSRD	9.32
ESRS	9.35
Reporting areas under ESRS for disclosure	9.36
Disclosure and the double materiality test	9.37
CSDDD	9.47
CONCLUSIONS, GUIDANCE, AND KEY PRINCIPLES	9.48

INTRODUCTION

Regulation of disclosure

9.01 As discussed in Chapter 1 from 1.44, the natural starting point for a small mining or oil and gas company at the exploration stage with just a few directors, limited funds, and a narrow scope of activities is likely to be what it is legally required to report – in other words, disclosures required by applicable laws. That disclosure requires certain processes such as a risk assessment. As mentioned in Chapter 1, disclosure laws generally have two main sources: company laws requiring directors to report on non-financial matters,[1] and laws of stock exchanges or market and securities regulators requiring listed companies

1 For example, *Companies Act 2006 (UK)* section 414A.

to disclose matters like material climate-related risks.[2] In some jurisdictions, that disclosure will apply to environmental, social, and governance risks.

Australia, USA, Canada, and the European Union examined

9.02 This chapter examines the requirements of regimes applicable in Australia, the USA, Canada, and the European Union. An important question in each case is whether the regime applies to all companies connected to it or whether there are exceptions for companies below a specified size or which are not listed on an exchange. A strong influence on the climate disclosure rules examined in this chapter, and in many cases their starting point, are the recommendations of the Task Force on Climate-related Financial Disclosures (TCFD), who issued their final report in 2017 (TCFD Final Report).[3] The structure used by the TCFD of four thematic areas 'that represent core elements of how organizations operate',[4] namely governance, strategy, risk management, and metrics and targets, resonates throughout this chapter.

9.03 Adding complexity are variations between jurisdictions in the wording of the regulations because of their function, history, and reliance on other sources. There are also variations in structural matters such as the role of federal regulation as opposed to state or provincial regulation. For example, in the USA, securities regulation is a federal matter under the control of the Securities and Exchange Commission (SEC). The disclosures required by the SEC are discussed in the later section on the USA. The SEC climate disclosure rules were intended to be phased in from fiscal years starting in 2025. They were intended to apply to SEC registrants that generally include companies listed on a securities exchange in the USA, such as the NYSE and Nasdaq.[5] But it remains to be seen whether President Trump changes that.[6] There are equivalents in other jurisdictions.[7]

---

2 For example, the SEC's new climate disclosure rules are being phased in from fiscal years starting in 2025, which will apply to companies listed on NYSE and Nasdaq. The Climate Disclosure Rules are set out in a new Subpart 1500 of Regulations S-K and new Article 14 of Regulation S-X.

3 Recommendations of the Task Force on Climate-related Disclosures, Final Report (June 2017) https://assets.bbhub.io/company/sites/60/2021/10/FINAL-2017-TCFD-Report.pdf (TCFD Final Report).

4 Ibid iv and Figure 2.

5 The Climate Disclosure Rules are set out in a new Subpart 1500 of Regulations S-K and new Article 14 of Regulation S-X.

6 Brian Schwartz, CNBC, 'A Trump SEC would aim to reverse climate disclosure rule, ratchet up ESG fights, sources say', CNBC 2 May 2024 https://www.cnbc.com/2024/05/02/trump-sec-would-end-climate-disclosure-rule-target-esg-investments.html?msockid=35c9f8602fd96394095dec112ed6622f.

7 For the Financial Conduct Authority in the UK and its listing rules, see the Corporate Reporting Authority's *TCFD and related reporting requirements* https://www.icaew.com/technical/corporate

AUSTRALIA

IFRS and Australia's new climate disclosure rules

9.04 The new Australian climate-related financial disclosures legislation that received the Royal Assent in September 2024 represents a significant shift in Australian law. The standards used are based on IFRS S1 (General Requirements for Disclosure of Sustainability-related Financial Information) (IFRS S1) and IFRS S2 (Climate-related Disclosures) (IFRS S2) with minimal variations.[8] This section is an explanation of IFRS S2 as well as the Australian rules.[9] IFRS S1 is examined at 3.59. The reason for this separation is that the ISSB developed IFRS S2 to run concurrently with IFRS S1, whereas in Australia the equivalents, AASB S1 General Requirements for Disclosure of Sustainability-related Financial Information (AASB S1) and AASB S2 Climate-related Disclosures (AASB S2) do not.[10] AASB S1 is voluntary, while AASB S2 is mandatory. Entities can nevertheless decide to implement AASB S1.

The Australian climate-related disclosure legislation

9.05 The Australian legislation is the *Treasury Laws Amendment (Financial Market Infrastructure and Other Measures) Act 2024 (Cth)* (*CRFDA24*). The relevant part of *CRFDA24* is Schedule 4, which sets out amendments to the *Corporations Act 2001 (Cth)* (*CAWA*) that require relevant entities to disclose their climate-related plans, financial risks, and opportunities in accordance with Australian Sustainability Reporting Standards (ASRS) made by the Australian Accounting Standards Board. The first ASRS were also issued in September 2024 and consist of AASB S1 and AASB S2.

Amendments to Australian companies legislation

9.06 Before we look at the implications of the standards, we should briefly highlight the significant amendments made by *CRFDA24* to *CAWA*. Many obligations

-reporting/non-financial-reporting/nfi-and-related-uk-reporting-regulations#subheading-1b69cf8a-19c7-47be-8abd-bd58ba341dcd.

8 KPMG, *Australian Sustainability Reporting legislation and standards finalised*, Reporting update (23 September 2024), 24 RU-12 https://kpmg.com/au/en/home/insights/2024/09/24ru-12-australian-sustainability-reporting-standards-legislation-finalised.html.

9 For the IFRS Sustainability Standards, see the IFRS website at https://www.ifrs.org/issued-standards/ifrs-sustainability-standards-navigator/.

10 Australian Sustainability Reporting Standard AASB S2 (Australian Accounting Standards Board, September 2024) https://standards.aasb.gov.au/sites/default/files/2024-10/AASBS2_09-24.pdf (AASB S2).

flow from the contents of an annual sustainability report set out in *CAWA* section 296A. The annual sustainability report has to be prepared in addition to the financial report.[11] It is important to understand that notwithstanding the *CRFDA24* terminology refers to sustainability, at this point the contents of the report are limited to climate matters. A main feature of the basic contents of the sustainability report set out in *CAWA* section 296A(1) is the climate statements for the year with accompanying notes, additional statements, and the directors' declaration. Under *CAWA* section 296A(2), the climate statements of the year are 'the climate statements in relation to the entity required by sustainability standards made for the purposes of this subsection'. Those standards are the ASRS. Under *CAWA* section 296A(5), the Minister may require a sustainability report to include 'statements relating to financial matters concerning environmental sustainability'. That has not yet occurred.

9.07 A new section 285(1) is substituted in *CAWA*. It adds to the existing provision that says that all companies and other relevant entities must keep financial records and some must prepare financial reports. It does that by now saying that some of them must also keep sustainability records and prepare sustainability reports. Which entities must do that is dealt with in *CAWA* section 292A, explained at 9.08. If an entity must prepare a sustainability report for a financial year, it must keep sustainability records that 'correctly explain and record its preparation of the substantive provisions of the sustainability report'.[12] A substantive provision is 'anything required to be included in the sustainability report under subsection 296A(1), other than the directors' declaration mentioned in paragraph 296A(1)(e)'. A sustainability report will have to be audited by the auditor of the financial report.[13]

9.08 The implementation of the regime is being phased in. The reporting commencement date is 1 January 2025 for the largest entities, called Group 1 Entities, which are entities that meet two out of three of the following at the end of the financial year: consolidated revenue of A$500 million or more, consolidated gross assets of A$1 billion or more, and 500 or more employees.[14]

---

11 *CAWA* section 285(1).

12 *CAWA* section 286A(1). Sustainability records are defined in *CAWA* section 9 to include 'documents and working papers needed to explain the methods, assumptions and evidence from which the substantive provisons of sustainability reports are made up'.

13 *CAWA* section 301A. The form of the audit opinion is set out in *CAWA* section 307A. The auditor must form an opinion on whether the report is in accordance with the Act, whether the auditor has all necessary information, explanations, and assistance, and whether the entity has kept sufficient sustainability records to enable the report to be prepared and audited.

14 Group 1 Entities also include companies registered, or required to register, for the *National Greenhouse and Energy Reporting Act 2007 (Cth)* (*NGERA*) and that meet a publication threshold in section 13(1).

Groups 2 and 3 contain smaller entities and their reporting start respectively on 1 January 2026 and 1 January 2027. The criteria for Group 3, which represent the minimum levels for an entity to have to report, and which are set out in *CAWA* section 292A(3), are two out of the following at the end of the financial year: consolidated revenue of A$50 million or more, consolidated gross assets of A$25 million or more, and 100 or more employees. It is not a requirement that the entity is listed, and it does not apply automatically to listed entities. What that means is that small exploration companies may not have to comply.

CAWA section 296D sets out required disclosures for the climate statements and notes, which must be in accordance with the sustainability standards. These start in *CAWA* section 296D(1)(a) with a requirement to disclose for a financial year any 'material financial risks there are for the entity' or 'material financial opportunities relating to climate there are for the entity'. In both cases, the requirement is determined 'by sustainability standards made for the purposes of this paragraph'. In addition, if required by the sustainability standards, the climate statements must disclose metrics and targets relating to Scope 1, 2, and 3 greenhouse gas emissions, related governance, strategy, or risk management information, and a scenario analysis. For the first three years of the regime, directors are required to provide a declaration whether the entity has taken reasonable steps to ensure the substantive provisions of the sustainability report are in accordance with the legislation. After that time, directors will be required to declare that the substantive provisions of the sustainability report are in accordance with the legislation. **9.09**

Other reporting obligations of directors

As 3.50 mentions, *CAWA* section 298 requires the directors to file a review of operations.[15] One Australian publication explains that the review 'should complement the financial report.... The underlying drivers of the results and financial position should be explained, as well as risks, management strategies and future prospects. Forward-looking information should have a reasonable basis and the market should be updated through continuous disclosure if **9.10**

Registrable superannuation entities, registered schemes, and retail corporate investment vehicles are not included in Group 1.

15 See *CAWA* section 298.

circumstances change.'[16] Climate change risk is one of the things mentioned that could have a material impact on future prospects.[17]

The structure of AASB S2

9.11 The structure of AASB S2 is that after an introduction about the AASB, it sets out the main requirements briefly, the application date (it applies to reporting periods beginning on or after 1 January 2025), a comparison with IFRS S2, its objective, scope, and then the longest part containing core content. Appendices follow, with Appendix A setting out defined terms, Appendix B containing application guidance, Appendix C dealing with effective date and transition, and Appendix D setting out general requirements for disclosure of climate-related financial information. AASB S2 was developed by the AASB 'by incorporating the content of IFRS S2, including the IFRS S2 paragraph numbering'.[18] There are modifications to take account of the Australian legal and institutional environment. So, there are some Australian-specific paragraphs (11 in total, mainly in the appendices) which have 'an Aus prefix' and some deletions. As mentioned above, the main difference is that the ISSB developed IFRS S2 to run concurrently with IFRS S1, whereas in Australia the IFRS S1 equivalent, AASB S1, is voluntary. That has the consequence that some IFRS S1 paragraphs are replaced in AASB S2 with references to Appendix B of AASB S2.

Main requirements of AASB S2

9.12 The main requirements of AASB S2 (the opening paragraph is the same as that of IFRS S2) are:

> AASB S2 *Climate-related Disclosures* sets out disclosure requirements for an entity to provide useful information to primary users of its general purpose financial report about climate-related risks and opportunities that could reasonably be expected to affect the entity's cash flows, access to finance or cost of capital over the short, medium or long term.
>
> The main climate-related financial disclosure requirements relate to governance, strategy, risk management, and metrics and targets, including information about scenario analysis and Scope 1, Scope 2 and Scope 3 greenhouse gas emissions.
>
> The Standard also includes general requirements for the disclosure of climate-related financial information (see Appendix D). The general requirements include the conceptual

16 ASIC, 'ASIC highlights focus areas for 31 December 2022 reporting' (Media release, 22-333MR, 1 December 2022) https://asic.gov.au/about-asic/news-centre/find-a-media-release/2022-releases/22-333mr-asic-highlights-focus-areas-for-31-december-2022-reporting/.

17 Ibid.

18 AASB S2, 5.

> foundations for reporting such information, the location of disclosures, the timing of reporting and disclosures relating to judgements, uncertainties and errors.[19]

The disclosure requirements cover governance, strategy, risk management, and metrics and targets, including information about scenario analysis and Scope 1, Scope 2, and Scope 3 greenhouse gas emissions. The section of AASB S2 extracted above goes on to say that an entity applying AASB S2 is not required to apply AASB S1 *General Requirements for Disclosure of Sustainability-related Financial Information*, which is 'a voluntary Standard addressing sustainability-related financial information covered by AASB S1... Nevertheless, an entity may refer to AASB S1 for guidance in complying with the requirements of Appendix D'.[20]

The focus of IFRS S2 and AASB S2

The focus of AASB S2 and IFRS S2 is financial disclosures concerning climate-related risks. But as subsequent paragraphs will explore, the information requirements set out in the standards are extensive. The scope is circumscribed by paragraph 3 of IFRS S2 and AASB S2, which, under the heading 'Scope', says that it applies to: **9.13**

a) climate-related risks to which the entity is exposed, which are:
   (i) *climate-related physical risks*; and
   (ii) *climate-related transition risks*; and
b) climate-related opportunities available to the entity.[21]

Climate-related physical risks are defined as:

> Risks resulting from climate change that can be event-driven (acute physical risk) or from longer-term shifts in climatic patterns (chronic physical risk). Acute physical risks arise from weather-related events such as storms, floods, drought or heatwaves, which are increasing in severity and frequency. Chronic physical risks arise from longer-term shifts in climatic patterns including changes in precipitation and temperature which could lead to sea level rise, reduced water availability, biodiversity loss and changes in soil productivity.[22]

The definition goes on to explain that 'these risks could carry financial implications for an entity, such as costs resulting from direct damage to assets or indirect effects of supply-chain disruption' and that the entity's financial

19 AASB S2, 4.
20 Ibid.
21 AASB S2, para 3, 6.
22 IFRS S2, Appendix A, 19, and AASB S2, Appendix A, 15.

performance could also be affected by matters such as 'changes in water availability, sourcing and quality' and extreme temperature changes 'affecting the entity's premises, operations, supply chains, transportation needs and employee health and safety'.[23]

9.14 Climate-related transition risks are defined as:

> Risks that arise from efforts to transition to a lower-carbon economy. Transition risks include policy, legal, technological, market and reputational risks. These risks could carry financial implications for an entity, such as increased operating costs or asset impairment due to new or amended climate-related regulations. The entity's financial performance could also be affected by shifting consumer demands and the development and deployment of new technology.[24]

Climate-related opportunities are defined as:

> Climate-related risks refers to the potential negative effects of climate change on an entity. These risks are categorised as climate-related physical risks and climate-related transition risks.
>
> Climate-related opportunities refers to the potential positive effects arising from climate change for an entity. Efforts to mitigate and adapt to climate change can produce climate-related opportunities for an entity.[25]

Paragraph 10 of IFRS S2 and AASB S2 sets out requirements for the disclosure of information that enables users of general purpose financial reports to understand 'the climate-related risks and opportunities that could reasonably be expected to affect the entity's prospects'.[26] They include a description of those risks and opportunities and the time horizon in which they could reasonably be expected to occur. In identifying the risks and opportunities, the entity 'shall use all reasonable and supportable information that is available to the entity at the reporting date without undue cost or effort, including information about past events, current conditions and forecasts of future conditions'.[27]

9.15 The annual sustainability report will have to set out extensive information, which will require a significant amount of work. An indicator of the level required is the objectives and underlying requirements of IFRS S2 and AASB

23 Ibid.
24 IFRS S2, Appendix A, 20, and AASB S2, Appendix A, 16.
25 IFRS S2, Appendix A, 19, and AASB S2, Appendix A, 15.
26 AASB S2, para 10, 7.
27 AASB S2, para 10, 8.

S2. The objectives begin with the overall objective, which for AASB S2 (IFRS S2 is the same) is:

> The objective of AASB S2 *Climate-related Disclosures* is to require an entity to disclose information about its *climate-related risks and opportunities* that is useful to *primary users of general purpose financial reports* in making decisions relating to providing resources to the entity.[28]

That is elaborated in the core content part, where there are further objectives as follows:

Governance
The objective of climate-related financial disclosures on governance is to enable users of general purpose financial reports to understand the governance processes, controls and procedures an entity uses to monitor, manage and oversee climate-related risks and opportunities.[29]
Strategy
The objective of climate-related financial disclosures on strategy is to enable users of general purpose financial reports to understand an entity's strategy for managing climate-related risks and opportunities.[30]
Risk management
The objective of climate-related financial disclosures on risk management is to enable users of general purpose financial reports to understand an entity's processes to identify, assess, prioritise and monitor climate-related risks and opportunities, including whether and how those processes are integrated into and inform the entity's overall risk management process.[31]
Metrics and targets
The objective of climate-related financial disclosures on metrics and targets is to enable users of general purpose financial reports to understand an entity's performance in relation to its climate-related risks and opportunities, including progress towards any climate-related targets it has set, and any targets it is required to meet by law or regulation.[32]

Under each of these, the standard sets out further requirements of what is **9.16**
needed to achieve the objective. For example, paragraph 25, under the risk management objective, requires the entity to disclose 'the processes and related policies the entity uses to identify, assess, prioritise and monitor

28 AASB S2, para 1, 6. It contains a footnote saying that the terms 'primary users' and 'users' are used interchangeably in the Standard, with the same meaning.

29 IFRS S2, para 5, 5 and AASB S2, para 5, 6. The reader can assume that in the following footnotes the IFRS paragraph has the same number as the AASB S2 paragraph. The page numbers are slightly different.

30 AASB S2, para 8, 7.

31 AASB S2, para 24, 11.

32 Ibid.

climate-related risks'. The entity will also have to disclose information that enables users of general purpose financial reports to understand the effects of climate-related risks and entities on the entity's financial position, financial performance, and cash flows for the current reporting period and for the short, medium, and long term.[33] Greenhouse gas emissions have to be disclosed under the standard in accordance with the Greenhouse Gas Protocol: A Corporate Accounting and Reporting Standard 2024.[34] There are particular rules for asset managers, bankers, and insurers.[35] Entities must also disclose their climate-related targets.[36]

9.17 Appendix D of AASB S2 sets out 'General requirements for disclosure of climate-related financial information'. It has this to say about materiality:

> An entity shall disclose material information about the climate-related risks and opportunities that could reasonably be expected to affect the entity's prospects.
>
> In the context of climate-related financial disclosures, information is material if omitting, misstating or obscuring that information could reasonably be expected to influence decisions that primary users of general purpose financial reports make on the basis of those reports, which include financial statements and climate-related financial disclosures and which provide information about a specific reporting entity.[37]

It goes on to say that 'to identify and disclose material information, an entity shall apply paragraphs B13–19 and B21–37'. These are taken from Appendix B of AASB S1 and contain further matters to consider in determining materiality.

USA

The SEC

9.18 The SEC regulates securities pursuant to the *Securities and Exchange Act 1934 (US)* (*SEAUSA*) and the *Securities Act 1933 (US)* (*SAUSA*). *SEAUSA* requires disclosures for SEC registrants that generally include companies listed on a US securities exchange, such as the NYSE and Nasdaq. The SEC has publications relating to climate change disclosure going back to at least 2010.[38] New rules (SECCD Rules) are set out in a new Subpart 1500 of Regulation

33 AASB S2, para 15, 9.

34 AASB S2, paras 29 and B 23, 12, and 21.

35 AASB S2, from para B 58, 25.

36 AASB S2, para 33, 13.

37 AASB S2, Appendix D, paras 17 and 18, page 31.

38 See Commission Guidance Regarding Disclosure Related to Climate Change, effective date 8 February 2010 https://www.sec.gov/files/rules/interp/2010/33-9106.pdf.

S-K and new Article 14 of Regulation S-X (SECCCDIS2024).[39] Disclosures include annual and quarterly reports and now climate disclosure rules which are being phased in from fiscal years starting in 2025.

The SEC's new climate disclosure rules

SECCCDIS2024 will require SEC-registered domestic or foreign companies to include climate-related information in filing documents such as registration statements and periodic reports, such as 10-K annual reports. The SEC's summary in its commentary on the final rules (SECCD Note) is: 9.19

> The final rules will require information about a registrant's climate-related risks that have materially impacted, or are reasonably likely to have a material impact on, its business strategy, results of operations, or financial condition. In addition, under the final rules, certain disclosures related to severe weather events and other natural conditions will be required in a registrant's audited financial statements.[40]

The SECCD Rules leave the placement of the climate-related disclosures, other than the financial statement disclosures, largely up to the registrant. Financial statement disclosures (other than Scope 1 and/or Scope 2 emissions disclosures) are to be included in a separate, appropriately captioned section of a registrant's filing, or in another appropriate section such as Risk Factors, Description of Business, or Management's Discussion and Analysis of Financial Condition and Results of Operations.

The SEC says that they are requiring 'enhanced and more consistent and comparable disclosure about the material risks that companies face and how companies manage those risks by requiring': 9.20

- A description of any climate-related risks that have materially impacted or are reasonably likely to have a material impact on the registrant, including on its strategy, results of operations, and financial condition, as well as the actual or potential material impacts of those same risks on its strategy, business model, and outlook;
- Specified disclosures regarding a registrant's activities, if any, to mitigate or adapt to a material climate-related risk, or use of transition plans, scenario analysis, or internal carbon prices to manage a material climate-related risk;

39 The Climate Disclosure Rules are set out in a new Subpart 1500 of Regulations S-K and new Article 14 of Regulation S-X (SECCCDIS2024).

40 For the SEC's Final Rules commentary 17 CFR 210, 229, 230, 232, 239, and 249 [Release Nos. 33-11275; 34-99678; File No. S7-10-22] RIN 3235-AM87, see https://www.sec.gov/files/rules/final/2024/33-11275.pdf (SECCD Note) 1.

- Disclosure about any oversight by the registrant's board of directors of climate-related risks and any role of management in assessing and managing material climate-related risks;
- A description of any processes the registrant uses to assess or manage material climate-related risks; and
- Disclosure about any targets or goals that have materially affected or are reasonably likely to materially affect the registrant's business, results of operations, or financial condition. In addition, to facilitate investors' assessment of particular types of risk, the final rules require:
  - Disclosure of Scope 1 and/or Scope 2 emissions on a phased-in basis by certain larger registrants when those emissions are material, and the filing of an attestation report covering the required disclosure of such registrants' Scope 1 and/or Scope 2 emissions, also on a phased-in basis; and
  - Disclosure of the financial statement effects of severe weather events and other natural conditions, including costs and losses.[41]

9.21 The SECCD Note explains that the SEC's statutory authority under SAUSA and SEAUSA authorises the SEC 'to ensure that public company disclosures provide investors with information important to making informed investment and voting decisions' and accordingly gives it the power to promulgate the SECCD Rules.[42] Accordingly, 'such disclosure facilitates the securities laws' core objectives of protecting investors, facilitating capital formation, and promoting market efficiency'.[43]

9.22 Some of the differences between the final SECCD Rules and those proposed earlier are:

- Disclosure of Scope 1 and Scope 2 emissions is required only for large accelerated filers (LAFs) and accelerated filers (AFs) when material, with a phased-in approach. Smaller reporting companies (SRCs) and emerging growth companies (EGCs) are exempt;
- The phase-in period for the assurance requirement for Scope 1 and Scope 2 emissions for LAFs is extended, and only limited assurance is required for AFs;
- Disclosure of Scope 3 emissions is not required;
- Some climate-related disclosures are qualified based on materiality;
- The disclosure of financial statement effects of severe weather events and other natural conditions is focused on the notes to the financial statements.
- Disclosure of board oversight and executive management of climate risks, and board members' climate expertise is not required; and

41 SECCD Note 14.

42 Ibid 61.

43 Ibid.

- A safe harbour for private liability for certain forward-looking disclosures related to climate-related matters has been extended.

As the SECCD Note points out, certain of these disclosure requirements are similar to the disclosure frameworks of the TCFD, which focus on governance, strategy, risk management, and metrics and targets, and the global GHG Protocol.[44] The SEC notes that many registrants have elected to follow TCFD recommendations and the GHG Protocol and that building on those frameworks should mitigate their compliance burden.[45] But the SECCD Note points out that 'the rules diverge from both of those frameworks in certain respects where necessary for our markets and registrants and to achieve our specific investor protection and capital formation goals'.[46] The SEC rules are based on materiality under the traditional reasonable investor standard.[47] The SECCD Note says that consistent with Supreme Court precedent, 'a matter is material if there is a substantial likelihood that a reasonable investor would consider it important in determining whether to buy or sell securities or how to vote or such a reasonable investor would view omission of the disclosure as having significantly altered the total mix of information made available'.[48] 9.23

Therefore, Subpart 1500 of Regulations S-K and new Article 14 of Regulation S-X contain some familiar ground. Subpart 1500 has rules covering governance, strategy, risk management, and targets and goals. For example, the definitions in Item 1500 include: 9.24

> *Climate-related risks* means the actual or potential negative impacts of climate-related conditions and events on a registrant's business, results of operations, or financial condition.[49]

It then goes on to add definitions of physical risks, acute risks, chronic risks, and transitional risks. There are differences in the wording compared with IFRS S2. For example, chronic risks are defined as relating to 'longer term weather patterns, such as sustained higher temperatures, sea level rise, and drought, as well as related effects such as decreased arability of farmland, decreased habitability of land, and decreased availability of fresh water'.[50] IFRS S2 refers to

---

44 Ibid 25.
45 Ibid 26.
46 Ibid.
47 Ibid 105.
48 Ibid. The footnote in the text refers to 17 CFR 230.405 (definition of 'material') and also *Basic Inc. v Levinson* 488 US 224, 231, 232, and 240 (1988).
49 Subpart 1500 of Regulation S-K Item 1500.
50 Ibid.

'longer-term shifts in climatic patterns' and the specific examples are different. Both mention higher temperatures, but the emphasis is slightly different.

9.25 Item 1502 on strategy starts:

> (a) Describe any climate-related risks that have materially impacted or are reasonably likely to have a material impact on the registrant, including on its strategy, results of operations, or financial condition. In describing these material risks, a registrant must describe whether such risks are reasonably likely to manifest in the short-term (i.e., the next 12 months) and separately in the long-term (i.e., beyond the next 12 months). A registrant must disclose whether the risk is a physical or transition risk, providing information necessary to an understanding of the nature of the risk presented and the extent of the registrant's exposure to the risk, including the following non-exclusive list of disclosures, as applicable:[51]

Further disclosures under Item 1502 are extensive, including details of the risks, exposures, and costs. Item 1502 says that the registrant must 'describe the actual and potential material impacts of any climate-related risk identified in response to paragraph (a) of this section on the registrant's strategy, business model, and outlook, including, as applicable, any material impacts on the following non-exclusive list of items:'[52] It then goes on in paragraph (c) to require the registrant to:

> (c) Discuss whether and how the registrant considers any impacts described in response to paragraph (b) of this section as part of its strategy, financial planning, and capital allocation, including, as applicable:
> (1) Whether the impacts of the climate-related risks described in response to paragraph (b) have been integrated into the registrant's business model or strategy, including whether and how resources are being used to mitigate climate-related risks.

9.26 The relevant part of IFRS S2 has much in common in a practical sense with the SEC's strategy disclosure requirements. But there are differences in the language and the way that items are approached. IFRS S2 requires disclosure of 'the current and anticipated effects of those climate-related risks and opportunities on the entity's business model and value chain (see paragraph 13)'. It then requires disclosure of the effects on the entity's strategy and decision-making and its financial position, financial performance, and cash flows in the current reporting period and over the short, medium, and long term.

---

51 Subpart 1500 of Regulation S-K Item 1502.

52 Ibid, para (b). The items include business operations and products and services.

CANADA AND SASKATCHEWAN

Canadian Securities Administrators

The 10 provinces and three territories in Canada are responsible for securities regulations. Securities regulators from each province and territory together form the Canadian Securities Administrators (CSA).[53] The CSA 'is the umbrella organization of Canada's provincial and territorial securities regulators whose objective is to improve, coordinate and harmonize regulation of the Canadian capital markets'.[54] While the CSA coordinates initiatives on a cross-Canada basis, provincial or territorial regulators handle all complaints regarding securities violations in their respective jurisdictions.[55] Companies can be incorporated federally in Canada. So, before we look at securities regulation in Saskatchewan, we should look at the Canadian federal position on sustainability disclosure. **9.27**

Canadian federal regulation

On 9 October 2024, the Canadian federal government published a news release announcing its intention to amend the *Canada Business Corporations Act* (*CBCA*) to introduce mandatory climate-related financial disclosures for large, federally incorporated private companies, and to deliver 'Made-in-Canada sustainable investment guidelines'.[56] The development of investment guidelines follows commitments in the 2023 Fall Economic Statement and Budget 2024 to, among other things, develop a sustainable finance taxonomy identifying 'green' and 'transition' investment.[57] The purpose of the climate-related financial disclosures is 'to help investors better understand how large businesses are thinking about and managing risks related to climate change, ensuring that capital allocation aligns with the realities of a net-zero economy'.[58] The news release included a statement that the federal government is ready to work with provincial and territorial partners 'to ensure broad disclosure coverage across the Canadian economy' and also indicated that efforts will be made to **9.28**

53 The CSA's website is at https://www.securities-administrators.ca.

54 Ibid, *About Us*.

55 Ibid

56 News Release *Government Advances Made-in-Canada sustainable investment guidelines and mandatory climate disclosures to accelerate progress to net zero emissions by 2050* (9 October 2024 Department of Finance Canada) https://www.canada.ca/en/department-finance/news/2024/10/government-advances-made-in-canada-sustainable-investment-guidelines-and-mandatory-climate-disclosures-to-accelerate-progress-to-net-zero-emissions.html#.

57 Ibid.

58 Ibid.

harmonise any *CBCA* requirements with climate disclosure rules adopted by Canadian securities regulators. However, finalising the rules appears to be some way off, as the press release says that 'the government will launch a regulatory process to determine the substance of these disclosure requirements and the size of private federal corporations that would be subject to them'.[59] Earlier commentary suggests that rules will follow some at least of the recommendations of the TCFD.[60] In 2022, the Canadian Office of the Superintendent of Financial Institutions required federally regulated financial institutions to publish climate disclosures, with implementation starting in 2024.[61]

The Canadian Finance Taxonomy and Sustainability Standards

9.29 The taxonomy flowing from the 'Made-in-Canada sustainable investment guidelines' (the Taxonomy) aims to 'mobilize investment in support of Canada's net-zero transition by enabling investors to understand and communicate which key activities and investments will deliver a Canadian net-zero economy'.[62] It will be developed and governed by one or more external, third-party organisations and will first focus on the following sectors: electricity, transportation, buildings, agriculture and forestry, manufacturing, and extractives, including mineral extraction and processing, and natural gas.[63] The news release indicated that a taxonomy for two to three priority sectors will be released within 12 months of the commencement of work on the Taxonomy. The Canadian Sustainability Standards Board (CSSB) has recently released the final Canadian Sustainability Disclosure Standard (CSDS) 1 General Requirements for Disclosure of Sustainability-related Financial Information (CSDS 1) and CSDS 2 Climate-related Disclosures (CSDS 2). CSDS 1 and CSDS 2 are based respectively on IFRS S1 and IFRS S2.[64] They are now part of the CPA Handbook – Sustainability.[65]

9.30 In the meanwhile, companies are dealing with the impact of the 2024 'greenwashing' amendments to the *Competition Act* and the questions raised by those

---

59 Ibid.

60 Centre for Sustainability and Excellence *Canada introduces mandatory climate change disclosure for large companies* (18 October 2024) https://cse-net.org/canada-introduces-mandatory-climate-disclosure-requirements-for-large-companies/.

61 Ibid.

62 News Release (n 56).

63 Ibid.

64 Financial Reporting and Assurance Standards Canada (FRAS) *In Brief – A plain and simple overview of the recently issued Exposure Drafts of CSDS 1 and CSDS 2* https://www.frascanada.ca/en/sustainability/projects/adoption-csds1-csds2/cssb-in-brief-csds-1-and-csds-2.

65 For the Handbook and the standards see https://www.frascanada.ca/en/sustainability.

amendments, which require adequate and proper testing.[66] As a result of the proposed amendments, Cenovus removed environmental issues from its 2023 Corporate Social Sustainability Report 2023.[67]

Saskatchewan

The securities legislation in Saskatchewan is the *Securities Act 1988 (S)* (*SAS1988*). It is administered by the Financial and Consumer Affairs Authority of Saskatchewan (FCAAS), which took over the Saskatchewan Financial Services Commission.[68] Disclosure in Saskatchewan is awaiting regulations to be developed with the CSA. **9.31**

THE EUROPEAN UNION AND THE CSRD

CSRD

The European Union's Corporate Sustainability Reporting Directive (CSRD) was introduced to overcome a lack of consistent and comparable data arising from its predecessor, the Non-Financial Reporting Directive (NFRD).[69] The CSRD is one of a series of measures introduced in the EU.[70] The CSRD aims to improve the disclosure process so that investors and consumers can better understand and compare an organisation's ESG impact. Through measures like the CSRD, Europe's 2050 climate-neutrality target, and European Green Deal initiatives, the EU aims to achieve climate neutrality by 2050 and 'cleaner, more sustainable and energy-efficient industries which thrive in the **9.32**

---

66 Competition Bureau Canada *Environmental claims and greenwashing* https://competition-bureau.canada.ca/how-we-foster-competition/education-and-outreach/environmental-claims-and-greenwashing.

67 See 8.35.

68 *The Financial and Consumer Affairs Authority of Saskatchewan Act (S)* section 3(1).

69 The Non-Financial Reporting Directive (2014/95/EU) required large public interest entities with over 500 employees (listed companies, banks, and insurance companies) to disclose certain non-financial information. There is also Regulation 2019/2088, the Regulation on sustainability-related disclosures in the financial services sector (Sustainable Finance Disclosure Regulation (SFDR). There is also Regulation 2020/852 to establish a framework to facilitate sustainable investment (EU Taxonomy).

70 There is Regulation 2019/2088, the Regulation on sustainability-related disclosures in the financial services sector (Sustainable Finance Disclosure Regulation (SFDR). There is also Regulation 2020/852 to establish a framework to facilitate sustainable investment (EU Taxonomy). In 2024, the Corporate Sustainability Due Diligence Directive, Directive EU 2024/1076 (CSDDD), came into force. The CSDDD sets out a corporate due diligence duty for large companies to identify and address adverse human rights impacts (such as child labour) and environmental impacts (such as pollution) in their own operations, those of their subsidiaries, and in their 'chain(s) of activities', and requires them to have a climate change mitigation transition plan https://www.corporate-sustainability-due-diligence-directive.com.

EU and global markets'.[71] The CSRD applies to what it describes as undertakings. Those to which it applies must:

> include in a dedicated section of their management report or consolidated management report the information necessary to understand the undertaking's impacts on sustainability matters, and the information necessary to understand how sustainability matters affect the undertaking's development, performance and position. Undertakings are to prepare this information in accordance with sustainability reporting standards starting from the financial year indicated in Article 5(2) of Directive (EU) 2022/2464 for each category of undertakings.[72]

9.33 Compliance is being phased in. Undertakings (or 'entities') already required to comply with the NFRD have to start complying in the 2024 financial year, reporting in 2025. They include all entities listed in an EU-regulated market with 500 or more employees. Large EU-based undertakings, whether listed or unlisted, that meet two of the following three criteria on any two consecutive balance sheet dates have to start complying in the 2025 financial year. The criteria are: at least €25 million in total assets, at least €50 million in net turnover, or at least 250 employees (average) during the year.

9.34 Small and medium-sized undertakings (also called small and medium-sized entities, or SMEs) listed on an EU-regulated market have to comply from the 2026 financial year. Undertakings from third countries have to comply from the 2028 financial year if they have annual EU revenues of at least €150 million in the most recent two years, and also own a large EU-based undertaking, or an EU-based subsidiary with securities listed on an EU-regulated market exchange, or an EU branch office with at least €40 million in net turnover.

ESRS

9.35 In 2022, the European Financial Reporting Advisory Group (EFRAG) released its first set of European Sustainability Reporting Standards (ESRS).[73] The ESRS outline the metrics companies must report and how to report them to comply with CSRD disclosure requirements. The EFRAG developed the

---

71 Council of European Union, *European Green Deal* https://www.consilium.europa.eu/en/policies/green-deal/#:~:text=of%20the%20GDP.-,Key%20goals%20of%20the%20Green%20Deal,balance%20in%20nature%20and%20ecosystems.

72 Commission Delegated Regulation (EU) 2023/2772 of 31 July 2023 supplementing Directive 2013/34/EU of the European Parliament and of the Council as regards sustainability reporting standards. The Annex is EFRS 1.

73 EFRAG's website says that its activities have two pillars: a financial reporting pillar providing input into the IFRS standards and a sustainability reporting pillar developing draft EFRS. See its website https://www.efrag.org/en/about-us.

ESRS to align with the TCFD and GRI. Furthermore, the EU Taxonomy Regulation, which took effect in 2021, requires companies to disclose the sustainability performance of their activities and must reflect this information in their CSRD disclosures. In December 2023, the ESRS were published in the Official Journal of the EU as legally binding.[74] There are 12 ESRS in all. As European Sustainability Reporting Standard 1 (ESRS 1) points out, there are three categories of ESRS: cross-cutting standards, topical standards (environmental, social, and governance standards), and sector-specific standards.[75] In February 2024, the EU institutions agreed to postpone by two years the deadline for adopting sector-specific standards. Sector-specific ESRS are expected to be released by June 2026, but the postponement does not impact the CSRD effective dates. The CSRD will contain information that financial entities require to comply with the Sustainable Finance Disclosure Regulation (SFDR),[76] and will help financial advisers and market participants meet these SFDR obligations.

Reporting areas under ESRS for disclosure

The Disclosure Requirements in ESRS 2, in topical ESRS, and in sector-specific ESRS are structured into the following reporting areas: 9.36

(a) **Governance** (GOV): the governance processes, controls and procedures used to monitor, manage and oversee impacts, risks, and opportunities (see ESRS 2, chapter 2 *Governance*);

(b) **Strategy** (SBM): how the undertaking's strategy and business model interact with its material impacts, risks, and opportunities, including how the undertaking addresses those impacts, risks, and opportunities (see ESRS 2, chapter 3 *Strategy*);

(c) **Impact, risk and opportunity management** (IRO): the process(es) by which the undertaking:
   i. identifies impacts, risks, and opportunities and assesses their materiality (see IRO-1 in section 4.1 of ESRS 2),
   ii. manages material sustainability matters through policies and actions (see section 4.2 of ESRS 2).

(d) **Metrics and targets** (MT): the undertaking's performance, including targets it has set and progress towards meeting them (see ESRS 2, chapter 5 *Metrics and targets*).[77]

---

74 Commission Delegated Regulation (EU) 2023/2772 of 31 July 2023, supplementing Directive 2013/34/EU of the European Parliament and of the Council as regards sustainability reporting standards https://eur-lex.europa.eu/legal-content/en/TXT/?uri=CELEX:32023R2772.

75 Ibid, which sets out European Sustainability Reporting Standards 1 (ESRS 1). See para 1.1.

76 For SDFR, see n 70.

77 ESRS 1, para 12.

Disclosure and the double materiality test

9.37 The ESRS have disclosure requirements and also minimum disclosure requirements. In ESRS 2, the minimum disclosure requirements are broken down into those in section 4.2 regarding policies (MDR-P) and actions (MDR-A), and those in section 5 regarding metrics (MDR-M) and targets (MDR-T).[78] ESRS 1 requires the undertaking to apply the minimum disclosure requirements 'regarding policies, actions, metrics and targets together with the corresponding Disclosure Requirements in topical and sector-specific ESRS'.[79]

9.38 Before we look more closely at disclosure, we should look at the assessment of materiality and the double materiality standard that all CSRD reporting must meet.[80] The starting point is that 'performing a materiality assessment (see sections 3.4 *Impact materiality* and 3.5 *Financial materiality*) is necessary for the undertaking to identify the material impacts, risks and opportunities to be reported'.[81] That is further elaborated in paragraph 13, which says:

> ***Materiality*** assessment is the starting point for sustainability reporting under ESRS. IRO-1 in section 4.1 of ESRS 2, includes general disclosure requirements about the undertaking's process to identify ***impacts, risks*** and ***opportunities*** and assess their materiality. SBM-3 of ESRS 2 provides general disclosure requirements on the material impacts, risks and opportunities resulting from the undertaking's materiality assessment.[82]

Materiality assessment will require engagement with stakeholders.[83]

9.39 EFRS 1 says that double materiality has two dimensions: impact materiality and financial materiality.[84] The terms 'material' and 'materiality' are used throughout ESRS to refer to double materiality, unless otherwise specified.[85] It explains them as follows:

> ***Impact materiality*** and financial materiality assessments are inter-related and the interdependencies between these two dimensions shall be considered. In general, the starting point is the assessment of impacts, although there may also be material ***risks*** and ***opportunities*** that are not related to the undertaking's ***impacts***. A sustainability impact may be financially material from inception or become financially material, when it could

78 Ibid para 13.

79 Ibid para 12 and ESRS 2 paras 1 and 2. ESRS 2 can be found at https://www.efrag.org/sites/default/files/media/document/2024-08/ESRS%202%20Delegated-act-2023-5303-annex-1_en.pdf.

80 ESRS 1, para 21.

81 Ibid para 25.

82 Ibid para 26.

83 Ibid para 24.

84 Ibid para 37.

85 Ibid.

> reasonably be expected to affect the undertaking's financial position, financial performance, cash flows, its access to finance or cost of capital over the short-, medium- or long-term. Impacts are captured by the impact materiality perspective irrespective of whether or not they are financially material.
>
> In identifying and assessing the ***impacts***, ***risks*** and ***opportunities*** in the undertaking's ***value chain*** to determine their ***materiality***, the undertaking shall focus on areas where impacts, risks and opportunities are deemed likely to arise, based on the nature of the activities, business relationships, geographies or other factors concerned.[86]

What this means in a practical sense in comparison with those systems that focus on financial impacts is that impacts are captured irrespective of whether they are financially material.

Impact materiality is elaborated in paragraph 43, which says that: **9.40**

> A sustainability matter is material from an impact perspective when it pertains to the undertaking's material actual or potential, positive or negative impacts on people or the environment over the short-, medium- or long-term. Impacts include those connected with the undertaking's own operations and upstream and downstream value chain, including through its products and services, as well as through its business relationships. Business relationships include those in the undertaking's upstream and downstream value chain and are not limited to direct contractual relationships.[87]

Examples of matters that may have an impact which are not yet financially material could include matters like environmental protection, employment and diversity, social responsibility, human rights, bribery, and corruption. That will lead undertakings to set out their policies in areas like diversity, so that their impacts can be tracked. They must also share their sustainability targets, progress towards achieving them, and how those targets support a transition to a sustainable economy and achieving net zero emissions by 2050.

Financial materiality is elaborated in paragraph 48, which says: **9.41**

> The financial materiality assessment corresponds to the identification of information that is considered material for primary users of general-purpose financial reports in making decisions relating to providing resources to the entity. In particular, information is considered material for primary users of general-purpose financial reports if omitting, misstating or obscuring that information could reasonably be expected to influence decisions that they make on the basis of the undertaking's sustainability statement.[88]

ESRS 1 goes on to state in the next paragraph:

---

86 Ibid paras 38 and 39.

87 Ibid para 43.

88 Ibid para 48.

> A sustainability matter is material from a financial perspective if it triggers or could reasonably be expected to trigger material financial effects on the undertaking. This is the case when a sustainability matter generates risks or opportunities that have a material influence, or could reasonably be expected to have a material influence, on the undertaking's development, financial position, financial performance, cash flows, access to finance or cost of capital over the short-, medium- or long-term.[89]

9.42 ESRS 2 sets out disclosure requirements that apply to 'all undertakings regardless of their sector of activity (i.e., sector agnostic) and apply across sustainability topics (i.e., crosscutting)'.[90] ESRS 2 covers the reporting areas defined in ESRS 1 General requirements section 1.2 Cross-Cutting Standards and reporting areas.[91] Undertakings are also required to apply the Disclosure Requirements (including their datapoints) set out in topical ESRS as listed in Appendix C of ESRS 2.[92]

9.43 There are disclosure requirements in ESRS 2 and also minimum disclosure requirements. An example of the former is in relation to strategy, where it says that 'the undertaking shall disclose the elements of its strategy that relate to or impact sustainability matters, its business model and its value chain'.[93] It goes on to say that the objective of the requirement is:

> To describe the key elements of the undertaking's general strategy that relate to or affect sustainability matters, and the key elements of the undertaking's business model and value chain, in order to provide an understanding of its exposure to impacts, risks and opportunities and where they originate.[94]

Subsequent paragraphs require further information to be disclosed about products, markets, employees, revenues (including from fossil fuels), and sustainability-related goals.

9.44 An example of minimum disclosure is provided by policies adopted to manage material sustainability matters.[95] The objective of this requirement is 'to provide an understanding of the policies that the undertaking has in place to prevent, mitigate and remediate actual and potential impacts, to address risks

89 Ibid para 49.
90 ESRS 2 para 1 Objective.
91 Ibid.
92 Ibid.
93 Ibid para 38.
94 Ibid.
95 Ibid section 4.2 from para 60.

and to pursue opportunities'.[96] The undertaking is required to disclose information about policies adopted to manage material sustainability matters.[97]

The disclosure shall include the following information: 9.45

(a) a description of the key contents of the policy, including its general objectives and which material impacts, risks or opportunities the policy relates to and the process for monitoring;
(b) a description of the scope of the policy, or of its exclusions, in terms of activities, upstream; and/or
(c) the most senior level in the undertaking's organisation that is accountable for the implementation of the policy;
(d) a reference, if relevant, to the third-party standards or initiatives the undertaking commits to respect through the implementation of the policy;
(e) if relevant, a description of the consideration given to the interests of key stakeholders in setting the policy; and
(f) if relevant, whether and how the undertaking makes the policy available to potentially affected stakeholders, and stakeholders who need to help implement it.

The CSRD requires a third party to audit and assure the sustainability information and data included in the report. Initially, compliance will require the auditor to provide limited assurance, mainly based on the organisation's own statements. However, within the next three years, the CSRD will introduce a requirement for reasonable assurance, relying on the auditor's examination and understanding of the organisation's operations, processes, and controls. 9.46

CSDDD

The Corporate Sustainability Due Diligence Directive (CSDDD) also needs to be borne in mind in preparing disclosures. It applies to large companies or companies from third countries with substantial EU operations from July 2027.[98] The CSDDD covers the six steps defined by the OECD Due Diligence Guidance for Responsible Business Conduct: (1) integrating due diligence into policies and management systems; (2) identifying and assessing adverse 9.47

96 Ibid para 64.
97 Ibid para 65.
98 Those are companies referred to in Article 2(1), points (a) and (b), which refer to (1) large EU limited liability companies and partnerships with at least 1,000 employees and at least €450 million turnover (net) worldwide. These are about 6,000 companies; and (2) large non–EU companies that have €450 million turnover (net) in the EU. These are about 900 companies. But see also the higher thresholds referred to by the European Commission, *Frequently Asked Questions about the Corporate Sustainability Due Diligence Directive (CSDDD)*, 29 July 2024 https://www.corporate-sustainability-due-diligence-directive.com. Other companies' compliance is from 2028.

human rights and environmental impacts; (3) preventing, ceasing, or minimising actual and potential adverse human rights, and environmental impacts; (4) assessing the effectiveness of measures; (5) communicating; and (6) providing remediation.[99] The core due diligence duties for companies in the scope of the Directive are described as including the following actions:

- Integrating due diligence into the corporate policies and risk management systems.
- Identifying adverse human rights and environmental impacts in the company's operations as well as those of its subsidiaries and its business partners in the chain of activities; and prioritising them according to their severity and likelihood.
- Addressing negative impacts that have been, or should have been, identified, where necessary in the order of prioritisation. Companies have to prevent and/or mitigate potential impacts and, when negative impacts have already occurred, bring them to an end or, if not immediately possible, at least minimise their extent. Companies also have to provide remedies if they caused the adverse impact or contributed to it through acts or omissions.
- As a measure of 'last resort' when all other actions have failed, and where severe impacts are at stake and only where these impacts outweigh the foreseeable negative consequences of disengagement, companies are required to suspend or terminate a business relationship.[100]

CONCLUSIONS, GUIDANCE, AND KEY PRINCIPLES

9.48 A starting point in understanding the disclosure rules discussed in this chapter is the principles set by the TCFD. All the regimes discussed in this chapter refer to them – the Australian rules in CRFDA24, the USA's SECCD Rules, the EU's CSRD, and standards like IFRS S2. The themes of the TCFD are aimed at the areas of governance, strategy, risk management, and targets and metrics. All the regimes discussed in this chapter and the reports reviewed in Chapter 8 deal with these areas.

9.49 The TCFD was formed by the Financial Stability Board, an international organisation with its headquarters in Basel,[101] 'to develop voluntary, consistent climate-related financial disclosures that would be useful to investors, lenders, and insurance underwriters in understanding material risks'.[102] Its purpose was 'to help identify the information needed by investors, lenders, and insurance

99 European Commission, *Frequently Asked Questions about the Corporate Sustainability Due Diligence Directive (CSDDD)*, 29 July 2024 https://www.corporate-sustainability-due-diligence-directive.com.

100 Ibid.

101 For the website of the Financial Stability Board, see https://www.fsb.org.

102 TCFD Final Report, iii.

underwriters to appropriately assess and price climate-related risks and opportunities'.[103] Its focus was financial disclosure and key features of its recommendations were that they are 'adoptable by all organizations and includable in financial filings'.[104] Rules based on IFRS S2, such as CRFDA24, continue that focus on financial disclosure and financial impact. The CSRD has a double materiality test, so its focus is on impact as well as financial impact. The SECCD Rules are based on materiality under the reasonable investor standard (see 9.51).

There are other areas of difference. An important one is materiality. CRFDA24 and IFRS 2 say that 'an entity shall disclose material information about the climate-related risks and opportunities that could reasonably be expected to affect the entity's prospects'.[105] That is explained as 'information is material if omitting, misstating or obscuring that information could reasonably be expected to influence decisions that primary users of general purpose financial reports make on the basis of those reports'. The SEC rules are based on materiality under the traditional reasonable investor standard.[106] The SEC says: 9.50

> A matter is material if there is a substantial likelihood that a reasonable investor would consider it important in determining whether to buy or sell securities or how to vote or such a reasonable investor would view omission of the disclosure as having significantly altered the total mix of information made available.[107]

The SEC's materiality test therefore has a sharper focus on decisions regarding buying or selling securities or voting, with a residual category of the total mix of information.

All of the regimes discussed in this chapter require substantial additional information and data. That approach started with the TCFD and is the reason why the reports reviewed in Chapter 8 are so extensive. The test for whether a regime applies to a company having a connection with a regime is dealt with in the checklist. 9.51

103 Ibid.
104 Ibid Table 1.
105 See n 37.
106 See ns 46 to 48.
107 Ibid.

CHECKLIST

1. As with the checklist at the end of Chapter 8, the first question is which laws apply to your company, the directors of your company, and any securities listed on a securities exchange, if any? More than one set of laws may be applicable if, say, a company is incorporated in one jurisdiction,[108] has securities listed on an exchange in one or more countries, and carries out substantial operations in another country. For example, an Australian incorporated company that has securities listed on ASX and NYSE and has a subsidiary with substantial operations in the EU will have to comply with CFRDA24, the SECDD Rules, and the CSRD. So, the first question determines which laws possibly apply. It is then necessary to check those laws for their reporting and disclosure rules and to determine if any threshold and other conditions for the application of the rules are met.
2. In Australia, the implementation of the regime is being phased in. The reporting commencement date is 1 January 2025 for the largest entities, called Group 1 Entities, which are entities that meet two out of three of the following at the end of the financial year: consolidated revenue of A$500 million or more, consolidated gross assets of A$1 billion or more, and 500 or more employees.[109] Groups 2 and 3 contain smaller entities and their reporting start respectively on 1 January 2026 and 1 January 2027.
3. The criteria for the Australian Group 3, which represent the minimum levels for an entity to have to report, and which are set out in CAWA section 292A(3), are two out of the following at the end of the financial year: consolidated revenue of A$50 million or more, consolidated gross assets of A$25 million or more, and 100 or more employees. It is not a requirement that the entity is listed, and it does not apply automatically to listed entities. What that means is that small exploration companies may not have to comply.
4. The SECCD Rules apply to SEC-registered domestic or foreign companies and are being phased in from 2025. They are generally companies listed on a US securities exchange such as NYSE or Nasdaq.
5. The EU's rules are also being phased in. Undertakings (or 'entities') already required to comply with the NFRD have to start complying in the 2024 financial year, reporting in 2025. They include all entities listed in an EU-regulated market with 500 or more employees. Large EU-based undertakings, whether listed or unlisted, that meet two of the following three criteria on any two consecutive balance sheet dates have to start complying in the 2025 financial year. The criteria are: at least €25 million in total assets, at least €50 million in net turnover, or at least 250 employees (average) during the year. Small and medium-sized

---

108 Incorporation is not the only test. See n 99.

109 Group 1 Entities also include companies registered, or required to register, for the *National Greenhouse and Energy Reporting Act 2007 (Cth)* (*NGERA*) and that meet a publication threshold in section 13(1). Registrable superannuation entities, registered schemes, and retail corporate investment vehicles are not included in Group 1.

undertakings (also called small and medium-sized entities, or SMEs) listed on an EU-regulated market have to comply from the 2026 financial year.

6. Undertakings from third countries have to comply with CSRD from the 2028 financial year if they have annual EU revenues of at least €150 million in the most recent two years, and also own a large EU-based undertaking, or an EU-based subsidiary with securities listed on an EU-regulated market exchange, or an EU branch office with at least €40 million in net turnover.
7. If none of these rules or rules of other countries apply, is that situation going to change, say, because you are about to list on Nasdaq?
8. Finally, if you want to start preparing sustainability reports anyway, perhaps because it is required by your strategy, consider the requirements discussed in this chapter and the examples given in Chapter 8 to design your approach.

10

THE FUTURE OF SUSTAINABILITY LAW IN MINING AND ENERGY

INTRODUCTION: THE CURRENT APPROACH 10.01
The five themes 10.01
Theme 1: Mining and energy regulators do not test sustainability as such 10.02
Theme 2: Mining and energy regulators test environmental and safety matters 10.06
Theme 3: Compulsory disclosure of sustainability is increasing 10.09
Theme 4: Material on reporting and good practice is increasing 10.10
Theme 5: Companies are producing sustainability reports 10.12
REDUCING THE DISCLOSURE AND REPORTING REGIMES 10.13
Multiplicity of regimes 10.13
Reduction and simplification 10.16
Meeting the energy transition 10.17
REIMAGINING SUSTAINABILITY LAW IN MINING AND ENERGY 10.18
Mining and energy regulators are increasing their focus on sustainability 10.18
Other forces for change 10.19
A rationale for sustainability law 10.23

INTRODUCTION: THE CURRENT APPROACH

The five themes

10.01 Five themes are explored in this book, and this section summarises the conclusions reached. The impact of greenhouse gas produced by fossil fuels has become a matter of increasing concern, which has produced three results: governments seeking to reduce emissions, the growth of renewable energy like wind and solar, and concern by investors about the impact of climate change on their investments, causing enhanced disclosure by entities of climate risks and opportunities. At the same time, there has been considerable development in environment, social, and governance (ESG) reporting driven by a number of factors, including companies and their directors maintaining their social licence to operate and the attractiveness of their companies to institutional investors. Institutional investors are increasingly focused on the sustainability of their investments and, as a result, test not only climate change and environmental risk, but also social risks. Legal sanctions through increased regulation of areas like safety, human rights, modern slavery, and tax transparency have added to that focus.

Theme 1: Mining and energy regulators do not test sustainability as such

Sustainability seemingly does not play a large part in what mining and energy regulators do. For example, they do not require development and other required plans to demonstrate that operations are sustainable (nor do they monitor compliance with the Sustainable Development Goals (SDGs) as a surrogate for sustainability) or economic.[1] There are solid historical reasons for that situation. The initial emphasis of mineral laws, which extends back over many centuries, was to recognise the rights of miners and to allow mining to occur in an orderly manner. **10.02**

Oil and gas have been developed commercially at scale for a little over a century and a half, and oil and gas laws initially had similar objectives to mineral laws. But that changed as oil and gas became economically and strategically more important, producing the result that some states nationalised their oil and gas and all made their oil and gas regulations more stringent in an effort to reduce waste. In some jurisdictions, such as Western Australia, the rigour associated with mining and fossil fuel development has increased through requirements for mine or field development plans. The review of a plan of operations is a common feature of mining and fossil fuel regulation. **10.03**

The development of renewable energy in the form of wind and solar has occurred over the last 50 years, and that has been regulated differently because there are not the same property ownership issues with solar and wind as are found with minerals and hydrocarbons. However, access to land or sea areas, planning, environmental, and safety issues are important. **10.04**

Sustainability as a concept can be traced back many centuries in some parts of the world and has been embedded in some areas such as forestry or the practices of indigenous peoples. But it only came into the mainstream in the 1970s largely because of the rise of the concept of sustainable development, which combined environmental, social, and economic ideas of sustainability with a desire for development. Over this period, development, pollution, and population pressures resulted in the loss of natural habitats, species, and biodiversity. Concern about the environment grew, resulting in treaties protecting internationally recognised vulnerable areas, habitats, endangered species, **10.05**

1 There are a few exceptions. For example, the Norwegian petroleum regulators review project economics.

and biodiversity. Domestic statutes mirrored those treaties and also introduced environmental protection legislation. Environmental impact assessment became a commonly used tool of environment and mining and energy regulators.

Theme 2: Mining and energy regulators test environmental and safety matters

10.06 It is therefore not surprising that over the last 70 years, mining and oil and gas regulators have focused increasingly on environmental protection and management, rehabilitation, and decommissioning. They also focus on occupational health and safety. These are also concerns of renewable energy regulators.

10.07 There are several contributing factors to this position apart from the factors mentioned in Theme 1. First, the history of mining and oil and gas development has been one in which the company had the right to exploit the resource once acquired, whether from the private sector or the government. Second, governments have generally been ill-equipped to second-guess operational decisions made by the companies, and have not had the ability or desire to do so. In most cases, government regulators are not as well resourced in terms of skilled people and experience as the companies. They have generally relied on a royalty or tax system, or both, to give the government a return. There are exceptions in those countries where the country maintained a direct interest in the resource, such as happened in Norway and Indonesia.[2] Third, environmental damage and personal injuries arising from operations can cause potentially huge costs for the host country and also damage its reputation as a place to carry on business. Hence, those are areas where regulators have been given the resources by government to supervise operations more effectively.

10.08 The question was posed at 1.01 whether the rules implemented by mining and energy regulators are just regulatory red tape or whether they have the potential to improve the availability and quality of minerals and energy. The answer given here is that, over recent decades, mining and energy regulators have taken important steps to reduce waste, reduce environmental damage, and improve safety, and that is certainly true in the leading mining jurisdictions examined in this book. In those jurisdictions, there is evidence of the

---

2 The Norwegian Offshore Directorate is an example of an entity that seeks to match and challenge the skill and expertise of the companies. Its driving force is 'to realise as much as possible of the resource potential on the NCS, thereby generating the greatest possible values for the broader society. The Directorate must contribute to prudent production of Norwegian petroleum resources.' Norwegian Offshore Directorate *About Us* https://www.sodir.no/en/about-us/.

increased use of standards requiring best practice and measures to test the viability of projects. In summary, those rules improve the quality of minerals and energy produced because there is less waste, improved practices, and fewer burdens for later generations to bear. In an ideal world, those things would also improve the availability of minerals and energy, and clearly, they have the potential to do so. But unfortunately, those things will not necessarily be as true, or true at all, in some other jurisdictions. Those jurisdictions can produce minerals and energy more cheaply because they are not following best practices, particularly in relation to environmental protection. Until there is global enforcement of standards or purchasers insist on products satisfying environmental and other criteria, that problem will persist. Also, there are plenty of examples of increasing red tape in areas like environmental reporting and consultation of stakeholders. It is also clearly an issue with the disclosure and reporting regimes mentioned in other themes.

Theme 3: Compulsory disclosure of sustainability is increasing

Compulsory disclosure has increased over the last 15 years in relation to the **10.09**
impacts of climate change. The regimes that require compliance are mentioned below under the sub-heading Multiplicity of Regimes and in Chapter 9 and they commonly require the use of the disclosure rules mentioned here. Disclosure rules that companies are adopting also include those developed by the GRI aimed at multi-stakeholders. Rules on disclosure of the financial impacts of climate change risks and opportunities were developed by the Task Force on Climate-related Financial Disclosures (TCFD), which was formed in 2015. In 2021 the IFRS Foundation created the International Sustainability Standards Board (ISSB). The ISSB developed IFRS Sustainability Disclosure Standards IFRS S1 dealing with sustainability and IFRS S2 with climate change, taking up TCFD recommendations. As set out at 2.29 in August 2022, the ISSB assumed responsibility for the Sustainability Accounting Standards Board (SASB) Standards when the Value Reporting Foundation (VRF), the global non-profit foundation that previously maintained these standards, merged with the IFRS Foundation. Its website says, 'The SASB Standards help companies identify and disclose material information about sustainability-related risks and opportunities in the absence of specific IFRS Sustainability Disclosure Standards.'[3] SASB Standards have been commonly referred to by companies.[4]

3 See https://www.ifrs.org/issued-standards/sasb-standards/#:~:text=The%20SASB%20Standards%20are%20a,of%20Sustainability%2Drelated%20Financial%20Information.

4 See Table 8.1 in Chapter 8. On climate change risk, see the SASB Climate Risk Technical Bulletin 2023 Update. Table 1 on page 9 maps climate risk by industries according to whether they are

The public sector is considering financial reporting based on IFRS through the work being done by the International Public Sector Accounting Standards Board (IPSASB). The European Union has taken things a stage further with its Corporate Sustainability Reporting Directive (CSRD), which uses a double materiality test that looks at sustainability and climate change impacts as well as financial impacts.

Theme 4: Material on reporting and good practice is increasing

10.10 There are three groups involved in this area. First, there are the standard-setting organisations like those responsible for GRI, IFRS, public sector accounting standards, and accounting standards boards in various countries. There are also organisations like the ISO setting standards, and organisations setting standards specific to particular industries or practices.[5] Then there are rating organisations who rate performance.[6]

10.11 In parallel, organisations have taken an interest in the UN's Sustainable Development Goals since they came into effect in 2016 and in sustainability more broadly. They have suggested principles for good practice, voluntary disclosure, and reporting. Examples of those organisations include Ipieca (formerly the International Petroleum Industry Environmental Conservation Association), the International Council on Metals and Mines (ICMM), and the World Gold Council.

Theme 5: Companies are producing sustainability reports

10.12 Companies are producing sustainability reports which cover environmental, social, and governance matters. They generally deal with governance, strategy, and risk management and contain metrics and targets. The nine reports of companies examined in Chapter 8 had a number of features and goals in common.[7] There were also significant differences in style and emphasis, some of which can be attributed to the focus of their business and its particular risks. But the important point is the alignment of goals in certain areas – examples

---

physical, transitional, or regulatory https://sasb.ifrs.org/wp-content/uploads/2023/11/SASB-Climate-Risk-Technical-Bulletin-2023-0823.pdf.

5 There are numerous examples ranging from industry-based standards like NORSOK for oil and gas (https://standard.no/en/sectors/petroleum/norsok/?utm_source=google&utm_medium=cpc&utm_campaign=norsok_en&gad_source=1&gad_campaignid=59413212&gclid=EAIaIQobChMIvub52afdjQMVKTkGAB1g7BExEAAYASAAEgIhZ_D_BwE) to specific standards relating to processes like tailings management (https://globaltailingsreview.org/global-industry-standard/).

6 See 2.35.

7 See 8.07.

are water usage, injury reduction, and improving diversity. Companies which have significant operations in the EU or have securities listed on stock exchanges there, and therefore comply with the CSRD, have the longest and most detailed reports.

REDUCING THE DISCLOSURE AND REPORTING REGIMES

Multiplicity of regimes

The multiplicity of disclosure and reporting regimes is a cause for concern. The regimes can be split into several levels. At the top level, informing the form and content of ESG, sustainability, and climate change reports are the GRI and now IFRS, with the former focused on multi-stakeholders and the latter on financial disclosure.[8] The KPMG 2022 Report and the reports examined in Chapter 8 suggest a strong take-up of the GRI with larger companies.[9] However, adoption of the GRI and IFRS is not generally compulsory unless it is a requirement of a separate regime. **10.13**

The regimes which require compliance are conditional on a connection with a jurisdiction or a stock market in a jurisdiction, or both. Examples are the SEC rules, the CSRD, the Australian federal climate change rules, and the rules of stock exchanges. In some cases, for example, the Australian climate change disclosure rules, they are based on IFRS. Generally at a lower level, because they are focused only on specific aspects of a report, are standards relevant to processes, activities, or specific areas: examples range from the treatment of tailings to reporting on human rights, safety, nature, and modern slavery. In some cases, a jurisdiction will develop its own rules or guidance.[10] There are indications of efforts to combine various standards, for example, GRI and IFRS.[11] **10.14**

Underlying the regimes is company law and the duties of directors. Company law is the foundation for reporting and disclosure because it generally applies to all companies incorporated in a jurisdiction or registered as a foreign company. There are fewer exemptions for small companies than is the case with the disclosure regimes mentioned in the previous paragraphs. The duties of directors, particularly their duty of care, and whether they have to consider **10.15**

8 See 2.27.
9 For the KPMG 2022 Report, see 1.45.
10 For example, Canada has its own tailings standard, which is used by Cameco. See 8.18.
11 See 2.27.

the interests of society and stakeholders other than shareholders are pivotal in determining their approach to sustainability.[12]

Reduction and simplification

10.16 According to some commentators, the number of regimes that companies are actually applying is reducing. The reports examined in Chapter 8 show GRI, SASB, IFRS, and TCFD recommendations being the most followed. It is likely over time that out of those four, GRI and IFRS will remain, with some hope that they will produce a merged regime. The big four in terms of bodies setting standards are the SEC, EFRAG, ISSB/IASB, and GRI.[13] What is also apparent is that reporting and disclosure regulations introduced initially can be both complex and labour-intensive. That is one reason that regimes have cut-off points so that smaller entities do not have to comply. The European Union found that with its package including the CSRD. It is expected to publish an Omnibus Simplification Package (Omnibus) in February 2025 aimed at consolidating existing EU corporate sustainability reporting requirements.[14] The EU Commission President, Ursula von der Leyen, announced the intention to introduce the Omnibus on 8 November 2024 with the intention of reducing the bureaucratic burden.

Meeting the energy transition

10.17 As companies and governments struggle to meet their targets for matters like the use of renewable energy and limiting greenhouse gases, those targets will be adjusted. There is already speculation of how the Trump administration will do that.[15] Views were sought by the author as to the future of sustainability in mining and energy. Most people said that they believed that positive change would occur.[16] The biggest concern expressed was with the democratic process and the short-sighted view of politicians focused on a short electoral cycle and lack of government accountability for objectives.

---

12 Discussed from 3.46.

13 Industry interviews, January 2025.

14 Those requirements are contained in the CSRD, the EU Taxonomy Regulation (the Taxonomy Regulation), and the Corporate Sustainability Due Diligence Directive (CSDDD).

15 Brian Schwartz, CNBC, 'A Trump SEC would aim to reverse climate disclosure rule, ratchet up ESG fights, sources say', CNBC 2 May 2024 https://www.cnbc.com/2024/05/02/trump-sec-would-end-climate-disclosure-rule-target-esg-investments.html?msockid=35c9f8602fd96394095dec112ed6622f.

16 Industry interviews, January 2025.

REIMAGINING SUSTAINABILITY LAW IN MINING AND ENERGY

Mining and energy regulators are increasing their focus on sustainability

It is inevitable that mining and energy regulators will increase their focus on sustainability. The first reason for that increase is the natural expansion of the interests of those regulators. As mining and energy regulations have developed, so too has their focus on the environment and safety. These are two of the pillars of sustainable development: environmental and social (through health and safety). There are examples of the expansion of the environmental focus. The definition of the environment has been expanded in some places to include aesthetic, cultural, social, and economic considerations.[17] In Australia references to ecologically sustainable development have been inserted in the EPBCA and mining acts such as that of Victoria. In Canada, fostering sustainability is a purpose of the *CIAA*, the federal environmental legislation. The social aspects examined by mining and energy regulators are also expanding through requirements for stakeholder engagement, protection of heritage and the position of indigenous people, and requirements to consider local communities. The second reason is that regulators are enforcing standards dealing with a growing range of activities, such as treatment of tailings, waste, water quality, and decommissioning, to name just a few. While these various items are not generally given the overall label of 'sustainability', they all test matters relevant to the sustainability of mining and energy operations. **10.18**

Other forces for change

We can identify at least four other forces for change. The first is government policy. Government sustainability reporting requirements are expanding. So too are policies for particular activities like emissions, procurement, and alternative energy.[18] Those policies will have an influence on reporting by mining and energy regulators and also their consideration of the energy used by mining and oil and gas projects. What can be seen from the CSRD as an example is that there is a trickle-down reporting effect. Banks that lend for energy projects have to also report on the sustainability performance of their borrowers. Regulators are having to report on their own emissions,[19] and in some cases report on the emissions of projects they regulate.[20] **10.19**

17 For example, Environmental Protection Act 1986 (WA) section 3(2).

18 Ibid.

19 See 3.39.

20 An example is reporting emissions to clean energy regulators such as Australia's Clean Energy Regulator. See https://cer.gov.au/schemes/national-greenhouse-and-energy-reporting-scheme.

10.20 The second force is the advance of disclosure regimes and the standards on which they are based. These regimes are extending beyond climate change to sustainability and beyond financial impacts to include double materiality. Examples of the first are IFRS S1 and the EU Taxonomy. An example of the second is the CSRD.

10.21 The third force is the approach taken by companies. The sample of nine companies in Chapter 8 showed in each case that sustainability is a vital element of their business, although the rationale is different. Many are embracing the energy transition and the shift in the world economy to decarbonise and making that an essential part of their business. Companies in that group include Cameco, Conoco, TotalEnergies, and the renewable energy companies Iberdrola, Vestas, and CSI. The strategies of the first three vary, with Cameco producing uranium and focusing on nuclear power, Conoco focusing on the energy transition through its 'Triple Mandate to reliably and responsibly meet demand, deliver competitive returns on and of capital and achieve our net operational emissions ambition',[21] and TotalEnergies growing its renewable energy portfolio. Barrick is an interesting case, with its focus on sustainable development and the SDGs based on wanting to be the partner of choice in the countries and communities where it operates.[22] MinRes is an example of a company that believes that acting sustainably will improve its business for the long term.

10.22 The fourth force for change is the growing body of rules and case law dealing with human rights and related areas like modern slavery. The human right to a certain quality of life has led to a series of cases against governments and companies in relation to their greenhouse gas production.

A rationale for sustainability law

10.23 The problem that we are left with is that the meaning of sustainability is contested. Definitions based on the definition of sustainable development are common: 'development that meets the needs of the present without compromising the ability of future generations to meet their own needs'.[23] At 1.09, a definition of sustainability in mining and energy was suggested, a critical part of which was a mining project continually improving its performance and the total quality of life and the ecological processes affected by it. Theme

21 Chapter 8, n 80.

22 Chapter 8, 8.13 n 22.

23 Brundtland Report Chapter 1 and 5.

3 discussed the increase in compulsory sustainability disclosure. The disclosure regimes commonly contain tests of financial or material impacts, although they usually do not contain a definition of 'sustainability'. An example is in the CSRD:

> A sustainability matter is material from an impact perspective when it pertains to the undertaking's material actual or potential, positive or negative impacts on people or the environment over the short-, medium- or long-term.[24]

From that one can conclude that something is unsustainable if it has a material actual or potential negative impact on people or the environment. It is suggested that that disjunctive test is correct for determining what is unsustainable, but a conjunctive test is needed for determining what is sustainable – that is, something is sustainable if there is a material actual or potential improvement for both people and the environment (or ecological processes, to use the wording from 1.09). This book argues that sustainability requires these two elements – people and the environment – to be linked and one should not be advanced to the detriment of the other. They are often linked in environmental legislation, but without clear guidance on what, if any, environmental detriment is considered material or acceptable. Sustainability also requires a holistic view. Hence the suggested definition in Chapter 1 that to be sustainable a mining or energy project must 'continually improve its performance, the total quality of life and the ecological processes affected by it'. What 'total quality of life' means in a practical sense is that a sustainable project will not provide short term benefits but cause medium or long-term detriments.

The implication for sustainability law in mining and energy is that there are **10.24** practices that are sustainable because they make actual or potential improvements for people and the environment. There are rules that provide penalties for acting unsustainably, such as causing pollution. What has not occurred yet in mining and energy is using the word 'sustainability' as an umbrella term for practices and rules setting out unsustainable or sustainable behaviour. But the list of those practices and rules will continue to grow. At some point, a tipping point will be reached when the expression 'sustainability law' is used to describe the principles and rules governing them.

24 European Sustainability Reporting Standards 1 (ESRS 1), 43 at 9.32.

INDEX

accountability, meaning of 3.12
Agenda 21 4.04
amenity 1.22
  landscapes 1.15
ammonia 1.02
AngloGold Ashanti 4.29, 4.32
artificial intelligence (AI) 1.03
audit 9.07, 9.46
Australia 1.06, 1.31, 1.35, 1.38, 10.18
  company reporting 1.46
    Australian Accounting Standards Board (AASB) 2.31, 8.21, 9.05
    regulation of *see* Australia *under* regulation of company reporting
    Stock Exchange 3.51, 3.54, 3.56
  corporate governance 3.56
    directors 3.03, 3.42, 3.43, 3.45, 3.47–49, 3.50
    review of operations 3.50, 9.10
  development approvals 7.01, 7.05, 7.07
    Western Australia *see under* Western Australia
  environmental approvals 6.01, 6.03, 6.10–13, 6.16, 6.18–19, 6.20, 6.64
    Western Australia *see under* Western Australia
  governance 3.05, 3.13, 3.17, 3.29
    corporate *see above*
    ministerial responsibility 3.15
    planning policy 3.34
    state-owned resources 3.28
    statutory objectives 3.36, 3.37
  Minerals Council of 2.19
  New South Wales 3.34
    public interest test 5.10–12
  registration of companies 2.36
  renewable energy 2.15, 2.18, 3.40, 3.41
    Western Australia 6.54, 6.55, 6.61–63, 7.30, 7.33–34
  Standards 2.16
  Stock Exchange 2.37, 3.51, 3.54, 3.56
  Western *see separate entry*
Australian Energy Producers (AEP) 2.21
Australian Securities and Investments Commission (ASIC) 2.36, 3.51
Australian Sustainability Reporting Standards (ASRS) 9.05, 9.06
  AASB S1: sustainability 9.04, 9.05, 9.11, 9.12
  AASB S2: climate 9.04, 9.05, 9.11–12
    focus of IFRS S2 and 9.13–17
AXPC ESG metrics template 8.32

banks 10.19
Barrick Gold Corp 8.02, 8.12, 8.13–16, 8.28, 10.21
batteries 1.07, 8.39, 8.48
BHP Group 1.36, 1.42, 4.29, 4.30
Biden, J. 2.17
biodiversity 1.11–12, 1.15, 1.22, 1.27, 2.06, 3.37, 7.21, 10.05
  company reporting 8.21, 8.22, 8.29, 8.30, 8.34, 8.35, 8.44
  SDG 15: Target 5 4.13, 4.16
  Wales 3.21
Bloomberg 2.24, 2.40
  ESG Data 2.35
Bosselmann, K. 4.09
BP: Energy Outlook 2023 Edition 1.40
Brazil 1.35, 1.41, 2.14
Brookfield Renewable Corp 1.42
Brown Weiss, E. 5.04–05, 5.07, 5.20
Brundtland Report (1987) 1.08, 1.13, 1.19, 3.20, 4.03, 4.06–09, 5.03, 5.23
building materials 1.07
Butler, J. 6.26

Cadbury Report (2012) 3.06–07
Cameco Corp 8.02, 8.12, 8.14, 8.17–19, 8.22, 10.21
Canada 1.06, 1.31, 1.35, 1.38, 10.18
  company reporting 1.46, 9.02, 9.27–31
    Canadian Accounting Standards Board (AcSB) 2.31
    Toronto Stock Exchange 3.51, 3.55
  corporate governance 3.07, 3.55
    directors 3.03, 3.42, 3.43, 3.45, 3.48

development approvals 7.01, 7.05, 7.06, 7.07
  Saskatchewan *see under* Saskatchewan
energy policy 2.18
environmental approvals 6.01, 6.03, 6.05–07, 6.16, 6.18–19, 6.20, 6.64
  Saskatchewan *see under* Saskatchewan
governance 3.13, 3.16, 3.17, 3.37
  corporate *see above*
IFRS 2.29
Mining Association of 2.19
pollution offences 6.15
renewable energy 1.41, 1.42, 6.54, 6.55, 6.59–60, 7.30, 7.32
  tax credits 2.18
Saskatchewan *see separate entry*
SDGs: 2023 VNR 4.19–21
Standards Council of 2.16
Toronto Stock Exchange 2.37, 3.51, 3.55

Canadian Association of Petroleum Producers (CAPP) 2.21

Canadian Securities Administrators (CSA) 3.51, 9.27, 9.31

Canadian Solar Inc 1.42, 4.37, 8.02, 8.39, 8.48–50, 10.21

Canadian Sustainability Disclosure Standards (CSDS) 9.29

Canadian Sustainability Standards Board (CSSB) 9.29

Cenovus Energy Inc 8.02, 8.23, 9.30

Chevron 1.39

Chile 2.14, 2.29

China 1.03, 1.35, 1.38, 1.40, 2.29, 2.37
  Accounting Standards for Business Enterprises (ASBEs) 2.31
  renewable energy 1.40, 1.41, 1.42

China Shenhua Energy Co Ltd 1.36

climate change 1.37, 2.06
  cumulative effects of projects 6.16
  examples of company reporting 8.04, 8.07, 8.10, 8.17, 8.21, 8.25, 8.26, 8.34, 8.44, 8.56
  healthy environment, right to 5.21
  IFRS S2 *see under* International Financial Reporting Standards (IFRS)
  law 1.55
  UN Framework Convention on 2.02
    COP21: Paris Agreement 1.54, 2.02, 2.04
    COP28: Dubai 8.25
  see also regulation of company reporting

coal 1.36

Columbia Center on Sustainable Investment (CCSI) 4.27–28

company reporting 1.04, 1.09, 1.10, 3.62, 10.12
  directors: duty to report 1.48, 3.42, 3.50, 8.03, 9.01
  examples 8.01–02, 8.56, 10.21
    best practice, guidance on 8.54–55
    common features 8.07–11
    flexible options 8.53
    mining 8.10, 8.12–22
    oil and gas 8.10, 8.23–38
    process and guidance 8.04–06
    renewable energy 8.10, 8.39–52
    reporting required by law 8.03
  human rights *see* company reporting *under* human rights
  KPMG Survey of Sustainability Reporting (2022) 1.45, 2.24–25, 4.25–26, 4.33, 10.13
  multiplicity of regimes 10.13–15
    reduction and simplification 10.16
  obligations: ESG and other approaches 1.43–51
  purpose of report 1.51
  regulation of *see separate entry*
  SDGs *see* company reporting *under* Sustainable Development Goals (SDGs)
  securities exchanges 1.48, 2.38, 3.07, 3.51–56, 8.03, 9.01, 9.03, 10.14
  small/smaller companies *see separate entry*
  see also Global Reporting Initiative (GRI); International Financial Reporting Standards (IFRS); Task Force on Climate-related Financial Disclosures (TCFD)

computing 1.03

ConocoPhillips Inc 1.39, 8.02, 8.23, 8.31–34, 8.56, 10.21

Constellation Energy Corp 1.42

corporate governance 3.01–04, 3.51, 8.44
  Cadbury Report (2012) 3.06–07
  directors 1.06, 3.04, 3.06, 3.62, 3.63, 8.10
    board or committee 3.08, 3.10
    duties 3.03, 3.42–50, 9.09, 9.10, 10.15
    duty of care 3.46–49, 10.15
    duty to act in good faith and in interests of company 3.45
    duty to act within powers 3.44
    duty to report 1.48, 3.42, 3.50, 8.03, 9.10
    trustees 3.03
  outline 3.42–43
  securities exchanges 3.07, 3.55–56
  sustainability 3.08–11, 3.61, 3.62, 3.63
    committee 3.08, 3.10, 8.53

see also company reporting
corruption 1.04, 2.05, 9.40
cost–benefit analysis 1.17, 5.12, 5.24, 6.16
COVID-19 pandemic 4.17, 4.22
culture and regulation *see under* governance
customary international law 5.18

de Sadeleer, N. 5.14
Decleris, M. 5.14
democracy 10.17
Denmark 1.42, 8.47
development approvals 3.33, 6.02, 7.01–03, 7.37–38
background to 7.04–08
mining
Nevada 7.09–11
Saskatchewan 7.12–15
Western Australia 7.16–17
oil and gas 7.18
Nevada 7.18, 7.19–21
Saskatchewan 7.18, 7.22–23
Western Australia 7.18, 7.24–29
renewable energy 7.30
Nevada 7.30, 7.31
Saskatchewan 7.30, 7.32
Western Australia 7.30, 7.33–34
development, definition of 1.26–27
development finance *see* finance, sustainable
disclosure *see* company reporting
double materiality 1.43, 9.38–41, 9.49, 10.20
Dworkin, R. 1.33, 1.34, 1.55

ecological systems 1.11–12, 1.22, 3.21
ecosystem accounting 2.33
education
SDG 4: Target 7 4.13, 4.17
electricity 1.02
networks 1.32, 6.55
constant and adequate supply of power 1.07
right to supply of 5.22
Elliott, J. 4.01
energy mix 1.07, 1.37, 1.40, 2.18
environmental approvals 1.17, 4.05, 6.01–02, 6.64–65, 8.46, 10.05
mining 6.21–23
Nevada 6.21, 6.22, 6.23, 6.24–29, 7.10
Saskatchewan 6.21, 6.22, 6.23, 6.30–35
Western Australia 6.21, 6.22, 6.23, 6.36–39
oil and gas 6.40–41
Nevada 6.40, 6.41, 6.42–44
Saskatchewan 6.40, 6.41, 6.45–49
Western Australia 6.40, 6.41, 6.50–53
renewable energy 6.54–55
Nevada 6.54, 6.55, 6.56–58
Saskatchewan 6.54, 6.55, 6.59–60
Western Australia 6.54, 6.55, 6.61–63
review of significant projects 6.54
Australia: federal review 6.10–13, 6.18–19
Australia: state level review (WA) 6.14, 6.51, 6.63, 7.16, 7.25, 7.34
Canada: federal review 6.05–07, 6.18–19
Canada: Saskatchewan review 6.08–09, 6.17
EIAs, public interest and sustainability 6.16–20
other offences 6.15
public consultation/participation 3.32, 6.06, 6.08, 6.14, 6.20
two streams 6.03
US: federal approval 6.04
environmental-economic accounting 2.32
Equator Principles 2.34, 7.36
equity 1.16, 1.20–21
intergenerational *see separate entry*
intragenerational *see separate entry*
Euronext 2.37
European Financial Reporting Advisory Group (EFRAG) 9.35, 10.16
European Sustainability Reporting Standards (ESRS) 9.35
ESRS 1 9.35, 9.37–41, 9.42
ESRS 2 9.36, 9.37, 9.42–45
European Union 1.46, 8.26, 8.40, 8.47, 9.02
Corporate Sustainability Due Diligence Directive (CSDDD) 9.32, 9.47
Corporate Sustainability Reporting Directive (CSRD) 1.43, 2.25, 8.07, 8.26, 9.32–34, 9.35, 9.48, 10.12, 10.13, 10.23
audit 9.46
double materiality test 1.43, 9.38–41, 9.49, 10.20
small and medium-sized entities 9.34, 10.16
trickle-down effect 10.19
environmental impact assessments 6.16
finance, sustainable
Taxonomy 2.34, 8.24, 8.26, 8.40, 8.47, 9.35, 10.20
Green Deal 2.17, 8.26, 9.32
IFRS 2.29
simplification 10.16
Sustainable Finance Disclosure Regulation (SFDR) 9.32, 9.35
ExxonMobil 1.39

federalism 1.31, 6.03
fertilisers 1.07
finance, sustainable 2.34, 4.15, 7.35–36
  Canadian Taxonomy 9.28, 9.29
  EU Taxonomy 2.34, 8.24, 8.26, 8.40, 8.47, 9.35, 10.20
Financial Stability Board (FSB) 2.28, 9.49
Fitzmaurice, M. 5.07
forests 1.25, 1.26
Fortescue Ltd 1.36
France 1.37
free mining 1.06, 7.05
Freeport-McMoRan Inc 1.36
future
  current approach: themes 10.01
    1: testing sustainability 10.02–05
    2: testing environmental and safety matters 10.06–08
    3: compulsory disclosure 10.09, 10.23
    4: reporting and good practice 10.10–11
    5: sustainability reports 10.12
  disclosure and reporting
    energy transition 10.17
    multiplicity of regimes 10.13–15
    reduction 10.16
    simplification 10.16
  rationale for sustainability law 10.23–24
  reimagining law 10.18–24

G250 1.45, 1.46, 4.25
General Electric Co 1.42
Germany 1.41, 2.07, 4.25
Glencore Plc 1.36
Global Compact 2.05, 2.40, 4.36, 8.21, 8.40
Global Reporting Initiative (GRI) 1.44, 2.24, 2.25, 2.26, 2.40, 8.07, 8.16, 8.21, 8.32, 8.40, 8.48, 9.35, 10.09, 10.13, 10.16
  GRI 2: General Disclosures 2021 8.05, 8.53
  IFRS Foundation 2.27, 3.58, 10.14
  KPMG 2022 Report 1.45
governance 3.62–63
  corporate *see separate entry*
  culture and regulation 3.26–27
    definition of culture 3.26
    policy on mining and energy operations 3.28–34
    policy on sustainable procurement 3.39
    renewable energy 3.31, 3.35, 3.40–41
    reporting requirements 3.39
    state-owned resources 3.28, 3.35–38
  general principles
    corporate 3.06–07
    government 3.12–17
  government 3.01–05, 3.26–27, 3.62, 10.19
    development approval 3.32, 3.33, 3.41
    general principles 3.12–17
    judicial review 3.17
    ministerial responsibility 3.15–16
    oaths on taking office 3.14
    pipeline of projects 3.31
    planning policy 3.34
    policy on mining and energy operations 3.28–34
    public consultation 3.32
    public policy sustainability objectives 3.39
    public trust 3.38
    renewable energy 3.31, 3.35, 3.40–41
    reporting requirements 3.18, 3.39, 3.41, 3.62
    statutes with(out) objects clause 3.13, 3.36–38
    Welsh example: sustainability 3.13, 3.18–23, 3.27, 3.62
  introduction 3.01–25
  securities exchanges 3.07
    and market regulation 3.51–56
Greenhouse Gas Protocol 2.16, 9.16, 9.23
greenwashing 1.06, 9.30
Guterres, A. 4.14–15

Hawke, B. 6.12
health and/or safety 1.15, 1.30, 1.33, 1.48, 6.55, 8.04, 8.54, 10.01, 10.06, 10.08, 10.14, 10.18
  Australia 2.14, 2.15
  Canada 2.14
  examples of company reporting 8.07, 8.13, 8.16, 8.22, 8.30, 8.31, 8.36, 8.44, 8.49, 8.51
  United Kingdom 2.14, 2.15
  United States 2.14, 2.15
Heffron, R. 5.08
holistic approach 1.16, 10.23
human rights 5.21–22, 10.01
  company reporting 1.48, 2.05, 10.14
    EU: due diligence 9.47
    examples of 8.07, 8.16, 8.30, 8.51
    impact materiality 9.40
    social pillar 1.48
  quality of life 10.22
hydrogen 1.02, 1.32, 2.22, 3.40
hydropower 1.41, 2.18

Iberdrola SA 1.42, 4.37, 8.02, 8.39, 8.40–45, 10.21
India 1.41, 2.29

indigenous peoples 4.30, 7.04, 8.14, 8.35, 8.36–37, 10.05, 10.18
environmental approvals 6.06, 6.07, 6.08, 6.20, 6.22, 6.61
Indonesia 2.14, 10.07
industry bodies 1.49
in mining 2.19–20
in petroleum and energy 2.21–23
see also individual industry bodies
industry lobby groups 1.06
institutional investors 8.43, 10.10
intergenerational equity 1.21, 4.08, 4.09, 5.01–05, 5.10, 5.24, 5.25
creeping intergenerationalisation 5.16–23
defining needs 5.06
ecologically sustainable development, principle of 6.11, 6.12
environmental impact assessments 6.16
making fair decisions 5.13
soft law 5.14–15, 5.16, 5.17
valuation and apportionment 5.07
Intergovernmental Forum on Mining, Minerals, Metals and Sustainable Development (IGF) 2.13, 2.40
International Accounting Standards Board (IASB) 2.29, 10.16
International Council of Minerals and Mines (ICMM) 1.49, 2.20, 2.40, 2.41, 8.16, 8.53, 8.54, 10.11
International Court of Justice (ICJ) 5.18
International Energy Agency (IEA) 2.11, 2.18, 2.40, 2.41
International Finance Corporation (IFC) 2.10, 2.34, 4.33
Sustainability Practices 1.09, 3.08, 7.35
definition of sustainability 1.09, 3.09, 7.35
International Financial Reporting Standards (IFRS) 2.28, 2.40, 2.41, 8.48, 10.13, 10.16
Foundation 2.29
GRI and 2.27, 3.58, 10.14
S1: sustainability 1.43, 2.29, 3.07, 3.58, 3.59–61, 9.04, 9.11, 9.29, 10.09, 10.20
S2: climate change 1.43, 2.29, 3.07, 9.04, 9.11, 9.29, 9.48, 9.49, 9.50, 10.09
focus of AASB S2 and 9.13–17
SEC's new disclosure rules and 9.24, 9.26
US GAAP and 2.30
International Organization for Standardization (ISO) 2.16, 10.10
International Public Sector Accounting Standards Board (IPSASB) 1.44, 3.39, 10.09
International Renewable Energy Agency (IRENA) 1.41, 2.40, 2.41
International Sustainability Standards Board (ISSB) 2.27, 2.29, 3.58, 9.04, 9.11, 10.09, 10.16
International Union for Conservation of Nature (IUCN) 4.02
intragenerational equity 1.20, 4.09, 5.01–03, 5.17, 5.24, 5.25
costs and benefits 5.10–12
fair distribution 5.13–15
distributional equity and energy justice 5.08–09
Ipieca (formerly International Petroleum Industry Environmental Conservation Association) 2.23, 2.24, 2.40, 4.33, 8.32, 10.11
Reporting Guidance 1.49, 1.50, 2.23, 8.04, 8.06, 8.38, 8.54
Iran 1.38
Iraq 1.38

Japan 1.41, 2.37
Jinko Solar Holding Co. Ltd 1.42
justice, energy 1.20, 5.08–09, 5.16–23

Khalfan, A. 4.03
KPMG Survey of Sustainability Reporting (2022) 1.45, 2.24–25, 4.25–26, 4.33, 10.13

least developed countries 8.28
licence to operate
social 1.10, 3.25, 8.20, 10.01
sustainable development 3.25
local communities 10.18
see also indigenous peoples

materiality, determining
AASB S2 9.17, 9.50
EU: CSRD 1.43, 9.38–41, 9.49, 10.20
SEC's new climate change disclosure rules 9.23, 9.49, 9.50
medicines 1.07
milestones, list of 1.54
Millennium Development Goals (MDGs) 4.10, 4.11, 5.17
Mineral Resources Limited 8.02, 8.12, 8.14, 8.18, 8.20–22, 8.56, 10.21
mining or fossil fuel energy project
phases of 1.29–31

differences with renewable energy projects 1.32
MSCI 2.24, 2.40
ESG Research 2.35

natural capital accounting (NCA) 2.03, 2.32
natural resources
minerals and energy as 1.24–28
net zero emissions 1.04
Nevada 1.31, 8.13
development approvals 7.01, 7.04, 7.05, 7.37–38
oil and gas 7.18, 7.19–21
renewable energy 7.30, 7.31
environmental approvals 6.01, 6.64
mining 6.21, 6.22, 6.23, 6.24–29, 7.10
oil and gas 6.40, 6.41, 6.42–44
renewable energy 6.54, 6.55, 6.56–58
good faith 3.45, 3.48
mining and petroleum statutes 2.14
regulators 2.14
Revised Statutes 2.36, 3.42, 3.43, 3.48
Newmont Corp 1.36
NextEra Energy 1.42
Norway 1.38, 2.16, 3.37, 10.07
nuclear power 1.36, 2.18, 8.17

OECD (Organisation for Economic Co-operation and Development) 1.24–25, 1.27, 2.09, 3.12, 9.47

Peel, J. 4.06
Petrobras 1.39
PetroChina 1.39
Philippines
Minors Oposa case 5.20
SDGs: 2022 VNR 4.22–24
planning or zoning regulations
competing uses of land 3.34
renewable energy 3.41, 6.55, 6.58, 6.61, 6.62, 7.30, 7.31, 7.32, 7.33
policy-setting 2.16–18
polluter pays principle 4.05
poverty 1.19, 4.14
precautionary approach/principle 4.05, 6.11
premium, green 1.04
Preston, B. 5.10–12, 6.12
principles and rules, meaning of 1.33–34
profitability 1.14–17
public consultation/participation 3.32, 6.06, 6.08, 6.14, 6.20
public interest 3.12, 3.38, 5.10–12, 6.04, 6.07, 6.09, 6.17, 6.56
public sector 1.44
International Public Sector Accounting Standards Board (IPSASB) 1.44, 3.39, 10.09
see also governance

Qatar 1.38, 2.14

rating and ranking bodies 2.35, 10.10
Rawls, J. 5.08
Redgwell, C. 5.16
regulation of company reporting 1.46, 9.01–03, 9.48–51, 10.09
Australia 9.02, 9.48
amendments to companies legislation 9.06–09
climate-related disclosure legislation 9.05, 9.48, 9.49, 10.14
directors' declaration 9.09
focus of IFRS S2 and AASB S2 9.13–17, 9.50
IFRS and new climate disclosure rules 9.04
main requirements of AASB S2 9.12
other reporting obligations of directors 3.50, 9.10
small exploration companies 9.08
structure of AASB S2 9.11
Canada 9.02
Canadian Securities Administrators 9.27, 9.31
federal regulation 9.28
finance taxonomy and sustainability standards 9.29–30
Saskatchewan 9.31
European Union 9.02
Corporate Sustainability Due Diligence Directive (CSDDD) 9.32, 9.47
Corporate Sustainability Reporting Directive (CSRD) *see under* European Union
European Sustainability Reporting Standards (ESRS) 9.35–45
small and medium-sized entities (SMEs) 9.34
Taxonomy Regulation 9.35
materiality, determining
AASB S2 9.17, 9.50
EU: CSRD 1.43, 9.38–41, 9.49, 10.20
SEC's new climate change disclosure rules 9.23, 9.49, 9.50
United States 9.02
emerging growth companies (EGCs) 9.22

Securities and Exchange Commission (SEC) 1.47, 3.51, 9.03, 9.18, 9.19–26, 9.48, 9.49, 9.50, 10.14, 10.16
smaller reporting companies (SRCs) 9.22
regulators 2.14–15, 2.18, 2.40, 2.41, 2.42, 10.02–08, 10.18, 10.19
corporate 2.36
development approvals *see separate entry*
environmental approvals *see separate entry*
fair decisions 5.13, 5.15
functional separation 3.28, 3.31
history 3.29
role of 3.12, 3.27
securities exchanges 3.51
Canadian Securities Administrators 3.51, 9.27, 9.31
SEC *see* Securities and Exchange Commission (SEC) *under* United States
statutes without objects clause 3.36
renewable energy 1.02, 1.03, 2.15, 8.25, 8.26, 10.04, 10.06, 10.17
company reporting: SDGs 4.37
development approvals 7.01, 7.30–34
energy mix 1.37, 1.40
environmental approvals 6.54–63
governance 3.31, 3.35, 3.40–41
incentives, financial and tax 2.17–18
snapshot of sector 1.37, 1.40–42
supply chains 1.10
transition costs 1.06
see also solar power; wind power
Responsible Mining Foundation (RMF) 4.27–28
Rio+20 conference (2012) 2.03
Rio Declaration (1992) 4.04–05, 5.17
Rio Tinto 1.36, 4.29, 4.31
risk management 7.36, 8.09, 8.33, 9.02, 9.09, 9.23, 9.48
AASB S2 9.12, 9.15, 9.16
IFRS S1 3.61, 9.15, 9.16
statutory objectives 3.37
rules and principles, meaning of 1.33–34
Russia 1.35, 1.38, 2.29

safety *see* health and/or safety
Sands, P. 4.06
Saskatchewan 1.31
Business Corporations Act 2021 2.36, 3.42, 3.43, 3.48
company reporting, regulation of 9.31
development approvals 7.01, 7.04, 7.05, 7.37–38
mining 7.12–15
oil and gas 7.18, 7.22–23
renewable energy 7.30, 7.32
environmental approvals 6.01, 6.64
mining 6.21, 6.22, 6.23, 6.30–35
oil and gas 6.40, 6.41, 6.45–49
renewable energy 6.54, 6.55, 6.59–60
review of significant projects 6.08–09, 6.17
good faith 3.45, 3.48
mining and petroleum statutes 2.14
offences 6.31
regulators 2.14
Saudi Arabia 1.35, 1.38
Saudi Aramco 1.39
Sax, J. 3.38
Scotland 3.18
securities exchanges 1.48, 2.37–38, 8.03, 9.01, 9.03, 10.14
governance 3.07, 3.51–56
Segger, M.-C. C. 4.03
Shell 1.39
simplification 10.16
slavery, modern 1.04, 1.10, 1.48, 2.05, 10.01, 10.14, 10.22
small/smaller companies 1.46, 8.03, 9.01, 10.15, 10.16
in Australia 9.08
small and medium-sized entities (SMEs) in EU 9.34
smaller reporting companies (SRCs) in US 9.22
social costs 1.09, 1.15
social inclusion 1.13, 5.02
see also equity
social licence to operate 1.10, 3.25, 8.20, 10.01
soft law 1.34, 4.38, 5.14–15, 5.16, 5.17
solar power 1.07, 1.28, 1.32, 1.40, 8.24, 8.39, 8.42, 8.48, 10.04
China 1.41
development approvals 7.01, 7.30–34
environmental approvals 6.54–63
governance 3.35
supply chains for equipment 1.10
United States 1.41, 2.22
South Africa 2.19, 2.29
South Korea 2.29
Sovacool, B. 5.08
sovereignty over natural resources 4.04
Spain 1.41, 1.42
statistics: snapshot of sector 1.35–42
stewardship 1.51
Stockholm Declaration (1972) 1.18, 4.02

strategic environmental assessments (SIAs) 6.16
Sustainability Accounting Standards Board (SASB) 2.25, 4.01, 4.10–11, 8.07, 8.17, 8.32, 8.40, 8.47, 8.48, 10.09, 10.16
  Standards 2.29, 8.21, 8.38, 8.53, 10.09
sustainability, meaning of 1.04, 1.06, 1.08, 4.01, 4.09
  Canada 6.05, 6.18
  ecological systems and biodiversity 1.11–12
  elements 1.22–23
  IFC Sustainability Practices 1.09, 3.09, 7.35
  proposed definition 1.09, 10.23
  social and economic pillars 1.13
Sustainable Development Goals (SDGs) 1.10, 1.13, 1.54, 2.01, 3.38, 4.38–39, 5.02, 5.15, 10.02, 10.11
  company reporting 5.02, 8.06, 8.07, 8.08
    mining 4.25–32, 8.14, 8.16, 8.21, 10.21
    oil and gas 4.33–36, 8.27, 8.29
    renewable energy 4.37, 8.40, 8.47
  early history and UN 4.02–05
  electricity, right to supply of 5.22
  goals 1–17 4.12
  Secretariat 2.04
  sustainable development 4.01, 4.02, 4.04, 5.24, 10.05
    Brundtland Report 1.08, 1.13, 1.19, 3.20, 4.03, 4.06–09, 5.03, 5.23
    customary international law 5.18
    flexible nature of 4.06–09
    soft law 4.38, 5.14, 5.16, 5.17
  UN: reporting on 4.12–17
    Canada 2023 VNR 4.19–21
    high-level political forums and VNRs 4.18–24
    Philippines 2022 VNR 4.22–24
  World Bank 2.10
Sustainable Development Solutions Network (SDSN) 2.04
Sweden 2.07
System of Environmental Economic Accounting (SEEA) 2.32
  Experimental Ecosystem Accounting (SEEA EEA) 2.33

Task Force on Climate-related Financial Disclosures (TCFD) 1.43, 2.24, 2.28, 2.29, 3.07, 8.16, 8.17, 8.21, 8.40, 8.47, 9.23, 9.28, 9.35, 9.48, 9.49, 9.51, 10.09, 10.16
  Final Report (2017) 2.28, 8.05, 9.02
  formation of 2.28, 9.49
  themes 1.44, 8.05, 9.48
Task Force on Nature-related Financial Disclosures (TNFD) 2.24, 8.21, 8.34
taxation 10.07
  incentives 2.16, 2.17, 2.18
  transparency 10.01
TotalEnergies SE 1.39, 4.35–36, 8.02, 8.23, 8.24–30, 10.21
Trump, D. 6.04, 9.03, 10.17

UNESCO (United Nations Educational, Scientific and Cultural Organization) 2.08
United Kingdom 1.41, 2.36
  corporate governance 3.55, 3.56
    Cadbury Report (2012) 3.06–07
    directors 1.48, 3.03, 3.04, 3.42–50, 8.03
    strategic report 1.48, 3.50
  customary law in stannary districts 7.05
  directors 3.03, 3.04, 3.42–50
    duty of care 3.46
    duty to report 1.48, 3.42, 3.50, 8.03
  Financial Conduct Authority 3.51
  Financial Reporting Council
    UK standards and IFRS 2.31
  governance 3.05, 3.13, 3.17
    corporate *see above*
    ministerial responsibility 3.15
    statutory objectives 3.37
    Wales: WFGW 3.13, 3.18–23, 3.27, 5.23
  London Stock Exchange 2.37, 3.51
    disclosure 3.53, 3.55, 3.56
  mining and petroleum statutes 2.14
  offshore regulation 2.15
  regulators 2.14, 2.15
  UK Oil and Gas Industry Association Ltd 2.21
United Nations 2.01
  conferences 1.18, 2.02–03, 4.02, 4.04, 5.17
  Department of Economic and Social Affairs (UNDESA) 2.04
  Development Programme (UNDP) 2.07, 4.33
  Environment Programme (UNEP) 2.06, 2.23, 3.25
  governance 3.01
    sustainability 3.24–25
  human rights 2.05
  Sustainable Development Solutions Network (SDSN) 2.04
United States 1.06, 1.31, 1.35, 1.38, 1.41, 2.07, 2.29

company reporting 1.46, 9.02
Generally Accepted Accounting Principles (GAAP) 2.30
SDGs 4.25
Securities and Exchange Commission (SEC) *see below*
Delaware
public benefit corporation 3.49
development approvals 7.01, 7.04, 7.05, 7.07, 7.08, 7.18
Nevada *see under* Nevada
Energy Association (USEA) 2.21
environmental approvals 6.01, 6.03, 6.04, 6.16, 6.20
Nevada *see under* Nevada
Environmental Protection Agency 1.11, 6.04, 6.28, 6.40, 6.42
governance 3.05, 3.14, 3.17, 3.29
corporate 3.42, 3.43, 3.45, 3.48, 3.49
ownership of minerals 3.35
petroleum: rule of capture 3.30
public trust 3.38
Inflation Reduction Act (2022) 2.17
Nasdaq 2.37, 3.51, 9.03, 9.18
Nevada *see separate entry*
New York Stock Exchange 2.37, 3.51
disclosure 3.52–53, 9.03, 9.18
nuclear power 1.37
offshore regulation 2.15
pollution offences 6.15
registration of companies 2.36
renewable energy 1.41, 1.42, 2.18, 2.22
Securities and Exchange Commission (SEC) 1.47, 2.30, 2.39, 3.51, 9.03, 9.18, 10.14, 10.16
new climate disclosure rules 1.47, 9.03, 9.18, 9.19–26, 9.48, 9.49, 9.50
state corporate law 2.36
US Oil and Gas Association (USOGA) 2.21

Vale SA 1.36
Vestas Wind Systems AS 1.42, 4.37, 8.02, 8.39, 8.46–47, 10.21
voluntary national reviews (VNRs) 4.18–24
von der Leyen, U. 10.16

Wales
Well-being of Future Generations (Wales) Act 2015 (WFGW) 3.13, 3.18–23, 5.23
Future Generations Commissioner 3.18, 3.19, 3.23, 3.27
Walker, D. 3.23
Western Australia 1.31, 10.03
Corporations Act 2001 (Cth) 2.36, 3.42, 3.43, 3.47–49, 3.50, 9.05, 9.06–09
development approvals 7.01, 7.04, 7.05, 7.37–38
mining 7.16–17
oil and gas 7.18, 7.24–29
renewable energy 7.30, 7.33–34
environmental approvals 6.01, 6.64
ALARP (as low as reasonably practicable) test 6.51, 6.52, 6.53, 7.25
mining 6.21, 6.22, 6.23, 6.36–39
oil and gas 6.40, 6.41, 6.50–53
renewable energy 6.54, 6.55, 6.61–63
review of significant projects 6.14, 6.51, 6.63, 7.16, 7.25, 7.34
good faith 3.45
mining and petroleum statutes 2.14, 3.36
pollution offence 6.15
regulators 2.14
wind power 1.07, 1.28, 1.32, 1.40, 1.41, 8.24, 8.39, 8.42, 8.46, 10.04
development approvals 7.01, 7.30–34
environmental approvals 6.54–63
governance 3.35
World Wind Energy Association 2.22
World Bank Group
Environmental, Health and Safety Guidelines 7.35
International Finance Corporation (IFC) *see separate entry*
World Bank 2.10
WAVES 50:50 Initiative 2.03
World Business Council for Sustainable Development (WBCSD) 2.13, 4.33
World Conservation Strategy (WCS) 4.02
World Gold Council 2.20, 2.40, 2.41, 10.11
World Summit on Sustainable Development: Plan of Implementation (2002) 3.24